MORAL ECONOMIES OF CORRUPTION

MORAL ECONOMIES OF CORRUPTION

State Formation & Political Culture in Nigeria   Steven Pierce

Duke University Press   Durham and London   2016

Printed in the United States of America on acid-free paper ∞
Designed by Courtney Leigh Baker
Typeset in Minion Pro by Westchester Publishing Services

Library of Congress Cataloging-in-Publication Data
Pierce, Steven, [date] author.
Moral economies of corruption : state formation and
political culture in Nigeria / Steven Pierce.
pages cm
Includes bibliographical references and index.
ISBN 978-0-8223-6077-3 (hardcover : alk. paper)
ISBN 978-0-8223-6091-9 (pbk. : alk. paper)
ISBN 978-0-8223-7454-1 (e-book)
1. Corruption—Nigeria. 2. Political culture—Nigeria.
3. Nigeria—Politics and government—To 1960.
4. Nigeria—Politics and government—1960– I. Title.
JQ3089.5.C6P54   2016
306.209669—dc23
2015029176

COVER ART: *All Fingers Are Not Equal,* © Victor Ekpuk

Duke University Press gratefully acknowledges the support
of the Department of History at the University of Manchester,
which provided funds toward the publication of this book.

For Elango

CONTENTS   Acknowledgments ix

Introduction: Corruption Discourse and the Performance of Politics 1

ACKNOWLEDGMENTS

Like many well-beloved children, this book was an accident. It came about as I moved between two big research projects, one on the history of land law, the other on the politics of criminal law. Indeed, the research that has gone into it was originally planned (and funded) for those ends. As I worked on the two projects, my mind kept drifting back to my many conversations with a remarkable man, Malam Isa Muhammad. In many ways, Malam Isa was an ordinary *talaka*, commoner; he was a farmer, and he was very poor. He was distinguished, however, by a razor-sharp intellect and a biting wit, and he had enjoyed a career as an activist in the Northern Elements Progressive Union and People's Redemption Party, left-wing parties during Nigeria's First and Second Republics, respectively. Spectacularly knowledgeable about the political history of his town, and about the travails of its poorer residents, Malam Isa was also gifted at sensing when I did not understand concepts to his satisfaction. His patience and generosity made all the difference to me in some trying times. And his insistence on telling me about his comrades' problems in his own terms is what ultimately led to this book.

While I was finishing my first book, Jim Brennan invited me to the African history seminar at the School of Oriental and African Studies (SOAS) at the University of London, which I took as an opportunity to revisit a point Malam Isa had pressed, and which I had not resolved to his satisfaction or mine. Among Hausa-speaking people in northern Nigeria, there seemed to be several different ways of talking about corruption, only one of which accorded with my own understanding of what the word entailed, and I presented a paper laying out the concepts and the problems they highlighted. The audience pushed me hard, helping me to think through the problem sufficiently to turn my paper into a proper article. Along the way, I was helped enormously by the editors and anonymous readers for *Comparative Studies in Society and History*, where it appeared. While I was a refugee from Hurricane Katrina, Shannon Dawdy invited me to the University of Chicago, where I presented a near-final version of the article. Ralph Austen made me rethink the basic logic of what I had written, while Jean and John Comaroff picked up on what had been almost a throwaway line and pointed out that it raised a book's worth of questions. The rest followed from there.

I owe profound thanks to countless people in Nigeria for their help, advice, patience, support, and criticism. I have benefited from my affiliation with and support from many institutions: Bayero University, and especially its Departments of History, Nigerian Languages, and Islamic Legal Studies, and from its Centre for Democratic Research and Training (Mambayya House); the Kano State History and Culture Bureau; Arewa House; and the Nigerian National Archives (Kaduna). Hajiya Aisha Shehu, head of research and documentation at HCB, and the Honorable Professor Haruna Wakili, then director of Mambayya House, provided me with institutional home bases and greatly facilitated my work. Usman Aliyu, as ever, provided wonderful research assistance, and a great many people shared their wisdom. Because of the somewhat sensational subject matter of this book, I have for the most part structured my narrative in a way that avoids oral history, and the interview material that is presented is for the most part noncontroversial. I am deeply, personally grateful to everyone who was willing to talk to me. I hope this text adequately signals my intellectual debts without placing anyone in a difficult situation.

This book was written while I was a member of the School of Social Science at the Institute for Advanced Study (IAS). I am grateful to Professors Didier Fassin and Joan Scott for their intellectual leadership and for the opportunity to participate in their seminars on moral issues and on secularism. My arguments were shaped and enriched by conversations with Didier and Joan and with my fellow members, especially Laurie Green, Kimberly Hart, Cecile Laborde, Tomoko Masuzawa, Jeffrey Stout, Judith Surkis, and Winni Sullivan. I made final revisions on the manuscript while a senior fellow at the Käte Hamburger Kolleg/Centre for Global Cooperation Research (GCR), University of Duisburg-Essen and on a sabbatical from the Department of History at the University of Manchester. My thanks to Drs. Alexandra Przyrembel and Volker Heins, who headed my research unit while I was at GCR, and to my colleagues while I was there, especially Sarah van Beurden, Morgan Brigg, Jaroslava Gajdosova, and Abou Jeng. I am equally grateful to my friends and interlocutors here at Manchester, Laurence Brown, Paulo Drinot, Pierre Fuller,

Anindita Ghosh, Bidisha Ray, Natalie Zacek, and Zheng Yangwen. I thank Professors Paul Fouracre and Hannah Barker, who gave permission for me to take my fellowships while they headed my department. My research has been generously supported by the U.S. Social Science Research Council, American Council for Learned Societies, Wenner-Gren Foundation for Anthropological Research, the British Academy, the University of Michigan, Tulane University, and the University of Manchester.

I am grateful for the challenging comments I have received from many audiences, at soas, the University of Chicago, Nottingham Trent University, the University of Birmingham, Vanderbilt University, ias, Indiana University, the University of Newcastle, Royal Holloway College, the University of Leeds, the University of Durham, gcr, and Queen's University Ontario, as well as at the annual meetings of the American Historical Association and the European Congress on World and Global History. While they probably don't remember it, Ibrahim Ado-Kurawa, Misty Bastian, Charles Piot, Rabi'u Shatsari, Linda Pollock, Mamadou Diouf, Lessie Jo Frazier, Mahmood Mamdani, Greg Mann, Abosede George, David Pratten, Michael Watts, and Rudi Gaudio have all made sharp comments that made me reconsider key aspects of my argument. The anonymous readers for Duke University Press and my editor, Miriam Angress, have vastly improved the book with their careful attention to my argument and its implications. With such interlocutors, this book should be much better than it is; the fault for that, of course, is mine rather than theirs.

I owe many people thanks for personal and professional support over the years. Frederick Cooper has been, as always, kind, helpful, and challenging for this project. Luise White is the soul of generosity and never hesitates to slap me when necessary. Gracia Clark and Adeline Masquelier have been voices of cool sanity and fiercely intelligent interlocutors. Phil Shea was extremely helpful as I was first thinking through this project; his loss impoverishes us all. Moses Ochonu and Sue O'Brien have long been the two people on whom I try out my ideas on northern Nigeria and whose approval gives me faith I'm onto something, and Leena Hoffmann has recently become another prized critic. Lisa Lindsay, Will Gould, Jonathan Saha, and Arvind Rajagopal have been patient as I repeatedly tried out my ideas on them. Kerry Ward has not only been another trusted critic but gave me the title for the book.

This work has been sustained by many others as well. Patrick Loomer and Ana Carden-Coyne have been wonderful friends all the way through the writing of this book. The loss of Stephen Vella still hurts, as does that of my grandmother, Betty Bowman. I can't adequately describe my debt to Anupama Rao. Her fierce brilliance is as formidable as her steadfast loyalty, and I hear her voice echo through everything I write. My parents, Robert Pierce and Barbara Bowman Pierce, have been my intellectual and moral anchors, and my sisters, Anne Pierce Shaum and Margy Pierce, have been the bedrock of my sanity. Siva Sithraputhran has experienced all the tumult that accompanied writing this book and edited more of it than any sane person would have cared to. I thank him for everything. Finally, Pierce Elango Sithraputhran changed everything. He has been mostly aware of the book as a nuisance ("Why are you looking at your computer; look at *me!*") and occasionally a convenience ("Stop looking at me; go look at your computer!"). He has taught me something of the fierce desperation Nigerian parents feel for their children's futures. I hope those children and he will together create a better future than the one we have made for them.

This book is for Elango.

Northern
Region

Western
Region

Eastern
Region

Map 1. Three Regions, 1939–1963

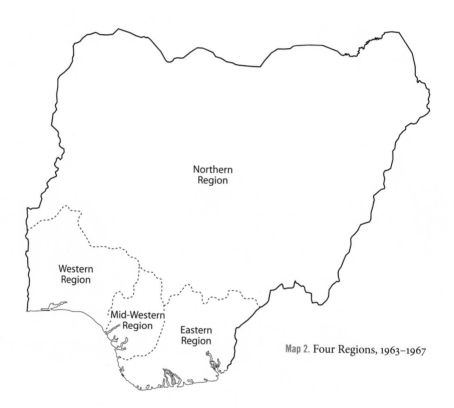

Northern
Region

Western
Region

Mid-Western
Region

Eastern
Region

Map 2. Four Regions, 1963–1967

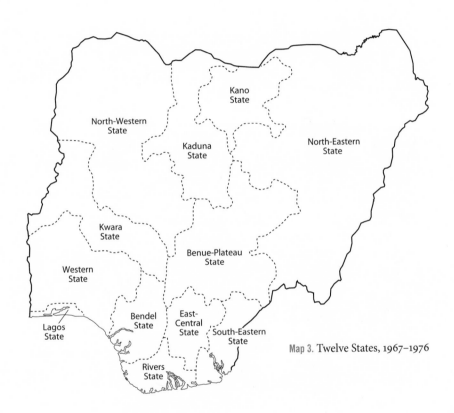

North-Western
State

Kano
State

Kaduna
State

North-Eastern
State

Kwara
State

Benue-Plateau
State

Western
State

Bendel
State

East-
Central
State

South-Eastern
State

Lagos
State

Rivers
State

Map 3. Twelve States, 1967–1976

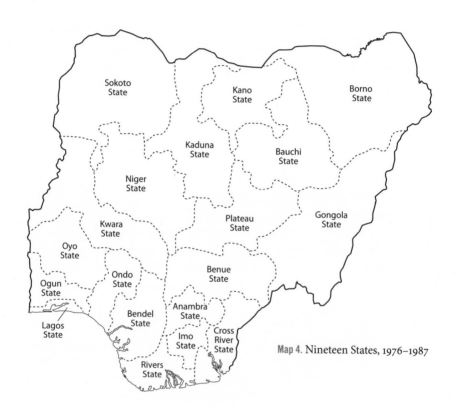

Map 4. Nineteen States, 1976–1987

INTRODUCTION

The messages are familiar to almost anyone with an e-mail account. During the early 2000s they became an international punch line. Often purporting to come from the relative of a Nigerian government official, they requested the recipient's help to transfer vast sums of money out of the country. In return for this assistance, the recipient would receive a significant percentage of the funds being transferred. Usually unsaid was that the money had been acquired corruptly and that the sender needed help in avoiding the attention of law enforcement. This high-tech update to the old Spanish Prisoner scam often appeared over the name of Maryam Abacha, widow of General Sani Abacha, who was Nigeria's military head of state from 1993 until his death in 1998. General Abacha had gained notoriety for the brutality of his regime and for personal corruption. As Nigeria moved to civilian government after his death, various estimates emerged of how much he and his family had taken out of the country—U.S. $2 billion, $3 billion, $8 billion, $9 billion. The Nigerian government sought international cooperation in 1999 to trace embezzled money, and in response Switzerland froze nearly $700 million in Abacha family assets.[1] The ensuing drama garnered immense press coverage, as the government repeatedly detained Mrs. Abacha and members of her family, and as talks between government lawyers, family members, international banks, and foreign governments resulted in considerable sums repatriated. The negotiations were fraught—the newspaper *Tempo* reported Mrs. Abacha was "snobbish and uncooperative" with government negotiators[2]—but Mrs. Abacha became something of an international celebrity, famous as mistress of a misappropriated fortune.

And thus the e-mails. Mrs. Abacha might not have been such a compelling signatory if her husband's regime had not already been known for human rights abuses. Most famously, the execution of the Ogoni activist Ken Saro-Wiwa brought the government to global attention. The story epitomized not just the regime's brutality but its corruption. Saro-Wiwa was known for his work in the Niger Delta, where the Ogoni people lived. They and other delta peoples had suffered the most from Nigeria's oil industry, losing great quantities of farmland to oil production and even more to the environmental degradation that went along with it. Worse, from their point of view, the revenues from oil were diverted elsewhere, to other regions of Nigeria and to the pockets of its rulers. Both inside Nigeria and internationally, General Abacha became synonymous with repression. As he became famous he was also equated with the political corruption for which Nigeria was already well known. The e-mails in Mrs. Abacha's name thus had various features to attract those with casual knowledge of recent Nigerian history: many had heard of vast sums stolen, many associated her name with that theft, and many had heard of her legal troubles. Other touches of verisimilitude may have passed many by: thus, the e-mails frequently had a return address that mentioned Gidado Road in Kano's elite Nassarawa neighborhood, where the Abachas famously own a house. But of course the e-mails did not come from Mrs. Abacha, and their recipients were not seriously intended to launder money. Anyone who replied was drawn into an extended correspondence, asked to send money to cover some of the expenses of regaining control of the fabled money, or even asked to come to Nigeria. There the target might be robbed, or subjected to elaborate dramas designed to extort large sums. In the first years of this century when this particular genre of e-mail was at its height of popularity, the senders were easily found. One could go into almost any Internet café in Nigeria and see the e-mails being written. When one sat down at a computer and woke the screen, if one didn't find porn it was often these e-mails.[3] There has since been a crackdown, and now in Internet cafés each computer usually has a printed warning sign informing users they will be ejected from the café if they write such e-mails or view obscene material. More recently, the advance-fee fraud e-mails tend to come from other countries. The confidence games emerging from Nigeria's Internet cafés are somewhat different—financial scams are more likely to propose private business dealings than money laundering, and many schemes have to do with Internet dating or identity theft. But although the specifics have changed, the object is the same, to convince the recipient to pay large sums of money in the hopes of eventual reward.

The genre of the Abacha e-mails became established long before the general came to power. The technology that brought it into being was the fax machine rather than the Internet. Nonetheless, a relatively anonymous medium of communication was not the only precondition for this confidence scheme. The scam depended on Nigeria's reputation for vast corruption. Mrs. Abacha was a compelling figure because of the Abachas' international notoriety, but in truth she only served as the embodiment for a well-entrenched stereotype. By the time fax machines were beginning to spool out stories of sequestered bank accounts and potential enrichment, the world had been hearing of florid Nigerian corruption for more than a decade. From the beginning of the oil boom in 1970, the Nigerian government notoriously spent vast sums of money, much of which was squandered and much of which was stolen. Both dynamics attracted lengthy international press coverage. The civilian rulers of the Second Republic (1979–83) received additional bad publicity when, in the aftermath of the oil glut and onset of the international debt crisis, the government was forced to admit that billions of dollars of government money had simply disappeared. Faxes and e-mails inviting their recipients to participate in looting Nigeria depended on the country's eruption into international discourse as a reservoir of corruption.

The e-mails in particular have also helped to confirm that reputation. Indeed, the e-mails have brought the Nigerian term "419" into international use. It invokes the section of the Nigerian criminal code outlawing confidence schemes. That section reads:

> Any person who by any false pretense, and with intent to defraud, obtains from any other person anything capable of being stolen, or induces any other person to deliver to any person anything capable of being stolen, is guilty of a felony, and is liable to imprisonment for three years. If the thing is of the value of one thousand naira or upwards, he is liable to imprisonment for seven years. It is immaterial that the thing is obtained or its delivery is induced through the medium of a contract induced by the false pretense. The offender cannot be arrested without warrant unless found committing the offence.[4]

Provisions of this kind were a feature of penal codes dating back to the beginning of the colonial period. They attempted to regulate a major headache for the new government. Termed generically "personation," the earliest versions involved people who dressed up in army uniforms or represented themselves as interpreters for British colonial officers and extorted money on the basis of their assumed positions. The colonial regime considered personation to be a particular threat to the legitimacy of the new British government and treated it severely.[5] Attempting to install a political order that was culturally alien, the British had every reason to fear criminals who appeared to be state actors. From the start the state reacted with particular ferocity to Nigerians who threatened the legitimacy of the new political order. Criminals engaged in personation and properly installed officials who misused their office were singled out for physical chastisement. The spectacle of public flogging was used to demonstrate the regime's disavowal of those who would use the symbols of state authority for private and dubious ends.

A semantic slippage from personation to the misuse of political office maps onto what might otherwise seem to be an idiosyncratic usage within Nigerian English: *both* confidence schemes and political corruption are referred to with the word "corruption." Naturally, most if not all Nigerian English speakers are well aware of international usages and of the nature of political corruption; nonetheless, Nigerian usages are somewhat broader. If anything, in Nigerian popular culture deception of individuals for personal enrichment is more morally dubious than the simple act of stealing money from the state or of exerting influence on behalf of those with whom one has personal ties. Indeed, these latter might, under certain circumstances, strike many as understandable or even laudable. As Daniel Jordan Smith suggests: "When Nigerians talk about corruption, they refer not only to the abuse of state offices for some kind of private gain but also to a whole range of social behaviors in which various forms of morally questionable deception enable the achievement of wealth, power, or prestige as well as much more mundane ambitions. Nigerian notions of corruption encompass everything from government bribery and graft, rigged elections, and fraudulent business deals, to the diabolical abuse of occult powers, medical quackery, cheating in school, and even deceiving a lover."[6] Such conceptual breadth is key to understanding the phenomenon overall—even and especially in the sense of abusing public office. The relatively wide scope of Nigerian usages masks some of what is specific to the place. It also encodes the long history of "corruption" both as a set of activities of Nigerian officials and as an international discourse for describing official malpractice, wherever it might be found. Taking the term "corruption" as transparent and straightforward implies that it has a universal set of meanings, but its vernacular application in Nigeria maps onto a distinctive local moral field. This book will argue Nigeria is not somehow exceptional or pathological in that. The semantic variability of "corruption" in Nigeria suggests something more interesting, which is that the use of the term lies at the center of how moral questions about the distribution of public goods are negotiated. In Nigeria, as anywhere else, talking about corruption is a way of talking about moral ills. What is distinctive in Nigeria is the specific history of how such public ills intersect with public evaluations of the state. More than that, the broader references in some Nigerian uses of "corruption" also points to long-term developments in how the term has functioned internationally.

The subject of this book is not 419 e-mails, nor is it a muckraking description of corruption in Nigeria. Rather, it is a history of corruption as a cultural category. It describes how corruption has taken on the forms it has, and it argues that the profusion of Nigerian corruption is partly explained by its cultural complexity. One reason Nigerian corruption is now omnipresent and florid is because "corruption" is a label bringing together a host of practices and moral imperatives. The challenge is that the label is used locally, but it applies to practices that transcend region, local moral communities, and traditions of moral discourse. Following how corruption has functioned in Nigeria historically requires focusing on something *other* than Nigeria's international reputation for corruption, or the reality of corrupt practices that pervade nearly every aspect of public life. Nonetheless the cultural imbrication of "corruption" ultimately provides insight into these two phenomena. This book's primary project is to trace historically the forms of political culture that have led to present-day Nigeria, plagued by corruption and notorious for it. Its point of departure is the contention that it is not entirely clear what "corruption" means. The history of Nigerian corruption reveals that "corruption" takes on a variety of meanings and refers to various phenomena. Corruption's meanings are multifaceted and polyvalent. At the most fundamental level, this book examines the polyvalence of "corruption." It traces how corruption discourse has changed across the past century. It considers the complexity of "corruption" as a conceptual category, and it attempts to map that complexity onto the history of corruption in Nigeria both as a set of concrete practices and as a clutch of ideas. Nigerians and international commentators decry the country's corruption, and rightly so. This book does not question the suffering corruption causes, nor the governmental dysfunction the label "corruption" indicates. These are real. The problems are urgent. But they have also changed across time, paralleling transformations in the political system and the economy. More than that, the vocabulary and traditions of discourse available for describing and evaluating these phenomena have also changed over time. The question asked here is of the political and cultural work done by people's calling such a complex of activities "corruption." That history is significant in its own right. Coming to terms with it is a necessary condition for dealing with the problem of corruption as it is generally understood.

The starting point of this project came while I collected oral histories about local government across the twentieth century. I noticed certain people did not tend to describe instances of bribe seeking, extortion, and embezzlement on the part of government officials as "corruption." Rather, many people consistently described such behavior as "oppression," acts that were *wrong* but that were nonetheless a common quality of people in government. Oppression is something to be expected from government officials, which is why it makes sense to avoid them as much as possible. This descriptive habit was most common among people who spoke only Hausa (rather than having substantial fluency in English as well), who did not have much Western education, and who were not strongly oriented toward Western culture. It is worth taking their formulation seriously, and not to dismiss it simply as a case of ignorance of the law or of appropriate governmental practice. Viewing certain official practices as being "oppression" rather than "corruption" is perfectly robust on its own terms. It enables moral evaluations of particular individuals. It is also part of a more complex whole, since the practices some would call "oppression" are also discussed by people who inhabit other conceptual universes. Both paradigms of malpractice-as-oppression and an international technocratic paradigm of malpractice-as-corruption should be taken as important ways of thinking about the morality of Nigerian political practice. Similarly, the formulation of "corruption" in Nigerian English in terms rather broader than those in American English should be taken equally seriously. Insisting on the polyvalence and the conceptual complexity of the label "corruption" is a way of starting to examine how particular social practices (stealing money from the government, for example) become conjoined with specific modes of describing them. The forms corruption has taken—and the manner in which it has become both all-pervasive and notorious—are encoded within the very complexity of corruption as a semantic complex. Observers variously evaluate "corrupt" practices and therefore make different moral claims on the officials in question. A multiplicity of interpretations helps to perpetuate the entire system. I will propose that part of the reason Nigerian corruption has taken on its current forms stems from its polyvalence, the manner in which social practice is inflected by translation between languages and frames of reference, by which it refracts through different and almost incommensurable social institutions.

But I have gotten ahead of myself. So far, my invocation of "international technocratic paradigms of corruption" has been somewhat loose, even while I have insisted on the specificity of Nigerian usages. This is partly because technocratic usages are themselves elusive. Consider one influential formulation: Transparency International (TI), the well-known nongovernmental organization, defines "corruption" as "the abuse of entrusted power for private gain."[7] The definition is useful in that it signals its own intellectual history even as it displaces almost all definitional bite onto other key terms. TI's definition is admirably open-ended, and it applies to all of the phenomena the organization wants to deal with. But unless one already has a good sense of what it means by every adjective and noun in the phrase, the definition is elusive. The key terms are "entrusted," "power," and "private" ("abuse" and "gain" are also challenging, for that matter). Below I will discuss these issues in more detail, but here it is worth noting that such technocratic definitions rest on particular understandings of what the state is and how its functionaries should discharge their duties. For technocratic commentators, corruption implies a deviation from the principles governing officials' behavior, and it also depends on a distinction between public and private: "corruption" labels not just divergence from official codes of conduct but divergence out of private interest. Technocratic paradigms are very different from those indexed by deception or oppression.

So this is my point of departure: some Nigerian paradigms of corruption are different from international norms, but together these three paradigms cover what one might term "corruption" in Nigeria. Where does that get us? How does one study corruption, especially if the conceptual universes available to describe it are divergent and sometimes incompatible? Is it possible to write a history of corruption if the word itself continually changes in meaning? The difficulties are yet more challenging. For while phenomena termed "corruption" constitute a discrete, albeit open-ended set of material practices (dressing up in army uniforms, gouging extra taxes from peasants, wiring government money to private Swiss bank accounts, sending deceptive e-mails), only some are "corrupt" in TI's sense. The various ways of thinking about corruption demonstrate that it is also a complicated array of discourses available for describing those practices. Instead of evaluating material practices as right or wrong, regular or irregular, one must consider descriptions of corruption to be a set of discourses that evaluate the moral qualities of concrete events. "Corruption" in this sense is a moral terrain on which debate is conducted. TI's definition is one strand in this much more complex discursive field, as are notions of corruption as oppression or deception. Related to but distinct from this formulation of corruption as a moral discourse is the fact that corruption is a set of legal doctrines under which particular events or practices can be adjudicated. Corruption is a legal category. And here, TI's definition maps onto formal laws fairly well, even if there are complexities in how those laws work in practice. These three registers of corruption—material practice, moral discourse, legal category—are sometimes parallel. They sometimes intersect. They sometimes are wholly independent.

If one wants to understand Nigerian corruption, therefore, one must understand that the label "corruption" is not a rigid designator. The term's meaning is not transparent. It refers to a variety of phenomena. Its meaning is contextually dependent, but more importantly its social utility stems in part from its protean qualities. Corruption's three registers—material, discursive, legal—are not three alternatives, each in its own domain the only possible meaning of "corruption." Rather, their complicated interdependence has structured the changing forms corruption has taken in modern Nigeria. This is a challenge to discuss, because it requires using the word "corruption" in a variety of ways, sometimes in scare quotes and sometimes not. For this reason, it is useful to borrow Jean-Pierre Olivier de Sardan's term "corruption-complex," although my use of it here is very different from his.[8] In this book I use it to designate the totality of phenomena encompassed by the term "corruption": practices that might be labeled "corrupt," the three registers in which "corrupt" practices subsist, *and* the various culturally embedded frames of reference through which this complex of practice and naming can be understood. A key contention of this book, then, is that the flamboyance of the Nigerian corruption-complex emerges directly from the ways in which its heterogeneous components have developed across the course of modern Nigerian history. As a matter of heuristic convenience, I shall use "corruption" with quotation marks in order to emphasize its status as a label. At times I shall also use the word uninflected, simply as a matter of narrative convenience.

A corollary to my formulating the problem in this way is the corruption-complex's cultural embeddedness and historical contingency. But those specificities pose their own challenges. To the extent that the corruption-complex is embedded in vernacular culture (which itself has changed across time, and continues to do so), the task of writing a history of how the complex emerged and was transformed is hideously complicated by Nigeria's cultural complexity. Contemporary Nigeria is a federation of thirty-six states; within those states live peoples speaking an estimated 250 languages. Each language might be considered to correspond to its own cultural vernacular, potentially with its own distinct manner of conceptualizing corruption. Some language groups may have more: a society such as that of Hausaphone northern Nigeria is extremely diverse, and has long been stratified by class, occupation, and geography. Moreover, the meanings of ethno-linguistic categories are fluid, and their boundaries porous. Their social implications have changed across time, and indeed even considering them to be *distinct* groups in many ways is a legacy of the colonial period. Reifying ethnicity is thus a mistake, and yet it has been a matter of life and death for many across Nigerian history. Ethnic groups are imagined communities in Benedict Anderson's terms, subject to change over time and subject to manipulation by individuals. It is sometimes possible to identify with different groups at different moments.[9] Despite their complexity, contingency, and fluidity, ethnonyms and linguistic groupings can serve as rough proxies for the contexts within which cultural understandings of phenomena like corruption take place. As such, every group potentially contains the history of a particular strand of Nigerian understandings of corruption. Perhaps some of these are more significant than others: the three largest ethnic groups (the Hausa, the Yoruba, and the Igbo) make up approximately 60 percent of Nigeria's population, and they have played a disproportionate role in Nigeria's history of ethnic politics. Even so, the history of Nigerian cultures is not reducible to those of the big three. Tracking the history of the cultural embeddedness of the Nigerian corruption-complex, therefore, is impossible in a straightforward narrative. A definitive history of the corruption-complex would need to attend to a myriad of vernacular histories, with all the nuance such would entail; that project is too complex for one volume to attempt at all. Yet the vernacular component of "corruption" is central to how corruption has developed across Nigerian history. In the interest of making a first approximation, therefore, this book will follow one of those strands, from the Muslim Hausa emirates of northern Nigeria as they have become incorporated into Nigeria as a whole. This is a very partial picture of the Nigerian corruption-complex but nonetheless is an important one. Muslim Hausa culture has been politically central to Nigeria from the start of internal self-rule onward. By following this strand of the corruption-complex, this book develops an approximation of what the history would look like for Nigeria as a whole, even though such an account would be almost infinitely more complex. It is thus an essay on how to go about the study of Nigerian corruption more than a history of the entire phenomenon.

Theorizing Corruption

It is all very well to insist that corruption can be understood only in cultural context and that contexts vary, but the formulation ducks a key problem. The entire discussion so far has implicitly relied on what I have been terming a technocratic definition of corruption. It has taken for granted that "corruption" (however defined) applies to a coherent, discrete referent directly describing what is going on when an official engages in "corruption." But does it? At times I have displaced this problem by calling activities that would fit under such a rubric "malpractice." But that is not entirely satisfactory. What features are common to practices that are described in technocratic terms as "Nigerian corruption" or "government malpractice"? What makes them distinctive or worthy of inquiry? What does "Nigerian corruption" have to do with political malpractice in other polities across human history, and to what extent can we equate different intellectual and moral systems for evaluating such malpractice? Is it appropriate, or even possible, to discuss Nigerian corruption as a discrete thing? A bureaucratic logic valorized distinctive codes of conduct for officials working within it; that logic came to Nigeria in tandem with a tradition of describing particular forms of misconduct as "corruption." But this was not static, a constant characteristic of British or western European culture. The import of bureaucratic norms to Nigeria took place in the late nineteenth and early twentieth centuries, at a time when the concept of corruption was in flux within Europe itself.

Western Europe by that time possessed a long history of using "corruption" and its cognates in other European languages metaphorically. In its basic sense, "corruption" denotes an apolitical, literal spoilage and rottenness. Any biological entity degenerates over time; bodies corrupt after they die. Such usages can be extended to describe governmental and public processes as metaphorically spoiled and rotten. A tradition dating from Aristotle and stretching to Machiavelli and beyond saw corruption as the diminution of virtue in the polity, a falling away of the citizenry from the principles of good behavior that had informed them in earlier times.[10] This use of the word "corrupt" was a political critique, or at least suggested principles for structuring a well-run state. Nonetheless, "corruption" in this sense did not have all the nuances it now has, nor was the metaphor necessarily employed to denote all occasions of government malpractice that might now be termed "corruption." Processes of degeneration were not universally correlated with sin, accepting bribes, improper reliance on patronage, and so forth,[11] nor was all condemnation of such practices necessarily understood through biological metaphors. Nonetheless, a powerful tradition had emerged of using such metaphors in this political sense.

Across the eighteenth and nineteenth centuries, political usages acquired new nuances through novel political struggles.[12] In keeping with earlier uses, "corruption" could designate a state of political affairs suffering from some species degeneracy, implying that society had been healthier in earlier periods before things went wrong. Physiocratic writing, for example, posited wealth as emerging from agricultural surpluses and economic problems as caused by the parasitism of merchants and artisans, whose activities degraded earlier states of prosperity. Similarly, Adam Smith and other political economists tried to understand how trade could be maintained to increase national wealth, avoiding distortions that had previously come to plague it. Such traditions of economic thought maintained continuity with earlier thinking about a degeneration of virtue: contemporary economic woes stemmed from an earlier system's spoilage. A novelty, however, had emerged in that such thinkers were not seeking a return to an earlier state of virtue but rather hoped for a different and improved future. Even as this occurred, however, practical politics and patterns of political and economic change pushed "corruption" in new and unexpected directions.

In the United Kingdom, the struggle against "rotten boroughs"—parliamentary constituencies that had declined radically in population and therefore had small electorates and were under the control of a local patron—helped to align ideas about political reform with a specific critique of patronage, which was then designated as "corruption." Reforms in hiring practices for the civil service, clergy, and military commissions, and in university admissions and appointments, similarly deployed "corruption" to criticize existing states of affairs.[13] In the United States, movements to pay public officials with salaries rather than fees and bounties and to combat patronage-based political machines adopted "corruption" as a powerful way of describing what was wrong with the system as it stood.[14] Both of these were instances in which projects of political innovation were dressed up as a return to regimes of morality that had previously prevailed. Because their novelty was also inarguable, such innovations helped to change the meaning of "political corruption" itself, somewhat diffusing the temporal trajectories the trope of rotting had implied. Nonetheless, it was especially the progressive movement in the United States at the turn of the last century that resulted in a new and detailed attention to what "corruption" might mean and how it might be ameliorated, and to the ways in which systems of patronage were incorporated into systems of government.[15]

A distinctive critique of corruption in empire infused "corruption" with yet more complexity. Imperial expansion across the eighteenth century led to a series of scandals. For example, officials of the British East India Company plundered India and then used their riches to buy honor and influence at home. Atrocities were committed against Indians. Almost worse, critics argued, British officials were conducting themselves in a manner that accorded more with "uncivilized" Indian mores than with the beneficence of rulers from a civilized Christian power. Not only that, men who had enriched themselves in such unacceptable ways were frequently from relatively humble backgrounds, but they were able to use their questionable wealth to climb the class ladder at home. Imperial administration debauched European officials and ultimately threatened to corrupt the mother country.[16] At the same time, the heat of the tropics and the allure of the various sexual delights available far from home threatened to debauch the European men and women who went there, creating a carnal corruption.[17] In imperial contexts, the language of corruption did not posit an earlier state of wholeness then spoiled by a process of corruption. Instead, the "advanced" mother country was endangered by the influence of its "primitive" possessions. An imperial dialectic of scandal and attempted reform combined with an ambivalence about the dangers of ruling colonies to push "corruption" in new and unexpected directions.[18] Corruption was no longer simply political degeneracy; it was beginning to imply a persistent primitivism, a lack of modernity, a state of not having achieved (or of having lost) key bureaucratic and procedural innovations in government. By the early twentieth century, Western states were still far from having eliminated all practices that could be called "corrupt," quite the contrary. However, an idiom for describing a particular genre of undesirable political forms was well established. "Corruption" was available as a term of critique. It pointed in many temporal directions at once, even as its means and application continued to shift.[19]

This process had relatively little purchase in Nigeria at the time of colonization, though many instances of annexation were justified by the claim that indigenous rulers had degenerated and become corrupt.[20] For the most part, however, the critique was applied to governmental processes that depended on an organization model brought to Nigeria only through colonial rule. Euro-American reformers had to this extent triumphed: by roughly 1900 "corruption" denoted a failure to live by the mores of a particular kind of bureaucracy. This usage valorized a bureaucratic code of conduct; it also naturalized distinctions between public and private and delegitimated political motivations on the basis of "private" interests. In the late nineteenth century, this distinction was still under negotiation and was more complicated in practice than in theory.[21] Nonetheless, at the start of the twentieth century when Northern Nigeria was colonized, the technocratic paradigm of corruption was still relatively close to its vernacular sense. The way it functioned as a political critique did not depend on a terribly elaborate theorization of the state or its history.

The antimonies of efficient bureaucracy and corruption were not the end of the story. "Corruption" continued to shift its meaning across the twentieth century, particularly as social scientists began to consider the problem in the years after World War II. Attention to corruption came as countries across Asia and Africa attained independence from colonial rule. Scholars accordingly attempted to plot a course toward modernity and political stability for these "new nations." The general rubric for this school of thought was modernization theory, which posited a universal sequence of political and economic development through which "precapitalist" systems of production like peasant agriculture gave way to industrial capitalism. The urgency of modernization theory stemmed from the ambitions of the emergent "Third World" and the fear of communist revolutions; the ambition was to achieve capitalism and democracy faster and with less social upheaval than the process had occasioned in the West. Frustrating the desires of citizens of new states might make socialism more attractive to them.[22] Corruption was a potential pitfall in the path to modernity. In this intellectual context, "corruption"—that is, officials not performing their duties properly but abiding by private interests—was a *technical* problem. Informed by a need to provide technical advice to the rulers of newly independent countries, scholars in this new approach avoided simple exhortations to progress but instead attempted to provide guidance about how progressive change might be accomplished. Moral proscription and political critique were insufficient as technical advice. An early attempt in this vein was a book entitled *Corruption in Developing Countries,* which acknowledged that corruption caused enormous problems but also argued that condemning it tout court was oversimple and unproductive. The authors proposed to address the "scarlet thread" of corrupt practices that plagued newly independent nations. They posited that the solution was to examine how corruption had been overcome in the West. This created a certain analytical problem, the authors admitted, because comparison and a "moralizing approach" might miss local systems of understanding, which were key to local practice. Indigenous culture needed to be taken into account, since only careful attention to corruption's social utilities would enable planners to address it effectively.[23] In this view corruption was neither an object of political critique nor a deformation of earlier, purer states of affairs. Rather, it was characteristic of a particular moment of social evolution, which all societies would face at one point or another. It had a social utility, and its many drawbacks might be ameliorated through a proper understanding of other societies' experiences.

An emphasis on local systems of knowledge and an acknowledgment that corruption could achieve important ends touched off a new literature considering corruption less as a moral problem than as a shortcoming in political systems, and as the consequence of relatively straightforward and recent historical causes.[24] A critical corollary was that corruption was the product of a certain stage of development. It was a sign of primitivism but for precisely that reason could be overcome through political development. One point of departure was a proposal by a former British political officer in Africa that corruption was the consequence of a clash between precolonial modes of political culture and new forms of the state that required a different mode of political comportment.[25] Others emphasized Ronald Wraith and Edgar Simpkins's rejection of moral condemnation, urging examination of such practices' historical or structural causes, rooted in local contexts.[26] Joseph Nye brought together these strands in an influential essay positing that there had been two primary approaches to the study of corruption, which he termed moralist and revisionist. He proposed retaining the insights of each approach by subjecting corrupt practices to cost-benefit analysis, as a way of determining the conditions under which corruption should be considered to be a barrier to political and economic development. Nye's article was important in its identification of two approaches to thinking about corruption, in its explicit reliance on modernization theory as a framework, and in its import into concepts of corruption a version of Weberian sociology then current among modernization theorists. Nye's definition of corruption bore a strong resemblance to earlier attempts, but its nuances were innovative: "behavior which deviates from the formal duties of a public role because of private-regarding . . . pecuniary or status gains; or violates rules against the exercise of certain types of private-regarding influence."[27] Nye's elaborate vocabulary imported a theoretical apparatus that today remains encoded as unarticulated assumptions when "corruption" is used in a technocratic sense.[28] Even though modernization theory lost explicit purchase after many decades' unrelenting criticism, the use of technocratic paradigms of corruption invokes this rather more rarified conceptual system. The corruption literature borrowed from modernization theory a historical argument suggesting corruption was ultimately the product of a confrontation between traditional and modern political culture. More recent uses of technocratic definitions also involve this conjectural and (as I shall argue in this book) rather problematic history. Nye is important in this regard because his definition most clearly signals the underlying assumptions of the paradigm.

Using technocratic terminology not only suggests the critic is a disinterested technocrat; it also presupposes an entire developmentalist history of the problems under discussion. The scholarly redefinition of corruption made a reformist critical vocabulary into an entire past, present, and future: "tradition" gives way to a problematic present, which may be redeemed in a modernized future. Describing political corruption thus systematizes and theorizes an analytic object for the purpose of justifying technical interventions in the evolution of capitalist modernity. The irony is that this intellectual apparatus was grafted onto a discursive tradition that emerged from idiosyncratic political struggles in countries whose histories have little to do with difficulties in countries like Nigeria today. Instead of remaining an objective description of a universal process of human development (much less an abstract set of neutral paradigms), "corruption" evolved as a way of critiquing political practices in

eighteenth- and nineteenth-century polities, mostly in Europe. Modernization theorists and other sociological commentators in the 1960s and 1970s may
have relied on a somewhat teleological view of how states develop or should
develop, but the long-term legacy of their paradigms does not lie in that conjectural future history. Rather, their redefinition of "corruption" helped to create a novel "political unconscious,"[29] which moved from individual instances
in which corruption was identified to an implicit and inarticulate conviction
that corruption had a consistent set of causes and at least potentially a consistent set of solutions. For this reason it has had profound political and cultural
consequences.

Social Science and Corruption in Practice

While the category of corruption was acquiring new weight, incisive field studies such as those of M. G. Smith and Simon Ottenberg developed a detailed
picture of how political elites emerged as intermediaries between domestic
economies and the international market as a consequence of political structures that came about during the colonial period. Smith's study of colonial Zaria,
for example, focused on long-term patterns of oppressive conduct on the part
of Zaria's aristocracy. Smith identified a long-term increase in what he termed
"the use of public office or authority for private advantage and gain"[30] ever since
a reformist jihad at the beginning of the nineteenth century. During the twentieth century, colonial rule brought greater centralization of government and
a larger role for it in managing economic life, both of which greatly increased
corruption's incidence. More immediately influenced by neo-Weberian approaches, Ottenberg viewed corruption in local government as being the consequence of a set of structures organized around modern bureaucratic principles.
These were staffed by people whose political culture dictated more personalistic
and reciprocal modes of decision making. The clientelist nature of their political support and the centrality of the state in providing opportunities for
enrichment combined to make diversion of state resources to private ends easy
and inevitable.

In the years following this pioneering work, the literature on corruption
flourished, to such an extent that it is difficult to represent its entirety.[31] Nonetheless, the period from the 1970s onward was not simply a halcyon time for
secondary literature on corruption; it was also when Nigeria became almost
synonymous with the term. To the extent that scholarly literatures have
informed technocratic vernaculars, some overview of the former is useful.
Roughly, one can perceive three major approaches to writings in the traditions

arising from the conjunctures of the 1960s. The tradition that has had great-est influence on technocratic approaches to corruption since the heyday of modernization theory emerged from economics. Many of these scholars fol-low Susan Rose-Ackerman in treating corruption as "an illegal or unauthor-ized transfer of money or an in-kind substitute" for which the "'bribee' must necessarily be in a position of power, created either by market imperfections or an institutional position which grants him discretionary authority."[32] Corrup-tion is conceptualized as a particular form of rent seeking—attempting to gain economic benefit by acquiring access to already-existing wealth rather than creating new—potentially constrained by an appropriately designed system of incentives. The trick is to prevent anticorruption mechanisms from imposing greater economic costs than does corruption itself.[33] For development plan-ners this is extremely useful in that it provides a package of potential fixes to specific forms of corruption. Rose-Ackerman herself suggests a battery of poli-cies that might, in different combinations, lower the incidence of corruption in many societies.[34]

Despite this obvious utility, microeconomic approaches provide little in-sight into why particular states of affairs obtain in the real world, tending to take institutional arrangements as instantiations of policy choices arrived at by decision makers after weighing them against alternatives. This may cre-ate a robust predictive model, but it does not accord very well with the pro-cesses through which these arrangements came about. On one hand, such approaches are well suited to reform, or at least to the design of policies ad-dressing the need for reform.[35] Accordingly, such approaches greatly influence policy—within governments, the donor and business communities, and civil society groups like Transparency International. On the other hand, like their modernization theory predecessors, they tend to naturalize the current state of affairs as a moment in a developmental sequence or to imagine a solution that could simply be willed into being.

A tradition emerged in political science somewhat at odds with this em-phasis. Such scholars emphasized the patterning of political relationships.[36] As the initial celebration of African independence gave way to more sober and critical assessments of African states' thorny problems during the 1970s and 1980s, scholars like Colin Leys and Sayre Schatz argued for the impor-tance of political elites in maintaining African states' dependent position in the world economy as a consequence of the elites' drive to maintain access to lucrative opportunities diverting state resources toward themselves and their families.[37] The sociologist Peter Ekeh made a very influential suggestion that postcolonial Africa was characterized by the coexistence of two distinct public spheres, one of primordial cultural ties whose moral claims were similar to the intimate ones of the private sphere, and a second of civic involvement equivalent to the Western public sphere but which was perceived as fundamentally amoral. Africans, Ekeh argued, experienced the claims of the primordial public sphere as exerting great moral force but perceived the civic public sphere as simply a realm to be exploited.[38] Together the emphasis on the peculiar incentives dependent economies created for political elites and culturalist accounts of how such elites perceived their sociopolitical responsibilities enabled the emergence of an important literature on politics in countries like Nigeria.

Such approaches ascribed corruption and political instability to the persistence of patrimonial ties within modern state structures, often under the rubric of patrimonalism or neo-patrimonialism.[39] One of the most influential studies of Nigerian politics emerged from this tradition. Richard Joseph's *Democracy and Prebendal Politics in Nigeria* looks systematically at how the politics of patronage (and specifically the ethnicized distribution of state offices) both constituted and fatally undermined the course of politics in Nigeria's Second Republic (1979–83).[40] One of Joseph's key insights was that constitutional structures did not just exacerbate ethnic cleavages. Rather, the two had a mutually constitutive relationship. Patron-client ties were the sine qua non of Nigerian politics. Constitutional structures and patterns of politics determined how patronage could be exercised. Patronage largely followed ethnic boundaries, and since the state distributed most economic opportunities, political competition was inevitably a struggle over resources more than policy. Communal sentiments became a primary idiom for this competition.[41] More recently, William Reno made analogous arguments about the ways in which the politics of clientelism (or, in a later book, warlordism) have inflected the practice of politics and as a consequence have created corruption almost as a by-product.[42]

This literature has corresponded to much wider discussions on the African state which locate many of its dysfunctions in the inadequacies of institutions put in place during the colonial period. Local administration became the responsibility of officials granted resources inadequate for their political needs, or for their need for public consumption as understood in local political culture. Instead of acting as guardians of the public interest, African elites have accordingly pursued the interests of their home regions, of their families and patronage networks, and (quite frequently) of cities over rural areas.[43] One influential strand of thought was that the African state was weak, lacking the mechanisms of enforcement and control usually thought to characterize the modern state and maintaining its existence largely because of an international system that presupposed all territories are governed by a state, thus propping up institutions that had little popular legitimacy or efficacy.[44] More than approaches from economics, this approach answers critical questions about why African states face the dilemmas they do. But if the conclusions scholars taking this approach draw do not always offer obvious packages of reformist solutions, they nonetheless suggest how corruption might be overcome. Scholars who emphatically reject the supposition that African political problems emerge from a failure to develop nonetheless often rely on an implicit model of (European) states from which African ones deviate. Even where African states might be celebrated as hybrid, as having distinctive forms of politics, European forms remain as an ideological point of comparison, a norm, or an unmarked category—a great irony, since "corruption" emerged as a political critique rather than as a supposed developmental stage. Treating it as designating something coherent and real, which states might be plagued by or not, naturalized an ideological portrait of the noncorrupt state as a *European* state, when the conceptual category had emerged as an implicit complaint thus did not exist in the real world. Political case studies often lose track of the local systems of meaning through which "corrupt" practices emerge and from which they take on a large portion of their social significance.

Such questions, however, are at the center of an ethnographic literature on corruption that has emerged relatively recently. Much of this work moves away from neo-Weberian assumptions about the nature of state institutions or the significance of a clash between patrimonial and bureaucratic political logics. Rather, ethnographers have taken an actor-centered approach, considering how individual people understand the situation of corruption within which they find themselves. In their research on Ghana, for example, Brenda Chalfin and Jennifer Hasty describe how "corrupt" practices are understood in cultural context. Chalfin's fine-grained examination of the Ghanaian customs service demonstrates how customs agents and other state officials constitute "the state" in a particular location while being dependent on local political and economic relationships enabling them to exercise their authority and to extract "corrupt" revenue for themselves. Hasty's fieldwork working as a journalist in southern Ghana enabled a uniquely insightful account of how both "corrupt" practices and political condemnation of corruption depend on fundamentally similar expressions of desire for access to resources not available to particular actors.[45] Daniel Jordan Smith on southeastern Nigeria,[46] Janet MacGaffey on Congo/ Zaire, [47] and Olivier de Sardan and Giorgio Blundo's comparative project on Benin, Niger, and Senegal have all provided particularly noteworthy ethnographic studies of corruption.[48] Also important is the influence of the anthropological literature on gift giving and prestation. Following Marcel Mauss's seminal account of the gift as a total social fact, the organizing principle of exchange and thereby of social life in pre-market societies, anthropologists have debated the relationship between "pure" gifts and ones that demand reciprocation, and how this relates to other patterns of obligation and hierarchy in human societies.[49] Smith in particular provides a wonderfully detailed portrait of the emergent nature of "corrupt" transactions in particular locales, as a basic logic of prestation is enacted under the demands of bureaucratic authority, an intersection of reciprocity and what Christopher Fuller and Veronique Benei have termed the "everyday state."[50] Of particular note is recent work by Akhil Gupta, who has developed an important ethnography of corrupt state practice in India. He demonstrates the centrality of corrupt and irregular practice in the relationship between ordinary people and the frontline officials of the Indian state, and most importantly shows that *narratives* of corruption are a primary way in which the state itself is discursively constructed through talk of corruption.[51]

Such approaches provide a crucial addition to a literature that has tended to see "corruption" as one phenomenon that variously manifests itself around the globe, or that represents a particular developmental conjuncture. This strength can also be something of a weakness, since it leaves somewhat shadowy the question of how one might pay attention to the local meanings of a global phenomenon, or of the relationship between such socially situated practices and the state structures they emanate from and influence. As Rose-Ackerman notes, "Ethnographic research tends to concentrate on cultural and social expectations to explain the prevalence of personalistic ties and quid pro quo transactions" to the exclusion of looking at the dynamics of "grand" corruption, its systematic qualities, or the central role played by the state."[52] The danger of taking an actor-centered approach to corruption is that doing so tends to de-emphasize its consequences or what is specific to it. In one sense, this criticism is simply a familiar condemnation of anthropological relativism—which in fairness is not a position any serious scholar espouses. But that begs the question of how to deal with it analytically. Is "corruption" simply a series of family resemblances, or is there something more profound linking corruptions together? One useful approach has been taken by historians, who have tended to look at particular contexts and at how the phenomena deemed "corrupt" operated and changed over time.[53]

Along those lines, one of the most influential bodies of literature about the African state considers features that might be termed "corruption" and emphasizes how the specific histories of African states have produced a somewhat unusual state form. Authors like Jean-François Bayart, Mahmood Mamdani, Achille Mbembe, and Jeffrey Herbst have all insisted on examining the *longue durée* trajectories of African states, locating contemporary dysfunction in long-term patterns of politics, political accommodation, population structure, culture, and geography.[54] Such authors' appeals to history often work better as broad-brush characterizations than as detailed descriptions of any particular case. Even accounts that insist on the unlovely legacies of jamming together African political traditions and European political institutions and that decline to valorize European practices as advanced or intrinsically better can end up implicitly importing European models by positing them as actually existing in Europe or elsewhere. Whether or not one supposes a European model of the state is that with which "normal" states should accord, such approaches tend to reify European states as according with aspirational accounts rather than hard facts. The ideological figure of the bureaucratic state, which emerged in projects of political reform crosscutting intellectual traditions describing and enabling reformers' ambitions, becomes taken as an objective description of "normal" states rather than a charter myth some states invoke or a model to which they aspire. "Corruption," in short, is difficult to deal with because it is epistemically shifty: it creates urgent social problems, but its meaning is fluid and subject to change over time. It is a moral discourse as much as it is an objective reality.

How to Do Things with Corruption

Corruption is real. We know that, but that is not because corrupt acts occur and we know they are "corrupt." Corruption is now a global concern because corrupt acts occur *and are labeled "corrupt."* These acts of labeling are polyvalent, varying from time to time, place to place, and even situation to situation, even as they invoke a particular intellectual tradition that is not identical to all traditions for critiquing government malpractice. Changes in the entailments of "corruption" help to produce both the persistence of particular forms of political malfeasance and the perpetuation of a hierarchy of states and political forms. Across the past century invocations of "corruption" in global arenas have moved beyond reformist discourses about degenerate political forms. Increasingly they have invoked an implicit schema of political and social development. At the same time, other, oftentimes more local discourses about the rightness and wrongness of state actions have also acted to inform discussions of "corruption." In this process, such discourses performed political work, but that work has changed over time. This book is thus a history of the practical polyvalence of corruption discourse, and it is a history of the political work "corruption" has done in Nigeria.

Formulating the problematic in this way emphasizes corruption's quality as what might be termed "a political performative." That term is taken from J. L. Austin's notion of performative speech acts.[55] Austin noted there are things people say that have effects in the world simply by being uttered—the celebrant of a wedding saying, "I declare you husband and wife," for example. It is not always straightforward to distinguish what separates performative speech acts from other speech acts, but the notion of speech that does things simply through being uttered is fruitful, particularly when discussing politics. Even more useful is a distinction Austin makes between what he terms illocutionary speech acts and perlocutionary speech acts; the former are speech acts accomplished purely through being uttered, the latter acts accomplished because the words are spoken.[56] If I am a judge passing a sentence, it is an illocutionary act for me to say, "I sentence you to be hanged." My uttering the words accomplishes the act of sentencing. My words also have perlocutionary force in that they will result in the defendant's death by hanging; the sentencing is illocutionary, the hanging perlocutionary. In this instance, the discursive aspects of the corruption-complex function as a political performative, and the challenge for political analysis is to sort out what happens in the gap between the illocutionary and the perlocutionary, somewhere between "I say the town clerk stole money" and his removal from office in disgrace. People talk about corruption in order to achieve specific political ends, which are accomplished in and through the act of labeling. At least when discussing the trajectories of the Nigerian corruption-complex, the material practices of corruption become imaginable and therefore possible because of well-established discourses about corruption. If corruption is central to Nigerian politics *and* talk about corruption is as well, it follows that corruption itself depends on the discourses critiquing it. For this reason, corruption cannot be "solved" until we appreciate its status as a political artifice and political performative.

The cultural history of "corruption" is thus the history of a complex semiotic trajectory. Even in the context of the domestic politics of Western countries, "corruption" has been deployed to shifting political ends. An academic shift to neo-Weberian paradigms in the 1960s helped to bring in an implication of primitivism, which international technocratic parlance continues to employ if sometimes covertly through the idiom of development. As the performative work of "corruption" shifted internationally, Nigerians appropriated the term for their own ends; some accorded with international norms, and some did not. At the same time, vernacular modes of describing government malfeasance intersected and coordinated with technocratic language. The result was a multi-stranded public discourse articulating moral claims within the larger ideological project of the state.

Such a formulation raises as many questions as it answers. To shift attention from corruption conceptualized as objective practices to the amalgam of material practices, discourses, and legal regulation I have termed the corruption-complex is to emphasize moral systems, the political vernaculars that collectively constitute people's understanding of corruption in the world. As I shall argue at length in part I of this book, the moral systems through which government officials have been evaluated can sometimes dictate practices that are also possible to understand as "corrupt." This ambiguity and complexity is an integral aspect of the Nigerian corruption-complex and how it has changed over time. But following such patterns of change is challenging, both methodologically and theoretically. One useful approach to such issues is the literature on moral economy, which will be discussed at length in chapter 4. While there is considerable diversity in different authors' formulations of moral economy, the commonality is that they focus on how groups of people evaluate particular forms of conduct: the mechanisms for setting the price of bread, for example, or the conduct of scientific research. Instead of asking whether an action or procedure is moral, the study of moral economy looks at how such questions are negotiated socially. The question is not whether I personally think the price of bread is fair but whether the broader public within which I am included does, how those collective evaluations are negotiated, and how they then influence community action.[57]

Moral discourses about official conduct exist everywhere. In Nigeria they long predate the colonial period, which means they also long predate the formation of a single, countrywide public sphere. A plethora of Nigerian discourses on corruption is thus partly the consequence of the many languages and cultures from which Nigerians come and within which they continue to live. The story of how hundreds of different normative systems came together to create the multiple political performatives constituting today's responses to corruption is too complex—and too evanescent—to be written as one history. The following chapters attempt something simpler. Part I follows the consolidation of the corruption-complex in Hausaphone northern Nigeria across the colonial period. It then takes the story into the postcolonial period, even as Hausa political culture became intertwined with other modes of politics. The result is less a definitive history of the Nigerian corruption-complex than an extended essay about what enabled it. Part II consists of two thematic essays, each exploring a topic of critical importance to the study of the corruption-complex in Nigeria: chapter 4 looks at moral economy and chapter 5 at the ideological contours of the state. The arguments in these chapters are not intended to be definitive but instead to suggest some ways my approach to the study of corruption may be used elsewhere in Nigeria and beyond. Another way of looking at it is that part I provides the empirical material that supports conclusions presented in part II. This structure suggests several strategies for reading the book. Part I may be of more interest to those looking for the specifics of Nigerian society. The chapters in part II and the conclusion may be of greater comparative and theoretical interest. Although the argument is cumulative, the chapters can largely be read separately.

This book attempts to go beyond the view that corruption is a discrete problem that could be solved by sufficient effort—by providing officials with appropriate incentives or by somehow creating a "modern" political culture. Viewing corruption as the persistence of patron-clientage or patrimonialism in the bureaucratic state creates an uninspiring policy prescription: corruption can be combated by sufficient sincerity. While there might be a certain utility in such an approach, that utility does not lie in actually ending corrupt practices. The adoption of a historical, nonteleological view suggests something more interesting: it demystifies ideas about the state and potentially deromanticizes Western state formation. Corruption discourse is a way of articulating moral claims and of imagining alternative futures. For all the real and urgent pathologies the word "corruption" designates, a careful attention to the corruption-complex's historical, cultural, and conceptual career may ultimately point less toward bureaucratic regularity than toward democratic accountability.

PART I. FROM CALIPHATE TO FEDERAL REPUBLIC

ONE. A TALE OF TWO EMIRS

Colonialism and Bureaucratizing Emirates, 1900–1948

In January 1851 Emir Bello of Katsina received a visit from a young German on an exploratory mission for the British government. His visitor, Dr. Heinrich Barth, posed the emir with a dilemma. Barth's companions had parted ways with him, going instead to Katsina's rivals. One went east to the empire of Borno, which had resisted the jihad that had brought the emir's regime to power. The other went to Maradi, a city founded by the Katsina dynasty the jihad had displaced. Barth himself was on his way to Kano, Katsina's trading rival, and ultimately to Sokoto, the capital of the emir's overlord. The presence of this European in Katsina presented Emir Bello with both opportunities and dangers. As ruler of Katsina, he was entitled to presents from travelers coming through his land. Europeans had access to valuable things: manufactured goods unavailable through normal sources, rare medicines, powerful weapons. Receiving such presents from Barth was doubly desirable when hostile powers (not to mention formally friendly rivals like Kano) might be trading in such goods with Barth's friends. But the emir was no mere shakedown artist. He had a reputation to protect as a just Muslim ruler who fostered the traders on whom his land's prosperity depended. He owed obedience to Sokoto, which was doubly important since its sultan had deposed Bello's predecessor for disobedience a few years previously.[1] And thus his challenge: how could the emir use Barth's presence to best advantage?

The emir's ten days of negotiations with Barth are recounted in the latter's extraordinary travel narrative. The drama demonstrates important and enduring qualities to political life in the region. While the caravan in which Barth traveled was still encamped several miles from the city, the emir came to greet him. Soon thereafter the emir sent his European guest a present of a ram and two calabashes of honey. This was, Barth remarked, "an honor which was rather disagreeable to me than otherwise, as it placed me under the necessity of making the governor a considerable present in return. I had no article of value with me, and I began to feel some unpleasant foreboding of future difficulties."[2] The ten days that followed confirmed his worst fears.

The morning after that initial meeting, Barth confided to the leader of his caravan he had very little appropriate to present to the emir—only razors, cloves, frankincense, and two red caps. The bulk of his possessions having been diverted along another route, he did not even have enough money to purchase a formal gown as a present. The caravan leader warned him the emir "had made up his mind to get a large present from me, otherwise he would not allow me to continue my journey."[3] Visiting the emir, Barth made a present of the caps, razors, cloves, frankincense, a piece of calico, some soap, and a packet of needles. Barth then announced his intention to go to Kano and thence to Borno. There, he explained, he would be reunited with the bulk of his possessions, which had been diverted east. Having access to these goods would enable him to travel west to Sokoto to meet with the sultan. The emir replied that he would be foolish to allow Barth to leave when his companions had gone to Maradi and Borno. Tactfully, the emir forbore pointing out that Barth himself planned a journey to the latter. It was out of the question to allow Barth passage when he had done so little to acknowledge Katsina's dignity, and when he clearly intended to dispense favors elsewhere. Barth was instead separated from his caravan and provided with a house inside the city as an involuntary guest of the emir. Barth's obligation to produce a more spectacular present then deepened when the emir sent him another ram and two ox-loads of grain. In Barth's next meeting with the emir, the discussion expanded from the issue of adequate presents to Katsina's ruler from a visiting dignitary and began to consider Barth's legal status in the country. Barth presented the emir with letters written on his behalf by the sultan of Agadez, which he hoped would convince the emir to allow him onward passage. Emir Bello and his advisors, however, insisted on another interpretation:

> According to the sagacious interpretation of these men, the purport of
> the letter was to recommend me expressly to this governor as a fit person

to be detained in his company. All my representations to the effect that [the sultan] had recommended me in exactly the same terms to the governors of Daura and Kano, and that I had forwarded a letter from Agades to the Emir el Mumenin in Sokoto, informing him that, as soon as we had received new supplies from the coast, one of us at least would certainly pay him a visit, which, under present circumstances, robbed and destitute as we were, we could not well do, were all in vain; he had an answer for every objection, and was impudent enough to tell me that a message had been received from Maradi, soliciting me to go thither; that as Bornu had laid hold of one of my companions, and Maradi of the other, so he would lay hold of me, but of course only to become my benefactor. . . . Seeing that reply was useless and that it was much better to let this lively humorist go through his performance, and to wait patiently for the end of the comedy, I took leave of him and returned to my quarters.[4]

Barth felt trapped. His resources inadequate to satisfy the emir, he realized pretexts might be manufactured to detain him indefinitely. His next move was to try to find a sponsor in local politics. He had been placed under the protection of the expatriate who informally coordinated the affairs of non-Africans in the city. Acquiring a loaf of sugar, Barth reviewed his letters of introduction with this protector, who pledged to support his interpretation of their import, on the understanding that Barth would return to Katsina later after he had been reunited with his possessions. At that point his friends would be rewarded.[5] The strategy was not immediately successful; at his next meeting with the emir he was greeted with a demand for 100,000 cowries (Barth calculated this was equivalent to £8, more than he had with him), which the emir justified as adequate reciprocity for the gifts of foodstuffs Barth had received from him.[6] Ultimately, instead of money the emir received a caftan and a carpet, along with various medical goods: "a few powders of quinine, of tartar-emetic, and of acetate of lead, and . . . a small bottle with a few drops of laudanum." Although the emir then demanded two additional medicines—one for "conjugal vigor" and the other for war (i.e., rockets)—he ultimately allowed Barth to leave, despite disappointment in these last wishes.[7]

By itself the encounter between Barth and the emir has little historical importance. It outlines, however, a political logic of enduring significance. The issue at stake was not finding a fee for services to be rendered, nor was Emir Bello's conduct an exercise of government authority that could be termed proper or improper. The questions were deeper, and the transactions more profound. What was Barth's status in the emirate with regard to the sultan of

Agadez or the sultan of Sokoto? What kind of present was an adequate gesture of respect for the emir, and what were appropriate forms of reciprocity between him and a distinguished visitor? It is a sign of Barth's extraordinary lack of ethnocentrism that he narrates this encounter in a straightforward way. Frustration comes across, but so does his presentation of himself as enmeshed within a web of reciprocal transactions. He was annoyed by the emir but recognized himself as a political inferior. More than that, Barth's narrative underlines the centrality of reciprocal prestation in the governance of the Sokoto Caliphate.

Goods were not simply goods; they were tangible symbols of political position. Their transfer as presents was a means of representing and consolidating political relationships. Medicines, gowns, and carpets were not just useful in their own right; they coordinated Barth's (and by extension Britain's) political position in the central Sudan, and Katsina's position vis-à-vis its overlord, allies, and enemies. Relationships between states were manifested in flows of people and commodities. Katsina sent money and goods and slaves to Sokoto. This was part of a routine process of tax collection, but the symbolism was dense. On his installation, Emir Bello had paid the *kudin sarauta* new officeholders give their overlords, and he regularly sent gifts as "greetings" (*gaisuwa*). Barth's encounter is not just important for its snapshot of the tangible aspects of mid-nineteenth-century diplomacy or because it portrays political culture in some untouched past. Rather Barth's experience is a window onto one moment, with a specific set of historical actors, institutional constraints, and economic considerations, and it demonstrates a mode of politics transformed but persistent in other historical contexts. The manner in which the political culture of mid-nineteenth-century Katsina was incorporated into modern Nigeria is a condition of possibility for more recent practices, which are frequently called "political corruption," and which I suggested in the introduction should be understood as part of a distinctive "corruption-complex" of material practices and discourses about those practices. But it would be anachronistic to suggest the same for the 1850s.

Barth suggests the emir's actions are not entirely admirable even within his own frame of reference:

> Notwithstanding the injustice of every kind which he daily commits, he has some sentiment of honor; and feeling rather ashamed for having given me so much trouble for nothing, as he was aware that it would become known to his fellow-governors, and probably even to his liege lord, the Emir el Mumenin, he was anxious to vindicate his reputation.

It was from the same motive that he begged me most urgently not to tell any body that I had made him the presents here, adding that he would afterward say that he had received them from me from Kano.[8]

There is no hint in the text the emir was "corrupt" in the modern sense of the word—frustrating, disingenuous, perverse, greedy, oppressive, unjust. But not *corrupt*. Emir Bello committed injustice but retained "some sentiment of honor." And critically, Barth did not accuse him of misusing his office, just of causing Barth "trouble for nothing." Even in Barth's frame of reference this was no violation of a set of bureaucratic rules. Barth was, perhaps, not entirely fair to the emir. Aside from noting tensions with Maradi and Borno, he did not acknowledge the complexity of Bello's political position. The emir's grip on power was not entirely secure. His predecessor had been removed from Katsina's throne, and the deposed emir remained in the region, threatening to make common cause with Katsina's other enemies. Though Bello had been in power since 1844, he did not fully succeed in consolidating his authority until after 1853, when his predecessor invaded unsuccessfully.[9] At the time of Barth's 1851 visit, therefore, Bello was engaged in a struggle to install his own supporters in offices of state, to consolidate support among existing officeholders, and to stabilize his position within the caliphate and internationally. Barth's presence was potentially significant for doing so, offering the promise of decisive advantage, but any hopes the emir entertained were disappointed. Barth, for all his acumen, did not acknowledge this.

Despite its nineteenth-century details, this passage in Barth's narrative reads as surprisingly modern. It strikes a chord in anyone who has met repeatedly with officials and been frustrated by a constantly shifting set of requirements. In more recent times, official demands—which some would call "corrupt"— can be structured in a very similar way, with protracted discussions about supplicants' status, the government services necessary for their situation, and the appropriate recompense. For example, during a long research stay in Nigeria I had business in a government office and needed to receive an official document from the officials there. I was forced to visit the office multiple times across three weeks, as I met and befriended a variety of officials in the office, from the most senior to the quite junior. Our interactions were sociable, but friendly conversation served deeper purposes, working out how I was to apply for what I needed, and how much it would cost, both in formal fees and other expenses. Eventually, my primary advisor, one of the more senior officials, determined my case would need to be decided by the relevant ministry in Abuja, the federal capital. In order to expedite my case, I would need to pay for a junior official to take my file there himself, covering his costs of travel, as well as other expenses he and his colleagues would incur on my behalf. The sums involved were substantial, and considerably greater than the published fees, but from my vantage they were not wholly extortionate. As Daniel Jordan Smith has suggested for southeastern Nigeria, this kind of intricately negotiated encounter is all-pervasive but generally perceived as problematic,[10] not unreasonably, since so many resources must be devoted to such demands. How did a politics in which negotiation between superiors and inferiors involving significant material transactions become "corruption" and become a problem?

Hausa States and the Sokoto Caliphate

Emir Bello ruled a state with a venerable history. Katsina had long been famous as one of the *Hausa bakwai*, the seven ancestral Hausa city-states. These polities (the major states of Kano, Katsina, Zaria, and Gobir along with the more minor state of Daura, the Kano vassal Rano, and Biram in what is now Hadejia) claimed descent from a common ancestor-hero who had saved the city of Daura from a snake and married its queen. The Hausa states shared the Hausa language, many aspects of culture, and many elements of their constitutions. In their governments, the king was assisted by a constellation of subordinate officials (the *masu sarauta*, lit. "possessors of office").[11] Some of these offices were reserved for men and some for women, for royals and nonroyals, for free people and slaves (and sometimes eunuchs), though the specific offices and rules for filling them varied from kingdom to kingdom and across history. In addition to their functional offices, the masu sarauta played a key role in territorial administration. Every settlement under a kingdom's control owed allegiance to some officeholder, who assumed responsibility for collecting its taxes and administered its affairs through intermediaries called *jakadu* (sing. *jakada*).

Officeholders gained income from two sources. As a perquisite of office, they possessed large plantations staffed by slaves, whose incomes went to them personally. They also retained a portion of the taxes they collected from settlements inhabited by free people. When an officeholder first attained office, he or she would also make a payment (kuɗin sarauta) to the king, and subordinates regularly made presents (gaisuwa) to their superiors. Kings established and maintained their authority through their ability to appoint and remove officeholders and to grant slave plantations. Gifts thus went both ways, and the demands of superior officials were balanced by their ability to give patronage.[12]

Hausaland became incorporated into the great trans-Saharan trading routes beginning in approximately the eleventh century CE, and Islam came into the region along with traders. Widespread Islamicization came slowly, and it played out differently in the various states; where in Kano the aristocracy converted before ordinary people, in Katsina the reverse happened. Everywhere, this was a feature of the fifteenth and sixteenth centuries, if not later. Toward the end of the eighteenth century, however, Islamicization took a new turn. Some centuries previously, a group of nomadic pastoralists, the Fulani, had come into the region. Though the nomadic Fulani kept to an indigenous religion, some of them settled down in cities, and among those a number became renowned as devout religious scholars. One of these latter, a man named Usman dan Fodio, became a close advisor to the king of Gobir and later a bitter opponent. Dan Fodio and his followers ultimately fled the Gobir capital of Alkalawa and then launched a jihad against the kingdom, which was quickly joined by Fulani in other Hausa states and even beyond. Although most of the states the jihad made war on were officially Muslim, the jihadists declared that the practice of Islam in them was syncretistic and improper. They had great success. Most Hausa states were conquered, and their Hausa dynasties replaced by Fulani emirs subject to Usman dan Fodio, who presided over the empire from a new capital built at Sokoto.[13]

In the decades that followed, the new caliphate systematized the practice of Islam, particularly in cities and larger towns. Wars persisted with enemies beyond the empire's frontiers—kingdoms founded by displaced Hausa dynasties (such as Maradi or the Zaria successor at Abuja), other chieftaincies, and confederations. The jihad and then the continuing state of war intensified practices of slave raiding and slave holding that were already well established. Hausaland had long exported significant numbers of slaves, and its aristocracy depended on slave labor. Larger numbers of war captives expanded these sectors of the economy and also fostered a tendency of emirate authorities to sponsor slave raiding. Under Islamic law it is illegal for Muslims to enslave Muslims, but it is permissible (indeed, meritorious) to enslave pagans, who might thereby be convinced to convert. Across the nineteenth century, parties of quasi-official slave raiders increasingly targeted settlements within the caliphate's borders as well as beyond them, often depending on the flimsy justification that the settlements being raided were only nominally Muslim and had slid back to idolatry.[14]

At times, practices like the *bori* spirit possession movement were persecuted, and women's public role eroded as offices that had been female were filled by men. In both cases, the emphasis was on ensuring that government and officially sanctioned religious practice sufficiently accorded with Islamic norms. The new Fulani emirs were subject to Sokoto, owing the sultan taxes and tribute, appointed and overseen by this supreme authority. With the intensification of Islam as a principle of governance, a moral vocabulary for assessing governmental conduct became increasingly available to ever-larger numbers of people. And (especially since the jihadists burned documents that might have demonstrated pre-jihadic Islam was less syncretistic than they had claimed) a larger number of surviving documents and oral histories has allowed a detailed reconstruction of government practices in the nineteenth-century Sokoto Caliphate. Orthodoxy and obedience were key ways of characterizing official conduct. Officials were regularly deposed for a variety of offenses—oppressive conduct, failing to forward a sufficient share of tax. And yet, corruption was not an obvious idiom for describing these shortcomings. That began to change with the start of the colonial period.

Colonialism and Indirect Rule

In the aftermath of the Conference of Berlin, where Great Britain was allocated a vaguely delineated territory covering much of what is now Nigeria, the British government granted a charter to the Royal Niger Company to establish a protectorate over what is now northern Nigeria.[15] The company's interests lay in trade, and accordingly its protectorate established effective control only in the extreme southern portion of Northern Nigerian territory along the Niger and Benue Rivers, which facilitated trade to the south. Major powers like Borno and the Sokoto Caliphate remained independent, their manufacturing sectors producing textiles and leather goods for the Middle Eastern and north African markets and their traders relying on caravans across the Sahara desert. While this trade (along with the considerable profits to be made selling slaves) made them prosperous, it did not prove attractive for European commerce. Toward the end of the century, French and German activities intensified along Northern Nigeria's frontiers, and Britain increasingly worried about the possibility of their encroachment on what was supposed to be a British sphere of influence.

Despite these dangers, the company was disinclined to establish more of a presence further north. Accordingly, the government canceled its charter and declared a royal protectorate in 1900. It appointed Sir Frederick Lugard as its first high commissioner but gave him strict instructions to avoid unnecessary military conquest. British taxpayers were unenthusiastic about subsidizing new African colonies even while appreciating the glory of imperial possession, and there was little convertible currency to be gained in the northern emirates. Only an external subvention would make a European administration self-sustaining, and London's object was a presence as small and cheap as was compatible with keeping territory out of French or German hands. Lugard and his subordinates, by contrast, were determined to make names for themselves as heroes of the empire by presiding over imperial expansion. Missionaries enthusiastically supported their imperial ambitions in the hopes of gaining access to the vast territory's population, which had been blocked by emirate authorities. Missionaries and colonial officers were joined by antislavery campaigners, who considered Africa to be the last frontier for abolition.[16] This confluence of forces provided political cover as Lugard and his subordinates found casus belli against emirates that remained independent in the first years of the protectorate, directly annexing the major emirates by 1903. This form of expansion was controversial—an influential group of Liberals advocated imperialism through trade rather than direct conquest—but Lugard and his supporters managed to make themselves political conquerors.

The marginal financial situation of the British regime created a practical problem of how to govern a vast territory with a relative handful of European officials—nine when the protectorate first was declared.[17] The solution was to evolve an extreme version of the near-universal imperial tactic of governing through indigenous political institutions.[18] In the Sokoto Caliphate and Borno, therefore, Lugard retained the precolonial political structures more or less intact, replacing monarchs who had fought the invaders and demanding that their successors swear allegiance to Great Britain. Since these officials could be supported by local tax collection, the resulting regime would need relatively little in the way of convertible currency. But an ideological difficulty emerged in the metropole. Direct annexation had been justified to the British public by lurid accounts of Nigerian misgovernance. The Fulani emirs were represented as tyrants, sponsors of slave raids that terrorized the population and degenerate inheritors of a once-proud imperial tradition. The African masses (in this portrait) desperately needed European governance, which was not immediately compatible with retaining the structures of emirate governments intact. Lugard's skills as a propagandist helped to paper over this contradiction, and has had a legacy of enshrining his system of indirect rule as a coherent and innovative policy that Britain extended to all its African colonies, enabling a distinctive form of colonial rule. Lugard's extensive writings[19] and those of his admirers[20] fleshed out indirect rule as a theory of imperial administration uniquely suited "to tribal government, in order to secure maintenance of law and order through the least disturbance of tradition by the imposition of civilized authority,"[21] as the journal *Nature* ecstatically described it.

Existing governments were corrupt (in the older sense of the word), but they also had many admirable traits. Africans would not easily accept European systems of rule because they were conservative and hidebound. It was much better, Lugard argued, to retain familiar systems, which would be cultivated and gradually modernized under British tutelage.[22] Scholars have debated the importance of indirect rule—how interventionist it was in practice, how much autonomy native authorities enjoyed, how different British indirect rule was from French practices of direct administration.[23] These questions are difficult to answer. More productively, one can say that the British indirect rule dictated the terms in which policy debate was conducted, constraining what was politically possible. Preserving tradition was unassailable, but indirect rule also implied a mandate for change and reorganization, often cast as a means of preservation. Indirect rule elevated tradition (and culture more generally) to being a central principle of government.[24]

Whatever colonial policy was called—and whatever its political implications in Britain—the regime faced pressing administrative problems. The political staff genuinely was spread thin. The protectorate was organized as a group of provinces, each headed by a political officer termed the resident. Provinces generally contained several divisions, and each district was headed by a district officer who reported to the resident. For example, Kano emirate was large enough to constitute its own division, and Kano city was also the headquarters for Kano province. Until 1926 Kano province also contained Katsina division (which administered Katsina, Daura, and Kazaure emirates) and Katagum division (with responsibility for Gumel, Hadejia, Katagum, Misau, Dambam, and Jama'are).[25] Residents and district officers had wide-ranging supervisory responsibility. They spent much of their time touring the rural areas of their territories and reviewing the administrative decisions of emirate authorities. Precolonial territorial administration was almost opaque to British review, especially since conveying directives and collecting taxes did not generate paperwork. A target of immediate hostility was the system whereby officeholders administered settlements while continuing to live in emirate capitals. The jakadu who enabled this system to work were assailed by officers as personally immoral and arbitrary, their vices the cause of much of the oppression in precolonial administration. In truth, they attracted British hostility for a system of administration that was complex, personalistic, and negotiable, all of which made it difficult to monitor. To compound the difficulty, the jakada were slaves, which was something of an embarrassment to the avowedly abolitionist government.

As a result, the colonial government engaged in a thoroughgoing reorganization of territorial administration during its first years in charge, implemented at different times in different emirates. Rural settlements were grouped together geographically and then placed under one officeholder, who then was responsible for administering this new contiguous district. District heads retained the responsibilities implied by their emirate offices, but they were also expected to spend the bulk of their time living in their districts and personally heading territorial administration. In theory, they did not retain jakadu on their staffs, but practice was more complicated. At the same time, the categories of tax collected from the population were consolidated and simplified, and their absolute incidence increased considerably.[26] Difficulties emerged almost immediately. Soon after the reorganization took effect, officials were switched from being compensated through a share of tax revenues to being salaried employees of the government. However, salaries were far too low for officeholders' responsibilities to their constellations of clients. Moreover, salary levels were set according to British officers' assessments of individual officeholders' job descriptions rather than through indigenous conceptions of rank and propriety. This was deeply problematic, since it created a class of officials in dire need of money. It also placed them geographically in rural areas and with staffs of unprecedented size, which increased their ability to monitor rural areas and to place pressure on the people living there.

The advent of British supervision superimposed a very alien set of bureaucratic imperatives on Nigerian officialdom, often with no explicit recognition that change had occurred. The intensely personalistic system of precolonial administration had placed a premium on an officeholder's ability to control subordinate officials. Emirs and other masu sarauta needed to consolidate their positions so they could control the apparatus of governance, but this was not always possible when British officers demanded explanations for their decisions, explanations that needed to be structured by particular forms of bureaucratic logic. Discourses of corruption emerged in this conjuncture: a practical and material administrative reorganization in which officials in rural areas, who had new powers and a real shortage of money, confronted an ideological context in which the use of office to "personal" ends counted as corruption. But one should be clear about the distinctive characteristics of this moment. A corruption-complex had emerged, simultaneously dictating and proscribing "irregular" behavior in office. This pathologized indigenous political culture, but it also dictated an erratic colonial response to activities that might be considered irregular.

In early 1921 the emir of Zaria, Aliyu d̛an Sidi, was removed from office because of charges of corruption and misuse of his authority. The colonial government concluded he had diverted food intended for prisoners, selling it for his own profit. He had allowed prisoners to die from neglect, and he retained a thief in his personal retinue. More generally, the government claimed, he had prevented his subjects from complaining to the colonial government through threats and intimidation. The abrupt end of Emir Aliyu's reign was a reversal of fortune. In many respects he was an unlikely candidate for charges of malpractice and immorality. When he had assumed the throne in 1903, he was considered relatively friendly to British authority and also to the activities of missionaries within his emirate. Accordingly, he enjoyed good relations with colonial officers and local missionaries. Emir Aliyu was renowned for his piety and continues to be well known as a devotional poet of great power and sophistication.[27] In the early years of his reign the emir had succeeded at balancing the internal considerations of emirate politics against the tensions emerging from his relationship to colonial authorities and to the missionaries active in the southern part of his kingdom. However, contradictions built up between emirate politics and Aliyu's need to keep a good relationship with external actors. The deposition illustrates how British characterizations of governmental malpractice only partially reflected the political logic of Aliyu's administration but nonetheless began to constitute what would become a familiar narrative of corruption and official malfeasance.

From the time of the jihad, the Fulani emirs of Zaria had always occupied a delicate position. The roots of Aliyu's difficulties lay in the troubles that toppled his predecessor, Emir Kwassau. Aliyu assumed the throne in 1903 after a six-month interregnum following Kwassau's deposition. The latter's acceptance of a protectorate and his eventual removal from office had stemmed from a set of internal political challenges.[28] From the time of the Fulani jihad, Zaria's throne had alternated between three main dynasties. When the throne was vacant, Zaria's electoral council would propose a candidate from each dynasty to Sokoto, which tended to alternate between dynasties. Emir Kwassau was an exception to this rule. He was the son of his predecessor, Emir Yero, and therefore represented a second appointment for the Bornawa dynasty. Sokoto was disinclined to allow Kwassau's appointment and instead intended to appoint an elderly member of the Mallawa dynasty. Zaria's Fulani aristocracy suspected this candidate would be a puppet for the powerful *galadima* of Zaria, who was ethnically Hausa and thus undesirable from their standpoint.

When the *waziri* of Sokoto came to make the appointment, the emirate's office-holders and military supported Kwassau instead, and they made it clear that turbaning the other candidate would be resisted by force. The waziri therefore went along with Kwassau's irregular election, but the new emir's power was shaky. He was undermined by the continued tenure of the Hausa galadima, a domestic challenge compounded by sour relations with Sokoto. Indeed, soon after Kwassau's ascension the emir of Kontagora—a close ally of the sultan of Sokoto—invaded Zaria, prompting Kwassau to accept the protection of British troops and thus beginning the colonial period in Zaria.[29]

Accepting a protectorate allayed an immediate threat to his regime, but Kwassau immediately faced a whole new series of dangers. It was obvious to all that the British planned further military conquests. Christian missionaries were entering the emirate to evangelize its peoples. As a subject of Sokoto and a just Muslim ruler, Kwassau was caught in a bind; loyalty to Britain was incompatible with his moral duties to Sokoto and to Islam. Attempts to temporize won him few friends. He continued to share military information with his Fulani colleagues,[30] which Lugard interpreted as an "inability to refrain from his innate 'munafiki' [*munafunci*, hypocrisy, treachery]," and he also attempted to circumvent the galadima's right to collect taxes from the settlements under his control.[31] This double betrayal led the British to conclude "that he was a thoroughly bad man, possessed of great cunning, wholly unscrupulous, and by nature cruel and treacherous."[32] He was deposed for these sins and because of charges he was involved in continued slave dealing.[33]

Lugard played the politics of the deposition carefully, as he developed a procedure that he could bill as a continuation of precolonial procedures of governance. He asked Sokoto to select the new emir. The sultan's choice of Aliyu brought the Mallawa dynasty back to power. But Aliyu immediately faced the same dilemmas of balancing his obligations as a Muslim ruler of Zaria against the dangers of removal by British officials, though he enjoyed an initial degree of success. As Lugard reported in the immediate aftermath of his installation: "I was somewhat prepossessed by this man, who appeared quiet and dignified, and showed some anxiety to grasp the principles upon which he was to rule in the future. His fear was chiefly lest the Resident should be misinformed by tale-bearers hostile to him, and he insisted that so far as he was able, he would act up to my instructions, and that any default would be from ignorance and not of intention."[34] The emir's concrete actions and ability at diplomacy convinced the British he was ruling in accordance with Lugard's instructions, and as a result bearers of hostile tales were not believed. He allowed the school that the Church Missionary Society (cms) ran in his emirate to flourish in Zaria city itself. Kwassau had initially restricted missionaries to another town and ultimately chased them out, exiling them until just before the Kontagora invasion.[35] In 1905 Lugard wrote with satisfaction about relations between the emir and the head of the mission, Dr. Walter Miller: "The Emir himself has apparently formed a close friendship with Dr. Miller, and invites a frank expression of his opinions on social abuses which come under his notice." Indeed, Miller reported that he had "met with nothing but courtesy from the Emir and people, and not only has there been no hostility, but the people have manifested a desire 'to read, to hear, and to consider.'"[36] Aliyu personally accepted instruction in Roman script, though by the time he achieved fluency in that writing system, missionaries were already becoming frustrated at Muslims' disinclination to send their children for a Christian education.[37] Meanwhile, British political officers viewed Aliyu as relatively tractable and open to the modernizing imperatives of the new colonial administration. But even during this initial period of harmony contradictions began to accumulate.

Although there is little direct evidence of Aliyu's stance toward colonial authority, Sani Umar has brilliantly demonstrated that his poetry indicates an attempt to articulate a mode of maintaining his moral and religious bona fides while cooperating with British authorities sufficiently to remain in office. Umar suggests that Aliyu's *Wakar Zuwan Birnin Kano* (Song of Going to the City of Kano) and his *Wakar Diga* (Song of the Digger) offer key insight into his assessment of the contemporary political situation and of how it might be ethically interpreted. *Zuwan Birnin Kano* was written on the occasion of a durbar in 1912 held to welcome Lugard back to Nigeria as governor-general of the amalgamated protectorate. But while the poem pays intricate attention to the assembled dignitaries, provocatively there are only two mentions of Europeans, and no reference to Lugard himself. The poet instead provides a complex mapping of political power in Northern Nigeria as it was manifested in the positions taken up by the visiting emirs (and their host, Kano's Emir Abbas), and the appearance of other Northern Nigerians from outside the caliphate as well as within: the former are described with an acute eye to their political importance, the latter as subject peoples or as prey to the caliphate's predators. The provocative representational absence of colonial power from this intricate portrait of political power is paralleled in *Diga*, which describes the building of the rail line up to Kano, across much of Zaria emirate. In *Diga*, Aliyu describes the terrible power of the technology behind the railway and notes people's fearful reaction to it, but he ascribes this power ultimately to Allah rather than any human agency—suggesting that those who felt fear "have forgotten God, who created us all, including the European who made the digger"—neatly eliminating colonial power as anything but a channel for Allah's will.[38]

Aliyu's poetry demonstrates an ambivalence toward colonialism, as well as an ability to convey it to discerning readers without alienating the foreigners he needed to keep placated. A similar sophistication is evident in Aliyu's strategies for establishing political control. Any emir of Zaria needed to consolidate his control over the machinery of emirate governance.[39] Political expediency required appointing members of rival dynasties to high office, but emirs needed to do so carefully in order to keep their own political authority. And in the precolonial period, incumbents had done so with varying degrees of success. Too many rivals in too-influential positions would undermine an emir's ability to exert his will. Access to office—even and especially offices below the emirship—was not just a means of gaining political power. It also was potentially a way of acquiring economic resources. One might be given money and property when one assumed office, or one might accumulate them while in office. After one's death or deposition, however, the emir might take all or part of those resources, but not if they had been granted as heritable by one's heirs. Different royal lineages tended to follow different strategies in this; Aliyu's Mallawa dynasty tended to grant supporters resources when appointing them to office, but they also confiscated a large portion after dismissing them. Getting access to state resources was thus critically important for the emir's ability to gain the loyalty of his officeholders. As Aliyu assumed the throne, he not only needed to ensure his control of his subordinates; he also needed to ensure he had sufficient resources to make the political networks that also circulated economic resources on his behalf. This political dilemma was intertwined with the difficulties posed by the British. Although their ability to oversee the emir on a daily basis was limited, official appointments were much easier to monitor. And the British did not consider dynastic considerations a valid reason for appointment. Even less were they an excuse for deposing an incumbent. Thus although Aliyu succeeded in dismissing the chief alƙali of Zaria as well as the powerful galadima, he was forced to reappoint dynastic rivals to other offices after he tried to dismiss them without a justification the British found acceptable. Almost worse, the British regularly made him dismiss members of his own family when they were charged with corruption and misuse of office.[40]

To compound these issues of tenure in office, the British policies to reorganize, regularize, and make transparent the system of territorial administration being implemented across the protectorate created problems for the Zaria aristocracy. The masu sarauta detested the creation of districts and the move of officeholders out of Zaria city, but the more serious corollary was the British move across the first decade of colonial rule to change systems of official remuneration. In the precolonial period, officials had enjoyed revenues from their own estates, but they also retained a portion of the taxes they collected before passing the remainder to the emir (who himself retained a portion and sent the other part onward to Sokoto). This system persisted into the first years of colonial rule, but the British quickly attempted to move to another basis, in which village and district heads collected taxes and then passed them along to their superiors in their entirety. In place of the percentage of tax previously theirs, they received a government salary, in theory commensurate with their official responsibilities. At the same time, the system of taxes was radically simplified. In the precolonial period, taxes had been collected under a number of headings, but in the colonial period these were consolidated into a tax on farmland and a tax on cattle. (An "industrial tax," *kudin masu sana'a*, had a relatively low incidence, since it only applied to men who did not own farms as well.) These developments presented individual officeholders with a difficult set of dilemmas. By virtue of their offices, they had considerable responsibilities as political leaders. An officeholder was, by definition a *babba mutum*, a big man (in contradistinction to a *karamin yaro*, a small boy), but his responsibilities were not so much generated by the demands of administering towns as they were related to the importance of his central office. His following of clients was not equal to all of the villagers in his district but had more to do with politics in the capital. The salary structure that was put into place did not readily reflect the hierarchies undergirding Zaria politics. Since this set of political developments was going on at the same time that district heads were moving out into the districts and assembling a whole constellation of district officials to aid them, and since a new and intensified tax system was coming into force, the net effect was to enable—indeed to create—the incentive for a much intensified system of extracting money from the peasantry. The stakes of appointment and deposition thus became even higher as resources that went along with officeholding were renegotiated.

This was an opportunity for Aliyu, but also a problem. Patronage was a critical tool in consolidating an emir's power, but it also made policies that could be interpreted as oppression or the irregular extraction of tax revenue almost universal among officials. Aliyu's ability to dominate existing *masu sarauta* and aspirant officeholders was heightened, but the machinery of emirate government could generate as much scandal as British officials wished to read from it. Still, while Aliyu remained in favor administrative difficulties received official remark chiefly as problems with Aliyu's subordinates, not as the fault of the emir himself. District and village heads might be charged with embezzlement and misusing their offices in other ways, but the emir was unbesmirched.

An immediate point of tension, for which no euphemization was possible, concerned the judiciary.[41] During the precolonial period, the court system had been relatively limited in scope. The emir maintained a judicial council, and there existed also courts presided over by the chief alƙali and subordinate alƙalai. With the advent of colonial rule, lower-level courts were inaugurated in most district capitals as well, their alƙalai under the supervision of Alƙalin Zaria rather than the emir. The extension of the court system was meant to aid in the regularization of rural administration, since officials who got in trouble with the law were increasingly sent to court.[42] As a way of gaining control over the judiciary, Aliyu had appointed his own candidate as Alƙalin Zaria a month after taking office.[43] But as time passed, the emir's direct authority declined vis-à-vis the expanded judiciary, and he therefore attempted to reassert his influence. In 1916 he moved the incumbent alƙali to the office of waziri (which he had only recently revived), in the hopes that a new alƙali's need to consolidate his own hold on the office would diminish his capacity to interfere with Aliyu's own power. Given British notions of judicial independence, any dissatisfaction in how justice was meted out in this new regime left Aliyu personally open to criticism, but he weathered British disapproval. Rather than recoiling with horror at such machinations, British officials tended to the position that, whatever its shortcomings, Fulani administration and the way the courts worked in practice were far superior to any realistic alternatives. Responding to a criticism of the court system from Miller, an officer wrote, "No one but an antiquarian or fanatic would desire to re-write the Sharia. It reflects the ideas and ideals of an age different to that in which we live. It can neither be emended nor corrected. Any school boy could criticize it and compose legal quips and dilemmas from it. It is however a code—which adapted or ignored according to environment and liberally interpreted—commands the respect and obedience of all the 5,000,000 Moslems who surround Dr. Miller and his household."[44] On the specific issue of judicial independence, even during the investigation of Emir Aliyu the acting lieutenant governor wrote that although "it is of course most improper of the Emir . . . to influence the judiciary" nonetheless the "selection of Alkalai and members of Courts should be by the Emir with the advise [sic] of the Alkali"[45]

A more serious conflict began when charges arose that Galadima Idris was dealing in slaves,[46] which resulted in his removal from office and eventual conviction for enslavement and perverting the course of justice. He was sentenced to two years in prison. The attorney general, however, declared that the conviction for slave dealing was improper and that the galadima's only real crime was counseling and procuring the commission of a perjury.[47] The case that got the galadima in trouble was somewhat complicated. A girl of slave origin had gone to court looking for a certificate to recognize her freedom. The court acknowledged a payment made to her former master from a man with whom she proposed to live as a concubine. A payment from a woman or her fiancé to her master would have been perfectly licit because it enabled the woman to obtain her freedom. The issue in this case was that the woman was becoming a concubine rather than a wife. "Concubine" is a slave status. Courts supervising transactions that ended in concubinage were ipso facto engaged in slave dealing because they had acknowledged a transfer in custody. Officials like the galadima who facilitated such cases were therefore guilty of slave dealing as well. The acting lieutenant governor argued forcefully that this placed officials in an impossible position: the distinctions between marriage and concubinage were tenuous, particularly for a woman of slave origin.[48] The charge of slave dealing made little sense in its legal or cultural context; the galadima's real crime was trying to facilitate a set of transactions some British officials did not fully understand, which did not map easily onto a bright-line distinction between "slave" and "free."

The galadima's legal woes might not have badly harmed the emir, but a more serious problem emerged from different quarters. The missionary Walter Miller had decided the emir was a tyrant and needed to be deposed, and he had waged a long campaign to publicize Aliyu's abuses and dethrone him. Miller had long been ambivalent about Fulani rule in northern Nigeria. As early as 1903 he had proclaimed "the Fillani *is not, will not be* and *cannot* ever be loyal to the British Government."[49] Across the first decade of Aliyu's rule, Miller's purported friendship with him had faded. Writing many years later, Miller claimed "a very warm place in my heart for the picturesque old tyrant," explaining, "Race, heredity, and circumstances had badly moulded a character which might have given great things to the world."[50] He went on to describe an initial interaction, when Aliyu was acting *wombai* and aspiring to the emirship after Kwassau's deposition. Miller claimed that Aliyu had sent a messenger to him with the present of a turkey and the request that Miller should intervene with British authorities and recommend Aliyu's appointment to the throne. Miller refused the present ("thus greatly outraging native etiquette," he noted) and declined to offer assistance. Despite Miller's refusal to help, Aliyu was appointed anyway. This touched off "a reign of eighteen years which was a long drawn out torture to the people of the province."[51]

From the vantage of fifteen years later, Miller emphasized that the British administration was blameless for this: "That he was able to live such a double life, combining so much that was useful and efficient with what was so terribly evil and oppressive, yet remain largely unchecked by the able Residents . . . is a tribute to his skill in avoiding detection rather than a reflection on their ability as rulers."[52] The contents of this retrospective condemnation are striking: despite constant assertions that Aliyu was a terrible tyrant, Miller only details a few crimes: he sponsored "highway robbers" when wombai, took a free woman as a concubine (Miller noted darkly she died in a suspicious fire after the matter had garnered unfavorable publicity), mistreated prisoners, and imposed brutal regimes of forced labor on the populace.[53] Miller was nobody's fool, and his concern for human suffering comes across as very genuine. Nonetheless, it is significant to note what attracted his outrage and why. Of Aliyu's support for "highway robbers," the activities in question sound like those of slave-raiding parties, who genuinely did terrorize the countryside,[54] but which had at least arguable legitimacy. To a British audience, the story of Aliyu's machinations with the turkey was amusing; considered in context it reflected badly on Miller, as he admitted himself with the mention of "native etiquette." In the uncertain climate of early colonialism, it would not have been clear to Wombai Aliyu how British colonial hierarchies worked, and the head of the CMS mission was relatively accessible and also had obvious connections to the colonial government. The present of a turkey was a gesture of respect to a dignitary of whom one was requesting an important favor. How else was one to maneuver for political position? Who was being obtuse and improper, Aliyu or Miller? What is striking about the other crimes Miller enumerates is how unexceptional they were: the sexual exploitation of women, political interference in the court system, brutalization of commoners in order to mobilize forced labor. These were all accusations colonial officials were able to ignore when it suited their purposes. They were also not new developments in the last years of the emir's reign.

The year 1920 was a watershed, but why? Relations between the emir and Dr. Miller by then were thoroughly sour, though if one discounts the latter's having becoming disillusioned as a result of information he had not known previously, the reasons are not entirely clear. Indeed, Miller's own account of his relationship with the emir emphasizes the constancy of the emir's sins, leaving unmentioned the earlier period in which Miller was describing him to Lugard in hopeful terms. Although there is little direct evidence for a reason, it is worth noting that Miller's hostility did seem to increase during the second decade of colonial rule. One possible change is the 1910 passage of the Land and

Native Rights Ordinance, which placed land tenure in most of the protectorate under the control of local emirs, which would have made the mission itself vulnerable to Aliyu's goodwill. As Miller's hostility became more and more public, relations between the emir and the provincial administration were increasingly ambivalent. The resident (and later the acting resident) suspected the emir was guilty of the same slave-dealing sins as the galadima. Dr. Miller continued a steady stream of complaints about the emir's oppression of Hausa commoners, which culminated in an eighteen-page dossier.[55] And the emir's continuing attempts to maintain his control over the mechanisms of emirate governance increasingly appeared a questionable use of his authority.

The governor, Sir Hugh Clifford, was initially skeptical of the gravity of the situation. While on tour in the north, he was informed of the galadima's deposition, but his response was moderate. He directed the acting resident to summon the emir to the northern capital in order to inform him that the administration was deeply disappointed in his conduct and expected much better from him. According to the acting lieutenant governor, Aliyu's response to this admonition was unconciliatory. The acting resident then reported that upon Aliyu's return to Zaria the emir held a meeting of his council in which he included an official the British had ordered deposed. This may have been the emir's fatal mistake, for it convinced the lieutenant governor of Aliyu's tendency to defy British orders. The administrative response, however, was not formulated as a countermove to the emir's defiance. It was bureaucratic, launching an investigation of misconduct in office. The difference was that now the administration was less inclined to dismiss accounts of his wrongdoing than it had been previously. Scenting blood, the members of the emir's judicial council also came forward alleging the "cold blooded murder" of prisoners.[56] And at that point a number of other reports of oppression also began to come in from both masu sarauta and commoners.[57] The governor therefore ordered the acting secretary for the north to investigate the charges fully.

As the secretary's investigation progressed, the acting resident, Captain Byng-Hall, prepared a report detailing his objections to the way Emir Aliyu administered justice, highlighting the government's long-standing concern with his attempts at exerting control. Byng-Hall painted a dire picture of a court system dominated by a savvy and unscrupulous tyrant determined to subvert the rule of law. Byng-Hall asserted that the creation of the emir's judicial council in 1912 had given the emir an opportunity to exercise power without constraint. In the precolonial period, the emir had been present in a court presided over by an alƙali who had been appointed by Alƙalin Zaria and therefore enjoyed a considerable degree of judicial independence. Byng-Hall emphasized, "The Emir had no judicial powers at that time, except so far as punishing, i.e. deposing—his office holders and chiefs." Although the institution of the judicial council initially appeared a continuation of this earlier system, it was actually very different, since it placed judicial power in the hands of the emir, who had much more power than his precolonial predecessors because of the British administration standing behind him. "Being an exceptionally clever chief," the emir installed puppets on his judicial council and proceeded to deliver any verdict he saw fit. Even worse, the emir had taken to interfering in the court of Alƙalin Zaria as well. In one case, the emir had sent a man to be tried in the Alƙalin Zaria's court, with instructions to give him a heavy sentence because he was a well-known thief. The man had been employed by the emir, but Aliyu did not submit any actual evidence that he was a habitual thief, and so ultimately the alƙali passed a sentence far too heavy for the relatively simple case of theft before him.[58]

The acting lieutenant governor agreed that the current function of the judicial council gave the emir too much power and indeed that "it was largely the fear of this improperly run Court which prevented natives reporting the gross wrongs perpetrated by the Emir Aliyu."[59] However, even at this late date the substantive lieutenant governor was more nuanced. He minuted that "Capt Byng-Hall is new to administration in the Mohammedan emirates" and did not entirely comprehend how autocratic emirs were in the immediate precolonial period. He was skeptical that any written legal procedures would alleviate the problem, suggesting instead that regular supervision from the political staff would prevent the emir from getting away with any too-glaring subversions of acceptable legal procedure.[60]

If the dissatisfaction about Aliyu's conduct of the judiciary ultimately proved minor, the same was not true about other charges against him. The governor reported to the Colonial Office the emir's recall to Kaduna "had the effect of putting courage into the Chiefs and people of Zaria who now began forthwith to prefer a number of charges against the Emir."[61] This evidence enabled investigators to conclude the emir had committed various offenses, including the deaths in custody ("murders of a particularly inhuman character") of four prisoners in the emir's prison, severe floggings, threats made against anyone inclined to report the emir's crimes, the diversion of prisoners' grain for the emir's own purposes, and allowing a "notorious thief" to live in his house.[62] A somewhat darker allegation was that the emir was behind several attempts to poison Captain Byng-Hall, the last of which "made him unconscious for a time and very ill for several days." For that charge, at least, there was no admissible evidence. The emir was again called to Kaduna, where he vigorously rebutted the accusations against him, but to no avail. The acting lieutenant governor ruled that the charges against him were proven, which led the governor to order his deposition. Aliyu was therefore deposed and a Bornawa candidate was installed in his place.

The strange trajectory of Emir Aliyu's woes indicates a dynamic of enduring significance: the moment he lost the administration's support was when he insisted on determining the personnel to be included on his council and when he was unconciliatory about the charges against him. Nonetheless, the justification for his removal was not that he was too restive or too arrogant. Rather, the record depends on a shifting series of accusations about malfeasance, malpractice, and misappropriation. Every one of these was, at some moment, dismissed as unfounded or insufficient to warrant deposition. But ultimately, they helped to constitute a pretext, albeit a nebulous one. Emir Aliyu was removed for corruption, even if it was not clear *how* his corruption had manifested itself in legally admissible ways.

Governor Clifford ruefully admitted that British supervision of Emir Aliyu's government had "been most perfunctory and inefficient." Shortages of staff as a result of World War I explained a part of it, but previous residents should have been more diligent in their inspections of the prisons and the emir's court. The Colonial Office, agreed, responding, "Every effort must be made by the Provincial staff to put an end to serious malpractices of the kind which the present enquiry has brought to light."[63] The next month, reporting his installation of the new emir, the governor described the speech he gave after the emir had taken his oath of allegiance, explaining to those assembled that "tyrannical conduct . . . would inevitably be punished." At the same time, he happily conveyed the resident's report that "that since the news of Aliyu's deposition has spread large numbers of people have flocked back to Zaria who had abandoned their homes in the town owing to the fear which Aliyu had inspired. His deposition has apparently been hailed with great satisfaction by Chiefs and people alike."[64] And administration proceeded under the new emir.

The drama sums up the ways in which the colonial regime had constituted "corruption" as a charge that could be used to depose officials, though it was not applied consistently or universally. Emir Aliyu had the misfortune of Dr. Miller's proximity and, across the 1910s, his hostility. Nonetheless, the emir retained the administration's support until relatively late in the day. Captain Byng-Hall's animosity increased his vulnerability, as perhaps did a recent scandal over flogging in Northern Nigeria in which Miller played a muckraking role. That humanitarian scandal may have left the governor and his subordinates disinclined to protect a potentially embarrassing official.[65] Whatever the proximate cause in this case, patterns of conduct that pervaded the northern emirates were treated as "corruption" only when committed by officials the administration desired to depose, a process whose logic has little to do with the bureaucratic logics "corruption" indexes. But while the case of Emir Aliyu presents a useful case study of the political complexity underlying such charges, a more humble case might illustrate better the more quotidian stakes of the colonial corruption-complex, both as a set of practices and as a potential accusation.

Missing Taxes or Taxpayers in Kacako

In 1924 Mohama Sani, formerly the village head (Hausa *dagaci*) of Kacako in the Sumaila district of Kano emirate, went to the northern capital of Kaduna to make a complaint to a British official, the secretary of the Northern Provinces. Sani reported that he had been improperly forced to resign only a year after taking office. He had been appointed just as tax collection was getting under way in the autumn of 1922.[66] He claimed to have discovered shortly after his appointment that the official list of taxpayers included a number of dead people whose farms had been abandoned. These dead people would have been liable, he said, for tax totaling roughly £40. He had duly reported the discrepancy to Kano's Emir Usman, but he was told that he was personally liable for the 1922–23 shortfall. However, the error would be rectified for the 1923–24 tax season. Sani borrowed the £40 he owed, and the district head, who held office as the *makama* of Kano, sent a revenue official to inspect the farms in question. The resulting adjustment in the tax list did not correct all of its errors, and there was another shortfall for 1923–24. As collection got under way in 1923, Sani returned to the emir to report his dilemma, only to be told he would again be liable for the missing tax. Sani declined to go further into debt, and he was detained in Kano. He was later deposed.[67]

A political officer visited Kacako on tour in November 1923. Commenting on his report, the district officer noted he did not think Sani's resignation had been entirely voluntary, since Sani was initiating a complaint before Emir Usman against servants of the district head. As it turned out, Sani charged that district head's son Muhammadu and two of his servants had received gowns as compensation for helping get Sani's tax list revised. Although the *charge* was demanding gowns—that is, accepting bribes—Sani was later to report to the secretary that his *grievance* was that the revision was not made. Muhammadu proved his innocence by taking an oath, so no further action was taken against him. Or rather, no temporal action was taken against him: he died within the month; swearing a false judicial oath was held to lead to damnation but also to more immediate, earthly misfortune such as premature death. Muhammadu's two servants did not take exculpatory oaths and on the basis of Sani's complaint were convicted of bribery. There matters remained for seven months, until Sani made his trip to Kaduna and swore out his complaint.

The emir's conclusions about Muhammadu and his servants did not satisfy the British staff, and the secretary queried the Kano provincial office, which insisted on further investigation. In July, the emir sent a party out, which included both Sani and a member of the revenue department, to enumerate abandoned farms and their tax liabilities. They returned with a list whose total non-collectable revenue was £16.3.3. Sani objected to this conclusion, complaining that the revenue official had refused to look at an additional list of abandoned farms he possessed, so a second party was sent out, discovering more abandoned farms. These would have paid £13.7.4½ in tax. The resident suspected that this latter list comprised farms that had not been abandoned in 1922–23, so he was inclined to discount it.[68]

At this point, Sani made an explosive allegation. He produced a second supplementary list of farms, all duplicates of holdings on his original list. He claimed the district head had ordered him "to collect the sum shown as additional to the amount recorded in the Official Tax lists." Although the total liability from this supplementary list was £20.11.6, he reported having paid only £13.6.9, saying he did not collect this sum from the taxpayers but took it from his own pocket. The government took this allegation very seriously: the resident "used every possible means to try and trace the writer of these lists and [has] compared the calligraphy with those of the District Head's Malams, the Village Head's Malam, and the Members of the Central Revenue Staff but without result. Appellant has no evidence as to how the lists came into his hands and all the persons named by him (including the D.H.) have taken oaths that they know nothing of the papers and have never seen them before."[69] The implication of Sani's claim was that the district head or his staff was attempting to collect tax from certain households twice over, once on account of the official tax list and a second time from the mysterious supplemental list. According to Sani, the £13-odd he passed on was out of his own pocket rather than extralegally extorted from put-upon peasants, but the resident's report leaves ambiguous whether this bit of self-sacrifice was voluntary or not. The resident concluded that Sani had been unjustly deprived of his office but also admitted restoring him was not feasible. His tenure in office and his subsequent complaint had won him no friends in the emirate hierarchy. If he were reappointed, "sooner or later trouble would inevitably ensue." Moreover, his successor had already been turbaned, and it would have been an injustice to deprive the new village head of office through no fault of his own. Instead, the resident ordered Sani be given £20 in compensation for the loss of office, in addition to £16 for his out-of-pocket payment for 1922–23. Half of the latter was to be paid by the district head, half by the emirate treasury. The resident concluded his report by noting the entire incident showed serious deficiencies in emirate administration. Tax records had been demonstrated to be riddled with errors, but worse, the central administration had declined to rectify them until the resident had intervened personally.[70]

This conclusion was relatively sanguine, and it appears more calculated to withstand casual scrutiny than to come to terms with any serious structural deficiency. Sani's allegation about the second supplementary list implied certain unfortunates were being squeezed by a double tax burden, whose surplus would presumably go to the district head or the emir. The resident implicitly acknowledged the gravity of the charge through his reaction in forcing district and emirate officials to take oaths of innocence. Nonetheless, in the absence of any confession, the resident simply dropped the matter. But attention to any aspect of this resolution underlines how unsatisfactory it really was. Sani's own figures indicated he was £42.17.4½ out of pocket, but the resident was inclined to discount the supplementary list of abandoned farms—because, he avowed, the odds were that they had only been abandoned for the 1923 growing season. He also discounted the farms on the mysterious second supplementary list— due, he claimed, to his inability to identify the list's origin. If no one could identify the list's calligraphy, there was no reason not to conclude Sani had manufactured it himself. But this reasoning is not compelling. There is a more obvious reason for the resident's skepticism; the tax liabilities on the two lists were almost identical: £13.7.4½ and £13.6.9, only 7½d different. The resident's inclination to ignore both suggests he was inclined to view the serial production of the two lists as an attempt to claim essentially the same compensation twice. Under this assumption, when frustrated in his attempt to claim reimbursement for taxes paid on recently abandoned farms (which presumably he had collected in 1922–23, before they were abandoned), Sani managed to generate a compelling claim to scandal. In either case, he really wanted £13-odd, increasing his claim from £16 to £29.

A less comforting but more likely possibility is that Sani was telling the truth and really was £42 out of pocket. Sani's claim to have paid villagers' spurious tax liability from his own pocket shows admirable charity and public spiritedness—but what if he actually had initially attempted to collect the tax? Farmers unable to pay their tax bills were generally forced to abandon their farms. Closer to Kano, officials sometimes took advantage of that fact to obtain farms they would allocate to followers or use for their own purposes.[71] In less land-hungry regions like Kacako, such farms simply went out of cultivation. But if farmers faced with a double tax bill had fled before paying during the 1922–23 tax season, Sani would have been faced with a £26-odd liability *and* a collection of farms abandoned just at the start of 1923, which perfectly accords with the allegations made in his complaint.

The whiff of scandal emanating from the district head's son, Muhammadu, grows stronger when one considers that the district head himself was deposed for embezzlement at precisely the time his son Muhammadu was tried for accepting bribes. Makama Aminu had been criticized earlier for administering his large district ineffectively, and the provincial administration used the excuse of another accusation of tax embezzlement to remove him both from the district headship and from his central office.[72] Indeed, Dokaji Abubakar, the noted historian of Kano emirate, reports Makama Aminu presented a great contrast to his father and predecessor, Makama Dahiru. Where Dahiru was "famous for kindness," in Aminu's time the people of his district "feared him very much indeed."[73] At least according to Sani's testimony, Muhammadu was not implicated in the problems with assessment. Instead, he was capitalizing on Sani's urgent need to get the abandoned farms off his tax list. Presumably Muhammadu's present was more lavish than the gowns given his servants, but Sani's strategy did not succeed. The tax list remained unrevised, and Sani was deposed. Only then did he move forward with his complaint to the emir about the gift giving. And it was only after his relatively open invitation to revise the tax list and quietly overhaul its questionable contents was rejected by the revenue official that Sani proceeded with his more shocking revelations. By then, the district head had been deposed. The reform went further, in response to claims that the district was too unwieldy even for a head more competent than the unfortunate makama. It was divided in two and Kacako put under a newly appointed official, the Dan Darman.[74] The somewhat disingenuous refusal of emirate officials even to entertain the notion that there was something wrong with the £13 tax liability and with the farms abandoned after the 1922 harvest suggests one of two things. Either they were attempting tactfully to overlook further evidence of the previous district head's malfeasance, or someone else in the emirate hierarchy was implicated in the scheme to double-tax certain inhabitants of Kacako. The resident's resolute inattention to these sinister possibilities after his initial attempt to ascertain who had produced Sani's second list suggests he was acutely aware of the scandal that might cut deep into the emirate hierarchy.

The resident's attempt at euphemization was masterful. The only time his report to the secretary of the Northern Provinces even uses a term that might suggest corruption was one instance in which he states Muhammadu's servants were convicted of receiving "bribes."[75] Other than that, his investigation simply noted Sani had suffered an "injustice" and that the case had "unsatisfactory features," including that revenue records were "defective" and emirate authorities only corrected them under pressure. He attributed this to the emir's anxiety that Sani's successor as village head of Kacako might unfairly lose his office. The resident was nobody's fool, and none of these aspects of the case would have escaped him. Despite the fact that the district head—already deposed for corruption—provided a ready-made scapegoat for all of these intimations of malpractice, both the resident and emirate authorities chose to avoid blaming him. Why? The claim that it was an overdelicate sense of justice for Sani's successor is hardly convincing. The £20 compensation paid for Sani's loss of office did not entirely compensate him for the £26 he may have lost from the double-counted households, much less offset the injury of losing his office. Instead, the resident clearly lacked the political desire to pursue a line of investigation that might ultimately implicate the emir himself, or at least demonstrate the previous district head was not simply an individual bad apple but rather was part of a much more systematic set of problems in rural administration.

Northern Nigeria and High Colonialism

In one regard, this vignette simply illustrates the difficulties of being a village head, caught between a set of rural realities and the demands of a complex and powerful administrative apparatus. But it also marks an important point of transition in the logics of Nigerian discourses about malpractice in the Nigerian government. The political pressures on Sani were not entirely dissimilar to the difficulties that had plagued officials for two decades already. Sani took office at a time when systems of rural administration had become reasonably systematized and, at least formally, were bound by a certain form of bureaucratic rationality. The language of complaint and accountability only imperfectly conceals the multiple dramas from which Sani's case emerges. His yearlong career as village head—a position he could have assumed only at considerable personal expense—was personally ruinous, but the damage was deeper. Sani was obviously a man of means, since he was able to borrow substantial sums to make up the shortfalls in his tax collection. The erstwhile owners of the abandoned farms he discussed, whatever the precise circumstances of their dispossession, were obviously not so lucky. The lingering question is, what went wrong? Who got in trouble, and why? The case of Emir Aliyu demonstrates a political logic in which a set of relatively constant administrative (mal)practices, many of which were structurally determined, resulted in verified charges of corruption only when other political considerations led British political staff to assess the emir as a liability rather than an asset. "Corruption" in other words did not describe anything distinctive in the emir's conduct but rather was a label that served as post hoc justification for a separate political calculation.

In this case, the administrative decision to offer Sani only partial compensation required ignoring malfeasance at multiple levels. Under other circumstances this malfeasance might have been called corruption. The investigations undertaken in direct response to Sani's complaint did not find evidence of systematic problems in the administration, even though *other* undertakings (deposing the makama, splitting the district, conducting a reassessment) demonstrated an awareness of organizational shortcomings. Putting aside the issue of the "real" reasons for the deposition of the makama of Kano, the district head deposed for embezzling tax revenues and whose son's servants were convicted of extorting bribes from Sani, the case is notable for the government's stern inattention to matters of malfeasance and irregularity. No attempt was made to trace the owners of the abandoned farms or to investigate whether villagers really were being dunned for taxes twice over. The government pursued the relatively minor issue of intermediaries who demanded presents for lobbying their superiors for administrative favors (which, ultimately, was the crime of Muhammadu's servants). This was prosecuted, but a systematic problem with the machinery of taxation got nothing but an abstract assurance of official concern and a mild admonishment to the emir. Anything more extreme would have been politically delicate, an acknowledgment that the tax system had grave administrative problems. But that should not obscure what is truly novel about this specific conjuncture. Without publicly acknowledging wrongdoing, the government did address some of the issues involved. The Makama was deposed, the district reorganized as two, and a political officer was dispatched in 1924 to do a thorough reassessment of its tax burden.[76]

Other cases of corruption from the period—such as Emir Aliyu's alleged crimes—were similarly confined to somewhat minimal questions of misbehavior and individual acts of wrongdoing, even if these were interpreted through a rational-legal framework. The problems with tax collection, by contrast, were embedded within a new administrative logic. The bureaucratic context of these malpractices represented a new referent for the potential charge of corruption. The colonial period had already occasioned wide-ranging reorganization, and by the second decade of the protectorate this began to extend beyond issues of administration and of the political structure of the new districts. Methods of tax assessment and collection were radically reworked, sometimes with dramatic consequences, and at the same time the structures of emirate governance began a systematic transformation that would result in their ultimately paralleling structures of the colonial government in Kaduna. Some of these developments were central to the problems Sani had encountered.

Tax revenue had always been central to the colonial government's plans for the region. During the first decade of colonial rule, the hope was that peasant producers would begin to grow cotton as a cash crop, which would then be exported along the railroad that was extended to Kano in 1911.[77] A gradual consolidation of the precolonial land tax and the charitable donations (*zakkat*) collected from Muslims formed the basis for a unified land tax that was assessed under the general rubric *haraji* (Ar. *kharaj*). When the Report of the Northern Nigeria Lands Committee was codified by the Land and Native Rights Ordinance in 1910, land rights in the region were systematized, allegedly along traditional lines, in a way that was meant to accord with the paradigms of land rent propounded by the American socialist Henry George, whose theories had influenced Northern Nigeria's second high commissioner, Percy Girouard, and one of the most senior residents, Charles Temple. Accordingly, Northern Nigeria's land tax was designed to collect the value of agricultural produce that emerged from the natural fertility of the soil and from any publicly funded improvements (accessibility to the rail line, public irrigation projects, etc.). Output beyond that dictated by natural fertility and improvements was the result of a farmer's own efforts and so should not be taxed, lest industry not be sufficiently rewarded.[78] The theory required a tax system that would reflect what was naturally there, which required very careful monitoring of individual farmers' situations and landholdings. Beginning in 1909 in areas close to major urban centers, a land survey began to be conducted of farmers' individual holdings, which were surveyed by a staff of African officials who calculated farm size by pacing them out. They recorded these measurements on maps, which were then revised to reflect subsequent transfers of ownership or usufruct.[79] The survey process was called *taki* ("footstep") assessment, and the surveyors were called *taki malamai* (*malam* being the term for Islamic scholars, which by extension is used for all educated people and more generally as an honorific).

The difficulty was that these maps frequently bore a somewhat attenuated relationship to actual farm tenures. The taki malams frequently demanded bribes from farmers. Those who paid would be listed as having smaller farms than they actually possessed; those who did not were listed with larger farms and thus larger tax bills. These methods also allowed higher-ranking officials to intervene in the process, adjusting maps and tax bills for their own purposes. In this way, an elaborate bureaucratic edifice both covered over and enabled various kinds of administrative malpractice.[80] When the system of taki assessment was first used to set levels of taxation in 1911, it was intended to be applied only in densely populated areas around well-established major cities like Kano, Katsina, and Sokoto. These were areas where land hunger was acute and where the infrastructural improvements (like roads and the railway) made peasant agriculture a more profitable concern than it was in more outlying areas. For this reason, agricultural production was imagined to be more closely tied to the acreage farmers could place under cultivation. A more systematic regime of tax assessment was unlikely to increase the marginal costs of extending acreages sufficiently to decrease overall production.[81] And initially, areas like Kacako were supposed to be assessed through a less bureaucratic system, in which individual village heads were given an overall tax burden for a village, based ultimately on the adult male population, which they then allocated as fairly as they could. However, the system of taki assessment resulted in greatly increased notional revenues. That is, officers repeatedly discovered that with taki assessment farming families' theoretical tax burden remained constant, but villages' and districts' total liability substantially increased, leading to much greater revenues overall. In practice this indicated vastly greater tax burdens on farming families, which was a particular problem given the overall increase in tax assessment since the beginning of the colonial period. Nonetheless, with this incentive structure, taki assessment was extended ever further well into the 1920s,[82] including to Kacako.

The taki assessment system began to generate complaints almost immediately, leading also to recommendations that especially the less densely populated regions should be moved back to lump-sum assessment. Indeed, that was proposed in the reassessment report of Sumaila conducted in 1924, which ascribed some of the problems in the land tax to the administrative complexities of taki assessment, and others to the personal failings of the taki malam on staff.[83] Accordingly, beginning in 1924 a more complicated, reformed system began to be put into place. The taki malamai were gradually removed altogether from their duties in outlying districts. In theory this was because they were so far away from supervision that their malpractices were difficult to detect. In their place, assessment reverted to the earlier system of lump-sum assessment, in which a village head was assigned a total tax to collect from a village and then shared it out among the families under his control using his own discretion. When reapplied to the outlying village, it resulted in higher overall tax receipts, which suggests that by the 1920s small-scale farmers had learned to minimize their burdens under taki assessment. Officials anxiously outlined a procedure for reverting to the older style of assessment: a British officer would conduct a census of all households in the district in order to determine the adult male population and to get a sense of a town's general level of prosperity. Then the officer would compare the district under consideration with the tax levels of similar districts and with the tax incidence the district had paid under the taki system. The overall level of tax would be set to approximate the previous revenues as closely as possible, and then individual incidences would be distributed accordingly. Meanwhile, densely populated districts would be moved from taki assessment to the more methodologically sophisticated revenue survey, whose surveyors measured farms using chains and more modern survey techniques.[84]

Taki assessment and the revenue survey created an appearance of bureaucratic rationality while maintaining personalistic, negotiable modes of rule.[85] Across the 1910s, the colonial government concentrated on installing an administrative infrastructure that, at least in theory, ensured regularity and accountability in governance. Officials' decisions were recorded and could then be monitored by their superiors. Taki assessment was not the only part of this new infrastructure. Records of tax collection began to be kept, and *hakimai* were warned that any sums collected that were not reflected in these ledgers would be considered evidence of a crime. [86] Taxpayers and other people who owed money to the government began to be provided with receipts. Courts were increasingly required to keep records, though initially in Arabic, a language few colonial officers could read. In this way, rural administration and the judiciary were supposed to become more easily monitored by the British colonial staff and more accountable to the populations they administered.

Similarly, the central organs of emirate administration were gradually reorganized. A major point of departure was the establishment of emirate treasuries, into which the proceeds of tax collection were to be deposited. The first official colonial-era *bayt al-mal* was instituted in Katsina in 1907 as the formalization of an arrangement in which Katsina's ma'aji kept the emir's treasury. Up until 1907, the ma'aji kept these funds at his house. With the reform, the practice continued but in a formalized way and under new accounting control: half of the tax revenue was passed directly to the British colonial administration while the remaining half remained in the new bayt al-mal and was deposited into bank accounts. One portion was used to pay the salaries and fund public works projects; the other was transferred to district and village heads. The new approach was extended to Kano in 1910. This was such a success that the governor ordered it implemented in all emirates the following year.[87] At the same time, other functional divisions within the emirate hierarchies were also being systematized and deepened. One of the other major offices of state, the madaki had during the precolonial period been the commander of the cavalry, but with the inauguration of the district system, the new structures of territorial administration were placed under his control, and he also administered the process of revenue collection. The galadima, who had long functioned as a key administrator, retained responsibility for the emirate administration's functional organs such as prisons, sanitation, and public works.[88] In this process, departments of the emirate hierarchies began to parallel those of the British secretariat running the northern government in Kaduna, and indeed some of them began to be headed by British officials.[89]

In the years after World War I and before the onset of the Great Depression, these functional organs of the emirate government became increasingly important. Especially in the second half of the 1920s, new initiatives in medicine, public works, and rural sanitation increased the expenditures of emirate departments considerably. In this period, however, the most significant effects were in the domain of tax collection. In this arena, the institution of receipts given taxpayers provided them, at least in theory, with a means of defending themselves from illegal demands. Nonetheless, as Michael Watts suggests, the procedure for making complaints was "Kafkaesque."[90] In that regard, the manner in which the British political staff and superior emirate officials monitored those on the front lines of rural administration shows some fundamental continuities with the earlier period of less bureaucratic administration.

Emir Aliyu's deposition was justified as being a direct response to crimes he committed, even though none of the crimes for which he was held legally responsible was sufficient itself to warrant his losing office. Instead, the colonial government seems to have decided in 1921 that retaining him in office was more politically troublesome than removing him would be. Even in a moment when emirate governments were being remade along a bureaucratic model, the records of Aliyu's deposition do not reveal much evidence of his "corruption" as being composed of a deviation from the rules supposedly governing his office. Rather, "corruption" was a gloss for an array of charges made against him. It was a form of political critique, and it indexed moral failings. But it was not used coherently or consistently, and it did not easily map onto more recent implications of the term. Similarly, though new bureaucratic systems of rule in theory provided a set of adequate mechanisms for ensuring administrative regularity and for detecting and dealing with deviations from proper administrative procedure, in fact signs of malfeasance were often determinedly ignored for decidedly personalistic reasons.

The tax system is instructive to the extent it provides an illustration of the principles of rural administration that had emerged by the 1920s, outlining how official malpractice was imagined to occur. The implementation of such principles provided, at least in theory, a means through which such malpractice might be controlled. The dual system of taxation (revenue survey in densely populated regions, lump-sum assessment elsewhere) was a matter of administrative practicability (since only close-in areas permitted sufficient monitoring of the surveyors) and also accommodated land of differing economic value (since far-flung locations could not market their cash crops as profitably, and they also enjoyed less in the way of infrastructural improvement that might make agriculture more efficient). From the 1920s onward, therefore, the legally sanctioned system was superficially transparent and provided both a mode of tax collection and a means of supervising its administrators. But that regularity and transparency were illusions.

The illicit was transformed in tandem with the licit. The advent of the regularized apparatus for conducting and monitoring tax collection inflected the ways in which revenue could be diverted into officials' own pockets. Or, more precisely, the reorganization that placed hakimai on salaries and required that taxes be collected as "public" money and deposited into the bayt al-mal helped to create an explicit class of malpractices as crimes where none had existed so precisely in the past. New groups of officials—such as those within the revenue survey—were also put in place, creating both an administrative apparatus that could be used to "corrupt" ends and a cadre of new consumers of corrupt rewards. Sani's deposition as village head of Kacako demonstrates these dynamics in play as early as 1924. Indeed, changing administrative structures both enabled material malpractices and determined the ways in which those malpractices were conceptualized and, to some extent, were dealt with. The administrative reforms of the preceding two decades determined the form of Sani's tax list. Before the colonial-era reform of local administration, Sani would have set individuals' tax levels in consultation with the jakada who represented Kacako's fiefholder, the predecessor of Kacako's *hakimi*, the makama of Kano. Instead of a tax list whose somewhat notional mapping of individual farms determined a family's tax liability, the dagaci and jakada would have collected tax under a variety of headings, adjusting liabilities according to specific circumstances. While these negotiations would have been somewhat flexible—and would doubtless have been accompanied by gift giving as gestures of respect and obedience—the primary effect of reform was to rigidify the levels of tax that emerged from being listed as cultivator of a particular amount of land and to define as "bribes" presents inferiors might give superiors. Extorting money from unlucky farmers became defined as misuse of office, and the possibilities for increasing the amounts collected were constrained by the bureaucratic requirements of the maps and tax lists. These, once generated, dictated the amounts that needed to be handed over to the hakimi and thence to the central administration. Collecting more therefore required either revising the lists, falsifying receipts, or double collection. And thus, the material forms in which money was extorted from farmers were transformed by the advent of colonialism.

The other transformation was the reorganization of government. The makama's move out from Kano city to the district capital at least partially displaced the old jakadu from their roles as intermediaries. But the makama's presence in his district capital (Wudil when Sani first became dagaci, Sumaila after the reorganization and Kacako's half of the district came under its new head) created a new body of government actors. The demands Sani received from the hakimi's son Muhammadu and his servants were enabled by the inauguration of the districts as a new level of government, with the district capital a new space where *dagatai* like Sani needed to negotiate the instruments of administration. While it is impossible to know the originator of the improper demands (Muhammadu? the hakimi? the emir? Sani?), it is clear that the forms the demands took, and their intensity, were determined by the reorganization of government.

As surely as material practices of exploitation shifted, so did the political logic behind charges of corruption. Adjudicating accusations of malpractice is always intensively political, and so the new politics of district administration inevitably dictated a new politics of corruption as well. It is striking here that the only crime Emir Usman was willing to consider was that of Muhammadu and his servants receiving bribes, and that the servants did not manage to prove their innocence through oath. (This may have been lucky for them; unlike their master they did not die the following month.) The issue of improperly refusing to adjust the tax lists was never taken up, and the issue of double-taxing households was treated so gingerly only the faintest traces remain in the archives. Thus, not only did the rank of the various protagonists help to determine their fates, but "corruption" only emerged as a charge in a limited (and less serious) subset of the ways it could have. This was despite the fact that the makama was almost immediately deposed for irregularities in other aspects of his administration. In order for "corruption" even to be explicitly articulated as a possible charge, the crimes in question needed to be among those the government could acknowledge as actually having occurred. And the double taxation of individuals was a step too far. The charge was so serious, the possibility it had actually occurred could not be contemplated.

At the same time, the semantic range of "corruption" could hardly remain unaffected. While as late as 1920 it clearly had a relatively freeform set of implications, denoting a wider range of crimes than the term does in early twenty-first-century international usage, the reorganization of government helped to change "corruption's" meaning by altering the nature of official malpractice. One potential reason for the memorialization of Emir Aliyu's deposition as stemming from his maladministration of the legal system was that he had been deposed for "corruption," which increasingly denoted *administrative* irregularity rather than tolerating slave dealers, taking concubines and burning them to death, or poisoning political officers. These irregularities, obviously, continued to be frowned on, but going forward they would be viewed more as criminal acts in their own right rather than manifestations of corruption. The functional transformation of emirate administration continued after the 1920s, but at a slower pace. The financial constraints of the Great Depression and then of administration during World War II greatly diminished the colonial government's ability to invest in new administrative infrastructure. For this reason, the fifteen years from 1930 to 1945 were more a matter of particular logics playing out than they were of fundamental departures. In 1922 the inauguration of Katsina College, a secondary school for boys, created a class of officials with advanced proficiency in English, and by the 1930s alumni were beginning to assume high office within emirate administrations. Accordingly, the paper flows within the emirate hierarchy and between emirate officials and British ones increasingly resembled those of bureaucratic institutions in the metropole. However, absolute levels of investment were substantially diminished.[91]

In this conjuncture, "corruption" had taken on a powerful if somewhat counterintuitive role. The emergence of a bureaucratic administrative state helped to give the charge the sense of an abuse of office. At the same time, the political logic of the colonial state made it as much a weapon as an objective crime. "Corruption" was only prosecuted—or even admitted as a possibility—in some of the cases it might have been. This development took place in parallel with administrative reorganizations that made malpractice more feasible and more likely. In short, as early as the 1920s, corruption had emerged as a problem in Nigeria and was simultaneously recognizable as a phenomenon that might be generalized around the world and enmeshed in local meanings and relationships. The story does not stop there. After World War II, the start of party politics across the country occurred in tandem with the inauguration of responsible government at the center, which brought politicians from all regions into competition with one another. That ethnicized and regionalized political competition, and the political economy of oil, would fundamentally alter government malpractice, even as "corruption" retained its status as an ambiguous and highly selective political weapon.

In this way, the early-colonial intermingling of personation and "corruption"—crimes that threatened to delegitimate the state and that were punished with public flogging—can be seen to have persisted, jointly transformed by a changing governmental order. Sani's complaint resulted in no floggings, nor did it directly result in any coherent finding of official malfeasance. The categories of those considered to hold public office were somewhat blurry, as the successful prosecutions only of Muhammadu's servants attested, but the selective nature of how the state addressed claims of corruption was already well along the way to its contemporary forms. Sani's sad career as a village head has little historical importance by itself, but it illustrates how deeply embedded corruption is in practices of government—not as a pathological deformation of a set of bureaucratic rules but as a natural consequence of the constitutive logic of basic government structures. Selective prosecution, ubiquity, and ambiguity of what even counts as corrupt are all qualities of Nigerian corruption even today.

TWO. THE POLITICAL TIME

Ethnicity and Violence, 1948–1970

In August 1950 a young member of the new Northern House of Assembly tabled a motion to empanel a commission of inquiry into the native authority system of Northern Nigeria. In the speech introducing his motion Abubakar Tafawa Balewa called the emirate governments corrupt and autocratic, noting that they systematically demanded bribes from ordinary Nigerians and that they ruled with no regard for popular consent. Emirate governance—and by extension the colonial system of indirect rule—he claimed, was incompatible with the modernizing ethos demanded by the postwar world. Calling the native authorities "the system which has outlived its usefulness so long that it now constitutes the chief barrier to our progress," he advocated a reform that would "retain whatever there may be of value in the traditional pattern" by means of "grafting modern ideas on the old stock." His proposal addressed the problems of an autocracy unsuited to modern conditions: "One of the biggest defects of the system is the complete ignorance of everyone from top to bottom about his rights, his obligations and his powers." Emirs were unsure of their proper roles. Common people, similarly ignorant, were never consulted about public affairs at all. A source of hope was the emergence of a "new class" of northerner created by "Western education and world conditions." Giving this class of northerner a formal political role would, Tafawa Balewa implicitly argued, be a critical part of salvaging emirate authority.[1]

The speech was provocative and bold, both as a political initiative and for the legislator personally. Tafawa Balewa came from relatively humble origins. His parents were servants of officials of Bauchi emirate, a position of practical privilege. But it was not the same as being a member of the aristocracy, and his ancestry was symbolically at a remove from the freeborn talakawa as well. His family's connections were sufficient to win him a place at Katsina College, Northern Nigeria's elite secondary school for boys mentioned in the previous chapter. Tafawa Balewa was one of the first cohort of Northern Nigerians educated there, and he was not the only graduate of relatively humble background. Because of ambivalence about Western education, emirs had often hesitated to subject their own families to the schools; nonetheless the boys who went (and who therefore ultimately benefited from the opportunities that became available to the Western educated) tended to have strong emirate ties. For a time after his graduation, Tafawa Balewa worked in the Bauchi native authority as a teacher and administrator. He then earned a teaching certificate from the University of London. When a new constitution was implemented in 1946, inaugurating a new, appointive regional House of Assembly, Bauchi's emir nominated him to it. This position provided the platform to launch his attack on emirate officials. Balawa had many allies among his colleagues in the Assembly, which was largely populated by men of similar outlook, self-consciously modernizing young men who also had strong emirate ties. Not coincidentally, membership in the regional assembly was heavily skewed toward graduates of Katsina College.

As newspapers such as Zaria's Hausa-language *Gaskiya Ta Fi Kwabo* gave Tafawa Balewa favorable coverage, these reformist parliamentarians joined the Jam'iyyar Mutanen Arewa (JMA, lit. Association of Northern People), which had been a cultural association. In that guise, the JMA had existed for several years already. It had vaguely reformist goals, which it made clear did not include national independence for the foreseeable future, and it too emphasized the reform (rather than the abolition) of emirate governance. This reformist but accommodationist stance helped to ensure at least a modicum of official toleration. It was a comfortable ideological home for Tafawa Balewa and his cohorts, for like them the JMA was skeptical about the more authoritarian qualities of the native authority system. It thus combined moderation with a commitment to modernizing change. Nonetheless, an organization that brought together a community of northerners outside the rubric of established emirate or religious auspices—and which leveled criticisms against the current order—was potentially subversive. Accordingly the government stance was ambivalent. This ambivalence was heighted when, with the addition of these reformist parliamentarians, the JMA incorporated itself as a political party the year after Tafawa Balewa's speech and also became known by its English-language name, the Northern People's Congress (NPC).[2]

The emergence of the NPC was as moderate a nationalist development as the colonial and emirate governments could realistically have expected. Despite Tafawa Balewa's emphasis on the shortcomings of emirate governance and the need for modernization and reform, his political program clearly envisioned a continued role for the native authorities and emphasized political continuity rather than revolution. By contrast, just before Tafawa Balewa's speech a group of relative radicals split off from the JMA, forming a more confrontational political party, the Jam'iyyar Neman Sawaba (Association Seeking Salvation), known by its English-language name of Northern Elements Progressive Union (NEPU). Its declaration of principles, which it called the Sawaba Declaration, developed a quasi-Marxist critique of class domination of the talakawa by the masu sarauta. The declaration identified "the shocking state of social order" that emerged from the emirates' nature as hereditary monarchies. More specifically, the declaration claimed the problem came from a class divide between the talakawa and the masu sarauta (whom NEPU termed "members of that vicious circle of Native Administration"). The Northern Elements Progressive Union condemned British colonialism for having supported emirate aristocracies, asserting "the entire Machinery of Government, including the armed forces of the nation exist only to conserve the privilege of this selfish minority group." Political parties, it claimed, "are but the expression of class interest." The Northern Elements Progressive Union proposed to represent the interest of the talakawa.

With fewer personal connections to emirate aristocracies, NEPU's leaders were less likely than those of the NPC to have high levels of Western education (though some, including NEPU's leader, Aminu Kano, were also Katsina College graduates and had postsecondary Western educations). More subversively, they had ties to nationalist parties from other regions, most notably Dr. Nnamdi Azikiwe's National Council of Nigeria and the Cameroons, whose base was in the Igbo-speaking southeast. A number of NEPU's leaders were also respected religious scholars and came from well-recognized scholarly lineages. Their center of gravity was in Kano and with the Tijaniyya sufi order, specifically a reformed branch that followed Sheikh Ibrahim Niasse of Senegal. Although not all NEPU leaders were reformed Tijanis (nor all reformed Tijanis sympathetic to NEPU—indeed their Nigerian political head was the emir of Kano), an emerging NPC/NEPU split did tend toward expressing a perceived opposition between the Tijanis and the Qadiri order of the founders of the Sokoto caliphate, and also a regional rivalry between Sokoto and Kano.[3] Although the NPC's reformist ambitions were potentially uncomfortable for emirate officials, NEPU's intertwined political and religious criticisms of emirate governance were potentially more dangerous to elites that wanted to prevent political pressure for substantial administrative change.

Bold and provocative as his comments in the House of Assembly were, Tafawa Balewa's intervention positioned him well for an era of electoral politics that was just beginning. Interdependent tropes of corruption and reform functioned as a way of consolidating Tafawa Balewa's own position as a figure in the emerging order; they also helped to articulate patterns of political transformation as they unfolded. In 1951 a new constitution made a majority of seats in the Northern House of Assembly subject to indirect election through a tiered system of electoral colleges. Meanwhile, the central legislative council in Lagos was expanded into an elective parliamentary chamber whose members were elected by the regional houses of assembly. The logistical demands of electoral politics, however indirect, helped to spur the consolidation of political parties everywhere. By this point national independence was clearly in the cards, though its terms and timetable were still unclear. The political parties in the north both responded to this new institutional pressure and to the potential challenges of developments in southern Nigeria.

Nationalist political parties had long existed in the south. By 1951 the dominant party across southern Nigeria was the National Council of Nigeria and the Cameroons (NCNC). The NCNC's real base of support was in the southeast part of the country, which at that point comprised the Eastern Region of Nigeria. In the Western Region, a new party called the Action Group (AG) was also founded in 1951, emerging from a Yoruba cultural association called the Egbe Omo Oduduwa, under the leadership of a brilliant young activist and barrister named Obafemi Awolowo. Quickly the NCNC lost much of its support in the west to the new regionally based party. Both southern parties were assertive about the prospect of national independence (in 1953, an AG member of parliament moved to declare "a primary political objective" self-government in 1956, which the NPC opposed, substituting "as soon as practicable" in place of 1956). In part because of nationalist pressure from the southern parties and left-wing pressure from NEPU, northern native administration officials formed an alliance with the new NPC, hoping thereby to domesticate the threat it might have represented. The Northern Elements Progressive Union soon made a tacit alliance with other nationalist parties and with a dissident party of minority ethnic groups in the southern portions of the Northern Region, termed the "Middle Belt." This political organizing quickly convinced both British and emirate authorities that the left-wingers were a far more pressing threat than the NPC could ever be. At the time the 1951 primary elections were held, NEPU was the only organized political party in the far north, and emirs saw NEPU challengers defeat many of their favored candidates in the selection process.[4] Another new constitution in 1954 brought ministerial responsibility to a federal government in Lagos and provided for direct elections to the federal parliament.

In 1950 it was not yet clear that party politics would emerge in the forms they did or that independence would begin to loom so large. Nonetheless, it was obvious that change was in the air and that the organs of emirate governance would need to adapt. Tafawa Balewa's speech suggested a course of action that reformed native authorities instead of abolishing them. However, his criticism of emirate institutions coupled with his humble origins to make him unacceptable to the masu sarauta as NPC leader. Instead, official support gravitated to Ahmadu Bello as leader of the party. Bello had not been one of the JMA's original leading lights, nor had he been one of the more significant politicians who transformed it into a political party in 1951. He had other advantages. Bello was a member of the Sokoto royal family. He held the Sokoto title of sardauna, and he was a descendant of the caliphate's founder, Usman dan Fodio. He was also a graduate of Katsina College and had been a teacher and native authority employee before his appointment as district head of Rabah in Sokoto. Charismatic, fluent in English, and highly intelligent, he was a reassuring figure both to worried emirs and to a British bureaucracy still ambivalent about the emergence of a Western-style political elite.

Delivered at this conjuncture, Tafawa Balewa's identification of autocracy and bribery as major shortcomings of the existing regime is revealing. It addressed a system in transition from the systems of administration that had emerged across the 1920s and that persisted through World War II to those that would superintend the transition to independence. Tafawa Balewa's empirical claims were unexceptionable, though one can understand the emirs' discomfort with the criticism their administrations received. Nonetheless, it was clear that the emirates of Northern Nigeria *were* autocratic (the main point of contention was whether this was for good or ill), and it was also difficult to deny that bribe taking and other forms of official malfeasance were quite common. Although the speech was not retailing unknown information, it was nonetheless noteworthy as a political performative. Giving the speech and publicly articulating its sentiments itself transformed what was politically possible. It signaled a new departure in Northern Nigerian politics.

Tafawa Balewa identified elite oppression of ordinary people as both an evil in itself and as a roadblock to modernization. Where British colonialists had proposed a superficially similar program, balancing a need for the "progress of the country" against a respect for "native tradition," Tafawa Balewa inserted a critique of corruption as it was then understood. His claim that "the giving and taking of bribes occupies the attention of all degrees to the exclusion of the ideals of disinterested service" inserted a novel idea into the familiar colonial dichotomies of indigenous and modern. By formulating his critique as addressing *corruption*, Tafawa Balewa suggested governmental reform would require constitutional change. Bringing the emergent NPC (and himself) to power was a logical corollary. By this point, modernization was popularly invoked as necessary, inevitable, and good. The postwar period was the occasion of a considerable systematization of what had hitherto been somewhat scattershot notions of economic change and a transformation toward modernity.[5] Tafawa Balewa not only suggested a political program with his allies at the head; he proposed a reformist agenda that would consolidate the new system of self-rule under their authority. The issue was not just one of a specific political struggle; it concerned the identity of Nigeria's postcolonial ruling class, and the ideological justification of its qualification to rule.

The proposal worked. Tafawa Balewa became Nigeria's first—indeed, as it turned out, its only—prime minister when that position was created in 1957. But something more interesting was at stake than the consolidation of a new political class, aligned with but not identical to emirate aristocracies. The political transformations of the 1950s created a new dynamic in which two bodies of Northern Nigerian officials, each subject to colonial control, shared responsibility for public affairs. Beyond this, it brought the political tensions of Northern Nigeria's ruling elites into direct interaction, and contention, with those of Nigerians from other regions. The emergence of the federal parliament and responsible ministerial government created an entirely new forum within which Nigerian political life was negotiated. These linked transitions had wide-ranging consequences for the corruption-complex as well. Material practices that could be labeled "corruption" would be transformed by the shifting constitutional structure. The advent of regional (and emerging from that of ethnic) competition at the center changed the incentives to exercise office for ends different from those of the regime's formal logic, and it transformed the normative terrain on which such practices were publicly evaluated. Ongoing instances of political malpractice that erupted into the public sphere or caused political crisis helped to change the legal status of such endeavors and indeed the nature of what people expected from political leaders. The result was the emergence of what one might finally term a truly national Nigerian corruption, emerging from the various political and cultural traditions that intertwined in Nigeria's federal center.

"Corruption" and an Emergent Political Class

The power of Tafawa Balewa's speech transcended its timely advocacy of a novel constitutional settlement. It suggested a new form of politics for the coming era. *Constitutionally,* the native authority/colonial dyad had accepted tradition and modernity as opposed categories. *Politically,* the regime had depended on Lord Lugard's old claim that colonialism's tutelary function demanded indirect rule as an expedient formula for the legitimacy of British rule: colonial interference was explained as the instruction necessary for improvement and social modernization. Tafawa Balewa's formulation demanded a new order: the old complementarity of the traditional and the modern had broken down; the myriad postwar changes, which had transformed the meaning of modernization and development, required a new politics as well. He accepted the long-established British claim that corruption and oppression were natural outgrowths of rulers' more primitive impulses, and he also accepted the claim that precolonial systems of rule had inherent strengths that should not be sacrificed. But instead of arguing for continuity with the native authorities' traditional practices, which could be ameliorated by colonial tutelage, he implied the new circumstances dictated more radical reform. Nigerians were ready to break with their traditional past because it had already broken down. Even while Tafawa Balewa's rhetoric suggested that corruption and oppression, like modernization and progress, were absolute qualities with fixed meanings, he also invoked the fact that contemporary politics had transformed what the positive terms meant. Where in the past they had implied economic transformation and adoption of European modes of living, they now had different political and social implications. Nigeria could not be modern unless people's welfare was improved. The revised position opened up the possibility of a progressive modernity under the direction of Nigerian officials. With the prospect of a new political order, "corruption and oppression" also shifted in meaning. In previous decades, corruption was held to be a natural consequence of the preservation of precolonial systems of rule; it was invoked as a problem demanding attention with regard to the failings of individual officials. Tafawa Balewa's innovation (at least for an establishment northern Nigerian politician) was to identify oppression—"corruption" in this emergent sense—as a systemic problem in need of systemic solution. The problem was less the immoral conduct of specific officeholders than an outmoded system of government. And ultimately, the solution was to grant power to someone like himself.

Tafawa Balewa's speech was a symptom of change rather than a catalyst for it. The old regime purported to be a faithful instantiation of the principles Lord Lugard had articulated in his policies of indirect rule as outlined in his *Political Memoranda* and *Dual Mandate*.[6] Governing practices had always been more complicated than this ideological representation would allow: the principle that indigenous practices would be permitted to persist was more a convenient fiction than an exhaustive description of practice on the ground. Instead, ideologies of indirect rule led to bureaucratic debates conducted in the idiom of political tradition. In the process considerable change was effected, sometimes deliberately and sometimes not.[7] The ultimate effect of indirect rule as a system of government was that the basic organs of administration remained more or less constant, even while their practices (and often the social logic behind them) were systematically transformed. The basic structures of indirect rule took on their general outlines by the end of the first decade of colonial rule. Categories of tax were consolidated. The district structure of local administration was worked out. The network of courts took shape. And as outlined in the previous chapter, the corruption-complex was a natural consequence of this politico-administrative conjuncture. Its material manifestations emerged from the structural imperatives on officials, and its discourses emerged from a discrete set of normative and legal doctrines indirect rule had instituted. By the 1920s, "corruption" was a self-evident reason to depose an official, even an emir, but the irony was that the references to particular acts grouped under that label were somewhat less distinct than a contemporary reading of the term would imply. The administrative reorganization of emirate government, the institutionalization of the distinction between public revenue and private income, and the bureaucratic elaboration of public office all tended toward making "corruption" refer to a more delimited set of crimes. Even so, a basic dynamic remained of using "corruption" as a strategy of accomplishing diverse political ends.

Careful attention to the corruption-complex thus provides a window onto the stresses and strains inherent in this constantly evolving system. Officials who found themselves in difficulty were enmeshed in a system that increasingly envisioned their official conduct as being in accord (or not) with a set of bureaucratic rules and with norms of behavior that rigorously distinguished between public and private resources. So were all officials. Misbehavior in office was described in terms of this ideological grid. The administrative apparatus of the native authorities helped to bring particular material practices into being, as with inflated tax assessments, and at the same time colonial rule created a normative apparatus for describing those practices. Just as significantly, indirect rule constituted the political conjuncture in which those normative codes could apply. Thus, not only was colonialism the context in which Emir Aliyu engaged in a particular set of political and economic actions; it also imposed a code of conduct that could be used to evaluate them. Moreover, the political struggle between Aliyu, his rivals in the emirate, British colonial officers, and the missionary Walter Miller was conducted in the idiom of (in) appropriate official action. Dubbing an official "corrupt" or not was as much effect as cause. Aliyu was only vulnerable to being called "corrupt" when he became a political liability to the colonial administration. Sani Kacako's overlord, the hakimi, was not found to be corrupt as a result of Sani's woes, even though he was politically vulnerable in other regards. All of this is to suggest that "corruption" both signaled the ideological limits of indirect rule as a doctrine of governance and provided a means through which it could be adjusted.

This process of constricting the referents of "corruption" even while retaining its deployment as a political weapon is illustrated by a somewhat later example, that of Tafawa Balewa's soon-to-be NPC superior Ahmadu Bello. He had been an unsuccessful contender for the throne of Sokoto when Sultan Hassan died in 1938. Appointed district head of Gusau and to the office of sardauna after the selection of Sultan Abubakar III, Bello had a rocky relationship with the British colonial administration in his new capacity. Gusau was a commercially dynamic town at a remove from Sokoto and with substantial numbers of southern Nigerian inhabitants. The areas surrounding Gusau had proven difficult to administer because of their distance from Sokoto. The administration proposed a new arrangement in which the fourteen districts in the region were placed under the supervision of an emirate councilor, who would reside in Gusau as a superordinate district head. Bello was selected for this honor. The plan was that his high level of Western education would allow him to provide close, modernizing oversight to his subordinates in these eastern districts, while his regular trips to the capital to attend council would facilitate ready communications with the sultan and political officers. As matters played out, the Sardauna preferred spending time in Gusau and the areas under his direct authority to being in Sokoto where he was subject to his successful rival, the incumbent sultan. He kept his time in the capital to a minimum.

British reports on the situation suggest increasing frustration across the several years following his appointment.[8] From their point of view, the Sardauna was too little involved in Sokoto politics and too inclined to supervise the activities of his subordinate district heads, or to do their work himself instead of teaching them proper methods. In the meantime, other forces began to move against him. In his autobiography, Bello reports his appointment to Gusau was "not lacking dark undertones and hidden motives." This was demonstrated in 1943 when a friend came to warn him of a plot against him: "When I asked what sort of plot, he said that people were being organized to lay complaints against me so that I would be involved in a court case."[9] Soon thereafter he heard that a group of cattle herders was being pressured to report he had extorted tax from them that he had not passed on to the Sokoto treasury. The cattle tax in particular was something of a sore point in Sokoto province. By the 1940s, Fulani pastoralists had become skilled at evading it, and officials in Sokoto were also known for inflating their assessments of the cattle herds. Both tendencies resulted in substantial shortfalls. These shortfalls had been the subject of a major investigation in 1937–38, which found huge discrepancies between the receipts given pastoralist taxpayers and the counterfoils recording the revenues collected and passed on. The latter were much smaller than the former, which suggested the district heads and their subordinates were retaining large sums for their own purposes.[10] The issue was still sensitive five years later, when Ahmadu Bello faced his accusers. He was especially vulnerable as a result of having already frustrated his British supervisors. He was tried in the sultan's court, convicted of embezzling cattle tax and of receiving bribes from herdsmen, and sentenced to a year's imprisonment. His conviction was overturned on appeal before the High Court in Zaria, but not until after a period of considerable anxiety and an expensive court case that required him to leave his home base in Sokoto.

The details of this court case are somewhat shadowy, but it is clear that Bello's rivalry with the sultan—the "dark undertones and sinister motivations"—singled Bello out for scrutiny, ensuring his conviction in the sultan's court, and winning his appeal. British complaints about his disinclination to visit Sokoto also point to a tense relationship with the sultan. That British officers recorded their frustration underlines his vulnerability to the charges against him. Complaints about an official tended to be phrased cautiously when that official's position was unimpeachable. The political machinations behind the case can only be inferred, but an obvious conclusion is that the Sardauna was prosecuted for conduct which was anything but unusual. One charge he faced had to do with gifts he received in the course of his duties in Gusau, many of which he regifted to others. Even if such behavior was not, strictly speaking, legal, it was part and parcel of the gifting relations a Sokoto official was expected to engage in. By folding the issue into the broader charges of corruption laid at Bello's feet, the prosecution demonstrated a further development in the formal criminalization of long-standing gifting practices. Where receiving gifts from Sani Kacako constituted a crime for relatively junior district officials while being ignored on the part of their superiors in 1920s Kano, a senior royal could be prosecuted for the same in 1940s Sokoto.

While the very nature of crimes susceptible to prosecution may have been shifting, there was also a selective quality to Bello's case. Whether or not he had actually diverted a portion of the cattle tax to his own purposes (a sympathetic biographer asserts there was "no evidence to suggest that the Sardauna misappropriated public funds, and he was regarded as scrupulous in separating private and public funds"),[11] Sokoto's regular problems with the cattle tax demonstrate many other officials had done the same thing, and relatively few of them had been prosecuted. The empirical conduct of individual officeholders had less to do with their being investigated and deemed corrupt than did their broader political context. Corruption was less a discrete set of practices, though it was that as well, than it was a free-floating charge that could be applied to individuals under the right circumstances.

The question of whether Bello *truly* misappropriated public funds is less important than the issue of how and why his actions might have been—and ultimately were not—found to be criminal corruption. The charge was a political weapon that could be used against an official who was vulnerable. Bello's longer-term vindication suggests something more. The case shows a transition in the corruption-complex, a shift in how corruption talk functioned as a political performative. The case's emphasis on the purely financial aspect of his misconduct demonstrates a constriction of the crimes that could be deemed "corruption" rather than simply criminality. The first part of the drama, up to Bello's conviction, is similar to that of Emir Aliyu. But ultimately the Sardauna was more than vindicated; his misadventure strengthened him in the long term. During this trying period, he made a number of key allies. The ciroma of Kano, who would become emir ten years later, was a key supporter. Many of his friends from his Katsina College days made it a point to visit him. Indeed, the legal case helped to galvanize this new class of educated northerners to understandable ambivalence toward existing native authorities. If a young man of elite lineage like Bello could find himself on trial, the older generation might pose dangers to any ambitious member of the new cohort. On his return to Sokoto, the Sardauna was moved from his position in Gusau and instead took over managing the Sokoto native authority's central office. This administrative role was a powerful position for an ambitious politician when widespread politics began a few years later.

The Sardauna's experience in 1943 reveals a system already in transition. The motor for change was the cohort of young men who supported Bello. His prosecution helped to consolidate an alliance that would enable the emergence of the NPC. Their support facilitated the Sardauna's appeal, and it also signaled new political possibilities, which would be manifested as representative politics created a forum for their consummation. Again, the shifting contours of the corruption-complex provide a window onto this more fundamental transformation. The corruption-complex had emerged as a key part of colonial systems of indirect rule—a charge and a legal category as much as a set of objective material crimes. The political changes that unfolded after Tafawa Balewa's speech led to a constitutional transformation, which then created a fundamental change in the corruption-complex as well. Before and during World War II, Nigerian officials were largely limited to the confines of the native authorities.[12] To the extent "corruption" was perceived to be an integral feature of Nigerian governance, it was as corruption existed or persisted as a feature of emirate governance. There were too few Nigerian officials elsewhere in the colonial administration for their malpractices to be viewed as a systematic problem rather than as an individual moral failing. British officials, by definition, were not corrupt.[13] One does not need to conclude from this that only Nigerian officials ever exercised their offices improperly or benefited from economic considerations in ways the rules did not allow. In practice, corruption was treated as an African attribute. The distinctions emerge in the different material positions of African and European officials and in the distinct political logics of applying "corruption" as a label emerging from normative or legal codes. For this reason alone, the transition to self-rule was a watershed in the history of Nigerian corruption. The very administrative locations in which material practices of corruption could occur were altered, as legislative bodies and responsible ministries were created and as increasing numbers of Africans entered the civil service. With these changes, African officials began to operate from new governmental locations.

At the same time, the administrative structures of the native authorities went through a revolution. The postwar emphasis on development as social welfare touched off major investment in roads, hospitals, schools, public health, and agricultural improvement.[14] Much of this investment was channeled through the native authorities. As the 1950s progressed and then gave way to the postindependence era, institutions of emirate governance were superseded by organs of the secular state. Elected councils were instituted in the districts, for example, and these were gradually transformed into the primary institutions of local administration, forming the precursors of today's Local Government Councils. In this process, hakimai gradually lost their direct administrative role. Meanwhile, regional governments took on direct responsibility for infrastructure.

At the same time that the transformation in government structure helped to alter the material contexts in which government practice took shape, party politics intersected with the emergence of a new print culture to create new valences to "corruption" as a potential charge that could be made against officials. The NPC (as opposed to its culturalist precursors) was brought into being by the inauguration of elective positions within regional and federal houses of assembly, as well as by the maneuverings of people wanting to channel (or blunt) the population's restiveness under emirate rule. Of almost equal significance to these constitutional changes was the emergence in the north of new communicative media. A northern Nigerian structural transformation of the public sphere was touched off in part by a Sierra Leonean named Samuel Cole-Edwards, who had originally come to Northern Nigeria to work with Lugard. His business interests had been destroyed by the Great Depression. Disillusioned by the government's response to this crisis (and by its ignoring his personal grievances), in 1930 Cole-Edwards founded Northern Nigeria's first newspaper, the short-lived *Nigerian Protectorate Ram*. With a small Anglophone readership, the *Ram* published relatively mild criticisms of British rule, which were little threat to the regime. It nonetheless prompted the administration to sponsor a pro-government outlet, *Northern Provinces News*, which published articles in Hausa and was distributed for free around the protectorate. The *Northern Provinces News* gave writers like Tafawa Balewa their first mass audiences. It also created a novel public forum, however propagandistic.[15] In 1938 this forum was consolidated with the establishment of the Gaskiya Corporation, a quasi-official body whose original charge was to engage in public "education" that would consolidate popular loyalty to the British Empire and would quiet fears of or hopes for German conquest. Gaskiya began publishing a Hausa-language newspaper, *Gaskiya Ta Fi Kwabo*, which provided a public forum for political debate to be conducted. Popular discourse about public affairs was not absent before, but a newspaper is structurally different from devotional poetry, sermons, songs, praise poetry, and other longer-established forms of public discourse that also had political valences. Although *Gaskiya* was aligned with the moderate opinions of the NPC, its elaboration of new forms of Hausaphone public debate created the possibility for mass politics and official practice.[16]

In addition to this new Hausaphone public sphere, the press that had been established along the coast for many decades was finding a larger northern audience in the postwar period. The spread of Western education meant there was an increasing cadre of people who could read English-language newspapers, and in this way a nationalist English-language press helped to consolidate a nationalist public sphere in the north. Where *Gaskiya*'s audience tended to align with the NPC and the political establishment—as befitted a quasi-government entity—the audiences of newspapers like Nnamdi Azikiwe's *West African Pilot* or the nationalist *Daily Comet* were frequently more sympathetic to the demands of NEPU. Scholars from Benedict Anderson onward have underlined the role print media have played in the consolidation and reconsolidation of particular political forms.[17] Of particular interest here is that the lively press emerging across the first half of the century was not merely instrumental in consolidating various national, regional, or ideological publics. The press also constituted a new forum in which discourses of corruption could circulate, and therefore in which the corruption-complex itself could take shape.

Corruption in Kano: Emirate, Region, and Emir Sanusi

Although the NPC emerged as a political party slightly after NEPU did, that initial disadvantage was quickly overcome by the benefit of the NPC's close ties to the region's aristocracies. It immediately became dominant in the Northern Region. In part because of the indirect system of elections in 1951, NEPU failed to gain any seats in the regional assembly, but the NPC continued its dominance in the 1954 elections, also aided by organizational problems in the opposition party. Power in the Northern Region guaranteed national power as well.[18] This is not, however, simply the story of an entrenched aristocracy that had converted its power into electoral success. The controversy Tafawa Balewa had touched off in 1950 signaled continuing points of tension. Northern People's Congress politicians shielded the northern aristocracy from the prospect of an independent Nigeria and changes that might threaten aristocratic power, but a number of them remained critical of at least some excesses of emirate rule, and some of them were of commoner or slave lineage. The aristocracy was not convinced of the necessity of transferring administrative authority from emirate structures to the regional assemblies and ministries, and aristocrats formed a key conservative constituency within the party leadership. Even when the transfer was to a regional government headed by a royal like Ahmadu Bello, tensions remained. These tensions played out in struggles that were conducted in the idiom of corruption accusations. Unsurprisingly, while the basic accusations may well have been accurate, they were also a way of expressing these much more fundamental varieties of political contest.

The abrupt end of the reign of Emir Sanusi I of Kano was a demonstration of this new state of affairs. Emir Sanusi had been emir since the end of 1953, when his father, Emir Abdullahi Bayero, died. British officials were initially hostile to his candidacy: the district officer of Kano identified him as "undoubtedly corrupt, more for power than for money, though the latter motive is close behind" and complained that he was an ultraconservative, by which the district officer meant unwilling to compromise about the powers exercised by the native authorities. The district officer argued that Sanusi would either need to be allowed to succeed his father as emir or be exiled, because his political support within Kano would make his continued presence there liable to catalyze violent protest.[19] His superiors, most notably the governor of the Northern Region, Sir Bryan Sharwood-Smith, admitted Sanusi was "fundamentally traditionalist in outlook and eager for power, lacking in scruples and progressive measures . . . inspired more by political ambitions than liberal outlook," but argued ultimately that there was little point in spending the political capital necessary to block his election.[20] Looked at askance from the start of his reign, Emir Sanusi continued to surprise.

The new emir was something of a reformer—he restored women's right to inherit houses and farms under Maliki law, for example[21]—and in his inaugural address he emphasized the need to modernize practices of emirate administration and for the reform of past injustices.[22] This emphasis brought him at least superficially into line with the position staked out by Tafawa Balewa and his fellow politicians several years earlier. Indeed, Emir Sanusi's support for the Sardauna during the latter's troubles when district head of Gusau helped to propel him to a role in formal electoral politics as well. As the NPC emerged as a political party he became a senior figure in it, serving as a minister without portfolio in the regional government. In 1961, after independence, he even served briefly as acting governor of the Northern Region. Emir Sanusi was no radical activist and indeed became known as a particularly brutal opponent of the NEPU opposition in Kano.[23] Accordingly, the left-wing party was vociferous in decrying both native authority oppression of talakawa[24] and his arbitrary arrests of NEPU activists.[25] Judges in Kano repeatedly convicted NEPU activists on relatively minor charges, sentencing them to substantial terms of imprisonment or beatings. Some were convicted of spurious charges of lèse-majesté. It quickly became difficult and dangerous to be active in opposing NPC hegemony, which helped to ensure the NPC would win all elections. In some ways modernizing and reformist, and a stern partisan of NPC power, Sanusi was more or less the ideal figure of an emir for independence, at least by the lights of the north's dominant party and the departing British administration.

There was a religious element to his reformist leadership. His reinstatement of women's inheritance rights, for example, was a canny step in blunting NEPU criticism: Kano's brief experiment with denying those rights was legally dubious. Maliki law is quite clear on the rights of a number of categories of women inheritors, most notably daughters, who should receive shares half the size that sons receive. Emir Usman had justified his exclusion of women in 1923 by noting Kano had been conquered in the Fulani jihad. Kano's status as conquered territory implied it was legitimate to abide by Hausa customary practices rather than the Maliki law of succession. Activists for NEPU attacked Kano's practice as evidence of the native authorities' lack of proper religious scruples. The reform helped to bolster the NPC's claims to being Islam's true protector in the region. Sanusi's status within the reformed branch of the Tijaniyya sufi order was a point of strength, but that too existed uneasily with the religious credentials of the NEPU leadership.[26]

Despite establishment and populist bona fides, all was not well. Emir Sanusi's long-standing alliance with Ahmadu Bello did not prevent tensions from emerging between Kano's emir and the senior leadership of the NPC. Various versions of the split have been retailed. Some suggest the tension arose between Sanusi and the Sardauna himself, sometimes centering on Sanusi's stint as acting governor of the Northern Region in 1961, where some allege he was insufficiently deferential to the premier.[27] Others say that relations between the two were always excellent but that the emir treated other prominent northern politicians with appalling disdain; essentially, the falling out emerged from a tension between two institutions, the emirship and the regional government.[28] It is also true there were considerable religious tensions between reform Tijanis like Sanusi, and Qadiris, which were only exacerated when the Sardauna attempted to create a new sufi order around the figure of Usman dan Fodio.[29]

Influential though he was, the emir evidently gained increasing numbers of powerful enemies, which made him particularly vulnerable when he found himself in difficulties soon after independence. In October 1962, public attention was riveted by a breaking news story: the Kano Native Authority declared it had a serious funding shortfall and needed a loan of £260,000 from the regional government if it was to meet that month's salary obligations.[30] This was a strikingly public admission of crisis, but it was not the first rumbling of trouble. For some months already, the regional government had been forced to take notice of fiscal and administrative difficulties in the Kano Native Authority. On 18 September, just before Kano admitted its shortfall, the government had appointed a British civil servant, David Muffett, as sole commissioner of an inquiry into emirate finances. Muffett was personally close to the Sardauna.

His charge as sole commissioner was to discover what had caused Kano emirate's perilous financial position. He chose a broad approach to this task and began investigating corruption and oppression widely construed, taking evidence from across the emirate. He received the regional government's enthusiastic support in this undertaking. Under pressure, the madaki of Kano issued a stern directive to masu sarauta and other officials of the Kano Native Authority warning that any attempt to interfere with witnesses and people trying to communicate their complaints would be dealt with severely.[31]

The inquiry leaked enthusiastically. The British deputy high commissioner in Kaduna reported in September 1962 that there were widespread "reports" of abuses. In his report the diplomat mentioned rumors that the emir was repaying misappropriated native authority funds, and that the commissioner had received overwhelming numbers of reports of extortion: "It is said that Native Authority officials seeking car advances had to pay the Emir £50, with corresponding payments for motor-cycle and bicycle advances; nomination as a candidate for the Regional elections cost the applicant £400; appointment as District Head or Alkali cost the individual £700–£1000. (An Alkali's salary is in the region of £400 per annum.) On Native Authority contracts the Emir has expected between 30% and 50% of the contract price. Indeed, the picture conveyed by such reports is one of organised extortion throughout every sphere of the Native Authority administration."[32] The outlines of the case were little surprise and tended to confirm accusations long publicized by NEPU activists. Officials did not waste much energy denying them. Indeed, many details required careful framing even to come across as problematic or corrupt. For example, the issue of the payments made by alƙalai and hakimai on their appointments sounds like kuɗin sarauta; comparing those payments to the offices' annual salaries would, in that context, have been something of a red herring, ignoring the ongoing situation in which official salaries were lower than social logic would have placed them. It also ignored the fact that such positions' formal compensation was not the whole story. An alƙali could doubtless have made considerably more than £400 in bribes. Similarly, the exchanges of £50 consideration for a car advance sounds like an updated version of reciprocal prestation. While obviously such exchanges violated a boundary between the Kano treasury and Emir Sanusi's private income, it was at best disingenuous to suggest the practice was exceptional, or indeed to maintain such arrangements violated long-standing norms.

In the logic of the inquiry, however, the only real question was whether the commission "will be able to bring [the emir's financial malpractices] to light." This was a political question, echoing the politics of Emir Aliyu's deposition in

Zaria forty years earlier. An inquiry into official malpractice got under way, but it was not until the emir was generally recognized as being politically vulnerable that substantial numbers of people became willing to testify against him, as had also been the case in Zaria in 1921. Under the new regime, however, the Special Branch of the federal police had been collecting information of emirate corruption, as had agents working directly for Ahmadu Bello. British diplomatic observers were convinced that the real question was how determined NPC forces were to depose the emir. The appointment of Muffett was held up as evidence of that ambition: he was "widely recognized as the Premier's favourite hatchet man." The deputy high commissioner speculated that an immediate show of force from the regional government had already emboldened witnesses to testify against Sanusi and would provide the government with sufficient evidence to remove him by convincing potentially reluctant witnesses they would be safe if they revealed details of Sanusi's malpractices. He would be removed from office and would therefore be unable to retaliate against them.[33] By the beginning of November, the deputy high commissioner reported so much scandal had been uncovered that the regional government really would need to depose the emir; his political power had eroded to such an extent that he was no longer able to keep scandal from surfacing.[34] The latter comment was perceptive, indicating an awareness that the issue was not Sanusi's having given grounds for complaint but rather his inability to prevent them from surfacing. The commissioner provided the government an interim report in November, which outlined evidence of substantial malpractice,[35] but there the matter remained for the next four months. In late January and early February, British diplomats reported Ahmadu Bello was having difficulty deciding what action to take. They reported rumors Bello owed Sanusi a considerable debt the latter would publicize if deposed. He was worried about losing the party leadership to a rival. He was afraid of spells being cast by the Kano palace. The rumors of magic led to a popular conviction the Sardauna had contracted leprosy as a result of the emir's spells, and he was obliged to make many public appearances and show off his healthy limbs in order to dispel the stories. Despite these anxieties, the government did eventually make up its mind, and the governor of Northern Nigeria accepted Sanusi's resignation in March. The government followed this development with a press release outlining a set of proposed reforms to the Kano Native administration that would, allegedly, prevent such abuses from occurring in the future.[36]

The episode is fascinating, less for the revelations made about improprieties in the emirate government than for the ways in which they were raised as issues for public policy and criteria on which Sanusi's continued tenure should be judged. As Alhaji Yakubu perceptively notes, "No doubt the Muffett Commission uncovered fraud, miscarriage of justice and general abuse and misuse of office by the emir, his officials and notable supporters. To many who were closely associated with the regional Government, these were not startling revelations; they were practices prevalent in many NAs."[37] He goes on to suggest that Kano was perhaps exceptional for the scope of its corruption, but that is easily explicable given its population and relative wealth. Indeed, even at the time the difficulties in the Kano Native Authority were not seen as extreme or exceptional. The Zaria Native Authority had gotten into very similar financial difficulties only a few months earlier, and its emir (the successor to Aliyu's successor) had been allowed to remain in office. Moreover, Sanusi's financial crimes were, quite overtly, broadly shared in the political class as well.

As Sanusi was officially excoriated for his mismanagement, the British were also complaining about Ahmadu Bello's "growing megalomania and squandermania." About the latter, "His presents increase in magnificence and frequency; his largesse abounds. One can only guess at the sources of income from which the largesse flows."[38] They did acknowledge Nigerian politicians needed to distribute money to their followings: "In the North it is traditional that great men like the Sardauna do give 'dash' to their dependents periodically and this is widely expected. Nevertheless the scale and extent on which the Sardauna is giving away money and presents at the present time has apparently started to get out of hand. [His permanent secretary] reckons that the Sardauna is now giving away money at the rate of at least £50,000 a year. This means he is undoubtedly indebted financially to several people, not least Leventis—a Greek-Cypriot of unsavoury character."[39] However complicated the corruption-complex at this moment in history, it was also clearly ubiquitous. What, then, made Sanusi vulnerable to the charges that brought him down?

Previous commentators have located the deposition of Sanusi in the context of his political career within the NPC, either directly in a fight with Ahmadu Bello, or more generally as he attempted to retain the prerogatives of the native authorities against political attempts to increase the direct authority of the secular state. They also point to Sanusi's prominence in the reformed Tijaniyya sufi order (he would become its head after his deposition),[40] which placed him in opposition both to traditional Tijanis in the region and to the Qadiriyya order, which was historically dominant in the Sokoto Caliphate. The latter rivalry also tended to recapitulate a rivalry between Kano and Sokoto, which Sanusi and Bello literally embodied as members of those royal lineages. Sanusi himself exacerbated the problem by pushing for a Kano state independent of the Northern Region. His timing was unfortunate; all three regions contained restive areas, and a more complex federal structure was being discussed. The NPC's federal dominance already faced challenges from southern Nigeria, the Northern Region, and from its own fractious Middle Belt, which was a center of opposition both in the federal parliament and in the regional assembly. Kano's restiveness in the Hausa heartland was not at all helpful. While all of these dynamics contributed to the government's determination to see Sanusi investigated and deposed, they do not fully bring into focus the role corruption (either as a material matter or as an ideological charge) played in the entire drama.

In this regard, Muffett's own explanation for why Sanusi was deposed is instructive. Muffett claimed the difficulty was less positive instances of corruption than it was his lack of legitimacy, and that the difficulty stemmed from the fact he should not have been appointed emir in the first place. According to Muffett, Sanusi's difficulty was that he was the son of his predecessor, Emir Abdullahi Bayero. This was a problem, because candidates for the Kano emirship were required to be sons of an emir, but a son was not supposed to be his father's immediate successor. For this reason, one of Bayero's brothers should have been appointed, or a son of his predecessor and uncle, Emir Usman. Only after an emir from one of these other branches of the royal lineage had reigned could a son of Bayero take the throne.[41] This proposal is somewhat disingenuous, overlooking several cases in the nineteenth century when an emir was immediately succeeded by his son, and ignoring the fact that Sanusi was only the fourth emir to reign since colonization.[42]

Muffett ascribes Sanusi's forced abdication to a lack of traditional legitimacy rather than to a naked power play or an exceptional instance of malpractice understood in bureaucratic terms. According to Muffett, Sanusi's political troubles emerged from the cultural basis of Kano's throne rather than from regional politics or from formal misuse of office. Muffett's article not only ignores his own role in the entire drama but implicitly claims the deposition was neither the result of a power struggle nor a response to corruption. It is unsurprising that a figure previously known as the Sardauna's "hatchet man" would be disinclined to acknowledge the possibility of political calculation in these events. But the latter omission is more telling. For if the sole commissioner himself did not consider Sanusi's alleged crimes to be the cause of his abdication, the obvious conclusion is that the commissioner either considered them not to have happened, unexceptional, or perhaps unexceptionable. Even if Muffett's claim about Sanusi's lack of legitimacy was unconvincing on its own terms, it points to something more interesting: the issue was not about corruption conceived in bureaucratic terms. It was about vulnerability. Whatever role the charge of corruption played in the drama, a key player did not view it as sufficiently compelling to explain his own actions. Corruption did not make the treasury shortfall into a scandal, and it did not determine Sanusi's resignation. The precise reason Sanusi was vulnerable is somewhat more elusive: Why did the Sardauna equivocate in January and February? Why was Sanusi targeted at all? The charges of corruption do not indicate anything about his actual conduct in office. Rather, they indicate rather more Machiavellian patterns of political maneuvering within the northern Nigerian political elite, making him vulnerable to deposition and at the same time pointing to the ideological basis of state politics at the time.

Even if the precise reasons for Sanusi's fall are not entirely clear, the fact he came out the loser in a confrontation with the Sardauna points to traditional rulers' eclipse by secular politicians in the governance of the Northern Region.[43] Even though emirate apparatuses would retain considerable degrees of direct responsibility for some time and maintain enormous influence to the time of this writing, by 1963 they were already administratively the junior partner to NPC politicians. When they came into overt confrontation, they would lose. And although traditional rulers retain considerable influence even today—as evidenced by the fact state officials are still wont to maneuver for traditional titles, and to intervene to appoint and depose particular officeholders—they are very much subordinate to other state officials. Charging Sanusi with corruption reveals this process of supersession was nearly complete by 1963, providing a window onto politics that would otherwise remain invisible. The continuities between this case and previous instances of the adjudication of corruption within native authorities only partially mask the basic fact that powerful chiefs like Emir Sanusi were losing their central political position.

For this reason, the key ways in which corruption and corruption allegations were negotiated and transformed became ever more centrally determined by federal politics than by local political culture. Thus, by the early years of the First Republic, the corruption-complex had taken on substantially new form. A logic of politics determined through forms of reciprocal prestation endured, as did an incompatibility with the bureaucratic logic of the secular state: the "private" resources officials could gain access to according to the rules of office were insufficient for their politico-social obligations. "Corruption" retained a role as a charge that could be leveled against officials, but its application was haphazard and partial. Far from being automatically a career-threatening scandal whenever it was committed or even when it was discovered, it channeled how officials might be attacked. These logics persisted, but other forces were bringing about a broader transformation. As "development" became the primary way in which social goods were delivered to the population, and as the shifting fiscal basis of the state made the financing and delivery of development money key political questions, the inauguration of a national parliament brought the material interests of different regions of the country into direct competition, touching off a mass politics of region and ethnicity. Concrete acts of corruption and official responses to the crime of corruption thus themselves took on new forms as a result of the politics of independence.

Party Politics and Centrifugal Federalism

The case of Emir Sanusi provides a sounding into a political process that was close to complete by the 1960s, as Northern Nigeria's native authorities were eclipsed by the political structures of the Nigerian state. "Corruption" was now more than a euphemized excuse for colonial intervention in local political hierarchies. It had become a label under which more fundamental political contests among Nigerians were conducted. A new federal arena, which created national-level politics for the first time, touched off profound changes. It was more than a new locale for an established set of politico-cultural logics. The corruption-complex was fundamentally changed, even while it retained much of its earlier character. The transformation was gradual and took most of the 1950s.[44] The Richards constitution of 1946 had begun to change regional politics, as the emergence of the JMA demonstrated. At the center, however, the governor and his executive council continued to exercise authority, though a representative legislative council did allow a role for some Nigerian politicians.

The center took on increasing importance in 1951 with the promulgation of the Macpherson constitution, which replaced the legislative council with a parliament. While the legislative council had included members from across the country, only a few were directly elected. The emergent political parties played little role in the others' appointment. The new parliament for the first time brought the complex chains of authority, patronage, and obligation that constituted political relationships in the north systematically into relation with analogs from other parts of the country.[45] As the NPC grappled with the question of how emirate aristocracies would give way to the institutions of the secular state and how the talakawa would find enfranchisement after centuries of subjugation to a tiny elite, southern Nigerians responded to distinct concerns. Many areas were under the control of native authorities analogous to emirate governments, though even there their authority tended to be less absolute than in the Sokoto Caliphate.[46] Labor regulation, education, access to public employment, and nationalism loomed large. Even in the southern part of the Northern Region, a political party called the United Middle Belt Congress (UMBC) emerged among "minority" and frequently non-Muslim groups. Its challenge to the hegemony of emirate aristocracies was different from that of NEPU, reflecting the distinct aspirations of groups who had frequently chafed at being subject to Hausa-Fulani-dominated systems of administration under colonial rule.[47]

During the early part of the decade, the most intensive political maneuvering took place outside of parliament, in party and constitutional negotiations. The new central parliament dictated the start of party politics, but their stakes remained relatively low. However, the Macpherson constitution was quickly superseded by the Lyttleton constitution in 1954, which provided ministers with greater responsibility and devolved more autonomy to each region, whose assemblies and regional governments enjoyed a corresponding increase in their power. With this development, the three major political parties consolidated their holds on their own regions and moved more directly to exercise their influence on the federation as a whole, as political contests at the center became a more pressing issue. Accordingly, the federal election in 1954 was seriously contested. The advent of responsible government brought into relief what had previously been easier to ignore: different parts of the country had enjoyed vastly different degrees of infrastructural investment. Western education was far more widespread in southern Nigeria, and peasant producers in the southern part of the country sold more profitable crops—southern cocoa and palm products were producing far more federal revenue than northern groundnuts and cotton.

Where Northern Nigeria had been a relatively stable geographic unit ever since the onset of colonization, Southern Nigeria had been slowly assembled, with the merger of several protectorates in 1900 and the addition of Lagos in 1906; it was then divided into the Eastern and Western Regions in 1939. National party politics started within a three-way federation whose character helped to define the parameters of political contestation. In the Northern Region, the NPC was rivaled both by NEPU and by the UMBC, but in part because both the native authorities and the colonial administration placed overwhelming support behind the conservative party, it attained absolute dominance. The other two regions also ended up under the domination of a single party. The displacement of the NCNC by the AG in the Western Region was uneven: although the AG was able to form the western government in 1951, it actually gained fewer federal seats in the west than the NCNC in the election of 1954, as the result of rivalries between different Yoruba towns. The NCNC also retained a center of support in the eastern portion of the region.[48] In the east, the NCNC retained absolute dominance, though the AG did manage some support, and small parties aligned with the NPC gained a following in "minority" non-Igbo areas. Each region was dominated by its own political party, and in each case the dominant political party had rivals whose base of support was inflected by ethnic and regional difference.[49]

These regional differences, combined with very different histories of political organization, translated into distinct positions on the question of constitutional change. For southern politicians, the primary question to be negotiated at the center was that of national independence—the first motion for national independence was made by Anthony Enahoro of the Action Group in 1953, a move strenuously opposed by the northern representatives. Even if southerners had not been eager to govern themselves, their political constituents were pressing for change, as were the assertive and eloquent educated elites, who communicated through a well-developed press, both English-language and vernacular, and who had well-developed ties with other African countries, the metropole, and beyond. Northern politicians perceived their region as being at a relative disadvantage. Their English-speaking elite was comparatively small, and only a few of these had postsecondary education. Moreover, the NPC party establishment was committed to maintaining the primacy of the northern elite, even if it was attempting substantially to alter the structures through which that elite ruled. But as constitutional structures for a federal government were proposed, these developments threatened the NPC's fundamental political commitments. Too-rapid national independence would ensure southern domination of central political institutions because not enough northerners had the kind of training that would allow them to take power. But given the NPC's determination not to allow NEPU and its political base to assume significant degrees of power, the emergence of a Westernized class would itself pose substantial political dangers.

The reasons for regional tension and competition were not mysterious. Ethnicity served as a proxy for regional origin, and regional questions had substantial material consequences. As Nigerian ministers gained autonomy, the question of where in the federation those resources should be channeled became one of increased salience and potency. The postwar years were a time of rising expectations. The stringencies of the Depression and war had given way to demands for greater material benefits for the colonized population, both from the people themselves and from the international community. Improved living standards required ever-greater involvement in world markets. Accordingly, the colonial government increased its expenditures on basic infrastructure, leading to a shift in the very paradigms for understanding such investment. Calls for hospitals and clinics, schools, roads, electricity, well drilling, and other forms of investment became widespread and were made as demands for development, but "development" in a new sense, which coupled ideas of economics and technical change with ideas of social welfare. Demands for development were a new mode of making claims on the state. Arguments over where to invest funds for development thus were ultimately ones in which different regions attempted to make claims on national resources for the local good.[50]

As the routes to temporal power shifted to electoral politics, appealing to nascent political constituencies became an item of politicians' acute concern. Since issues of social welfare had been folded into the overarching program of development, and since those goods were zero-sum and locally specific (only so many schools could be built, only so many roads surfaced, and all of these were in specific locations), the populist politics of social welfare pitted one area against another. And to the extent that resources were finite and social needs pressing, issues of where to target investments had the potential to touch off dangerous rivalries, particularly in a context where politicians' political base reinforced regional splits—as regional political parties inevitably did. Political life had played out as acts of patronage, but now patronage became increasingly inflected by region. In the institutional contours of Nigeria's federal system, the rivalries between regions took on ethnic overtones. Ethnicity could serve as a proxy for region. More than this, to the extent patronage is an affective relationship, the commonalities of culture made patron-client ties particularly easy to form between members of the same ethnicity. Any political system dependent on patronage tends toward ethnic exclusivism, but this three-way federal system of patronage greatly exacerbated that tendency. As parliamentarians and ministers debated these questions at a national level, party imperatives paralleled and helped to heighten the regional and ethnic divisions the federal structure reinforced.

The British deputy high commissioner's derogatory comments about the Sardauna's "squandermania" underlined an element of this dynamic, identifying Ahmadu Bello's flamboyant practices of distributing largesse as a pathology of governance. Insofar as the distribution of state resources was generalized to entire neighborhoods, towns, and constituencies, the very concept of "development" became the governing idiom for describing how those allocative decisions could be made. That is to say, the label of "development" was used to articulate the relationship between political calculation—as politicians attempted to ensure their support by bettering the lives of potential voters—and the allocation of national resources. As many authors have noted, retail politics tended to transform competition into a zero-sum game: winning candidates gained office, and through that they gained access to resources, which could then ensure their reelection. Losing candidates had no such resources and therefore were less likely to attract future voters. But that very logic also made incumbent politicians less likely to tolerate the possibility of electoral defeat, since the lack of future resources would make their return to office much less feasible.

By itself, this political tendency was ominous. The economic, historic, and cultural gulfs between different areas of the country exacerbated the difficulty, all the more so given how abruptly the regions were brought into political competition at the center. The potential for a redistribution of resources between regions coupled with the differences that already existed in their infrastructures to make issues of development more than a concern for individual politicians. Regions were aggrieved if they had enjoyed lower levels of investment during the colonial period (as had the Northern Region) or if they faced the possibility of paying more into federal coffers than they received from them (as was true of the two southern regions). Thus, from the very beginning of responsible federal government, there were already substantial structural tensions between the regions. These were exacerbated by the nature of the political parties that emerged. The NCNC had quickly made a political alliance with NEPU, and as the 1950s progressed, the Western Region's Yoruba-dominated Action Group made common cause with the United Middle Belt Congress, which had emerged among the smaller ethnic groups who inhabited the southern reaches of the Northern Region.

The problem of where development monies would be deployed pushed politicians toward regional and ethnic rivalry. A related problem emerged from the issue of revenue and its derivation. The critical shift at this time was the establishment of the commodity marketing boards in the postwar years. In 1947 the government established a marketing board for cocoa, and in 1949 this was extended to groundnuts, oilseed, and cotton. The boards' purpose was ensuring peasant producers a minimum price for their cash crops even during years of depressed world market prices. This was a pressing concern in the aftermath of the Great Depression. The colonial government had pressured Nigerian farmers to expand into cash crop production during the first decades of colonial rule, and it had invested significant sums of money in enabling the emergence of a cash crop sector. The Great Depression temporarily diminished the significance of cash cropping to government revenue. Lower demand and thus market prices diminished the revenue the government received through export taxes. Depressed prices to some extent undid colonial agricultural agents' efforts to expand production for export; the Depression ultimately shook farmers' confidence in producing cash crops as a route to individual prosperity.[51] Nigeria's future prosperity (and its utility to the British Empire) depended on its role as a producer of these goods, so it was important to restore farmers' confidence in the markets they were to supply. That, at least, was the idea behind the marketing boards. Their purpose was "to secure orderly marketing and give the producer the benefit of absolute price stability" by guaranteeing farmers a minimum price for the products during periods of low market prices.[52] The boards would build up the funds to enable this guarantee by paying slightly below market prices during good years. Substantial reserves were thus a necessary part of the system. While the marketing boards initially appeared to be a relatively minor development, they would have a transformative effect on the nature of the Nigerian state, and on development spending in particular. Before the boards, the state's primary source of revenue was duties leveled on international trade and taxes paid by peasant producers. From their early years, the marketing boards' reserves were invested in the United Kingdom, helping to finance postwar reconstruction. In 1954, however, the new constitutional order went along with a regionalization of administration and finance. The marketing boards came under the control of the regional governments, and the formula for distributing revenue was also altered, the first of many adjustments attempting to deal with the tricky question of how to balance different regions' contributions to national funds with their need for investment. The principles of the new system emphasized the areas from which revenue originated, which meant in practice that the Western Region received a much greater proportion of revenue; cocoa was the most lucrative export. With the regionalization of the marketing board, the Western Region enjoyed a period of relative prosperity and development.[53] As the boards developed substantial cash reserves, those funds became the primary financing mechanism for infrastructural investment, for the forms of "development" that increasingly were the government's claim to benefit the Nigerian population. As the boards became central to state financing, they also helped to create a new point of regional tension, since the revenues for the southern export crops of palm oil and cocoa were much greater than northern groundnuts and cotton. Given that the south had already benefited from much greater infrastructural investment across the previous decades, the north had a lot of catching up to do. But the south was providing the bulk of the income.

During the relatively buoyant period of postwar commodity prices, the marketing boards made the financing of new infrastructural investments relatively painless, albeit through what amounted to a heavy tax on producers of cash crops. The situation could not last forever. It intensified an already-existing political-economic dynamic. The Nigerian state mediated the relationship of Nigerian producers to the global economy, a form of state practice Cooper has called the "gatekeeper state."[54] That structural feature substantially predated the marketing boards, but they intensified the dynamic. As "development" became not just a preoccupation of economic planners but a social welfare issue affecting the regime's international legitimacy, the demands of electoral politics also made delivering development key to political success. The federal structure that emerged from Nigeria's successive postwar constitutions guaranteed that local demands for development would translate directly to contests between the three major parties in the center. With the charge of "corruption" already well established as a means of conducting political rivalries and substantial patronage demands on officeholders creating a need for substantial income, it is little wonder the corruption-complex was transformed by this new political-economic system and became central to it. The legacy of prewar administrative practice had already made material practices of corruption feasible and near-mandatory for Nigerian officials, and it had also made the accusation of corruption a key tactic for political competition. Ahmadu Bello's tribulations as Gusau district head demonstrated the dynamics were still at play for the new generation. They would accompany this cohort as it assumed positions in the emerging structures of the secular state.

During the first years of politics, the NPC manifested ambivalence about the federal government and the dangers it posed for existing political relations in the Northern Region. The north needed investment in order to catch up with the south (even just in terms of creating a sufficiently sizeable cohort of northerners with high levels of Western education) so as to avoid southern domination of government. This ambivalence was reflected in some of its choices of personnel. Ahmadu Bello, who was the party's leading light and, from 1954, was its president, remained based in the north, first as minister of works, and from 1957 as premier of the region. By contrast, Tafawa Balewa, who became Bello's deputy as the NPC's vice president in 1954, went to Lagos as a member of the federal parliament and government minister. In 1957, he became prime minister of the federation, leading an all-party coalition government. The NCNC's Nnamdi Azikiwe ultimately went to Lagos as governor general (becoming non-executive president when Nigeria became a republic in 1963) after stints in the Western Regional legislature and as premier of the Eastern Region. The AG's Obafemi Awolowo entered the federal parliament, becoming a minister and then in 1959 leader of the federal opposition when the AG left government.

Just as the NPC determined to slow the transition to full independence for as long as possible, other issues became increasingly relevant. Ministers obtained increasing responsibility for the disbursement of federal revenues just as those revenues were substantially increased by the profits of the state marketing boards while at the same time infrastructural investment was increased by the government's commitment to postwar development. The control of these resources therefore became a matter of acute political concern. A regionalization of the marketing boards in 1954 heightened this tension: cocoa was by far the most profitable export crop and the profits the Western Region obtained from it dwarfed those of the other regions, most acutely the north given the great difference in overall population.

This was no simple matter of bureaucratic decision making, or of issues of how most equitably to distribute revenues also generated in rather unequal ways. The practice of retail politics emerged from the political logic that had long obtained under other systems of government, which is to say it was essentially clientelistic and redistributive. Especially as parties moved into competition with one another (an issue that was particularly acute in the far north, with the NPC continually under fire from NEPU), having access to federal and regional largesse, both in formal development projects and in the resources that could be irregularly extracted from them, was a critical ingredient for political success. The possibility of losing elections became ever more dangerous to political parties dependent on their access to government office as a means of cultivating their own constituencies.[55]

The consequence of these patterns of political competition was a ratcheting up of regional tensions, which was expressed in ethnic terms. An initial point of tension was in the reception northern members of parliament received in 1953 after they had acted to block the motion calling for self-government by 1956. Nationalist crowds disgusted at the northern position gathered and treated the northerners with great disrespect, an insult quickly answered by northern violence against AG organizers during their political tour of the north. But insults and violence were not conducted only in an idiom of policy debate over national independence or regional rivalry over economic resources. Each of the three regions was dominated by one of the three biggest ethnic groups, and each major party therefore became associated with that ethnicity—the NPC with the Hausa-Fulani, the NCNC with the Igbo, and the AG with the Yoruba. Communal tension was then exacerbated as the process of politics itself became increasingly violent. When AG politicians were attacked in the north, the ostensible grievance was less that they were purveyors of a policy the masses disliked or representatives of an economically advantaged region. It was as Yorubas and servants of Yoruba interests. All political parties maintained youth wings, which had substantial ties to groups of unemployed young men willing to act as political thugs for their party leaders. In the course of postcolonial politics, thuggery of this form attained disturbing dimensions, which then became immediately ethnic as well. As this took place, mass riots made ethnicized violence more general, and much more deadly. While it would not be accurate to suggest that politicians touched off violence through their most volatile supporters, which then became ethnic riots—the relation was not so direct, so unilinear, or so easily comprehensible as that—nonetheless, there is a certain trajectory here worth taking into account.[56]

After the federal election of 1959, the NPC controlled most but not all of the northern seats in the federal parliament, the remainder going to NEPU and the UMBC. The NPC's failure to win all northern constituencies dictated a coalition government: the Northern Region enjoyed a slight majority in seats within the federal parliament, and the NPC held a plurality in parliament. It therefore entered a coalition with the NCNC. Meanwhile, the AG announced what it termed a social democratic political program, and the Western Regional government invested substantial sums in initiatives like universal primary education. Because of the substantial autonomy regions enjoyed and because of the profitable nature of the Western Region's prime export, cocoa, its government had substantial resources despite its party's exclusion from the federal coalition. Although the AG did not have patronage to offer in the east or north, the example of its investments in the west did open the disquieting possibility it might chip away at NPC and NCNC dominance in their home bases. In the north, the threat was manifested through an alliance with the UMBC, but in the east, there remained a real possibility the AG might attract substantial support both from political radicals unhappy with Dr. Azikiwe's relatively accommodationist leanings or from members of ethnic minorities unhappy with Igbo domination of the Eastern Region. Both members of the ruling coalition therefore had reasons to attempt to neutralize future threats the AG and its leadership posed. And the corruption-complex provided precisely the techniques necessary to do so.

In 1962 tensions had emerged between Awolowo and his deputy, S. L. Akintola, who had succeeded him as premier of the west when Awolowo moved to the federal parliament. Akintola complained that Awolowo was continuing to attempt to govern the region from Lagos, and he himself increasingly advocated attempting to join the federal governing coalition. Awolowo, however, maintained a strong grip on his party and eventually sponsored a vote of no confidence in the Western Regional House of Assembly, seeking to replace Akintola with another AG leader more sympathetic to Awolowo's leadership. Awolowo's sympathizers made up a clear majority of the Western House of Assembly but Akintola's minority of supporters disrupted its proceedings and prevented the process from playing out. Eventually the federal police were called in. Courts ruled that Akintola should remain the premier. The case was appealed to the Privy Council in London, which found for Awolowo's majority faction of the AG. The federal parliament responded by removing the Privy Council's appellate jurisdiction. In the interim many members of the regional and federal parliaments defected from Awolowo's faction of the AG to Akintola's faction. Meanwhile, a cache of weapons was discovered in Lagos, which the federal government alleged was evidence of a plot masterminded by Awolowo to take over the government. He and a number of AG politicians were tried for treason, and Awolowo was ultimately sentenced to ten years in prison. The consequence of this drama was that the sitting Western Regional government lost a considerable amount of its popular standing. However, the federal coalition faced much less active competition from the western regime. However, the AG remained something of a threat to both members of the coalition, even though Akintola's faction party had chosen to join it. [57]

Corruption in the Western Region

The chaos of the Western Regional crisis emerged directly from the competitive logic of party politics in the First Republic, both internally as the Action Group debated whether it was better to join the government or remain in opposition and across the federation as the three major political parties maneuvered for advantage and for inroads into their rivals' home bases. Political and constitutional logic intersected with the new forms of government financing and with the mass politics of development as a means of conceptualizing public entitlement. The rest was ugly. The politics of the Western Regional assembly and rumors of coup plots were only the most dramatic end of a broader and more systematic shift in how government was negotiated. Where the case of Emir Sanusi exhibited considerable continuities with cases of corruption at earlier periods, the new domain of mass electoral politics and ministerial government dictated corresponding shifts in the corruption-complex, manifested in the role "corruption" played in the regional crisis. Accusations of corruption played a critical role in Chief Awolowo's sidelining and the destruction of the

Action Group. Looking at that process in more detail thus is a useful window onto how corruption was transformed in this period.

A drama that played out alongside the Awolowo/Akintola split and Chief Awolowo's treason trial began in May 1962. The Western Regional Marketing Board was discovered to be operating on an overdraft from the Bank of West Africa of approximately £2.5 million despite having taken in revenues of £68.6 million across the eight years of its existence. The marketing board's legitimate activities and investments did not seem to equal such substantial outgoings. As a consequence, the federal prime minister appointed a commission of inquiry to investigate where the money had gone. The Coker Commission took testimony across the rest of 1962, returning its report on 31 December. The commission's specific charge was to examine six statutory corporations that had received loans or other payments from the marketing board, thereby depleting the latter's funds.[58] The commission discovered serious irregularities in each corporation; these are documented exhaustively in its report. These irregularities were complex, ranging from questionable investments and sweetheart deals to money that had vanished entirely. While the details were bewildering, the commission's basic findings were more straightforward: marketing board funds had been improperly funneled toward political expenditures meant to bolster the Action Group. The party had subsidized its own activities with funds that were supposed to be devoted to stabilizing export crop prices and investing in development projects. The board had also deposited money into banks controlled by people with tight connections to the Awolowo faction of the Action Group, thereby profiting them personally. Some of these people had also received support for their businesses through grants from development authorities.

The Coker Commission's report was not shocking in and of itself. The diversion of marketing board funds had been talked about for years, and reports of misconduct included all regions. As with the case of Emir Sanusi, the only real question was whether the activities documented by the Coker Commission were any different from activities going on in the Northern and Eastern Regional governments. Indeed, Dr. Azikiwe had been the subject of a similar investigation in 1956, when he was premier of the Eastern Region. The allegations against him were that the Eastern Regional Marketing Board had deposited substantial monies in the African Continental Bank, which Dr. Azikiwe founded and which he and his family continued to control. That commission of inquiry found shocking irregularity in these business transactions and ruled that "his conduct in this matter has fallen short of the expectations of honest, reasonable people" and that "he was guilty of misconduct as a Minister."[59] Despite such criticism, Dr. Azikiwe was not prosecuted, nor did his political career suffer. Chief Awolowo did not emerge from his scandal similarly unscathed. The underlying issues in the Western Regional scandal were strikingly similar to those in the Eastern Regional affair: in each case, funds meant to stabilize producer prices or to fund development were diverted for politicians' self-interest. If anything, the Western Region's scandal was less personal: where Dr. Azikiwe benefited personally from official malpractice, Chief Awolowo seems to have benefited politically rather than personally. While some Action Group officials were found to have improperly benefited their own enterprises with funds taken from the Western Regional Marketing Board, Awolowo did not so immediately serve his own interests.

The authors of the Eastern Region Commission of Inquiry were if anything concerned to preserve Dr. Azikiwe's political career, but the Coker Commission had no similar compunction. The differences are evident in how the Coker commission framed the question of Chief Awolowo's culpability. Its report was published in four volumes, which describe in detail the testimony taken before it, and the reasons it arrived at conclusions about guilt or innocence. In this regard, the report is extremely compelling, at least so far as such reports can be: its conclusions and analysis are dry, dispassionate, but occasionally biting. Damning conclusions appear all the more so because they follow a list of particulars presented with disinterest. Testimony and evidence are weighed, reasonable conclusions drawn. The tenor is moderate; condemnations come only after dry conclusions about factual misstatements. Few figures come out well; some are adjudged dishonest and malign, others stupid or incompetent. This method is the report's power. Tracing what happened in particular transactions or deals ultimately can demonstrate particular officials' honesty or dishonesty, and thus their worthiness to remain in office or not. The report's conclusions about Chief Awolowo, thus, appear to emerge only from an incremental evaluation of the marketing board's financial history.

The report's topline conclusion was that Chief Awolowo orchestrated all financial malpractices in the Western Region. His deputy, successor, and rival, Premier S. L. Akintola, was adjudged largely innocent of wrongdoing. Akintola's vindication was not the most ringing endorsement ever made: "He . . . impressed us as a veritable deputy who all along the line had relied upon his leader. We are satisfied with his evidence to the effect that appointments to all political offices in the Region even during his tenure of office were made by him only with the consent of Chief Awolowo."[60] Chief Akintola could not be held responsible for his own government's financial mismanagement. By contrast, the report would argue at length for a portrait of the federal leader of the opposition as a spider whose web of corruption ensnared public monies to his party's nefarious aims. The conclusions of Awolowo's guilt and Akintola's innocence are doubly striking, since they were published in the immediate aftermath of Akintola's triumph over Awolowo and his faction of the Action Group. Interpreting the premier as a mindlessly loyal deputy took determination. Like Akintola's innocence, Awolowo's guilt emerged as a series of assertions and interpretive leaps carefully developed through an intricate narrative structure.

The report's rhetorical crafting is central to this process. To take an instance almost at random, the report contains an extended discussion of the regional government's acquisition of the land occupied by a village called Moba. The village was bought from its original owners for £11,000 by two officials of the National Bank of Nigeria who were also senior AG officials in October 1958. Shortly afterward, they sold it to a businessman for £150,000. This buyer sold it again, this time to the National Investment and Properties Company for £718,000 in July 1959. The regional government then requested a firm of valuers to assess the land, and it found it to be worth £850,000. Accordingly it paid that sum in June 1961. The company's managing director, Chief S. O. Shonibare, also a senior AG member, then made a series of payments to the AG's treasurer for slightly more than that total.[61]

The commission took testimony into these transactions and also into the conduct of the survey firm that came up with the valuation, concluding that the complexity of the transactions was a way to disguise the principals' intention to transfer government money to the Action Group. It also concluded that the survey firm had involved itself in numerous conflicts of interest and that its valuation was suspect: the relatively high valuation of the land presupposed the development projects the land was being acquired for. If anything this land was less valuable than other nearby plots. Chief Shonibare was held up for particular opprobrium and represented as having been the organizer of much of the fraud in this case—the surveyors' overvaluation of the property and the peculiar chain of ownership after the land's original sale.[62] Ultimately, however, Chief Awolowo was the responsible party: it was "entirely impossible that as the Federal President of the Party and as the evidence establishes the man in charge of and in absolute control of the Party funds he should be unaware of the whole plan and purpose."[63] While Shonibare was the managing director of the National Investment and Properties Company, Awolowo "organized [its] formation," and "the multitude of entries in his diary about [it] clearly demonstrate how much he had the matter of the National Investment and Properties Company Limited at heart. He it was who nominated the directors, and we are satisfied that the character Shonibare derived all his inspiration with regard to the affairs of the Management of that Company from Chief Awolowo."[64] The positive testimony cited in support of these conclusions is somewhat less than compelling. Claiming that Chief Awolowo had been concerned to acquire Moba quickly lest the federal government buy it first and realize the substantial profits to be made there, the witness reported he had gone to Premier Akintola to report Awolowo desired to acquire the land quickly, which the regional government then did as a matter of urgency.[65] That detail does support the conclusion that Awolowo rather than Akintola was the guiding light even in regional policy, but it also suggests he was deluded about the prospects for profit from the Moba undertaking. There is no reason to construe the evidence differently from the Coker Commission or absolve Awolowo (or the AG leadership more generally) from the charge of funneling government resources to their own ends. But at the very least Chief Awolowo managed to maintain what might have appeared plausible deniability to a friendlier tribunal.

The Moba incident illustrates a more general quality of the report: the rights and wrongs of the government's case against Chief Awolowo were less important than its general tenor. It is not unreasonable to suppose Awolowo was ultimately responsible for systematically diverting the marketing board's funds for the benefit of his party and his supporters—not just in a ministerial sense of collective responsibility but in the sense of having crafted the policy. Nonetheless, the specifics of the case against him were more suggestive than definitive, and they depended on a literal hermeneutics of suspicion: damning testimony was balanced by exculpatory testimony or by absence of other forms of direct evidence. Chief Awolowo's guilt in specific instances was demonstrated by the miasma of misconduct emanating from the totality of the transactions under investigation.

In this regard, the Coker Commission is similar to the Muffett Commission. Both investigations publicized malpractice and did so judiciously. Both are ultimately unconvincing, or at least they beg the question of why they attacked their specific targets while others remained relatively unscathed: the emir of Zaria retained his office in 1963; Premier Azikiwe did the same in 1956; the Sardauna of Sokoto's conduct as premier of the north was not investigated at all. Why Emir Sanusi and why Obafemi Awolowo? As was the case in much earlier times, the obvious answer lay in their vulnerability on other fronts. However, something novel was at play in the investigation of Obafemi Awolowo, emerging from the period's poisonous federal politics, and demonstrated by the commission's determined absolution of Chief Akintola.

It is far-fetched that a panel as distinguished as the Coker Commission would have reached its conclusions without any awareness of their political convenience to the government. The commission's findings required construing Chief Awolowo's actions as uncharitably as possible while remaining almost manically convinced of Chief Akintola's innocence. It was disingenuous to construe the latter as a "veritable deputy," given his actual conduct in office. The commission's report—and indeed, much popular Nigerian political history—tends to construe corruption as being a set of nefarious plots orchestrated by singular villains. In that regard, the image of an Awolowo who orchestrated all Action Group misconduct is a familiar trope. The more obvious conclusion would have been that sweetheart deals and public funds diverted to political parties and to corporations controlled by their members were a more-or-less universal feature of First Republic politics. If Akintola was less the architect of such schemes than Awolowo, that presumably has more to do with his subordinate position than with absolute innocence. And the commission's great enthusiasm for construing innocence and powerlessness on favored figures and damning others for their villainy almost certainly has more to do with the politics of 1962 than with such people's empirical actions.

Awolowo, by contrast, was portrayed as a much more sinister figure, who "was responsible for all the ills of the Western Region Marketing Board."[66] He was the architect of "the most infamous part of the set-up," and even when there was no direct evidence of his improper interference in any of the board's transactions, scrutiny of his diary showed he had held meetings about the board's beneficiary organizations. The tricky part was that "Chief Awolowo did not himself take any steps which will clearly show that he was involved in any matter; indeed in almost all the transactions in which the events revealed him as the motivating spirit, his name does not appear on the record. He always did everything through the hands of somebody else." Nonetheless, the commission continued, "We are satisfied by and large that Chief Awolowo knew everything about this diversion of large sums of money both from the National Bank of Nigeria Limited and the National Investment and Properties Company Limited into the coffers of the Action Group. His scheme was to build around him with money an empire financially formidable both in Nigeria and abroad, an empire in which dominance would be maintained by him by the power of the money which he had given out." The commission also referred darkly to "Chief Awolowo's continued association with foreign institutions, newspapers, or political associations" though it made no direct accusation about where such invidious contact might have led.[67] In the context of Awolowo's trial for treason, his association with foreign institutions needed little additional comment.

The report of the Coker Commission was not Obafemi Awolowo's greatest problem, unlike Commissioner Muffett's report for Emir Sanusi. In Chief

Awolowo's case, corruption was not the main explanation for his political relegation. Rather it was part of a much more systematic attempt to remove his influence in the run-up to Nigeria's federal elections in 1964. His regional powerbase was destroyed by the defection of Chief Akintola and his faction. His liberty, and his position as leader of the opposition, were taken away as a result of his treason trial. Nonetheless, the accusation of corruption attacked his legitimacy as a political leader. In that, it failed miserably. The AG's supporters were unimpressed by the findings of financial shenanigans. The basic logic is nicely captured in Wole Soyinka's description of the popular reception accorded Adegoke Adelabu, an NCNC leader from Ibadan whose mass following posed the greatest challenge to the Action Group and Chief Awolowo:

> Such was his hold on his followers that when, as a then regional Minister, he was accused of financial wrongdoings, he drove his newly acquired motorcar into Dugbe market and invited the throng to ride in it and treat it as their own, protesting: "This is what I bought with the money I am alleged to have stolen. It belongs to you all. Treat it as your very own property." If they could have done so, the ecstatic crowd would have lifted the car, with him in it, and danced round the town. It was, however, one of those long, gaudy American limousines so beloved of the first-generation politicians, so they settled for carrying him shoulder-high all the way from Dugbe to Mapo Hall. . . . They proceeded to the living quarters of his main detractor, summoned him out, stripped him naked and ransacked his residence.[68]

It is striking that Awolowo's reputation—very much in western Nigeria, but more broadly as well—was not seriously harmed by the condemnatory words of Justice Coker and his colleagues. However one construes "corruption" as an activity or as a charge, the memory of Obafemi Awolowo seems to be determined primarily by assessments of the goods he brought to his political constituencies. And those, as a general principle, continue to be judged as substantial. Even his less politically inspirational subordinates, such as Alfred Rewane, are remembered less for crimes during the First Republic than for their subsequent activities. Rewane, like too many others, is remembered for his martyrdom during the regime of Sani Abacha more than shady business dealings during the 1960s. This is a pattern that would occur and recur in subsequent decades.

Toward the end of 1963 the federal government conducted a national census. A census conducted in 1950–53 had found a slightly larger population in the Northern Region than in the two others combined, and this finding had been the justification for the northern advantage in parliament. The new enumeration discovered an inexplicably large increase in the Eastern Region's population, an increase large enough to destroy the north's popular majority. This result was attacked as fraudulent by northerners and westerners, and the census results were canceled and rerun the following year. The only difference in 1964, however, was that the other regions, especially the north, vastly overreported their populations as well. The country returned to using the results from the census of 1953, conducted under British auspices. Meanwhile, the ruling coalition substantially changed Nigeria's federal politics by carving a new region out of the Western Region, centered on the non-Yoruba areas in the region's east. This new region, named the Mid-Western Region, promptly elected an assembly dominated by the NCNC.

This political maneuvering was a dispiriting prelude to the federal elections held in 1964. The NCNC and Awolowo's faction of the AG allied with the dissident parties of the north—the UMBC, NEPU, and a new Kano People's Party that supported Emir Sanusi. The NPC campaigned in tandem with Akintola's faction of the AG, which by this point he was calling the Nigerian National Democratic Party (NNDP). It became clear before the election, however, that the dissident coalition was unlikely to prevail, and it therefore called for a boycott of elections, though this ultimately proved successful primarily in the Eastern Region. The outcome was somewhat unfortunate, at least from the standpoint of the NPC's opponents. The lack of competition allowed them to increase their margins in many northern and western constituencies and to defeat a number of NEPU and AG MPs. But after the election, the NCNC again entered into coalition with the NPC and NNDP, and the government lurched along, through an election in the Western Region in 1965, which was marred by wholesale fraud and an unconvincing though overwhelming NNDP victory. It is not clear where the federal government would have gone after this. It was overthrown in a military coup on 15 January 1966. A number of politicians, including Tafawa Balewa, the Sardauna, and Akintola, were assassinated in the process.

The coup was masterminded by a group of young army officers, mostly Igbo, and it was not carried out with uniform success. As it turned out, the politicians who were killed in the coup tended to be members of the NPC or NNDP.

Although the plotters had also intended to assassinate President Azikiwe and Michael Okpara, the premier of the Eastern Region, these Igbo NCNC politicians were spared because of a series of accidents. Suspicions, particularly northern suspicions of an Igbo plot against them, were heightened when the figure who emerged as military head of state was the army commander, General J. T. U. Aguiyi-Ironsi, who was also Igbo. General Ironsi quickly identified Nigeria's federal structure as behind many of the country's problems, and he therefore attempted to ameliorate them by abolishing the regions and establishing a unitary state. The reform did not get implemented, because the Ironsi regime was toppled in a second coup in July, led by northerners. General Ironsi and many of January's plotters were killed in turn, and a northern-dominated military regime took control under the leadership of Lieutenant Colonel Yakubu Gowon, who was from the Middle Belt. As military governor of the Eastern Region he appointed Lieutenant Colonel Chukwuemeka Odumegwu-Ojukwu, who would shortly become internationally famous.

The counterpoint to this drama of political sectionalism was a series of increasingly deadly riots, beginning with one in Kano in 1953. The Kano riot had been touched off by a series of confrontations among politicians—starting with the AG motion that year for independence in 1956 and then the harassment of NPC politicians by street gangs in Lagos following their opposition to the AG motion, and followed by the AG/UMBC tour of the northern provinces to garner political support. The riot in 1953 killed a number of southerners—ironically, mostly Igbo despite the AG's role in touching them off—but they were followed across the next thirteen years by many more, in both the north and the south and with both religious and ethnic elements to them. The violence came to a climax in September/October 1966, when the riots grew so systematic and so bloody that the substantial Igbo diaspora in the north fled en masse, even though the trains transporting them back to the Eastern Region were often attacked and their passengers murdered. Tensions continued to increase across late 1966 and early 1967, until in May 1967 the Eastern Region's military governor, Colonel Ojukwu, declared it independent as the nascent Republic of Biafra, leading to the brutal civil war that resulted in the death—by violence or starvation—of a significant portion of the eastern population.

The politics of Biafran secession were heightened by the ethnic politics of the Nigerian political economy. Rich oil deposits had been found in the delta of the Niger River. Though in the Eastern Region, the delta was not inhabited by Igbo people but by ethnic minorities. These groups were often hostile to the NCNC and had provided the NPC-dominated electoral alliance with some support during the federal elections in 1964. The NCNC had systematically quashed this dissidence, and more generally the region's lack of incorporation into NCNC politics had resulted in their receiving much less government money than other areas of the region. Relative deprivation meant that delta peoples were not great supporters of Biafran secession. One event immediately preceding Biafra's secession was Colonel Gowon's announcement that, like General Ironsi before him, he would attempt to ameliorate the centrifugal pressures of the regional structure by reforming Nigerian federalism. In place of the four regions, he instituted a system of twelve states, which were supposed to correspond to existing patterns of ethnic affinity. The Eastern Region was broken into three, and the state that would be dominated by Igbo was, by virtue of its geography, likely to be impoverished. The areas about to begin oil production were hived off into other states, and the Igbo state corresponded closely with the areas inhabited by Igbo people—inland, with few productive resources except for palm oil trees. (See Map 3.) Given Igbo grievances about the violence they had been experiencing, it was a provocative move, and it helps to explain Colonel Ojukwu's precipitate secession.

It is relatively straightforward to distill a story of ethnic sectionalism from this, but the more important conclusion to be drawn is of how these events completed the transformation of corruption as a political category. The basic dynamic illustrated by the deposition of Emir Sanusi remained at play. Malfeasance in office was a potent charge and could make an official's continued tenure impossible. But the case of Sanusi also demonstrates that malfeasance was not sufficient for deposition, and it is possible it was not necessary either. Across the colonial period, accusations of political malfeasance were only taken seriously by the government when the officials in question were already vulnerable. That basic political logic linked the cases of Emir Aliyu and Emir Sanusi. Both rulers almost certainly committed what could be interpreted as grave violations of the rules governing their offices. Nonetheless, that alone was not what ended their careers. Aliyu was the victim of a long campaign of vilification by the missionary Walter Miller, and Sanusi was undercut by political strains within the NPC itself. The continuities between the two cases, however, are dwarfed by the governmental transformation between 1921 and 1963. Where Emir Aliyu's real political constituency was the British political staff in the region, Sanusi's constituencies were more diverse. He took office at a time when the British were still potent political actors, though the records indicate their reduced scope for maneuver, given their disfavor of Sanusi's candidacy. The new emir was also subject to the constraints of the NPC hierarchy and to public pressure as well, epitomized by a thriving public sphere in both Hausa and English and by the political critiques advanced by NEPU and its southern political allies. Public opinion and opposition-party pressure became a serious vulnerability, however, only when Sanusi lost his base of support within the NPC. By itself this shift toward officials' dependence on diverse constituencies documents an important transition but a limited one. It has not been entirely appreciated how profound the change was as power within the northern elite shifted from the aristocracy of the Sokoto Caliphate and its officeholders to the NPC—even while that party's personnel largely emerged from the aristocracy. That transition was profound, in no small measure because it allowed narratives of corruption to take the forms familiar to a modern nation-state. Nonetheless, the case illustrates a process of transition only partway complete.

The scandals that wracked the First Republic at the federal level—even and especially when they centered on accusations of corruption and the misuse of office—took very different shape when they were tied to issues of interregional tension. Where Emir Sanusi's fall was due to his position within the NPC, Dr. Azikiwe's vulnerability stemmed from tensions within southern progressive politics and specifically the challenges that occasioned the rise of the Action Group and its supplanting of the NCNC in the Western Region. While the specific accusations against Dr. Azikiwe involved his violating the ministerial code as premier of the Eastern Region, his counterattack was to highlight AG malfeasance in the west. And, of course, the initiative was not successful. Azikiwe was not removed from office, and indeed he won the following election. Nonetheless, the *forms* of political vulnerability had begun to demonstrate the significance of regional and ethnic politics.

The Western Regional crisis, the Coker Commission, and the trial of Obafemi Awolowo illustrate a similar logic, though of course the coup plot Awolowo was alleged to have been involved in would not be classified as misuse of office. Nonetheless, the basic dynamic of interregional interest and political vulnerability is very similar. In this regard it is little wonder the outcome was different from the inquiry into Dr. Azikiwe. Where the latter had been able to depend on his party as a base of support, the former was faced with the rebellion of his chief deputy, Chief Akintola, even while the federal government and judiciary were controlled by the NPC/NCNC ruling coalition. Thus, already by 1962, the basic political logic of charges of political malfeasance had become largely federalized and regionalized.

Narratives of the end of the First Republic that emphasize politicians' misuse of office or the burgeoning of ethnic tension fail to appreciate some of the subtler transitions within the logic of corruption discourse. Across the federation, the First Republic had established a powerful dynamic of channeling federal resources to local constituencies. Given the coincidence of region and political party, this logic was always also ethnic, and it also helped to dictate a particular pattern to the diversion of state resources to private or extralegal ends, just as surely as the constitutive logic of the native authorities had in the early colonial period helped to dictate how, why, and under what circumstances emirs and their subordinates exercised their offices in irregular ways. To the extent that accusations of corruption became a tool that might be used by a politician's enemies even while the political system dictated some form of extralegal action by almost everyone, corruption discourse became something more than a mode of critique. "Squandermania" was a relatively insignificant material outgrowth of this political logic, at least during the 1960s. By the time the coup ended Nigeria's first experiment with democratic government, increasing levels of political violence and the use of ethnic terror had dwarfed simple instances of misuse of office. But given that violence and coercion had been a part of the repertoire of state officials for many decades before that, the change was one of degree rather than kind. At the same time, the political logic of the corruption-complex reached an end point in the secession of Biafra. Only in the aftermath of the civil war and reconstruction could a different distributional logic move corruption in new ways. In later years it would remain regionalized, but the pressure would become, at least to some extent, integrative rather than centrifugal. One long-term lesson of the civil war was the need to make the corruption-complex a means of giving elites access to federal largesse.

THREE. OIL AND THE "ARMY ARRANGEMENT"

Corruption and the Petro-State, 1970–1999

The repeated accusation in Fela Kuti's Afrobeat song "Army Arrangement" (1985) "Two-point-eight billion naira / Oil money is missing" might be taken at the leitmotif for Nigerian public affairs in the years since the start of the oil boom. "Army Arrangement" can be heard both as theme music and indictment of Nigeria's politics toward the end of the twentieth century. Its repetition of "oil money is missing" suggests a structural feature of government. More than that, it develops a complex web of references with ever-shifting political salience, given the contexts in which it was released and rereleased. Its critique of Nigerian politics and its discussion, sometimes overt and sometimes implicit, of political figures goes beyond simple representation. It depicts but also participates in a nearly forty-year history of politics and political corruption. As such, "Army Arrangement" is a window onto the transformation of Nigerian political life in the years after the civil war. Two intertwined transformations in Nigeria's economy and politics drove a change in the corruption-complex. The more obvious to external commentators was the economic transformation occasioned by the vast oil revenues beginning in 1970, which transformed the Nigerian state. Before oil became a significant source of income, governmental revenue was regionalized: it came primarily from taxes, the export of crops—cocoa in the west, palm oil in the east, and groundnuts in the north—and import duties. After the civil war, revenues from agriculture were dwarfed by oil receipts, which poured directly into federal coffers. Oil wealth allowed the government to maintain the naira at an artificially high level, serving to subsidize imports at the expense of some indigenous sectors. The strategy had limited success, at least if industrialization were the goal: import substitution is difficult when imports are effectively subsidized. The economic basis of state institutions became more centralized with the shift to oil exports, and Nigeria's new status as an oil rentier caused other sectors of its economy to stagnate. Nigeria's transformation heightened the stakes for control at the center, since the federal government controlled the country's primary source of wealth.[1]

The second transformation was equally significant. Even before the civil war broke out, Yakubu Gowon's military government had attempted to address the centrifugal tendency of Nigeria's previous federal arrangement. The twelve-state arrangement promulgated in 1967 was finally implemented in all parts of the country by 1970; it was more than a bureaucratic innovation. The politics of ethnic patronage that had bedeviled the First Republic emerged directly from the ethnic makeup of the three (and then four) regions. The twelve states created a new institutional calculus that government officials were forced to accommodate in distributing national resources, a logic that would extend to civilian politics when it restarted and aspirant politicians sought political constituencies. A federation of states constituted by ties of history and ethnicity offered new opportunities by underlining the possibility that yet more states might be created to accommodate disgruntled minorities within the existing arrangement. Lobbying for states was nothing new—it was a well-established feature of First Republic politics, as the creation of the Mid-Western Region and the lobbying for Kano state attested—but the new federal system demonstrated that lobbying for ethnic acknowledgment could succeed. It also established the form of arguments that might justify the creation of yet more states.

At the same time, the country implemented and standardized a third level of government, the Local Government Area (LGA); a similar logic emerged there. Affinity also justified claims to LGA status, as communities attempted to demonstrate their ties or lack of ties to one another. These institutional pressures had a further splintering effect on the identities that had political salience as aspirants to elite status at the top of a state lobbied for new states they might be better positioned to dominate. Nigerian politics has always been a politics of patronage; as Richard Joseph brilliantly demonstrates, the power of office and handing out offices has been at the center of Nigerian party politics, making the intersection between clientage and social ties like ethnicity of more enduring importance than ideology or policy. What made Nigeria's "prebendal" politics distinct from other forms of patronage was that state offices themselves became a form of wealth.[2] The forms federalism took after the civil war made institutional questions central for the politically pressing issue of where government offices and other goods might be available.

Nigeria's oil money supercharged this institutional conjuncture. The consequences went beyond a transformation in the country's political economy. The politics of patronage was transformed by the infusion of oil money, but could not have taken the forms it did barring Gowon's new version of federalism.[3] The changes affected politics and government practice, but *mal*practice was transformed as well. The corruption-complex thus took on new forms from this moment. Further, by becoming overt and increasingly visible to international commentators, it opened new, bigger, and more intensive opportunities for the irregular acquisition of money for private interests. The final result was to bring the Nigerian corruption-complex into more or less the form it retains at the time of this writing.

"Army Arrangement" and its enduring significance capture these complexities. Before the song's release in 1985, Fela was arrested and imprisoned on charges of currency smuggling. His imprisonment and declaration by Amnesty International as a prisoner of conscience gave the song an additional force as commentary on military governance.[4] Fela Kuti's son Seun, who took over his father's band, Egypt 80, began performing the song live after the former's death in 1997. The choice to perform "Army Arrangement" in the 2000s was provocative. Indeed, its performance in 2008 was especially fraught. The presidential election held in 2007 was the third under the Fourth Republic.[5] Like previous elections, it was plagued by irregularities. Widely called Nigeria's most fraudulent election ever—a real distinction given elections under the First and Second Republics—the candidate of the ruling People's Democratic Party (PDP), Umaru Musa Yar'Adua, was declared winner of the contest to succeed retiring President Olusegun Obasanjo. One of the leading opposition candidates was Muhammadu Buhari, representing the All-Nigeria People's Party (ANPP), as he had in 2003 as well. Buhari and another major candidate alleged President Yar'Adua had triumphed only through wide-scale vote fraud; many were inclined to believe these claims. The matter remained in litigation long after Yar'Adua took office. Like Obasanjo before him, Buhari was a former military head of state, and also like Obasanjo his record was the source of his political appeal. Both leaders had been imprisoned during the Abacha military regime in the 1990s, but where Obasanjo's appeal was having led a government that had voluntarily given up power—cynics said it was more that he was a westerner acceptable to northern power brokers—Buhari's appeal was his reputation for honesty and combatting corruption. Claims for his honesty were more compelling than claims for a record of good governance. General Buhari's military regime had been toppled in a coup after becoming repressive and unpopular while not managing to sort out the country's economic mess. His government's War against Indiscipline and War against Women were occasions of considerable brutality. But while his government was unpopular when it was toppled in 1985, it is remembered as less profligate and less rampantly corrupt than the Second Republic he displaced or the Babangida and Abacha regimes that followed. Buhari has capitalized on this reputation for discipline and rectitude; his presidential candidacies in 2003 and 2007—and indeed his 2011 candidacy for the Congress for Progressive Change, and successful 2015 candidacy for the All-Progressives Congress (APC)—centered on his criticism of the PDP's rampant corruption. Buhari's long career in electoral politics depends on reputation.

That image is a prime target for "Army Arrangement." Buhari came to public prominence in 1975, when he was appointed governor of North-Eastern state. He later became petroleum minister and head of the Nigerian National Petroleum Corporation. After Nigeria returned to civilian rule in 1979, allegations emerged that ₦2.8 billion had disappeared from the NNPC. Some claimed it ended up in Buhari's personal bank account. At the time, ₦2.8 billion was a notable sum. Initially inclined to leave the matter alone, Nigeria's new civilian president, Shehu Shagari, eventually allowed an inquiry to take place, and a panel headed by Supreme Court Justice Ayo Irikefe was empaneled in 1980, while a committee of the Nigerian Senate also investigated the allegations. The inquiry found no wrongdoing, though the former head of state declined to testify before it. "'Money no lost,' them shout again / Inquiry come close o." By 1983 the country's mood was ugly. The economic situation was dire as a result of the crash in world oil prices. Unable to pass a workable austerity policy, the National Assembly allowed Nigeria to go deeply into debt. The elections were no help. Notably violent, they were also blatantly rigged and thus conferred no additional legitimacy on President Shagari's administration. In this context, the Senate's ongoing probe into General Buhari's finances was no help. The matter became entirely academic when the army toppled the government and appointed General Buhari as the new head of state.

In the coup's aftermath, the National Assembly was dissolved, and the Senate committee reported no evidence of wrongdoing on Buhari's part or that of anyone else. Soon after taking power, the new head of state gave a defensive interview in which he claimed the allegation about the missing money came about because of the irresponsibility of the press. Buhari asserted his status as a simple army officer and claimed his regime sought only to rein in civilian corruption and to create the necessary conditions for real democratic accountability. Several months later, Buhari's government passed Decree No. 4, which severely curtailed press freedom and made it an offense to publish anything that "is calculated to bring the Federal Military Government . . . to ridicule or disrepute."[6] But while the general's coming to power shut down investigations into the NNPC's missing ₦2.8 billion, Buhari's government did investigate wrongdoing among many Second Republic politicians. Notably, President Shagari himself was cleared of all charges. Whatever suspicions still lurk about Buhari's having profited from his political positions, and however authoritarian his regime was in practice, General Buhari's twenty months in power were not as profligate as the Second Republic. His current reputation emerges from this relative rectitude and survived his tenure as chairman of the Petroleum Trust Fund during the military regime of Sani Abacha, an interlude that also proved a source of allegations about missing money. Versions of the ₦2.8 billion story continue to circulate. In the most lurid version, the Irikefe panel was an attempt to cover up the damning conclusions of the Senate report, which had been leaked to a reporter from the Nigerian Television Authority who covered the story on air. The Senate chairman was subsequently pressured to rescind the conclusions, and the story was scrubbed from the Senate record and the television archive. The reporter, who refused to retract her story, was forced into exile.[7]

Accusations about the missing money rankled. The government's Decree No. 4 declared Buhari's anger in legislative language. In an interview thirty years later, Buhari declared the money "couldn't have been missing. Not even the King of Saudi Arabia had the authority to issue checks in that amount." He went on to claim that Nigeria did not have enough money at the time to embezzle so much: "'At that time, Nigeria was exporting about 1.82 million barrels a day. And the cost of a barrel . . . was about $18. You work out ₦2.8 billion. How could ₦2.8 billion be missing and we still have money to run the country? So it was just a political.' He continued somewhat ominously, 'Well, later, Tai Solarin and Professor [Ayodele] Awojobi were confronted and Fela, the late Fela, to go and prove their case. They had no evidence, most of them took the newspaper cuttings of their allegations to the tribunal.'"[8]

"Army Arrangement" could hardly have been better calculated to defy Decree No. 4's ban on bringing officials into disrepute. It accused the head of state himself of stealing billions; the only fig leaf was that the song did not name General Buhari directly, simply relying on the 2.8 billion sum to make the connection. Given the regime's willingness to jail its critics, this was nonetheless a very notable accusation to make publicly. Seun Kuti's performance of the song was less dangerously provocative; it addressed Buhari as a civilian politician—and one in opposition—trying to advance his career in a civilian regime many already regarded as illegitimate. In this capacity, and as a representative of an opposition party, Buhari did not have the ability to menace Seun that he had possessed against the father. On the other hand, when General Buhari was head of state, he had not yet consolidated the reputation for honesty he later would acquire, nor was that reputation the basis for his public authority. Seun's attack on Buhari was thus safer than his father's had been, and the satire was perhaps more dangerous to its object if it was taken seriously. Then again, part of Buhari's allure is comparative: not only was the Fourth Republic seen as corrupt; the Babangida and Abacha military regimes that preceded it also were perceived as flagrantly dishonest. Buhari stood nearly alone in the pantheon of Nigerian leaders who genuinely fought corruption. The only other head of state who retained an unblemished character was Murtala Muhammed, and he was dead. Thus, Seun Kuti's version of "Army Arrangement" attacked the central weapon in Buhari's political arsenal.

The context of that earlier moment lessened the ad hominem implications of Fela's version. The song implied a fundamental quality of Nigerian governance: the alternation of civilian and military regimes continually invoked reformist ideals. Military regimes promised to restore a governmental integrity squandered by civilian politicians, while elected governments promised democratic accountability—and inevitably betrayed them. Neither brand of leadership, "Army Arrangement" suggests, ever seriously attempts to address the other's excesses. The absence of General Buhari's name made Fela's version as much an attack on all Nigerian governments as on the head of state himself. While Buhari obviously was targeted by the figure 2.8 billion and the specification of *oil* money, the central critique addresses a system that continually promises reform but never delivers it. The named villain is "Supervisor Obasanjo," the military head of state who had presided over the transition back to civilian rule. "Obasanjo plan am very well," in that the new civilian government elected "old politicians / Wey spoil Nigeria before." Earlier in the song, Fela describes civilians who had been sentenced to prison for illegal foreign exchange trades but were then released by the National Party of Nigeria (NPN) government. The "army arrangement" of alternation between military and civilian regimes meant that all government crackdowns on corruption were mere entertainment: "Obasanjo turn vocalist / Yar'Adua [Obasanjo's deputy head of state, brother to the future president] road manager." The military government had publicly arrested the currency traders, but the incoming Second Republic government released them after only a year in jail:

Them start to arrest everybody o
E no finish, e no finish . . .
Doctor, lawyer, hustlers
Engineer, photographers . . .
All of them Kirikiri [a Lagos prison]
Ten to fifteen years in jail
After one year inside jail
Civilian government take over
Them release all of dem
Them say dem be innocent o

Civilians ignored the sins of the military; military regimes forgave the civilians. Military rectitude was an elaborate show, without substance.

The inquiry into Buhari ended when the military came back to power. Fela's conclusion is that both the military and civilians loot the government, while attempts to investigate corruption and punish its perpetrators ultimately are inevitably stymied. By resurrecting "Army Arrangement" as Buhari tried to succeed Obasanjo for a second time, Seun not only undermined Buhari's reputation for honesty but questioned any possibility for political reforms driven by the Nigerian elite, civilian or military. By then, the alternation of civilian and military governments had receded somewhat as a possibility, but the inevitability of corruption in government loomed larger than ever. No one seriously proposed an "army arrangement" would benefit the country. The irony doubled in 2011, when the figure of 2.8 billion again made the news. This time, the release of Wikileaks cables publicized a set of accusations Obasanjo's Vice President Atiku Abubakar made to the U.S. ambassador to Nigeria. The vice president, whose relationship to the president had become strained, alleged the president had diverted U.S. $2.8 billion from the NNPC budget to buy arms in order to pacify militants in the Niger delta. The meeting took place on 8 February 2007, but the newspaper coverage began with the release of the cables in 2011.

The Kutis' continuing cynicism was more than understandable. In response to *Zombie*, an earlier album attacking the army, the military government sent more than a thousand soldiers to Fela's home in 1977. During the course of the raid, the singer's mother was thrown from a second-story window. Funmilayo Ransome-Kuti was herself a distinguished figure, an NCNC politician and reputedly the first Nigerian woman to drive a car, and the Kutis blamed her death the following year on the injuries sustained in this episode. Nor was Fela the only member of the family jailed under the military; one of his brothers was imprisoned at the same time as Fela's detention, though slightly later a second brother would serve as the federal minister of health.[9] Seun does not run such risks in the relatively more open environment of the Fourth Republic.[10] Even so, it is not clear what will be accomplished by critique alone: "The young Africans them get two ears for head / Them get two eyes too / Them dey see the things wey dey happen," which is all very well, but "Few people dey fat with big money / And the rest dey hungry."

"Army Arrangement" and its rehearsal of the allegations against General Buhari are notable for the song's portrait of how oil revenue began to inflect Nigerian politics across the 1970s and 1980s. During this period a novel set of political processes began to create a new national culture. Just as the inauguration of political competition at the center in the late-colonial period made possibilities for government malpractice because of the new salience of power at the center for determining the distribution of national goods, changes in this period also transformed the basic logic of political life. The consequence was a new politics of corruption. "Army Arrangement" is important not for documenting allegations against Buhari, which were (and still are) widely known— muckraking is not the point—but for underlining a complex dynamic of scandal and rehabilitation, fiercely brought up by the general's detractors, and even more fiercely denied by his supporters. The Kutis' taunt to General Buhari points to the ultimate meaning of corruption as a moral discourse. Seun's iteration posits the culpability of the entire political elite in the disappearance of oil revenue. Where Fela undermined what was by then an established narrative of Nigerian political life—civilian politicians reflected the popular will but also were rampantly dishonest; military rulers were authoritarian but reined in corruption—Seun's version is yet more dispiriting: both military and civilian administrations steal, and both systematically conspire to cover up their own culpability. Twenty-first century Nigeria is a sadder place than Nigeria in the 1980s.

"No Victors, No Vanquished": The Transformation of Corruption

The popular rage the missing ₦2.8 billion catalyzed presents a considerable contrast to the hope that characterized much of the 1970s. That decade was framed by two transitions: 1970 and 1979 were momentous years, marking the end of the civil war and then the return of civilian government after fourteen years of military rule. The earlier transition was the more extraordinary, marking the end of the civil war and of the escalating ethnic tensions and violence that had preceded it. Pogroms against Igbo people across the federation, their retreat to the Eastern Region, and Biafra's secession were neither a discrete regional dispute nor an instance of long-term and inevitable tension between implacably opposed cultural rivals. As the last chapter demonstrated, political competition that emerged at the start of national-level political competition under the Richards constitution in 1948 transformed an already-established dynamic in which politicians' diversion of state resources undergirded their political potency, which intersected with politicians' regionalized bases of support. In this process, accusations of corruption had become an integral part of this regionalized competition, while the overall dynamic helped to politicize regional rivalries as *ethnic* rivalries, as politicians negotiated the politics of patronage in culturalized and ethnicized terms. Although the coups of January and July 1966 ended that pattern of political competition, the wholesale politics of ethnicity and regional politics proved more enduring, and deadly. Subsequent events did not eliminate this quality to Nigerian politics, but they did alter the ways it played out in national politics. At the same time, the advent of military government and its persistence for the subsequent twelve years had the effect of shifting the impetus of ethnicized corruption from the practices of civilian politics to that of military rule as well.

The civil war ended on 15 January 1970, when a delegation of Biafran army officers led by the breakaway republic's vice president surrendered to Nigeria's military head of state, Yakubu Gowon. The military leader's response was conciliatory: he famously declared the civil war would have "no victor, no vanquished." In a subsequent radio address he announced that a reunited Nigeria would pursue a policy he termed Reconciliation, Reconstruction, Rehabilitation. His stated goal was a process of conciliation and rapprochement rather than an explicit attempt to punish Biafra's secessionist leaders.[11] Biafran leaders (aside from Colonel Ojukwu himself, who had gone into exile in Côte d'Ivoire) were welcomed back: "My Government has directed that former civil servants and public corporation officials should be promptly reinstated as they come out of hiding." Gowon emphasized the importance of equal Nigerian citizenship and the right of all Nigerians to live and work anywhere in the country. This may have reassured Biafrans, but it left unspecified how the ethnic cleavages causing the civil war would be addressed.

Ironically and ominously, the most immediate direct consequence of the federal victory was the full implementation of the twelve-state structure Gowon had proclaimed in 1967. Gowon's initial decree of the twelve-state structure in May 1967 had come in the aftermath of the anti-Igbo violence across the federation, the exodus of Igbos to the Eastern Region, and the coup against Ironsi's regime, which resulted in the deaths of the head of state and many of his Igbo subordinates. Gowon's new federal structure might have curbed the ratcheting up of tensions that led to such violence, while it also had the effect of potentially undercutting the position of Colonel Ojukwu, the Eastern Region's military governor, who would have become governor of the new East-Central state, vastly smaller than the old Eastern Region. It proposed a loss of territory and a concomitant loss of power for Ojukwu personally and was unacceptable for the largely Igbo elite that had dominated the region precipitating Biafra's secession. In ethnic terms, the structure could be justified in that the other two states carved out of the old Eastern Region were dominated by members of "minority" ethnic groups, while the Igbo now had a state of their own. However, Igbo partisans could not have helped noticing that the region's oil deposits were largely in Rivers and South-Eastern states and thus passed out from under Igbo control. *Both* the ethnic riots and the federal structure meant to accommodate ethnic diversity were easily understood as anti-Igbo, and both were tightly tied to questions of political control and who would have access to state resources. The end of the civil war, therefore, resulted in precisely the regional breakup Ojukwu was attempting to prevent, though by 1970 Biafra's military losses had long since removed the coastal areas from Enugu's control. Few truly mourned the end of the old regional structure, even if Ironsi's unitary state and Gowon's federal reorganization had each proven so costly, leading directly to countercoup and civil war.

Despite the contrast between abolishing federalism and increasing the number of states, both reforms achieved much the same centralizing end; the unitary state had devolved administrative responsibility from the regions to provinces while centralizing the civil service. The twelve-state system had a similar effect, with a devolution to states instead of provinces.[12] The unitary state prompted suspicion, particularly in the north. Already leery of Igbo advancement within the central civil service, a group of well-educated, relatively young men had attained high office within the Northern Regional government, and they were not inclined to trust the recruitment decisions of a regime perceived to be dominated by Igbos. Without a regional government dominated by a patronage network in which they were comfortably ensconced, this group faced bleak prospects for future advancement. Perhaps locked out of the federal civil service run by Igbo superiors, they would be forced to operate within the narrow confines of a provincial service. The twelve-state system was not necessarily more promising: military governors were appointed by the center, and they might hire subordinates from their areas of origin. Nonetheless, for northerners whatever shortcomings Gowon's government might have had, it was not dominated by Igbos.

The twelve-state structure addressed grievances that had festered within the old regions in part by opening up the possibility that more states would be created in the future. The superficial equality of the old north and old south each divided into six states broke down with a more detailed ethnic calculus. However, the justification for making these precise splits enshrined in Nigerian federalism a logic of ethnic sovereignty, which simultaneously reified ethnic groups and indicated the manner in which ethnic claims might translate into administrative recognition. It also moved Nigeria away from a federal structure that magnified the power of the three "majority" ethnic groups. Kwara, North-Eastern, and Benue-Plateau states were emphatically non-Hausa areas emerging from the old north; Mid-Western, Rivers, and South-Eastern states were southern but neither Yoruba nor Igbo.[13] Officially acknowledging that ethnic groups had the right to representation at the level of state government could signal reconciliation at a moment in which Igbo secession was the dominant political issue bedeviling Nigerian political life. Previously favored by the Eastern Region's government, in 1970 the Igbo inhabitants of East-Central state were the main audience for Gowon's "no victors" rhetoric. Devastated by the war, landlocked, and less fertile than many other areas, East-Central state desperately needed federal assistance, though at least Igbos wary of violence elsewhere knew they had a secure, Igbo-dominated home to which they could retreat. Meanwhile, the other areas of the federation enjoyed new benefits from the novel federal scheme. In addition to the minorities, the north's major city of Kano received its own state, and eastern Hausas also got a state autonomous from Sokoto domination. Lagos became its own state, but Yorubas who still smarted from having had the Mid-West carved out from their region managed to retain their territorial integrity otherwise intact. Such boundaries could thus equally be considered fair and unfair. The Igbos got one state of their own, the southern Yorubas two (if one took Lagos state to be a prize awarded to the Yoruba), and the Hausas three. Nonetheless, the new federal arrangements could be construed as providing benefits to all. Even if the Igbo were not economically advantaged by the new arrangement, they did have territory to call their own. The new federal structure blunted the poisonous system in which the big three ethnic groups dominated their own regions and competed in the center.

Civilian politics had been an inextricable part of that dynamic. The logic in which civilian politicians became entrepreneurs of ethnic conflict through their own need to cultivate territorial political constituencies had already been made irrelevant by military rule, but even before 1970 Gowon demonstrated himself a master of conciliation and inclusion in government. Reconciliation was easier when politicians were not maneuvering to win elections and prevent their enemies from doing so. Neither did it hurt that Gowon himself was a member of a minority ethnic group from the Middle Belt, and though he was a northerner he was a Christian. The redoubtable western leader Obafemi Awolowo had been freed by the military government in 1966 and made commissioner for finance the following year. As the war ended, some Biafran secessionists also were appointed to high office. As the political elite began to perceive all sectors might enjoy a certain degree of governmental enfranchisement, ethnic tension subsided across the country more generally. Without electoral politics driving maneuvers for local (and therefore ethnic) constituencies, the centrifugal politics that had haunted the First Republic were somewhat calmed, even as ethnicity continued to serve as a lens for interpreting political positioning. Gowon underlined his disinterested motives by announcing Nigeria would begin a transition to civilian government, which would be complete by 1976.

But even at this earliest and most hopeful moment of Nigeria's oil boom, accusations of corruption troubled the body politic, initially in forms similar to those established through the colonial period and the First Republic. These demonstrated potential fault lines and impeded the smooth functioning of state institutions. Too-slow and inadequate federal responses to the humanitarian crisis in the former Biafra were regularly attributed to corruption, but at this moment they reflected tendencies already well established. Thus, in the words of a rehabilitation commissioner, Samuel Ikoku, "deepening corruption and organized fraud" had led to a situation in which entire vehicles transporting relief supplies had disappeared in transit.[14] International concern at the humanitarian crisis in East-Central state segued into discussions of the use of development assistance, and resulted ultimately in a tendency to view corruption as having two manifestations:

> Two kinds of corruption thrive in Nigeria. The first comes from the traditional "dash" system of West Africa, where people expect or seek a tip, which they call a "dash," for their services. Many Nigerians fail to see why this system should cease just because they have become civil servants. If a government clerk hands a businessman some applications for a license, the clerk wants to be "dashed." The second kind is more Western and probably more harmful to a developing country like Nigeria. Men at the top expect a lucrative cut when they award a government

contract to a private businessman. It is difficult, of course, to document such bribery, but most Nigerians believe it happens all the time.[15]

This description nodded to the well-established technocratic paradigm of corruption as being a problem all countries had experienced during the course of modernization, and it tied into descriptions of Nigeria that had suffused international commentary during the First Republic: Nigeria was uncomfortably between tradition and modernity. Old practices persisted, but the country was more deeply troubled by the reaction of powerful officials to the demands of modern state structures. Nigerians were fully able to adopt this stance, but as the cases of Emir Sanusi and Chief Obafemi Awolowo demonstrated, the focus of attention was on particular officials. "Corruption" was a charge one leveled at opponents and enemies and overlooked among friends.

That dynamic persisted into the oil boom and has been particularly powerful in affecting how First Republic politics are remembered. Consider, for example, the enduring reputation of the First Republic's minister of finance, Festus Okotie-Eboh. Despite the great publicity his dealings had received in the domestic press during the 1960s, for the most part the minister had been discussed internationally primarily as a technocratic financial decision maker—in the words of the distinguished development economist Wolfgang Stolper, "despite his greed and corruption . . . a darn good finance minister."[16] His flamboyant corruption was not an issue for more than incidental international comment, and that mostly euphemized by references to his colorful African customs. The *Observer* commented just before independence that

> he is one of that group of new African leaders . . . who combine power with brilliant clowning. They seem to support the new adage: "All power is delightful; absolute power is absolutely delightful." . . . He is tall, fat, jovial, and obviously rich. His followers in the mid-west of Nigeria welcome him with a joyful shout, which means roughly "extravagant man!" He arrives in the Federal Parliament, accompanied by roars of laughter, wearing a straw boater, a huge brass pendant and a robe trailing several feet behind him. The robe, like that of his wife and followers, was designed by himself; it consists of several large, round portraits of Chief Festus.[17]

Coverage shifted after Okotie-Eboh's death, emphasizing the malpractice itself. Thus, the *New York Times* cited a "visiting foreigner" who described a meeting with Okotie-Eboh:

> "Excuse me a moment," said the genial Minister after the two had shaken hands. Chief Festus reached into his desk drawer. He withdrew 20 stacks

of £5 notes worth about $14,000. Then he buzzed his private secretary and told her: "Let's put this in my safe." His opening maneuver completed, he turned to his guest and said without batting an eye: "And now then, shall we talk business?" The late Minister was best known as the King of "Dash"—vernacular for bribery. And it was this odious reputation that prompted Nigeria's young army majors to put him high on their death list when they staged their lightning coup three weeks ago.[18]

Once he was safely out of power, it was a relatively minor change to recast Okotie-Eboh as "bad" or "corrupt" while still being a modern actor. What had been previously indicated by acknowledgments of his wealth or references to his flamboyance now was bluntly replaced by descriptions of bribes and ill-gotten gains. The implicit sociology behind the transition was more constant; during the first several years of the 1970s, technocratic discussions of corruption centered on the problems of an underdeveloped political culture and how that disrupted the urgent need to get resources for reconstruction and development.

In Nigeria, the complaints were somewhat more sophisticated, used for claim making. Accusations of corruption were politically performative; they placed the speaker in particular political locations, and they performed political work. Within such an optic, Okotie-Eboh was not simply a Westernized bad apple; he was tied into the social logic of his home area and his political base, of NCNC politics, and to the government of the First Republic. One's standing on the precise nature of his crimes depended on one's position relative to other political actors, and to the political networks he operated within. Thus, an influential leader from Okotie-Eboh's locality—who objected to his favoritism of one local ethnic group over another—recounted this scandal:

> Okotie-Eboh had acquired some new property in Sapele. He wanted the tenants to be moved out quickly, much more quickly than the law permitted. An Urhobo tenant by the name of Mr. Machine Orhorhoro, an Eku native, resisted hurried evacuation. Okotie-Eboh sent Itsekiri thugs to rough him up and to throw him and his family, along with their property, into the street. This matter was dragged into the courts and Okotie-Eboh was consistently found guilty by all courts all the way up to the Privy Council in London for the rough and violent treatment of Mr. Machine Orhorhoro.[19]

The criticism here was not for abuse of office per se, nor the diversion of public resources to private ends. Instead, it was of how someone with relatively little political influence was treated. Okotie-Eboh systematically favored members of his own Itsekiri group over those of Urhobos (this despite the fact that he was half Urhobo himself). Conversely, a fellow indigene of Warri recently called Okotie-Eboh "a jolly good fellow locked in the throes of splendiferous flamboyance and the theatrics of brummagem," protesting that he "was never found guilty of corruption by any court of competent jurisdiction and by any interventionist body on graft."[20] One should not fetishize technocratic and ethno-political frames of reference as purely "international" or "domestic." For example, the self-published memoir of Harold Smith, a British Labour Department official, excoriated Okotie-Eboh in personalistic terms, calling him "a cynical party hack intent on becoming rich very quickly. Already in the late 1950's he was a byword for corruption. Okotie Eboh was not a nationalist and in no sense an idealist. He was a large, fat, cheerful crook and he was much loved by . . . the Governor General, perhaps because he conformed to a stereotype which confirmed their low opinion of Africans in general."[21] Smith, like other colonial officers, tended to describe leaders' corruption or lack of it in terms of their personal qualities rather than as a consequence of the political and cultural systems in which they lived. In his account, Awolowo was not corrupt but was "extremely intelligent, wrote first class books, and taunted the British for their stupidity. At the same time he betrayed a love of democracy and touching faith in British fair play that was to lead to his downfall." Azikiwe was not corrupt but "an enigma. A charismatic and the first Nigerian national leader of note. He was seen as an egotistical, temperamental and flawed character by his political enemies, but revered by his Igbo followers."[22]

Even if the two ways of imagining and deploying the accusation of corruption intermingled, taken together they did create a coherent description and explanation of Nigerian politics. This took on new valences as a result of Nigeria's oil wealth. The new federal system changed the politics of resource distribution as a matter of region and ethnicity; oil revenue itself transformed the material underpinnings of corrupt actions; and Nigeria's burgeoning reputation for corruption created new constellations of corrupt possibility. The corruption-complex would never be the same. Its upward trajectory was stunning. Already in 1969 (when the civil war was still raging) Nigeria was exporting 540,000 barrels per day, but in 1970 that nearly doubled to 1,085,000 barrels per day.[23] In the years since, Nigerian production has fluctuated but always stayed substantially above that level. And while production increased to a level between 1 and 2 million barrels per day, the price of oil rose substantially with the oil shock of 1973, quadrupling by 1974, which further increased Nigerian revenues. Oil became increasingly important in funding the government:

in 1969 it was 16.6 percent of federal revenue, which increased to 25.9 percent in 1970. By 1974 it was 80.8 percent.[24] This change in government finances was stunning, more than a tenfold increase from 1970 to 1974. The quantitative change was profound to the point of becoming qualitative: financial shortages did not play the same role they had in earlier years. Oil made it possible to quiet sectional tension simply by paying off elites or aspirant elites across the country.

From the time of its final amalgamation in 1914, Nigeria's role in the international economy was as an exporter of agricultural goods. State revenue came from taxation, import and export fees, and from the marketing boards. Revenue allocation was a key political question, as indeed it has remained ever since. Commissions of inquiry met regularly to adjust the allocation of government revenues, in 1946, 1950, 1953, 1958, 1964, and 1969.[25] The issue was politically dicey because the products grown in different regions of the country were not equally lucrative, and the regions already had received quite different levels of infrastructural investment. The key difficulty was that palm oil and cocoa fetched much higher prices on world markets than groundnuts did. Southern Nigeria produced much more revenue than Northern Nigeria did. To compound the difficulty, the political accommodation between northern emirs and the British that had limited missionization and had maintained the aristocracy's economic influence also served to retard the region's access to education, Western health care, roads, and other forms of investment. As politicians took control—and as the country increasingly was dominated by northern politicians—the government was inclined to address the north's relative deprivation. However, because the south continued to produce more revenue, this involved a net transfer of resources. A "principle of derivation" (meaning that regions were supposed to retain revenues partly in proportion to their having provided them) was used to balance the competing concerns of allowing regions to retain their own revenues and of achieving equal development across the federation. Applying the principle caused controversy, and thus the recurrent commissions addressing the allocation formula. On one hand, the southern two (and then three) regions produced the more lucrative exports. On the other, the north also (at least according to the census) had the larger population and had been relatively disadvantaged in social spending up until independence. Both northerners and southerners could justifiably claim ill use. Compounding this difficulty, in common with many African states the Nigerian government had suffered from a tendency to redistribute resources from rural to urban areas. Until 1970, peasants were the producers of Nigeria's wealth, but infrastructural investment disproportionately benefited cities, which led cash crop production to stagnate across the 1960s—particularly the more lucrative cocoa and palm oil crops.

This recurrent problem took on a different political meaning as oil revenues transformed the government's revenue base, and it became a very different beast.[26] However, the issues of revenue distribution remained potent. As agriculture and import/export duties gave way to oil as the primary source of government revenue, the issue of the origin of revenue was diluted.[27] Oil revenues were paid into a federal account, and revenues were then transferred to the states. Across the 1970s, then, oil revenue became the primary funding source for government activity at both the federal and state levels. This transformation intersected with Gowon's ethnically generous approach to reconciliation, making it possible for elites across the federation to benefit directly from federal largesse. Moreover, the concentration of export revenue from oil rents resulted in a system in which the state was even more central to the economy than it had been previously, when it was superintending cash crop and other mineral exports. Unlike these earlier export regimes, a relatively small percentage of the Nigerian population was involved in oil production and therefore directly benefited from it. Nonetheless, at this early period, the net result of this prosperity was felt widely.

Oil revenues enabled a favorable exchange rate for the naira; imports became cheap. Even today, people reminisce about the standard of living that was possible during the 1970s. Those of relatively modest means were able to afford imported textiles and foodstuffs. Many were able to afford to buy cars or motorcycles, televisions, electric generators. My discussions of the 1970s with friends who were adult at the time were punctuated with the lists of consumer goods they had been able to afford. People doing the youth service required of university graduates could routinely buy bottles of imported wine. Ordinary families acquired expensive appliances. In the cities, there was a replacement of the indigenous *gari*, a dish made from locally grown cassava, in favor of bread made from imported wheat. Millet and sorghum were replaced by rice, which is much easier to prepare. Beyond the arena of consumer goods, oil money enabled an ambitious, even grandiose set of development initiatives, many aspects of which were poorly planned. All was not well, because agricultural production stagnated, and as a result ordinary farmers were cut out from much of this new prosperity. Buying cheap imports still required cash, and the flip side of a strong naira was that cash crops did not command high prices. As a consequence, therefore, having access to flows of government money became increasingly important to anyone's ambitions for material advancement.

The oil economy shifted the politics of resource distribution, providing funds to pay off enough groups to ensure a degree of relative communal quiet. The country embarked on a program of public works, all the more necessary in the aftermath of the civil war. The eastern states (and indeed, the Midwest as well) had sustained considerable damage. The advent of oil did not end officials' needs for illicit access to state resources. Military or civilian, Nigeria's governors were big men, and they needed access to money in order to take care of their followers. But there was enough money to keep revenues flowing to public works, even as substantial proportions were siphoned off to the demands of local politics. Oil revenues had another effect; they were made available for public consumption in the form of development investment. Oil revenue enabled development and other infrastructural projects, and these were contracted through the distribution of contracts. The process made Nigeria notorious. The massive resources newly available to the government, coupled with the popular demand for an investment in development infrastructure, resulted in what Bala Usman has called a "contractocracy,"[28] in which public works were contracted out to private organizations. The contract has become a primary means through which private individuals get access to state revenues, though it has proven an extremely inefficient way to run government affairs.

Although the civilian elite was relatively content with Gowon's approach to dividing the federal spoils, there was unanimity about the need eventually to return to civilian rule. In 1973 the Federal Military Government attempted to conduct a new census that would replace the one from 1952, which was still being used to shape government policy after the fiasco of the exercise in 1963, when large-scale fraud had forced the government to cancel the results of that census. To the country's horror, however, 1973 saw a replay of events from the previous decade: census returns demonstrated vast and entirely implausible population growth, a consequence of attempts by local officials who were maneuvering to claim aid on the basis of such growth. The sins of the First Republic persisted. A National Census Board conducted a national enumeration from 25 November to 2 December, but reports quickly leaked out that totals were being inflated in a number of states. Worse, as the board prepared its final evaluations, charges and countercharges proliferated of deliberate fraud among enumerators. Press coverage and rumors caused matters to go from bad to worse as the board attempted to complete its work: plots and counterplots across the country had a ratchet effect, as officials increased their totals ever higher to compensate for fraud being conducted elsewhere. One difficulty was in reconciling the new population totals with those projected from the results of the census of 1963, which required assuming a negative rate of population growth in some areas.[29] In the new enumeration, the six northern states were all in the top eight most populous. Popular reaction was furious, particularly in the southern states. The census's basic finding of more people in the north than in the south could be defended; more careful enumeration methods probably would tend to find more people in the north, given the suspicion with which people in the region received government agents. So returning to northern towns and counting more carefully probably would have discovered more genuine Nigerian citizens. The civil war would have tended to depress fertility in the south, disproportionately in the east, giving demographic stagnancy plausibility. Nonetheless, the overall findings were politically explosive.[30] Given the politics of revenue allocation and the fact that states that increased their share of the national population would receive a greater proportion of federal oil income, the north's smart rate of population growth was poorly received in the south. In his convocation address to the University of Ife, Obafemi Awolowo announced he was "irresistibly impelled to the conclusion that the so-called PROVISIONAL FIGURES are absolutely unreliable and should be totally rejected." More seriously, he complained that in the censuses of 1952 and 1963, the northern provinces had been claimed to have 55 and 54 percent of Nigeria's population. In the new census, that increased to 65 percent. He calculated that his home base in Western state would have had a population growth rate of .62 percent, while North-Eastern state would have had more than 7 percent population growth. "THIS JUST CANNOT BE TRUE," he thundered.[31] Before matters could get out of hand, the federal military government canceled the results of the census, and the country proceeded to rely on the results of the (also-discredited, but by now less controversial) census of 1963. The prospects of transition to civilian rule were not aided by such scandals. If nothing else, it was an extremely ominous sign that civilians were so obviously maneuvering for political position in such overtly unscrupulous ways. The First Republic seemed to be more a model for future behavior than a cautionary tale.

Increasing scandal plagued many of the officials of the Gowon regime, which intensified popular pressure for moving back toward civilian rule. One locus of discontent was the state governors, most of whom became notorious for stealing money. In October 1974 Gowon announced he would replace all military governors, but soon thereafter backtracked, explaining he could not deny them the pleasure of shaking Queen Elizabeth's hand when she came to Nigeria in October 1975.[32] With a year's grace, a number of the military governors proceeded to award many irregular contracts. At the same time, commissioners running federal ministries were also becoming the subject of scandals.

Taken together, these factors undermined the military government's ability to claim itself as a force for moderating political corruption. The lucrative possibilities of government provided the military with motives for postponing the transition to civilian rule. Having political power was profitable. Officers who held political positions such as governorships or commissionerships became anxious to retain them. Their comrades whose duties remained purely military began to hope for transfer to political office so they could hope to reap these rewards for themselves. At the same time, the vastly increased financial resources controlled by the government suggested that civilian politicians would be attracted by precisely the same logic. Given the unfortunate history of the First Republic, this suggested a new civilian administration would be even more corrupt than its disgraced predecessor. The behavior of civilians in power, the fiasco of the census, continual bickering among civilians, all suggested a Second Republic would be troubled. Disquiet over the prospects for a future civilian government was widespread. Indeed, in a famous speech at the University of Lagos in 1972 former president Nnamdi Azikiwe had suggested that "diarchy" might be a potential long-term solution to Nigeria's political woes, by which he meant that future Nigerian governments should formally institutionalize a role for the military and that power should be shared between soldiers and civilians.[33] While Dr. Azikiwe garnered a furious response—especially since the military government had not acquitted itself well in the administration of the census or in its ability to handle state governors—the diarchy proposal found supporters. And Gowon himself announced the indefinite postponement of the transition to civilian rule on Independence Day in 1974: "In spite of the existence of a state of emergency which has so far precluded political activity there has already emerged a high degree of sectional politicking, intemperate utterances and writings which were deliberately designed to whip up ill feelings within the country to the benefit of the political aspirations of a few."[34] Ten months later, a military coup occurred while Gowon was out of the country. Brigadier Murtala Muhammed emerged as the new military head of state and proposed to attack the scandals that had festered under Gowon in order to achieve a transition to civilian rule in relatively short order. Immediately, he replaced the twelve military governors and instigated a probe into their conduct in office. Only two were found innocent of any malpractice. Both the military governors and commissioners were investigated for corrupt practices, and most had considerable amounts stripped from them. General Ibrahim Babangida would subsequently return some of this wealth in 1993.

The probes were not restricted to the top levels of government. All in all, ten thousand officials were replaced—not all for corruption, some ostensibly for age or inefficiency. The new government announced that civilian rule would be inaugurated on 1 October 1979. To prepare for that, a civilian constituent assembly was announced, which would draft a new constitution, and seven new states were created. The earlier calculations about state creation as reflecting and driven by considerations of ethnicity were redoubled in this new exercise, and the same dynamic persisted in the creation of new local government areas as well. The Yoruba-dominated Western state was split into three. Igbo East-Central state was divided in two, as were Middle Belt Benue-Plateau state and Hausa North-West state. North-Eastern state, which was ethnically complex, was divided in three. The material basis of these ethnic and political decisions was clear. In Nigeria's new economic reality, in which oil money dwarfed all other sources of national income, public office became more important than ever, since oil money flowed directly into government coffers. With the prospect of a transition to civilian rule, the old principle that political success could be attained only through being able to channel monies to one's constituency gained a renewed vigor. This situation was to confirm corruption as a national-level political problem in Nigeria, rather than one negotiated primarily in terms of local political culture. At the same time, Nigeria also became inserted into international discourse as a quintessentially corrupt locale, a status it had not had so unequivocally before.

As this drama played itself out, a new political crisis rocked Nigeria. Murtala Muhammed had become extremely popular as a result of his widely publicized moves against corruption and his promise to leave power quickly, and because he had very effectively established a no-nonsense, unpretentious persona that played well across the country. Overestimating his ability to impose his will, he passed over for promotion a group of military officers who included a number with ethnic links to Gowon. These officers became a nucleus of discontent and began plotting a coup. The head of state also had dispatched with Gowon's practice of maintaining an elaborate security apparatus, and he was well known for making surprise appearances all over Lagos.[35] The lack of security proved fatal. On 13 February 1976, a group of officers ambushed his car as he drove to the office, killing him, his aide-de-camp, and his driver. Meanwhile, other plotters attempted to capture or kill other key officials, with limited success. Despite Murtala Muhammed's death, the coup failed, and he was replaced as head of state by his deputy, Lieutenant General Olusegun Obasanjo.

The failed coup attempt was dealt with savagely. The government tried and executed a number of Middle Belt officers suspected of complicity. The government suspected Gowon himself was involved in the plot—one suspicion was that the plotters intended to recall him as head of state—but he was in the UK studying at Warwick University and declined to return to Nigeria for trial. Despite the death of Murtala Mohammed the regime continued on its reformist way. The fraction of the army dominating the military government was based in the north, even though the new head of state himself was a Yoruba from the southwest. The government's preparations for the transition to civilian government continued as well. These involved convening a constituent assembly to write a new constitution. The constituent assembly ultimately decided on a presidential model of government, a federal system that bore a resemblance to that of the United States. At the same time, the military government overtly displayed its commitment to reforming instances of corruption, though rumors persisted of ongoing failures and the persistence of corruption. It was during this period that the army raided Fela Kuti's house, and when Buhari became the petroleum minister.

The Cement Armada

The multiplex transformations in Nigeria's political economy made the 1970s a watershed in the history of the Nigerian corruption-complex. The "cement armada" of 1974 is an apt example of its new forms. The incident was a turning point in the country's new reputation for extraordinary corruption, which has been a central part of how corruption has functioned subsequently. With its five-year Third National Development plan starting in 1975, the Gowon administration embarked on a massive program of road building and the construction of public buildings. Domestic supplies of cement were minimal, and in March 1974 the government supply agency ordered 2 million metric tons, which was then supplemented by an additional request from the defense ministry for military buildings. The armed forces had proposed projects estimated to require 2.9 million tons of cement, but the ministry eventually ordered more than 16 million metric tons. Teams of government officials negotiated contracts for Romanian, Greek, Spanish, and American cement; with world prices of approximately $40 per ton, the Nigerian contracts ran more toward $115 per ton.[36] An oversupply of overpriced cement became the least of the government's worries as half the world's supply of cement was diverted toward Nigeria. When the cement arrived, the cargo vastly outstripped the Port of Lagos's ability to offload it. For a year, the port was choked by the cement armada, forcing it to pay millions in demurrage fees as well, which could run to $4,100 per ship per day. Some ship owners sent partially laden ships in order to collect multiple demurrage fees, or they diverted their cargoes elsewhere but continued to collect fees as if their ships remained in the Lagos port. A poorly thought-through plan to solve the crisis by buying cranes for the port compounded the difficulty, since the cranes also had to be landed, and once they were in the port there were no personnel trained to operate them. Part of the consignment waited for more than a year. By the time all cement shipments were unloaded, large quantities were unusable. The scandal did not unravel fully until after the coup in July 1975 brought Murtala Mohammed's reformist regime to power. The new government appointed a commission of inquiry under Justice Alfa Belgore of the Supreme Court.

The tribunal's report was released at the end of 1976. Its conclusions were carefully measured and ultimately received relatively little publicity. Its topline conclusions were unsurprising: the prices paid for the cement were far higher than world market prices, and much more had been ordered than was necessary for all projected building works. The commission's terms of reference had been somewhat constricted: it focused on the reasons so much cement was ordered, the logistics of procurement, the issue of whether any government officials had benefited personally from the orders, and the dark suspicion that "any public officer either by design or in collusion with some foreign interests not only defrauded the Federal Government but also intended to sabotage [it]."[37] The conclusions were unflattering to a considerable number of officials but found only a handful were guilty of actual dishonesty. Most notably, then–head of state Olusegun Obasanjo had served as inspector of engineers for the military, but the report noted that he had moved to other responsibilities before the first cement contract was signed (27). His successor as inspector of engineers, Colonel A. H. Hananiya, was found to have had improper contact with aspirant cement contractors and appeared to have advocated for friends and acquaintances (27–28). More seriously, the report concluded the defense ministry's principal accountant, J. A. Ilori, had made many unusual alterations in contractual terms and had done so "induced by improper enrichment" (37–38). Ilori's immediate subordinate, Simon Enebechi, gave "cunning and untruthful" testimony and was determined to have acted improperly in order to receive bribes. The tribunal was particularly unhappy about the fact Enebechi had arranged for a "partner's wife" to lobby one of his superiors for a cement contract. "Using a female to obtain gain from a colleague" was "abominable" (40–41). Two diplomats came in for suspicion. The ambassador to Turkey, Brigadier George Kurubo, had improperly approved a contract, but he had left government; therefore the tribunal did not pursue the matter. The ambassador to the Netherlands, Alhaji Osman Ahmadu Suka, had a much more extensive record of lobbying for contracts and seemed to have received considerably more money (43–45).

The villain of the piece was Simon Enebechi's apparently lascivious superior. Charles Guernsey Lakin-Smith was a retired lieutenant colonel from the British army who had come to Nigeria in 1958 and continued in the civil service after independence. In 1974 he was the defense ministry's deputy secretary for development projects. He oversaw all of the projects for which cement was ordered, and he was found to have circumvented his superiors in getting contracts approved. Despite all this (and presumably despite special pleading from female visitors), the tribunal found no evidence he had "gained any financial benefit" from the fiasco (39–40). Rather, the tribunal darkly noted:

> Such action of Mr Lakin-Smith as came out during evidence before us can only be that of either a block-head or a man with a design. Mr Lakin-Smith certainly is not a block-head. He was apparently not acting to enrich himself improperly or to defraud the Government. We gave robust allowance for his education and his age which may tend to make him senile and blur his perspective. We take into consideration the pressure of work but all taken into account we find it hard not to come to the conclusion that his devoted service might be a mere insidious devise, buying time to gain confidence of the people he was working with but looking for an opportunity to release his sinister motive. We have strong belief that his integrity is debatable and his loyalty suspect. He had motive, a strong motive for his action, the exact nature of which is not easy to ascertain but we are unanimous that the motive cannot be genuine or in the best interest of the government or this country. (68–69)

The military government's white paper in response emphasized the fact that the report had cleared General Obasanjo, at that time the deputy head of state.[38] The extraordinary aspect of both the report and the white paper is how completely they worked around the relationship between the objectionable aspects of the cement armada and the elements of Nigerian political society that had given rise to it. A few Nigerians were guilty of improper conduct because of greed and a desire for material advancement. A somewhat larger group contributed to the problem because they were incompetent or, at least to some extent, derelict in their duties. However, the real mastermind was a British man, comfortably removed from the Nigerian political and social scene. The official explanation for the catastrophe was that the cement armada had been caused by factors beyond—and beyond the control of—Nigeria. While a certain amount of administrative reform could prevent a repetition of some of what had happened, the Belgore tribunal did not hint at any real structural problems with the federal military government's underlying logic. The official response to the debacle was not in itself terribly different from the responses to cases during the First Republic or late-colonial period. The scale was something new, as was the response it garnered internationally.

The cement armada was the first Nigerian corruption story to attract huge international attention. This was in part because of how it became newsworthy and in part as a result of lurid stories about the cement contracts behind the incident, which were both colorful and involved non-Nigerians. It had a gossipy appeal from the moment it broke in the press; in western Europe, eyebrows were raised even before congestion in Lagos gave the story a slapstick quality. The first rumblings of trouble had emerged as part of a British domestic scandal involving the business dealings of a British government minister, John Stonehouse. A spy for the Czech government,[39] Stonehouse was a privy councilor who had been a member of the Labour government until the Conservatives won the election of 1970. Not appointed to the shadow cabinet, he proceeded to engage in questionable business dealings, including an attempt to obtain a contract to supply Romanian cement (controlled at that point by Princess Jeanne of Romania)[40] to Nigeria. The contract went instead to a Nigerian named Sylvester Okereke, who mysteriously drowned in the Thames on 18 November 1974, before the contract was finalized.[41] Stonehouse faked his own suicide two days later and went to Australia under a false identity—he had evidently been planning this for some time and had arranged to meet his mistress there—but he was arrested on Christmas Eve on the suspicion of being Lord Lucan, the murder suspect who had famously disappeared earlier that year. The inquest over Okereke's death was held in February 1975. It brought these sharp dealings over cement into international consciousness at roughly the time the Lagos port began to run into trouble. At this point, however, the story was one of international wheeling and dealing rather than one of baroque misgovernance in Nigeria. Nonetheless, the story had appeal, with its scandal-plagued privy councilor/spy, shady Balkan princess, and drowned businessman.

The full extent of the scandal attracted international attention that autumn, after the new military government began to investigate the affair. The fiasco in Lagos's port was well established at that point. Murtala's government was already inclined to investigate malfeasance under Gowon—it had the simultaneous benefits of assisting the cause of good governance and bolstering domestic political support—and the regime was also attempting to divert further shipments of cement away from Lagos. For international commentators the cement armada was initially a piece of business news: the Nigerian government was attempting to renegotiate and reschedule supply contracts, to the outrage of international shipping firms and cement contractors.[42] The government's inquiry into the possibility corruption had played a role in allocating the contracts provided additional leverage against contract holders by suggesting the contracts themselves were of questionable legality.[43]

The staggering extent of the problem soon became the main story. Nigeria sent a delegation to the London freight market to ask the world industry to divert incoming ships. The delegation's leader reported 400 ships awaiting berths in Lagos, 250 of which were carrying cement.[44] Over the course of a few days, the coverage became increasingly derisive:

> It seemed a good idea at the time, although now . . . it's a little difficult getting anyone to admit it was actually their brainwave. There was this plan for a black cultural Olympics you see, which meant constructing a sort of cultural Olympic village. And of course Nigeria needs more roads and schools. So someone ordered a few million tons of cement. Then there were these army men with big ideas. No one at the moment seems quite sure what the big ideas actually were, but they called for a lot of cement. So let's see, that's four million tons of cement ordered by civilians in Nigeria and an incredible 16 million tons ordered by the military, with delivery of the entire 20 million tons within the year. No one noticed the flaw in the grand design until cement ships started arriving at the Apapa port in Lagos early this year and formed an order queue; and more arrived and more until today the queue was 400 ships long, and some of them have been waiting eight months.[45]

Writers quickly developed broader metaphors: "Like the greedy little boy whose eyes were bigger than his stomach," *Time* magazine reported, "oil-rich Nigeria, thanks to a colossal spending binge, is in one dreadful financial mess."[46] Not all coverage depended so completely on derision; nonetheless, a consensus emerged that the situation was the consequence of Nigeria's state of development. The *New York Times* quoted a Danish "shipping expert," who declared, "The Nigerians are the first and foremost to blame. . . . They bought the whole lot. But the developed countries should not have sold them all that cement. They knew better."[47] Less overtly pejorative than *Time* comparing Nigeria to a child, the *New York Times* story nonetheless framed the issue as one of Nigeria versus "developed countries" rather than particular officials and particular suppliers. The Nigerian government, meanwhile, proposed an approach different from handwringing about corruption and the difference between developed and underdeveloped countries. The problem was "'unscrupulous' and 'militant' suppliers who had ignored earlier orders to delay new shipments until the congestion could be cleared and the contracts investigated." In response the government planned to "suspend loading payments to all shippers who defied its instructions and would also suspend demurrage payments in Lagos 'to enable the Government to distinguish between fraudulent claims.' "[48] The threat was carried out, and subsequent international coverage was divided between bemused stories on individual prosecutions (as when Nigeria's newly appointed high commissioner to the UK, the luckless Osman Ahmadu Suka, was dismissed for having improper business dealings when he negotiated cement contracts while ambassador to the Netherlands[49]) and reports of shippers complaining of dishonored contracts.[50]

The history of the cement armada by itself would be a footnote, an early instance of what has become an established genre of stories of spectacular corruption and misgovernance. It is more important than that. It demonstrates a transformation in the Nigerian corruption-complex as profound as the changes in the distributional politics of region caused by Gowon's new federalism and his policy of reconciliation. The international attention to the cement armada helped to establish Nigeria as a country almost uniquely corrupt. It had the money necessary to order vast quantities of cement, and it suffered from problems of governance serious enough to cause such quantities to be ordered. The cement armada became internationally significant because it served as a demonstration of the possibilities available to Westerners of Nigerian corruption: the government was so handicapped by incomplete records it could not tell genuine contracts from spurious ones. Businesses around the world thus learned powerful lessons about Nigerian governance. The cement armada thus catalyzed illicit contacts between Nigerian officials and foreigners. Nigeria's reputation for corruption would ultimately enable the scammers of the 1980s and after to lure gullible foreigners with the prospect of illicit rewards.

The diversion of immense resources (literally hundreds of millions of naira) into building materials that were unneeded and eventually became unusable illustrates pointless expenditure going far beyond the "squandermania" for which Ahmadu Bello was excoriated. The point of government spending became only incidentally about the construction of buildings and roads. Rather, it became about the negotiation of contracts and the percentages of those contracts that could be diverted to the officials negotiating them.[51] But this transformation was more productive than it might initially appear. Even if oil revenues were spent on projects like the cement armada, they were having an integrative function. It will be many years yet before one can disentangle precisely who profited from the episode (and in truth, the identities of the direct beneficiaries are a question of somewhat limited interest). As the Gowon government moved to incorporate notables from around the federation into the governing elite, a wider spectrum of people gained access to the resources available through office. The oil wealth that had become available increased the lucrativeness of the contracts being parceled out. It also made it possible to divert huge percentages of government spending into these somewhat convoluted channels without bringing public business to an absolute standstill. The cement armada was embarrassing, and it was disruptive—not only were port facilities at Lagos overwhelmed; there was a substantial knock-on effect at Port Harcourt as well. At the same time, the cement negotiators' access to illicit resources achieved a sort of reconciliation by making it possible to pay off leaders who might otherwise be disenfranchised and therefore not supportive of national unity or of the regime in power. Rehabilitation (in the form of giving erstwhile opponents access to office) enabled reconciliation (in the form of loyalty to the federal government), even if the literal reconstruction was somewhat attenuated.

The postwar military governments thus presided over a substantial transformation of the corruption-complex. While the charge of corruption retained its performative power and thus was sustained only against officials who were already marginal or vulnerable, this long-term continuity persisted within a system whose constitutive logic became ever more dependent on the distribution and circulation of irregular revenues. An intensification of the scope of corrupt material practices fostered an international reputation for corruption, which might have been useful to some actors. Just as Weber argued for Protestantism that church membership in the nineteenth-century United States functioned to bolster some people's reputations, making them seem reliable business partners, Nigeria's reputation for corruption gave Nigerians a reputation for potentially having access to ill-gotten gains. That reputation by itself could be a source of opportunity.

Political Transition and the Maturation of the Corruption-Complex

Ruth First's famous contention that military coups cannot be explained by looking at broader trends in society or economy but rather occur for "army reasons" is neatly illustrated by the aftermath of the coup that toppled General Gowon.[52] The figures behind the coup were the same plotters who had brought Gowon's government to power in 1966, but this time they assumed office directly and retired the major figures in the previous government. The new head of state declared that his government intended to correct Nigeria's continuing problems with corruption and misgovernance to prepare for a transition to civilian rule, though the concrete details of how this would occur were a bit more elusive. In a secret cable, analysts in the American embassy commented:

> How hard new leadership will hit corruption issue not clear. It does not appear at this time that members former administration will be investigated or have their assets questioned. This would be politically dangerous for new leaders. At same time, they must somehow cultivate image of honesty among Nigerian public, who by now are extremely cynical on this point. Big loser in change of faces are civilians. New FMG [Federal Military Government] is completely military (if one includes police); no civilians named to any post as yet, although commissionerships have not yet been filled. There always has been some friction between military and civilians here, but move toward more completely military control after last several years' agitation for return civilian rule could lead to deepening cleavage between military establishment and other elements.[53]

The Americans' assessment was wrong; the government did probe outgoing commissioners and governors for fiscal improprieties, and most lost assets in the process. The broader point was accurate. The coup served primarily to change the incumbents in state offices and to underline a commitment to honest government without changing any underlying pattern. Nor is it clear the "army reasons" ultimately involved a more direct commitment to a transition to civilian rule. By pegging the date for the inauguration of a civilian regime on Independence Day in 1979, the Muhammed government postponed disengagement. And as "Army Arrangement" documents, the reforms the new government achieved did little to change the overall dynamics of political society.

The longest-lasting legacy to Nigerian political society lay in the innovations the military regime made as it planned the constitution of the Second Republic. Retaining and extending the federal system established under Gowon, the civilian constitution moved from the parliamentary system of Nigeria's First Republic to a presidential system with some resemblance to that of the United States, with a separation of powers between a bicameral national assembly, independently elected president, and judiciary.[54] Given the challenges of ethnicity and sectional politics, the critical aspect was in how federalism and officeholding were handled. A novel aspect of the new constitution was the stipulations for the election of the presidency, which required the winning candidate to demonstrate substantial support from more than one region by receiving more than a quarter of the vote in two-thirds of the states in the federation.[55] If no candidate both won a plurality and demonstrated support across Nigeria, a run-off would be held between the two top vote getters.

In this way, the constitutional drafters would preclude the sectional divisions party politics had created for the First Republic.

A disquieting development occurred as the ban on political organizing was lifted in September 1978 and political parties began to prepare for the start of party registration toward the end of that year.[56] More than fifty political associations attempted to register, but only five received final certification by the federal electoral commission. The process was arduous and required demonstrable national scope. As vetting took place and new parties emerged, many familiar faces regained prominence; most new parties bore a distinct resemblance to earlier organizations. Far from representing a complete break from the centrifugal politics of the First Republic, the emergent parties of the Second Republic seemed likely to recapitulate the same problems.

Obafemi Awolowo emerged immediately as a potential presidential candidate, and the Unity Party of Nigeria (UPN) grew around him. Its political base was in the southwest, and its political platform bore a great resemblance to that of the Action Group in the First Republic. Aminu Kano led the new People's Redemption Party (PRP), which bore a great resemblance to the old Northern Elements Progressive Union. In the southeast, a somewhat more complicated process played out, in part because of the region's most prominent political son, Nnamdi Azikiwe. Other southeastern politicians negotiated with one another and progressives from other regions in order to build the Nigerian People's Party (NPP) as an organization with national support, an attempt that paralleled the trajectory of the old NCNC. Azikiwe himself flirted with representatives from a political party with its base in the north. However, when it became clear that party would not anoint a southerner as its presidential candidate, Azikiwe turned back to the party organized by his natural constituency and became the NPP's presidential candidate. This process also created another national party. During the period in which the leaders of regional associations were negotiating the emergence of what would become the NPP, one of the most significant actors outside the southeast was a group around Waziri Ibrahim, a son-in-law of the former governor of the Northern Region and former minister in the NPC government of the First Republic. As the NPP became more firmly a southeastern organization and it became clear it would be Azikiwe's vehicle for contesting the presidential election, Ibrahim and his supporters split off from the NPP to form the Great Nigerian People's Party (GNPP). Ultimately, GNPP candidates achieved victories only in the northeastern states of Borno (Waziri's home) and Gongola, but it contested elections more broadly than the UPN, PRP, or NPP.

While the novelty of the GNPP did not translate into great success, the other major innovation came from the party that would emerge to dominate the Second Republic. The National Party of Nigeria (NPN) was the party of the northern establishment. In its personnel and its policies it strongly resembled the old Northern People's Congress, but its leadership included younger technocrats with a higher average level of Western education. This group, termed the "Kaduna mafia," has been influential in Nigerian politics ever since its emergence during the Gowon regime. A younger and more cosmopolitan leadership enabled the NPN to adopt what may have been its most long-lasting innovation, a scheme of "zoning" in which it distributed major party offices and nominations for office across the federation. Dividing the country into a set of geographic zones, party elders agreed that each zone would be represented in the party's senior offices: the party chairmanship would go to the west, the presidency to the north, the vice presidency to the east, and the presidency of the Senate to "minority" groups. By guaranteeing all regions would have representatives in powerful party positions, the NPN might appeal to constituencies across Nigeria. Zoning ensured the NPN would not remain limited to the NPC's concentration on the north, in part by integrating other regions and ethnicities into structures of party patronage. In this way, the NPN inaugurated a mechanism for reflecting the basic political logic of prebendalism: the party required distributing the spoils of office across the federation through the process of nomination and appointment. Although the NPN followed the NPC as the conservative party of the northern establishment, it also established a genuinely national following. This has had a long legacy. Constituent Assemblies charged with drafting later constitutions considered making regional distribution of offices a formal constitutional requirement, and recently the Nigerian House of Representatives held public meetings to consider adding a zoning requirement as an amendment to the Fourth Republic's constitution. Regardless, the party that has dominated the Fourth Republic has made a somewhat more elaborate system of zoning central to its own distribution of offices.[57] This is evident in the party's initial flirtation with Dr. Azikiwe as a presidential candidate, though it is difficult to imagine circumstances under which the NPN would actually have nominated an Igbo president, no matter how distinguished his resume. As it turned out, the question of the presidential nomination was decided from among northern candidates; the choice was Shehu Shagari, who had been an NPC minister in the First Republic.

The NPN's regional strength proved decisive. It won the presidency and a plurality in the National Assembly, as well as a plurality of governorships and seats in state assemblies. For the presidency, the UPN's Obafemi Awolowo was the only candidate to come close to Shagari in percentage terms. However, he achieved this by running up massive margins in the Yoruba southwest, while President Shagari's support was more evenly distributed. Beyond the presidency, electoral results bore a dispiriting resemblance to earlier patterns. The UPN dominated state elections and National Assembly seats in the western states, the NPP the Igbo heartland. The PRP won Kano state and the governorship of Kaduna state (whose legislature had an NPN majority), and the GNPP won its northeastern base. As the National Assembly convened, its members applied their experience from the parliamentary First Republic, and the NPN (which fell far short of an overall majority) announced a coalition with the NPP, recapitulating the old NPC/NCNC coalition.

The military returned to the barracks with the inauguration of the new president. Whatever shortcomings had been perceived in the reforms the Mohammed/Obasanjo regime claimed as its purpose, the civilians quickly demonstrated that the NPN's innovations in zoning gave the corruption-complex new force. Scandals abounded and rebounded. By its nature, corruption is difficult to quantify. Its quality of being an *accusation* as much as a concrete *practice* opens up the possibility that the change was less an overall increase in actual practices than it was a shift in the utilities of making claims in the idiom of corruption. But that there was an increase in the claims is undeniable.

The career of Umaru Dikko provides a useful illustration of the transformations in the corruption-complex that took place across the ensuing decade as these were driven by civilian politics, military coups, and the transformations in the oil economy. Dikko came originally from Zaria. First prominent in the 1960s, he held cabinet appointments in the state government of North-Central state (later Kaduna state) under the military government. Dikko became a prominent member of the "Kaduna mafia" of relatively technocratic northern politicians from a generation younger than that of Ahmadu Bello and Abubakar Tafawa Balewa. Dikko rose to the center of national politics through the role he played in attaining the NPN presidential nomination for his brother-in-law, Shehu Shagari, who had been a minister under the First Republic but who was not known for either charisma or political competence. Dikko's prominence was cemented by his political acumen in building the NPN through its zonal distribution of offices and thus ensuring relatively widespread popular support.

It is appropriate that such a measure should be Dikko's lasting legacy, since the entire logic of zoning was a perfect instance of "prebendal politics." A strategy billed as ensuring national integration and political appeal built spoils-based patronage into the very logic of government, ensuring that national resources were parceled out across the country. By dividing constitutional offices among indigenes of different regions, the zoning party guaranteed every region a powerful patron—if not the president, then the vice president or chairman of the party.[58] In addition to being a key supporter of the party's presidential nominee and an architect of its winning strategy, Dikko himself stood as a senatorial candidate from Kaduna state. He lost that election to a PRP rival, which was a mixed curse. Dikko received what was probably a more advantageous and powerful appointment when he became Shagari's minister of transport. This was potentially lucrative given the government's continued investments in infrastructure. The cement armada publicly demonstrated the principle that even the most ludicrous schemes to siphon money from the government in the guise of national development would have few repercussions. Dikko was in a position to enrich himself and to apportion largesse to allies. Dikko's execution of his official responsibilities is vividly described in the memoir of Gerald Funk, an American political consultant. The incident took place after Funk had been hired as a consultant for President Shagari's reelection campaign in 1983:

> I explained that, per the contract we had signed with Shehu Musa, Assistant to President Shagari . . . he, Dikko, was to provide . . . a large furnished house for our people, who would be coming and going for the next several months; to provide, in kind, 3 or 4 cars; to arrange for international telephone calls to be paid by him; to make lump-sum monthly payments of per diem expenses; to arrange for local and international transport on the national airline. . . . I knew that if we tried to get into the procurement business with those Yoruba sharks in Lagos, we would be bankrupt within a week. Dikko had read the document, he said, and he listened patiently. And he watched me intently. Then he said something to the effect that we could make it easier for us all, and more profitable for me, personally, if we just did it a little differently. He then went into another room, and brought forth a very large suitcase, full of large Naira . . . notes, more or less the equivalent of perhaps half a million US dollars. He said that should take care of housing and cars and per diem and local travel and telephones . . . all local costs . . . for all of my present and future crews . . . for now. And if I needed more, I should return.[59]

In addition to his ministerial office and party role, Dikko enjoyed another source of power and patronage; he chaired the president's task force on rice. That commodity was in short supply in 1979, after a decade of oil wealth had led to a neglect of agriculture and declining yields of indigenous crops. Readily available rice at affordable prices had thus become important for a considerable portion of the population, particularly city dwellers. Rice imports were crucial because the grain had quickly achieved vast popularity; its preparation was relatively easy, not requiring the laborious pounding of many of its rivals. The new civilian administration thus contracted to import major quantities of rice and to offer it for sale at subsidized prices. Dikko oversaw the effort. Somehow, however, relatively little rice actually reached market; dark rumors circulated that he had diverted it to his own warehouses, from which he and his cronies sold it onto the black market. Such rumors received confirmation after the coup, when vast warehouses were discovered around Lagos.[60]

As Dikko enriched himself through infrastructure contracts and rice imports, he retained his influential role as an NPN political tactician. The party's campaign of 1983 was less restrained than it had been in the election of 1979. The country was tense in the period leading up to it and the electoral process itself was violent: politicians and parties employed mobs of young men to intimidate their opponents, a tactic already familiar in Nigerian politics. Allegations of vote rigging, stuffed ballot boxes, and the substitution of filled boxes for authentic ones were rampant. When the results were announced, it was clear Dikko had done his work well, perhaps too well. The NPN won elections in areas that had previously been strongholds of opposition parties. It increased its seats in the National Assembly, nearly doubled the governorships it controlled, and consolidated its grip on state assemblies even in areas that had been strongholds of other parties.[61] Opposition political parties were horrified, and the population was taken aback at the landslide victory of a party whose popular support was at best shaky. The violence and thuggery that had been obvious across the electoral period had been such that it was difficult to maintain the elections had been free or fair. As with the election of 1964 in the First Republic, the country's rulers had consolidated their electoral position, but at the cost of any semblance of democracy. The election had manifestly been rigged. This accomplishment did little for Umaru Dikko's national reputation, and the man himself credits his electoral role as being behind his lack of popularity. When he testified in 1999 before the Oputa Commission on human rights violations, Dikko admitted that he, "being [Shagari's] campaign-director general, had to step on the toes of his political rivals and even his enemies who would like to see him destroyed. Naturally, there was no way those who contested against him and lost could like him or me." Calling the accusations of corruption in the Second Republic "imaginary," he insisted he was guilty of nothing other than working very hard while a government minister.[62]

Had the NPN not engaged in such tactics, it might have faced defeat. The government's political standing had started to erode in 1981, when the world price of oil crashed. The government's dependence on oil receipts made this an immediate crisis only compounded by the economy's dependence on subsidized imports of basic consumer goods. To compound the trouble, the government's ambitious development program had required loans. This national debt invited considerably more scrutiny as it became clear a number of Latin American countries were likely to default on their own (much greater) debt obligations. As a result, the government came under considerable pressure from international lenders, Western governments, and institutions like the International Monetary Fund.

The government's response had been feckless before the election. The National Assembly was reluctant to pass the austerity budget demanded by Nigeria's lenders. Despite its increased majorities after the election, the ruling party continued to do little to lift the malaise, and the fitful inquiry into General Buhari's finances was not calculated to win support from anyone. In the years since then, many military figures have alleged a coup had been plotted for a considerable period and that the former military head of state, Olusegun Obasanjo, had been asked whether he would return to power at a junta's head. This he refused. The military's current leadership was less reluctant. When the military took power on New Year's Day in 1984, Dikko fled the country, crossing incognito into Benin Republic and then flying to Europe. The military government's inquiry into his affairs suggested he was directly responsible for pocketing ₦1 billion (at the time the naira was worth approximately U.S. $1.50 at official rates), and it was determined to return him Nigeria to face trial. Part of the impetus may have been that Dikko very quickly appointed himself a spokesman for the civilian government displaced by the coup, telling the *Observer* that he was declaring war on the new military government, which could claim no superiority over its civilian predecessor:

> Everyone can be trained to use a gun. The junta in Lagos is made up of politicians in uniform who turned their guns on the elected Government they had sworn to defend under the constitution. The true professionals in the Nigerian Army will make the distinction between soldiers and politicians in uniform. Nigerians cherish liberty and democracy above everything else and will fight to restore them before long. . . . Whatever money a politician makes goes back to the people because he wants their votes. The military are talking about money because they can only think of their own bank accounts.[63]

This public stance as a democrat was made against the backdrop of the lurid stories emerging from the military's investigations of the scandals of the civilian administration. Dikko was personally implicated. Investigators in Lagos discovered warehouses filled with rice and other imported consumer goods that had been under Dikko's authority. Although these stores were supposed to have been distributed for sale at subsidized prices, they had been kept back in private hands and were being sold, the military claimed, at inflated prices. The chairman of the special task force has profited handsomely from his charge of making rice available to all Nigerians; in doing so, he had guaranteed most could not afford to eat it.

Dikko was not the only Second Republic official who had escaped Nigeria and persisted in making statements to the press, but he was probably the most flamboyant. Billing himself as an advocate for Nigeria's legitimate civilian government, the former minister's "jihad" against the military was little direct danger to the military government. The man himself had little domestic constituency to rouse from afar. Nonetheless, the new head of state was thin-skinned, and the military government's response was robust. On 5 July 1984 Dikko left his Bayswater flat for a walk. A party including both Nigerian and Mossad agents bundled him into a van and drugged him. Dikko was transported to Stansted Airport and kept continuously under sedation as he was loaded into a crate that also contained an Israeli doctor charged with monitoring his physical well-being. The crate was loaded aboard a Nigeria Airways plane bound for Lagos. Though the plane's cargo was under diplomatic immunity, a customs official asked to inspect Dikko's crate minutes before takeoff. When Nigerian officials protested the inspection, the official called in antiterrorism police, and the minister was discovered. A major diplomatic row ensued.

Nigeria persisted in demanding his extradition, but Dikko was granted limited political asylum in Britain. The British government's consideration of his case, however, was an occasion for scrutiny of Second Republic politics and of the military regime's conduct in office. The "minister in a crate" news hook made Dikko an attractive story to the international press in much the way the clogged port of Lagos had a decade previously. Nigeria's international profile was deepened and confirmed: the minister's florid corruption—a billion stolen personally! One instance among many of official corruption!—now was juxtaposed with a story about military brutality. The story reflected well on no one. Despite his being victimized by a military regime, Dikko was an unsympathetic protagonist. And while the military government pledged to look into its civilian predecessor's corruption and economic malpractice, both its brutality and continuing criticisms by Nigerians with an international audience prevented the military government from successfully claiming a reformist mantle. "Army Arrangement" became internationally famous, and this also was the time when the celebrated author and dramatist Wole Soyinka released an album entitled *Unlimited Liability Company* also dramatizing the country's corruption. While the natural audience for such efforts was Nigerian, they reached international ears and helped to make vivid the picture incidents like the cement armada had begun to paint. It is little wonder the 419 genre emerged at this time.

Dikko himself remained in Britain until the early 1990s, when he returned to Nigeria. At that point he tried to establish himself as a politician in the political transition then being orchestrated by General Sani Abacha's military government. Dikko's attempt at a political career was unsuccessful, though the issue at the time became moot: that transition effort came to nothing. Dikko did testify before a truth commission impaneled at the start of the Fourth Republic, where his main concern was that the officials who had orchestrated his kidnapping attempt had never apologized to him personally. General Buhari had declined to testify before the commission, but the then–minister of defense, General Theophilus Danjuma (who Dikko claimed had the links with Israel that brought the Mossad agents in on the plot),[64] did testify. The general disclaimed knowledge of the case, and the commission directed the two men to shake hands. At that point, it declared the issue resolved.[65] With the passage of another decade, Dikko achieved something of a rehabilitation, becoming the head of the disciplinary committee for the ruling party until his death in 2014.[66] He continues to have relatively little independent constituency but nonetheless to enjoy a proximity to the centers of power.

Dikko's fame eclipses the manner in which his career epitomizes the evolution of the Nigerian corruption-complex across the 1970s, 1980s, and 1990s. Rising to power and prominence as the civilian elite maneuvered to take power across the Gowon and Muhammed/Obasanjo military governments, Dikko was most effective at inventing a mode of retail politics that brought together the demands of a vast, heterogeneous country whose one universal political principle was patronage and which had the economic potential of an oil rentier state. Dikko's innovation, his durable political legacy, was the principle of zoning, enshrining in party politics the principle that office and power should be distributed around the federation. The logic of patronage long predated the emergence of the NPN, but the innovation has persisted. It is no coincidence that Dikko reemerged as a figure in the party that dominated the Fourth Republic until 2015, whose time in power depended on its ability to maintain support across the federation. Alongside this historical role, however, was also Dikko's florid corruption: suitcases full of naira notes, a preference for backroom deals, diverted warehouses of rice, scandalous infrastructure projects. Although the man himself denied them, the stories of Dikko's conduct in office outline a pattern of wholescale financial malpractice that would seem to apply to vast numbers of politicians before him and since. The formal parceling out of political office as a means of personal (and thereby, to some extent regional) enrichment was a major innovation within the corruption-complex, as was the emergence of the "army arrangement" in which successive regimes probed their predecessors while, in the main, finding them innocent or at least impossible to convict.

Military Centralization, Violence, and the Confirmation of the Corruption-Complex

General Buhari's government faced terrible economic challenges. The debt crisis remained, and pressures from Nigeria's debtors increased even as economic crisis made its need for continued international credit ever more pressing. General Buhari's regime quickly squandered the goodwill it had received simply from displacing the discredited Second Republic. But while it showed a robust ability to crack down on dissent and a willingness to flout international norms, the regime did not manage to institute the savage austerity policies the international community sought. Instead, it undertook probes, many of which were largely ineffectual, although it did imprison a number of Second Republic politicians—the vice president was sentenced to prison, while the president was placed under house arrest. At the same time, the government attempted to discipline the unruly Nigerian population. The War against Indiscipline attempted to modify aspects of public behavior, enforcing norms like lining up for buses and taxis, and not engaging in petty crime. The government also declared it would enforce Nigeria's drug laws rigidly, imposing the death penalty for drug smuggling. Such initiatives helped to lead to a second campaign, which was dubbed the War against Women. Initially inspired by several high-profile instances of women caught smuggling drugs in their "womanly parts," women became a major target for street harassment. These endeavors succeeded mainly in alienating the populace; a high-level coup toppled General Buhari in mid-1985, bringing General Ibrahim Babangida to power in his place. Babangida proved more politically adroit than Buhari. One of his triumphs—which earned him the nickname "Maradona" after the Argentinian footballer whose adept fielding paralleled Babangida's political agility—was to engage the country in a "national conversation" about whether to adopt a structural adjustment policy as the International Monetary Fund demanded. Although the national consensus clearly came out against it, Babangida proceeded to institute an austerity policy that deviated somewhat from international demands but that nonetheless placated debt holders. The naira declined, and imports became increasingly unaffordable. Rice quickly moved from being a staple to being a luxury again. As *West Africa* noted,

> When importation was banned, there was loud protest from the Nigerian public which gave the impression that it couldn't live another day without rice. As the price rose (partly artificial) many people decided to cut down on rice, and some gave it up completely even after prices fell. The same has happened to bread. When the flour mills shut down during their confrontation with government, prices of bread went up scandalously, to ₦3 and ₦5 a loaf. Nigerians this time did not waste their time complaining, many remembered that they had not grown up on a bread diet. According to one Lagosian, "I passed a decree banning bread from my house with immediate effect. The children missed it for a few days, but now they are satisfied with indigenous foods for breakfast."[67]

A similar adroitness allowed the regime to finesse the issue of what to do with Second Republic officials, a number of whom remained detained under Buhari's Decree No. 3. The government white paper declared an intention to "put behind us this unfortunate episode in [Nigeria's] history and move ahead with determination, and resolve that never again would these sordid events be permitted to occur."[68] Although rage remained against the excesses of the democratic regime, the tricky business of determining which officials to prosecute and which to clear proved too much, and a line was drawn under the whole episode. Fela Kuti's "Army Arrangement" was confirmed; the military ultimately acted to euphemize the corruption of the civilian era, even as the civilians had declined to look too carefully at problems that had emerged under the Muhammed/Obasanjo regime.

Even as Nigeria moved toward an era of greater political accommodation, unrest grew. A coup attempt in 1990 came very close to succeeding. It had progressed to such a point that its leader, Major Gideon Orkar, was able to broadcast an address over the Federal Radio Corporation, which among other things accused General Babangida of corruption, economic mismanagement, and homosexuality.[69] Unrest in the army was mirrored by tensions in other parts of the country. Riots had broken out toward the end of May 1989. The first one was at the Lagos State College of Education on 22 May, touched off by a student dispute with the administration. The next day students at Lagos State demonstrated in solidarity, and at the same time students at the University of Nigeria in Nsukka demonstrated in response to the shooting of a student who had been protesting living conditions. Protests about internal university matters were one thing. More troubling to the regime was an incident on 25 May, when students at the University of Benin set motor vehicles ablaze and tore apart government offices. Their grievances were less local: they were protesting the national Structural Adjustment Policy (SAP), which was supposed to be over. Joined by market women and jobless youth, the students marched to the prison, freed six hundred prisoners, and set it on fire. Four days later, a riot at the University of Ibadan resulted in at least one death and injured at least four police officers.[70] The riots spread further: not only did protests take place at colleges of education in Ondo and Bendel states, but the riots spread to villages near the universities as well. While these student riots paralleled self-limiting student riots over the price of gasoline in 1988, involvement by farmers, market women, and urban youth portended a much more volatile possibility, that student riots might extend beyond the universities. Many southern universities were closed.[71]

The situation continued to deteriorate. In early July, students at the Federal College of Education (FCE) in Warri led a protest march singing songs against SAP. This turned into a riot and spread to other towns. Student leaders announced they were also protesting the university closures. At the same time, the Nigerian Labour Congress condemned the university closures and called for the release of detained students, while the Ondo state congress of farmers did the same.[72] The government's response was two pronged: it created a committee to consider relief measures to address suffering caused by SAP. Jobs programs were created, food production was increased (in largely cosmetic ways), drug imports were subsidized, and the import duty on commercial vehicles was lifted for the rest of 1989. At the same time, there was a clampdown on dissent. The universities remained closed, and the government engaged in its own publicity campaign against the "sophisticated process of disinformation and destabilization [that] was behind the disturbances."[73]

Even as the population at large became disenchanted with a government whose relative poverty meant that the welfare initiatives inaugurated under the Gowon regime came to an end, the military elite (and its civilian collaborators) continued to do relatively well. Oil revenues were insufficient to raise all ships, but they could support a wealthy elite. While the Babangida regime would survive for another three years, ceding power in the aftermath of the aborted inauguration of the Third Republic, it would both clamp down considerably on dissent (intensifying a dynamic that was already well established: as early as 1986 the editor of the muckraking dissident *Newswatch* was assassinated by a bomb delivered to his office) and work ever more assiduously to pay off potentially dissident segments of military and civilian elites. The Babangida regime engaged in two rounds of state creation—an expansion to twenty-one states in 1987 and to thirty in 1991. This would be followed under Abacha by an expansion to the current thirty-six states in 1996. State creation was the logical outgrowth of an ethnic politics dating from the First Republic, in which areas that were not strongly represented in the group governing a state agitated for the creation of a new state they would dominate. The criteria for state creation were historical and cultural; what that meant in practice was that states could only be created to accommodate already-existing ethnic groups whose separate historical existence could be documented. The same process was at play in Local Government Area creation.

Where the federal politics of revenue distribution continued to play out in well-established patterns, the military government insisted on centralizing control of state resources ever more completely. This innovation is illustrated by the travails of one of its officials, who would then become a critic. This section concludes, therefore, with a discussion of the corruption trial of Tam David-West, who is now remembered to have been convicted and sentenced to twenty years' imprisonment for receiving the gift of a watch. Tamunoemi David-West had attained distinction as a professor of virology at the University of Ibadan by the time of his appointment as education commissioner in Rivers state during the Muhammed/Obasanjo regime. He returned to government under Buhari, as the military government's petroleum minister. Despite rumors that he might be replaced, General Babangida retained him when he came to power but moved him to the mines and power ministry in 1986 before dropping him from the cabinet altogether later that year.[74] During his time as oil minister, David-West was a notable economic nationalist and became internationally known for his role in pressing for an increase in Nigeria's OPEC quota.[75] After his departure from government, he became a critic of the regime and indeed in October 1989 he was detained under Decree No. 2, which allowed for the arrest of people who posed a threat to state security or the national economic well-being.[76]

Matters became more serious the following year, however, when he was arrested and tried in connection to a set of negotiations he oversaw with an American corporation called Stinnes Interoil. Stinnes had negotiated a contract with the civilian Shagari administration to extract Nigerian oil and reimport refined petroleum products. The contract ran through the end of 1983, and as that date neared the Nigerian National Petroleum Corporation signaled its willingness to extend the contract to 1984. The company attempted to negotiate some provisions of the contract, and in the interim the company did not make its fourth-quarter payment.[77] The details of the debts and payments are somewhat involved, but the basic issue was that Stinnes owed Nigeria approximately U.S. $157 million. Professor David-West chaired negotiations with Stinnes over its debts and eventually secured an agreement that it would pay approximately $100 million. Professor David-West insisted on leading the negotiations personally, against the advice of the chairman of the NNPC among others. He did not refer his decision to the Council of Ministers or to President Babangida.[78] In the course of the negotiations, Professor David-West was given a gold wristwatch and attended a dinner party hosted by a Stinnes official. Testimony from other NNPC officials present at the negotiations suggested that David-West had been friendly with Stinnes executives—most particularly the dinner-party host and the corporation's president—and that his decisions emerged from his private meetings with them. The crimes for which he was convicted required proving that the minister had improperly used his office and his discretion, to the benefit of Stinnes and the detriment of Nigeria, and that he had improperly benefited from this misuse of his power. Professor David-West was unable to demonstrate that he had President Babangida's blessing for the write-off of $57 million, and the testimony of the other officials demonstrated that the patterns of decision making violated established NNPC guidelines. The wristwatch and the dinner party constituted the other element of the minister's conviction, since they were the only direct benefits he could be demonstrated to have received.[79]

The conviction was greeted with considerable derision in the opposition press, as when the *Guardian* complained "where the tribunal saw criminal corruption . . . we see no more than naivete" and pointed to the ludicrous disproportion of a twenty-year sentence meted out for receiving the gift of a watch. The *New Nigerian* retorted, "It beats one hollow how a whopping 57 million dollars loss to the national treasury can be described as 'naively,' 'imprudence,' and 'excessive enthusiasm.'"[80] The unfortunate ex-minister was imprisoned for almost a year while his appeal was considered by an appellate tribunal and eventually overturned. The higher court noted that the connection between the wristwatch and the decision was "speculative."[81] In the long term, the position of the opposition press has won the day, and Professor David-West is remembered for having been convicted of receiving a ludicrously small bribe. Nonetheless, the prosecution, the defense, and popular memory all focus their attention on a side issue. While the question of Professor David-West's criminal culpability may have hung on the connection between the watch and the

$57 million, the more urgent question had to do with whether the minister had acted of his own accord. In his testimony at trial, David-West not only claimed to have attempted to telephone President Babangida and to have written memos on the issue but noted the *Concord* had covered the agreement as a "$100 million windfall for Nigeria." More to the point, he recounted regularly having seen the president for the next nine months while serving as minister of mines but never to have been queried on the issue, despite his memos and the newspaper coverage.[82] Ultimately, then, the question of David-West's vulnerability stemmed less from the goods he received from Stinnes than in how decision making was conducted within the Babangida government, and who might be blamed for multimillion-dollar losses. The question of culpability traced a more general process of centralization, and the accusation of corruption, more fully than ever before, traced the workings of an inner elite.

Military Government and Corruption

The Babangida regime ended as abruptly as it began. The transition the government had charted to civilian rule considerably resembled the path inaugurated by the Muhammed/Obasanjo regime more than a decade previously. The process of registering political groups came to an end when the government announced it would not certify any of the political groups but rather would create two competing political parties, one left of center and one right of center. The parties were duly created, and they elected candidates to the local government councils, state assemblies, governorships, and to the National Assembly. After preliminary returns showed the presidential election held 12 June 1993 had been won by the Social Democratic Party's Chief Moshood Abiola, the military government nullified the results. After several months of escalating unrest and international sanctions, Babangida stood down as head of state at the end of August, and the civilian leader of government business, Chief Ernest Shonekan, was sworn in as interim president. However, that November, the army chief of staff and defense minister, General Sani Abacha, led a military coup. His tenure as head of state would last five years, and the military regime would go on for another year before giving way to the civilian Fourth Republic.

While the twenty years between Abacha's coming to power and the time of this writing have been eventful—and while some aspects of that time have already been discussed or will come up in part II of this book—the basic contours of the corruption-complex remain largely intact. The Buhari and Babangida regimes are noteworthy in several respects. First, they completed a process of politicizing the military that was already well under way during the military regimes of the 1970s. While diarchy was never formally installed, and while the "army arrangement" has given way to a resigned consensus that neither civilian nor military regimes can correct the sins of their predecessors, a prebendelist logic of clientelism became much more deeply entrenched in military hierarchies. While the military was never free from the politics of region, ethnicity, or religion, the regional origins of particular military officers have become even more salient than in the past. While it is difficult with any accuracy to chart material changes in the levels of corruption, it seems inarguable that more money was diverted from the country by the Babangida and Abacha regimes than had been diverted under their military predecessors. Civilians were not necessarily the only profligate rulers Nigeria had—even if now people contend the military was not as wildly spendthrift as the politicians of the Fourth Republic.

The brutality the Buhari regime meted out under its War against Indiscipline and War against Women remained a feature of its military successors, as the crackdowns on the riots discussed above suggest. While this took place, governmental austerity also defunded schools, hospitals, and universities, while the country's infrastructure crumbled. At the same time, the devaluation of the naira made many consumer goods increasingly unaffordable for the bulk of the population. As Andrew Apter has argued, the decline in world oil prices caused a hollowing out of the naira: rampant inflation and a state that was a shell of its former self was the result. The years of the beginning of structural adjustment were also the time when Nigeria's 419 messages first became famous. Apter suggests this is because of a change in regimes of value themselves. Nigerian politics became a politics of illusion; the Nigerian money form similarly was demonstrated to be an illusion. For that reason, 419 became a prototypical business form. I would suggest that is only a part of the story, and that it is necessary to place these developments in much longer-term historical trajectories.

The Nigerian corruption-complex emerged from sets of local political strategies and accommodations that first took shape under British colonialism and under the system of indirect rule. They took on a recognizable form as those of a "corrupt African government" as the country achieved internal self-rule a decade before independence. And they came to fruition as Nigeria became an oil state, in both flush times and lean ones. Part I of this book has not been a history of Nigeria, or of Nigerian corruption. Rather, it has been an attempt to trace the career of the corruption-complex, and to point to critical conjunctures in its history. Even today, there is not one language of corruption, or one set of principles by which it can be judged. While all commentators can agree that corruption is wrong, the problem is identifying who is guilty of it. When the accused are able to assert they have done nothing wrong—as when Umaru Dikko claimed his only sin was working faithfully for President Shagari and staying at the office until three a.m.—they may not be believed. But a key element to domestic Nigerian stories about corruption, even when they accept basic distinctions between the public and the private, and bureaucratic notions of officeholding, is their lack of consensus over who is actually guilty of such things. Warri people tend to be much more forgiving of Festus Okotie-Eboh's failings than Abeokuta people. And this negotiable, open-ended, strategic quality to corruption discourse is not just some Machiavellian element of Nigerian politics. It also enables concrete material practices that then might be labeled "corrupt."

The intertwined logics of the oil economy and Nigeria's own emergent prebendalite federalism intersected with increasingly powerful international stories about Nigerian corruption. The cement armada and the government minister in a crate were powerful proof to foreigners that Nigeria was a country in which illicit government money was easily available. Although scholars have convincingly argued 419 e-mails are effective in part through their unconvincing quality—only the truly gullible will respond to them, which makes them an effective tool for identifying easy marks—the intensification of Nigerian corruption would not have been possible without an international context that allowed it to take place. And Nigeria's international image was the consequence of the scandals that bedeviled it across the 1970s and after.

PART II. CORRUPTION, NIGERIA, AND THE MORAL IMAGINATION

FOUR. MORAL ECONOMIES OF CORRUPTION

Nigeria's recurrent scarcity of petrol is a perennial struggle for members of its middle classes, and indeed for anyone who owns a motor vehicle. Although Nigeria is a major oil producer and has a number of oil refineries, the latter are frequently in disrepair, or domestic supplies are disrupted by unrest in the Niger Delta. Even when it has a sufficient supply for domestic consumption, distribution is a real problem. Petrol stations, which sell fuel at the official price, do not receive a supply adequate to remain open at all times. Considerable quantities get diverted to the black market. Anywhere one goes, the roads are dotted with tables laden with small plastic containers of petrol, with larger jerry cans of it underneath. This black-market petrol is usually at least twice the price of that in filling stations, and it is often adulterated, causing problems for any car habitually fueled with it. Even in normal circumstances, finding petrol at filling stations can be a challenge. Most stations stand empty, with an attendant or two selling oil and other maintenance supplies, sometimes with a couple of cars awaiting the next tanker truck. It is useful to know a station owner, who can tell you when a consignment is due. Ideally, one arrives at a station when the tanker truck is still refilling the station's reservoir, before too many other drivers have noticed the station has petrol. Especially if scarcity is bad, lines can get very long indeed. Of course, if one is friends with the owner—or can make arrangements with the workers—it is possible to jump the line, though this must be done carefully. Tempers are often short.

The worst period of scarcity I have experienced personally was in Kano in 1996, when petrol was desperately scarce, and that on the black market was very expensive and very bad. One would need to get in line days before a tanker was due, and fights were common. One particular frustration was that petrol was much more readily available in Kaduna state, just south of Kano but too far to be feasible simply for refueling. Soon thereafter Kano state's military governor, Colonel Abdullahi Wase, was killed in an air crash and a new governor assumed office. The scarcity ended abruptly. The late governor had become unpopular well before his death, and stories about his corruption abounded. During the scarcity, rumors often blamed him personally, saying he (and sometimes other prominent collaborators) had diverted Kano state's supplies of petrol, exporting them to Niger Republic. Whatever the truth of these stories, they found corroboration in other rumors, especially of discoveries made after his death: of a fleet of minibuses belonging to the late governor in his ancestral village that had been found packed with ₦50 notes; of vast sums that had been hidden various places around his house.[1]

The truth or falsity of these rumors is not the subject of this chapter, nor is it an evaluation of given officials' competence or integrity. Instead, my interest here is in how official conduct was evaluated socially. Colonel Wase has faded from memory, except for a hospital and a road named in his honor. While complaints about his corruption were rampant during his tenure, they are now eclipsed by complaints about his two civilian successors,[2] Rabi'u Kwankwaso and Ibrahim Shekarau. Corruption discourse is densest about the present and the most recent past; it tends to concern people who are still politically active. My only conversations about government malpractice during the colonial period have been with scholars, highly educated people, and NEPU and PRP activists. Similarly, the First Republic is remembered as a time of relative rectitude, though people are usually most nostalgic about the politicians from their own areas. Northerners admire the Sardauna of Sokoto and Prime Minister Tafawa Balewa. Westerners often idolize Chief Awolowo, and easterners Dr. Azikiwe. General Buhari's reputation for integrity has largely drowned out stories about missing oil money or outrage at political repression, but this may change across the course of his presidency. Many remember even the Abacha regime with a certain fondness, considering it now to have been more honest than its civilian successors. This is not simply historical amnesia enabled by the passage of time. Outrage over corruption is among other things a symptom of contemporary political relationships. Discussion of the relative merits of

Governors Kwankwaso and Shekarau also are manifestations of political loyalty: Kwankwaso and Shekarau have always represented rival parties. The latter defeated the former's attempt at reelection in 2003, served two terms, and in 2011 was replaced by his predecessor.[3] Colonel Wase, whatever his failings, is outside contemporary political contests. To the extent that discussions of corruption express contemporary loyalties or themselves accomplish political aims—that is, to the extent they are illocutionary or perlocutionary—Colonel Wase is irrelevant at this late date. There is a widespread consensus that almost anyone in office will violate bureaucratic norms. This is inevitable, even necessary and admirable. Politicians are expected to steal money and to grant illicit favors to friends and family. Outrage comes about when it gets out of hand. In Kano in 1996, most of my acquaintances agreed Colonel Wase was behaving outrageously. What norms were being outraged? What did it mean to violate the norms, and how did and does popular outrage manifest itself?

Norms in the Corruption-Complex

Nigerian dramas of petrol scarcity, like daily discussions about state-level corruption and the microstrategies one could use to respond to it, were the backdrop to my starting a set of oral history interviews with small-scale farmers in a small town called Ungogo near Kano, about the history of their interactions with state officials. As a result, I had a wide variety of conversations—formal interviews, informal chats, late-night conversations over beer—about the frustrations of dealing with people acting in an official capacity, inside the government and out. These discussions covered a broad time span, ranging from contemporary events to ancestors' long-ago experiences. Practices one might call corruption were a key feature in almost all of these stories. Stories of fantastic macrolevel corruption abounded; the governor's alleged minibuses were the tip of a corrupt iceberg. Interactions with bureaucrats almost always resulted in demands for bribes. Travel was complicated by the demands of police who needed to be bribed at roadblocks. University admissions often could be achieved from personal connections—which could make education difficult for the ill connected—and provided instructors with substantial numbers of ill-prepared (but well-connected) students.

Contemporary complaints about corruption echo stories from the past, such as the trials of Sani Kacako or the injustices trumpeted by NEPU, and thus oral histories of corruption map well onto the documentary record, even when that record is fragmentary or elliptical. During the colonial period, officials who measured farms for tax assessment demanded bribes. A farmer who could or would not bribe the surveyor might find himself listed as having a much larger farm than he actually possessed and thus liable for much more tax than he could afford to pay. Ward, village, and district heads could exercise a certain amount of discretion in distributing the burden of taxes or in levying tax rates on particular farmers. While this enabled them to adjust the burden to account for individual disasters, it also allowed them to inflate particular assessments, either to absorb the revenue directly or to bring tax bills above what particular farmers could pay, which would result in their farms' confiscation.

Farmers' oral histories of tax assessment often turned into catalogs of extortion. Annual assessments were often at five shillings or more over the level set by the state. Hostile officials drove farmers off their land through inflated tax bills or confiscated livestock as interim payment and later pretended to have received nothing. Other taxes were levied on adult men, and officials extorted additional money by categorizing young boys as adults or by levying taxes on men who had died. These stories were all from the memories of elderly people, or were told by younger men recounting what their elders had experienced. The land tax itself was abolished in 1979 when the PRP government under Abubakar Rimi came to power in Kano state, and so people's contemporary experiences with corruption take somewhat different form.

Discussions of local courts and official systems of dispute resolution placed at least as much emphasis on the bribes extorted from litigants as they did on juridical mechanisms themselves. Judges and territorial heads acting as dispute mediators were known for supporting the claims of those who paid the most, or those who were already clients. Some of these practices were systematic: officials inflated the absolute incidence of tax and then skimmed the excess. Others were particular: improper tax bills presented to specific unfortunates. Alkalai have great discretion over which witnesses to believe and which to impugn, which testimony to allow to be supplemented with oaths and which to let languish unsubstantiated. Prevailing in court is therefore a matter of marshaling a variety of resources, of which the "true" facts of the case are often less important than money and political standing. It is an article of common wisdom that one should avoid going to court as much as possible. In part this is because of people's disinclination to air their dirty laundry in public, but to go to court is to risk massive financial losses, as bribes and other forms of extortion grow to dwarf any potential gains from victory. In cases of inheritance, when surviving relatives are unable to agree on the proper division of estates, it is not uncommon to take cases to court but to conceal from the judge the full extent of the estate, so that any extortion misses the really valuable things.[4] Given the local government reforms that transformed the administrative apparatus of the old districts into today's LGAs, the number of officials whose favors one might need to curry has multiplied, even as the issues involved have shifted.

Descriptions of what might be interpreted as improper practice depended very much on individuals' relationships to particular officials. Thus, for example, one fairly conservative religious scholar who had close ties to the village head and was also sympathetic to the emirate government (represented in Ungogo by the district head) admitted that revenue officials sometimes committed malpractices, reminiscing that giving them a ram could result in a reported plot substantially smaller than it was in reality. The village and district heads, however, were both too pious and too well educated to stoop so low. Illegal practices were a product of their naïve trust: "They could not know because they believed in [their subordinates]." When malfeasance was brought to their attention, it was quickly corrected.[5] However, the village head was (in this man's opinion) less reliable than the district head, and he could be bribed, assuming the bribe was attempted carefully and sufficiently large. The village head, he said, was less likely to intervene in the process of surveying but rather tended to become involved in instances of dispute, particularly in a dispute over inheritance. He was adamant, however, that district-level officials, whose social standing and religious credentials were considerably more impressive, were not involved in such tawdry affairs. This insistence on the uprightness of the district head was somewhat extreme, but it was not uncommon among those sympathetic to the emirate establishment.

By contrast, people who had been members of NEPU and the PRP, Aminu Kano's left-wing northern political parties, saw official malpractice in terms of a class divide between talakawa and the masu sarauta, with the interests of the caliphate aristocracy gradually being taken over the by NPC, and more generally the northern political elite. The actions of subordinates were ultimately less important than those of high-level officeholders. The thrust of this critique helps to explain why the repression of NEPU in the 1950s was so savage. While the political accommodations between emirate officials and British colonial officers had previously tended only to censure as corrupt or incompetent people who were in trouble from their political superiors, NEPU focused on the responsibility of the very most senior members of the political hierarchy. As Northern Nigeria moved from a system dominated by this colonial caliphate to one in which caliphal officials were subject to the interests of NPC politicians, NEPU criticism threatened this emergent accommodation.[6] But class-based critique had its limitations. Although these parties did indeed prove important for exposing and ameliorating government corruption, politicians who gained office under their aegis have proven little better. For activists, the problem with political life is that commoners are oppressed, by the political elite, the rich, and members of the old aristocracy. In that regard, higher officials like hakimai are guiltier than lower-ranking ones like *dagatai*. In effect, therefore, there is no consensus on *who* is corrupt, even when everyone can agree on the fact that corruption has bedeviled Nigeria for decades.

The politicization of memory stems in part from local politics. But the memory of particular individuals' actions is only partly determined by political ideology or religious conviction. Just as significantly, someone's evaluation of past action stems from that person's position in the complex chains of patronage and clientage that subtend much of economic and political life. The rich and powerful gain prestige and political support through the largesse they are able to give clients. A person in need is therefore well advised to ingratiate him- or herself with a protector, who may be able to help out with employment, cash for medical and other crises, places at school or university, or just about anything else for which influence might be required. The protector gains prestige and a follower. Influence and largesse are not cheap: acquiring them can require diverting public monies to individual ends. Nonetheless, it would be difficult if not impossible for even the most technocratic politician to become politically prominent without being able to produce such patronage. Common sense in Ungogo would have it that relations with state officials are intrinsically problematic and that it is wisest to make sure that officials know little about one's affairs. Political sympathies, friendship, and patronage loyalties lead to differing assessments of who is oppressive and why, but a sense that contact with the state causes problems permeates popular discourse about interaction with the government.

Consider again Sani Kacako, the village head of Kacako who was deposed in 1924 and who was discussed in chapter 1. As is most often true in cases where the government dealt with improper conduct on the part of officials not being considered for deposition, these records are extremely elliptical. A careful reading reveals a telling logic to his deposition. In the final analysis, Sani's problem was that he failed fully to establish himself as client of the district head. Sani's documented troubles started with his failure to collect all of the tax his registers listed as payable. After several attempts at revision failed to eliminate his liability for the shortfall, Sani claimed he was being forced to collect it twice over from certain unfortunates. When, instead of paying up, the taxpayers abandoned their farms and left Kacako, the district head did not relieve Sani of his responsibility for the taxes but rather demanded he make good the shortfall from his own funds. But, as is clear both from oral testimony I collected and from the scandals NEPU publicized during the 1950s, emirate officials were fully capable of pursuing absconding farmers. In this case they chose not to do so. The village head was squeezed in a manner not entirely unlike that of his taxpayers. This reconstruction of a fraught set of negotiations is speculative: when recorded by colonial investigators, practices that violated the basic norms of colonial governance could be acknowledged only circuitously. Excessive candor would acknowledge flaws at the heart of colonial political accommodations. The micropolitics of these negotiations therefore remain invisible. The district head and his son were under pressures of their own, as attested by the facts that the son was investigated for this crime and that the district head was deposed the following year. Even if Sani did not receive satisfaction, his tormentors were not completely invulnerable. One reason the district officer gave for not reinstating Sani was the fact that his successor was already in office, which would make Sani's position invidious should he be restored. The implication was that the new village head already had powerful patrons—the new district head, or perhaps others in the emirate hierarchy. For this reason, the case could not be resolved in Sani's favor.

For a somewhat more desperate instance of lack of patronage, consider the case of an old man I shall call Malam Balarabe, who was in his seventies when I knew him in Ungogo during the late 1990s and early 2000s, just before his death. He lived in desperate poverty there, along with his wife.[7] Balarabe had inherited no land from his equally impoverished father, and as a young man during the 1940s supported himself as a wage laborer working on other people's farms. By delaying his first marriage, he was able to save up enough money to buy a small parcel of land and take up farming for himself. He managed to support himself and pay his land tax through cultivating his farm and continuing in wage labor. During this period he also managed to get married. After a few years, he took an extended trading trip that lasted some years and in the interim left his farm in trust with his "brother," a patrilateral cousin. When Malam Balarabe returned to Ungogo, his cousin, who had assiduously cultivated ties with the ward and village heads, refused to return his farm. Balarabe had witnesses willing to testify that he had only lent the farm to his cousin, which is a recognized form of land tenure that comes with the expectation of the farm's eventual return. However, Balarabe did not think a court case feasible or wise.[8] He could not afford the expenses, both institutional and extralegal, of a court case, and he feared deepening the hostility of his cousin's powerful patrons. His hard-won farm lost, Balarabe returned to supporting himself through wage labor. The ill will of the village head proved enduring, and he was unable to get allocated a farm through the head's good graces. Instead, he devoted himself to trying to find farms officials "did not know about." After several years of cultivating ties to prominent men around Ungogo, Balarabe did manage to get an even smaller plot than he had before. Part of his challenge was that he was attempting to establish himself as a respectable farmer at a highly politicized time. Although his search for a new farm was taking place at a moment of infrastructural improvements in the village—a school and clinic were being built, improvements made to sanitation, and so forth—land pressures were becoming more intense, and patronage was increasingly being accorded to followers of the NPC. For those not as well connected with the majority political party, matters were grimmer, despite the fact that the period was one of relative prosperity overall. Balarabe eked out an existence on this farm, his solvency always imperiled by tax bills assessed by officials unimpressed by his local standing or his potential utility to themselves. The village head regularly inflated Balarabe's tax bill, sometimes with dire consequences for his very poor family. Even in the time after the land tax was abolished, Balarabe and his family lived with the constant danger of economic disaster.

Malam Balarabe's dispiriting biography is extreme; few others in town were so poor or so put-upon. Nonetheless, his description of official actions was not unusual. Official self-interest and a tendency to ignore the theoretical legalities of administrative procedure were commonly accepted as typical government procedure. The case of Malam Balarabe and complaints about government officials more generally did not tend to be couched in technocratic idioms of deviation from institutionalized norms of bureaucratic office. To the extent that people offered a negative evaluation of official action, they tended to call it "oppression," *zalunci*, which has a connotation of being *bad* but is also naturally to be expected from those who hold office—with an important exception: people were happy to describe contemporary Nigerian politicians as "corrupt" or as thieves and to emphasize specifically their diversion of public money. That is to say, for the most part, vocabulary that emerged directly from concepts of corruption tended to be applied to politicians and bureaucrats in the modern state apparatus. (The one partial exception to this is that revenue surveyors were regularly described as receiving "bribes.") In Hausa the conception of official zalunci maps onto the basic linguistic distinction between masu sarauta and talakawa.[9] "Masu sarauta" means literally "possessors of office," but this only refers to titles within the constitutions of the Hausa states, emirships, and subordinate positions. Modern political office would only be called a "sarauta" figuratively. Although many sarauta are heritable or inhere in particular lineages, the basic distinction between commoner and aristocrat is a simple question of whether or not one has been appointed to office. "Talakawa" also has an implication of poverty, although factually not every talaka is poor. The structural relationship between masu sarauta and talakawa is very often, perhaps normally, one of zalunci. Those in power are expected to exercise this power with a degree of ruthlessness. However, there are other qualities that can temper the zalunci talakawa suffer from their superiors. Many have ties of patronage to some officeholder. Moreover, in this Muslim area, anyone who wishes to be a good Muslim must behave well, provide charity, and avoid oppressing others and making them suffer unnecessarily. So although zalunci is to be expected, it is also normally restrained by other forces, which the skillful or lucky talaka may use to his or her own benefit.

Such constraints are more than attempts to live by a set of religious or social codes, although the moral prescriptions of Islam are a very important set of principles many attempt to live by. But in terms of daily life, the more important social constraints are conceptualized affectively: behavior (generosity, oppressiveness, ostensible gestures of clientage) is the overt manifestation of personal qualities and particular emotional states. Thus, one of the most important qualities any person can demonstrate is *hankali*, [good] sense, which does not just imply a capacity for assessing situations sensibly but indicates appropriate comportment and not being carried away by turbulent feelings. A person who has hankali knows what he or she should do, and does it. A subordinate person should display *kunya*, modesty, which is both an emotion and a mode of comportment: averting one's gaze from the superior person, speaking respectfully, not using the name of a person with whom one has a name-avoidance relationship. Appropriately respectful behavior is not a matter of great subtlety; to show respect for a very important person such as an emir, one would ordinarily prostrate oneself while greeting him, and such bodily demonstrations of respect exist along a continuum of a handshake between equals to complete prostration.

These embodied affective and emotional strictures emerge from local moral discourses evaluating individual behavior, and as such they are much more likely to come up in discussions of official "oppressiveness" than in those on more recent or more national-level "corruption." Even here the distinction is not absolute. One version of the explanation of Emir Sanusi's deposition is that it emerged from a chill in relations with the Sardauna of Sokoto caused by Sanusi's arrogant behavior during his tenure as acting governor of the Northern Region. The truth or falsity of this story is beside the point; it is unnecessary to psychoanalyze the Sardauna or other members of the political elite to determine the *true* cause of the emir's deposition. The prominence of Sanusi's arrogance in the stories of his deposition, their emphasis on greetings, postures, and patterns of silence, are not necessarily signs of what happened but rather of how bad comportment can create vulnerability, can displace one from the chains of patronage and accommodation that allow continued tenure in office. The findings of corruption in the Kano Native Authority were only the proximate cause of Sanusi's deposition—they were not exceptional—the key is his vulnerability to such charges in the first place. Certainly, the predominance of stories of his disrespect in the oral histories of his deposition demonstrate its salience in popular memory. Hankali is a two-way street. Just as subordinates are expected to comport themselves appropriately, so are superiors. And a key part of that obligation is not to treat subordinates badly. Doing so is zalunci.

Zalunci is more than just bad behavior caused by turbulent emotions or by a failure to control one's actions as a sensible superior ought. It is an absolute evil that deserves condemnation by everyone who admits it has occurred. Officials' quotidian oppressiveness is also testified to by people's emphasis on the nakedly extractive quality of taxation, which surpassed the universal lack of enthusiasm with which people regard paying taxes. Their word choice here was instructive: in addition to talking about taxes' being "collected" (*karba*) or "paid" (*biya*), people often talked of taxes being "cut out" (*yanka*) or "pulled out" (*cire*). Sometimes even giving up one's farmland was not sufficient to avoid tax bills. Migrating into Kano city was insufficient, for the sufficiently ill connected could find themselves pursued and dunned for back taxes. Those still unable to pay were often beaten. For the most part people did not describe any extorted payments, however extralegal, as "bribes" (*rashawa, cin hanci*), or the oppressive state of affairs as "corruption" (*baci*), although as suggested above, particularly the term *cin hanci* did come up when describing the revenue survey in particular. From this, one can discern two overlapping conceptual systems that coexist in northern Nigeria, both of which negatively evaluate particular official malpractices but which condemn them in quite distinct ways. Zalunci is a failure of morality, a demonstration of bad character, an inability to control one's emotions. Corruption is a technocratic failure to abide by the norms of office and an inability to observe the distinction between public and private. Particular individuals subsist in overlapping but divergent domains, each of which describes and interprets official conduct. The matter is further complicated by the third conceptual system described in the introduction, that of 419. But since it did not come up explicitly in these contexts, it can be bracketed for the moment.

Ideas about appropriate conduct on the part of state officials are complex and somewhat contradictory. While a good and upstanding official should not be oppressive, he or she should also have largesse available to redistribute to a following of clients—sums far beyond what officials could expect to gain "legitimately" from their state salaries. This depends on an internal contraction. Zalunci is undesirable but also necessary; how else are officials to get the wherewithal to be "big men"? The revenue for patronage must be extracted from someone. But the conception is also distinct from a notion of corruption, which implies a certain kind of pathology in the state, even if one might appropriately describe the oppressive conduct of a state official as being "corrupt." But while "corrupt" behavior is antithetical to the functioning of government, zalunci emerges directly from it.[10]

The distinction between zalunci and corruption is neither absolute nor developmental: discourses about the desirability of officials' abstaining from oppression are not gradually giving way to those about the desirability of technocratic rationality. Rather, various aspects of the political logic of zalunci have been incorporated into the political history of corruption. They coexist, interpenetrating, and provide a means for evaluating political behavior. Both are modes of understanding similar phenomena, and the logic of northern Nigerian political culture simultaneously demands and condemns zalunci and corruption. Languages of zalunci and corruption are inflected by class, access to Western education, and orientation toward the institutions of the contemporary state. They are intertwined, sometimes parallel and sometimes perpendicular. But the intricate economy of these two modes of understanding is key to the dynamics of government practice, and malpractice. That is, a language of zalunci surely inhered in the political culture that was incorporated into the structures of the Nigerian state through the process in which emirate governance became a part of the colonial government and then was incorporated into (and was gradually replaced by) the bureaucratic structures of federal Nigeria. The political culture of Western governance had its own set of descriptions for government malfeasance and its condemnation. A language of zalunci and a language of corruption enjoyed a common subject matter. They were sometimes uncannily similar and sometimes oddly divergent. But the practices of malfeasance that are currently understood as "Nigerian corruption" required both normative systems as conditions of possibility.

The perception of official actions as unfortunate but normal is neither limited to farmers with little Western education nor applied only to the domain of traditional government. A highly educated friend with a professional, public-sector job, someone who has been eloquent in condemning corruption in government and Nigerian society, one day surprised me by going on at length about his desire to gain government office in order to provide for his children.

Failing such a job, he wanted to be given a government contract. Public works are generally assigned to contractors, but many of these contracts are handed out because of one's proximity to government officials and do not reflect any actual capability to fulfill the assignment on the part of the original contractor. Getting a contract therefore is a lucrative opportunity to get paid by the firms that will actually perform the services, which can recoup their money (and then some) with substantial cost overruns. My friend saw nothing hypocritical in the disparity between his political beliefs and his ambitions; it is an imperfect world, and life is full of compromises.

He was hardly alone in this. Nigerians have long been eloquent in attacking government corruption in these familiar terms. A relatively early example was future prime minister Tafawa Balewa's famous 1950 speech before the Northern House of Assembly. Balewa's call for a commission of inquiry into malpractice by the native authorities was resolutely technocratic in emphasis. It cited "the twin curses of bribery and corruption." Tafawa Balewa went on to argue: "Native Administration servants have monetary obligations to their immediate superiors and to their sole Native Authorities [i.e., emirs]. It would be unseemly for me to particularize further but I cannot overemphasize the importance of eradicating this ungodly evil. *No one* who has not lived among us can fully appreciate to what extent the giving and taking of bribes occupies the attention of all degrees to the exclusion of the ideals of disinterested service. Much of the attraction of a post lies in the opportunities it offers for extortion of one form or another."[11] Chapter 2 detailed how Tafawa Balewa's speech helped to consolidate the Northern People's Congress in power by replacing the personnel of the native authorities with holders of office in the secular state. A dual focus on electoral appeal (as against the class challenge offered by NEPU) and on consolidating political power undergirded Tafawa Balewa's proposal of reforming the native authorities. The problem, according to him, was not Nigerians who had political power per se but rather the specific personnel of the native authorities. Politicians such as himself and his confreres in the NPC could staff a government that would not succumb to those sins. The irony was the overlap between the NPC leadership and the aristocracy, the masu sarauta and their relatives. Although Tafawa Balewa himself was a commoner, the party was aristocratic. Ultimately, Tafawa Balewa was advocating a slight change in personnel (not entirely unlike the shift that occurred at colonization, when existing officeholders were replaced by others eligible for the same offices) and a transfer in administrative authority from the organs of emirate governance to institutions responsible to ministries that would shortly be taken over by Nigerians. The problem as framed in this speech was bribery and patronage. If the issue were actually curbing practices that affected the tal-akawa, Tafawa Balewa's prescriptions for change were remarkably limited. The personnel of the NPC could be trusted more than native authorities because they were members of a new political class, despite their intimate ties with the old. New forms of political comportment would follow from a new, "modern" mentality.

Tafawa Balewa anticipated the theoretical moves social scientists would make across the next two decades, positing corruption as a developmental stage susceptible to administrative solution. As corruption became an administrative matter, avoiding it was largely an issue of constitutional adjustment and exhortations to good behavior. In a subtler way, Tafawa Balewa's critique implicitly developed a new departure in the moral evaluation of official conduct, one which simultaneously engaged tropes of zalunci (or at least of oppression) and of technocratic corruption, mediated by a developmentalist contrast between the suffering of the oppressed talakawa and the bureaucratic crimes committed by their rulers. Tafawa Balewa proposed a disjuncture in modes of moral evaluation. The problem with the emirate authorities was their autocracy and venality, only exacerbated by the "helplessness" of the talakawa.

Political opinion in the sixty years since Tafawa Balewa's time has consistently condemned political patron-clientage and the malpractices of the elite, even while discussions of malpractice have often been conducted in regionalist idiom, as outlined in chapters 2 and 3. The critiques leveled at the Nigerian leadership as a whole demonstrate remarkable continuities with Tafawa Balewa's invocation of technocratic modernity. But to the extent one can find a consistent condemnation of patronage politics, its rhetoric has grown ever more apocalyptic. Thus, for example, in 2005 a columnist for Abuja's *Daily Trust* wrote a fascinating response to the arrest and trial of Mustafa "Tafa" Balogun, a former inspector general of police, accused by the Economic and Financial Crimes Commission of stealing ₦17.7 billion in 2002–4. The writer, Adamu Adamu, began by suggesting Balogun was noteworthy precisely because his crimes were *not* exceptional but rather symptomatic of the behavior of the entire political elite, which he framed as an ironic parallel to the neoliberal emphasis in recent years on privatizing state companies: "For Nigerian people there is no armour against thievery. It seems set to go on unchecked in all the top places. And the result of all the thievery has succeeded in privatizing Nigeria more than the combined efforts of the National Council on Privatisation. . . . Thievery had itself privatized not just a few government-owned companies and parastatals but everything with which it came into contact. It had virtually privatized the whole of Nigerian society—every nook, every corner and every straight line, if there was one."[12] The only difference between Balogun and his erstwhile colleagues, Adamu argued, was that the latter had not been placed on trial. The government had become a farce: "Doing one thing, preaching another and pursuing a different third. It is as if the assignment for government is to pretend to please, and, in reality, confuse and to finally perplex." For Adamu, all that had been public—not only the institutions of the Nigerian state and parastatals but public goods like oil revenue—have been diverted into the private hands of its rulers. Thievery would naturally result in "privatization" through politicians' patrimonial refusal to observe distinctions between public and private, which suggests Adamu's critique is conventionally technocratic. But his choice of "privatization" also invokes neoliberal reforms implemented in Nigeria since the start of structural adjustment that sought to privatize Nigeria's dysfunctional parastatal companies. Instead of ingenuously replicating technocratic narratives, therefore, Adamu signals a complex stance of acceptance and critique. In doing so he suggests a crisis going beyond material misconduct, bringing into question foundational paradigms of technocratic modernity.

The parallels and divergences between Tafawa Balewa and Adamu are instructive. Both implicitly pose a model of technocratic governance, in which patrimonialism does not distort government function and in which public resources are not diverted to private hands. Both posit that the governments of their day had fallen far short of that model. Where Tafawa Balewa's "ungodly evil" suggested a difficulty that might be overcome (in his case, by transferring responsibility from native administrations to a Northern People's Congress administration), Adamu posits a bleak landscape where every bit of Nigeria has already been stolen. There is an interesting claim implicit in Adamu's use of the rhetorical equation of "thievery" and "privatization." The latter is a consequence of the former, but one might discern a somewhat different stance from Tafawa Balewa's position. "Thievery" might seem an obvious equivalent to Tafawa Balewa's "ungodly evil," "privatization" implies something different.

The one optimistic note Adamu strikes is that the looting of Nigeria's public goods "has effectively done away with tribalism." The spoils of this massive thievery increasingly are divided by political families. This is achieved through alliances between them, and these transcend ethnic boundaries. Adamu's pessimism captures a general sense of crisis well known to anyone in Nigeria, a sense that the Nigerian government has reached a state of utter paralysis and is unable to do anything on behalf of the Nigerian population as a whole. There is a sense that the economic situation is increasingly desperate, and there is a nostalgia for the leaders of the past—including even the kleptocratic Sani

Abacha (though, interestingly, not Ibrahim Babangida, whose interventions in Fourth Republic politics perhaps preclude sanitizing his record). This begs the question of *why* this sense of crisis is so pervasive, and of when the crisis began. What standards have been violated, how, and when? When did malfeasance in office stop being simply an ungodly evil and become critical, privatizing every nook of Nigerian society? To what extent does this disenchantment reflect a more brutal disengagement from the ideals of technocratic modernity, and what might be the consequences? These are good questions but cannot be answered directly. While there is no question that much greater amounts of money are being stolen in the early twenty-first century than were being stolen in Tafawa Balewa's time, when there were no oil revenues, there is very little way to estimate anything like the precise percentage of GNP being diverted improperly from public to private hands.[13]

Tafawa Balewa and Adamu are noteworthy for their resolute inattention to the political pressures that might have driven officials toward behavior they condemn as corrupt. This is not unsurprising, given the contexts in which each man operated. Neither one could expect much sympathy for the political plight of the big man or aspirant big man, either from the impoverished masses for whom even an inadequate public-sector salary would be an improvement or from national and international public actors invested in the appearance of bureaucratic rationality. Especially in the period during which Adamu wrote, it would be difficult to justify the diversion of public revenues simply as a kind of culturalized public spiritedness. Tafa Balogun did not need ₦17.7 billion (U.S. $130 million at exchange rates prevailing in 2005) to redistribute to a following or to bolster his police position. But beyond arguing that the diversion of public money might be motivated by incentives beyond pure perversity and greed, urgent questions can be posed about how to conceptualize what seems to be genuinely a mounting sense of crisis. In this regard, Adamu's bringing basic processes of economic regulation into question implies a crisis in the moral systems regulating political life.

Moral Economies of Corruption

The conceptual complexes around the terms "zalunci" and "corruption" are different, but they exert similar normative force. Ideas about officials' oppressiveness and their corruption take as a baseline a set of principles about ideal official action: it should be beneficent and in the people's interest. It should abide by a set of external strictures, religious principles or the norms of bureaucratic office. However, any realist expects many officeholders to fall short of these ideals; the real world is not ideal. The norms indexed by "zalunci" and "corruption" structure a set of arguments about how to evaluate people's actions. These arguments within popular discourse are obvious instances of what has come to be termed a "moral economy." That term has been at the center of very important discussions about how groups of people exert power through moral suasion, and it has been particularly influential in debates about violence and rebellion. Famously applied to issues of corruption in Africa by J.-P. Olivier de Sardan, analyses of moral economies are potentially useful in explaining how the conceptual systems of the corruption-complex both constitute the conditions of possibility for material practice and also suggest the constraints placed on it by systems of social regulation. One challenge, however, is that analysts of moral economies have used the term in different ways, and thus it is first necessary to bring various scholars insights more precisely into conversation with one another.

"Moral economy" is the term E. P. Thompson famously adopted to describe the social logic of riots over the price of bread in eighteenth-century England. For Thompson, it was "a consistent traditional view of social norms and obligations, of the proper economic functions of several parties within the community."[14] In his account, bread riots had resulted from ordinary people's furious sense that the price of bread violated the most basic moral structures of social distribution. It was no coincidence they occurred at this point in the development of market capitalism. Until this period, the price of bread had been determined by a set of communal mechanisms that had a degree of popular legitimacy. As a result, sellers could be popularly perceived as moral even when food prices were very high. The advent of market mechanisms eroded this older system of valuation. Prices rose in response to supplies of wheat and the demand for bread, which was often unrelated to reasons ordinary people found compelling. When people could not afford food and the reasons for high prices were abstract, they responded with violence.

Thompson's account has been vastly influential, not least because it provided a way of thinking about evanescent collective decision making. At the center of his account of causation was the emergence of market mechanisms, a transformation Karl Polanyi had called the "great transformation." Until that point, as Polanyi put it, "Man's economy, as a rule, is submerged in his social relationships. He does not act so as to safeguard his individual interest in the possession of material goods; he acts so as to safeguard his social standing, his social claims, his social assets. He values material goods only in so far as they serve this end."[15] Polanyi substantiated his claim of a great transformation through a set of magisterial case studies, ranging from the ancient world to precolonial Dahomey. These uncovered an "archaic" mode of valuation common to traditional societies that radically circumscribed market mechanisms in the interest of other social values.[16] Polanyi's evidence for this transformation emerged from the case studies. This poses a difficulty. His empirical claims have not held up well; the cases were more heterodox than he asserted. As a result, it would not be safe to assume that a transition between moral economies and market economies has been a universal feature of human history. The distinction between "traditional" and "modern" societies remains elusive.[17]

To his credit, Thompson insisted his remarks were meant to apply specifically to eighteenth-century England, and thus could argue from evidence of traditional norms specific to that context.[18] A stark division of the modern from the premodern was not entirely comfortable for analysts of present-day peasant societies, but the concept of moral economy was powerful. It was famously extended to instances of peasant resistance in James Scott's *The Moral Economy of the Peasant*. Scott argued peasants are most likely to resist economic exploitation when they are left with too little to reproduce socially. Peasant rebellions emerge when farming families are left with too little to survive. What matters is not the absolute scale of what is taken but rather how much remains. Peasantries were famously averse to economic risk, which made them reluctant to embrace new agricultural techniques out of worries over subsistence. This made peasants the bane of development planners, but Scott's description of their moral economies implied they could be the populist heroes. He provided a principled way of extending the notion of a moral economy beyond eighteenth-century England. More important, he dispensed with a romantic view of the precapitalist past. The peasant was not archaically tied to traditional social systems but rather was rationally attempting to ensure familial survival. Didier Fassin notes another important distinction between the two paradigms. Thompson's account was of how concrete behavior was socially evaluated: merchants' decisions over pricing could set off violence. Scott by contrast was concerned with moral systems: his object was less actual uprisings than their conditions of possibility.[19] Moral economy became detached from a particular temporal or geographic conjuncture, allowing it to be applied anywhere a peasantry existed. The formulation retained a Polanyi-influenced opposition between peasant economies and capitalist ones. It also, as Janet Roitman has argued, reified an opposition between "culture" and "economy" sustainable only through dubious developmentalist assumptions.[20] Thus, although the absolute opposition between modern and traditional (or peasant and capitalist) is unsustainable, moments of eruption demand scrutiny, because they suggest a clash between normative systems that can be elucidated by critical attention to how they exist in their historical contingency.[21]

An approach for doing so is suggested by a somewhat different formulation of moral economy coming out of science studies. In a study of how early modern scholarly communities established and policed norms of evidence, Lorraine Daston suggested the answer was through a moral economy, "a web of affect-saturated values that stand and function in well-defined relationship to one another."[22] This usage is much broader than those describing spheres of production and exchange. Daston's expansion of moral economies beyond the contexts of violence and immediately economic transactions is most useful. Communities sit in judgment of activities of all sorts. As Fassin pointed out, while this expansion of the concept of moral economy into wider cultural domains reflects a need to analyze the social negotiation of complex normative codes, there is a danger of losing the political urgency of earlier formulations. Daston's depoliticizing emphasis disentangles the moral economy from a particular stage in what is imagined to be a universal sequence in the evolution of market forces. A moral economy can be conceived as how somewhat discrete social groups (English working classes, peasant communities, scientific communities) exert normative force on their members. But aside from reading mechanisms ad hoc from the cases such authors have discussed, it is not clear how an analyst of moral economies should go about looking for their means of exerting moral force.

A useful suggestion can be read from John Lonsdale's slightly different formulation. His essay on the moral economy of Mau Mau examines the historical emergence of the Kikuyu ethnic group as a unit of colonial governance, which he argues was also the process that constituted it as a community capable of exerting moral authority.[23] Colonial policies of land alienation and settler demands for African labor were implemented through policies of indirect rule that placed "traditional" chiefs in charge of local administration. These chiefs had to negotiate hotly contentious issues like the allocation of land and grazing rights. Because their authority emerged from their alleged grounding in "tribal tradition," ordinary people were able to get land rights only through making claims on the basis of membership in lineages and clans under a chief's authority. Not only did this system give these identities and memberships a new political salience, the chiefs' status as Kikuyu chiefs also brought the "Kikuyu tribe" into being as an immediately relevant category of identity, in which access to the means of making a living was negotiated. Ethnic identity became a basis for claiming entitlement to critical social goods. The colonial era brought into being the ethnic group as a new kind of moral community and mode in which people imagined themselves as social actors. Lonsdale thus provides the precise converse of the other discussions of the moral economy. Where Thompson, Scott, and Daston provide structural accounts of the conditions that can bring a moral economy into being, Lonsdale's history of a distinctively Kikuyu moral imagination cannot be disentangled from the specifics of Kenyan history, which provides a more detailed account of the mechanisms that might allow a moral economy to function. This intricate portrait of how political debate and contests over resources were refracted through the culturalist lens of emergent Kikuyu ethnicity is one of a specific moral economy in action. Lonsdale's portrait of the ethnic group as a moral community with its own distinctive dynamics retains precisely what is useful in Daston's culturalist account while also maintaining a politicized awareness about the urgency of allocative decisions and yet expanding this beyond the immediate context of market relations and surplus extraction that concerned Thompson and Scott.

A provocative suggestion for how to maintain this synthesis was advanced by J.-P. Olivier de Sardan, who proposed to "refer" to the notion of moral economy as formulated by Thompson and Scott as a way of identifying "certain *social norms* widely represented in modern Africa, which 'communicate' with or influence the practices of corruption."[24] Olivier de Sardan advocated studies of what he terms a "corruption-complex"—in a usage very different from mine—which includes "a number of illicit practices, technically distinct from corruption, all of which none the less have in common with corruption their association with state, parastatal or bureaucratic functions, and also contradict the official ethics of 'public property' or 'public service,' and likewise offer the possibility of illegal enrichment, and the use and abuse to this end of positions of authority."[25] For Olivier de Sardan, the corruption-complex is distinctively postcolonial and all-pervasive in government even though corrupt practices are also widely condemned. They are considered legitimate and even necessary by their perpetrators, and their moral evaluation depends entirely on the social location of the evaluator. The account depends on a structural logic not entirely unlike that proposed by Daston. Olivier de Sardan insisted his account was not culturalist, which would imply romanticizing (or vilifying) a reified figure of "African culture." At the same time he claimed the corruption-complex emerges from socially embedded forms of patron-clientage. This is not unreasonable, but it imports a particular form of culturalist analysis even while denying it has done so. Olivier de Sardan's key insight is that the analytic concept of moral economy is potentially applicable to cases like that of corruption in northern Nigeria. Collectively, then, Daston, Lonsdale, and Olivier de Sardan discard the old traditional/modern apparatus on which Thompson and Scott depended for a rather subtler suggestion that consensus and dissensus are human universals and that the complex patterning of debates over the appropriate and inappropriate are at the center of all mechanisms for social regulation. That is perfectly reasonable, but is it more than a somewhat convoluted truism?

Even more than their ability to focus attention on the cultural negotiation of distributive questions, paradigms of the moral economy may solve a conceptual problem: by concentrating on riots and uprisings, Thompson and Scott take as a point of departure instances in which the moral economy was outraged. But that creates a circular argument. It implies the moral economy is known in and through its abrogation. Bread riots happened when market prices diverged from the levels societal consensus deemed just. We know about the consensus because the riots took place. Peasants rebel when they do not have enough food to survive. We know about that ethos because we know the rebellions occurred. Under somewhat similar circumstances, Paul Ricoeur said he preferred the term "hermeneutic" to "circular," and there is something to be said for it here. Nonetheless, is moral economy more than a heuristic device? If so, how can it be known in Nigeria when despite omnipresent discontent at the ubiquity of corruption there have not been uprisings directly targeting it?[26] Eighteenth-century bread riots and peasant uprisings are almost the obverse of contemporary Nigerian disquiet over corruption: the violence in Nigeria today is only indirectly targeted at official malfeasance.

The paradigm of the moral economy as a "web of affect-saturated values," as Daston suggests, poses a significant challenge, since these values are somewhat abstract. How should one conceptualize this web of values? The issue is clear enough in a bounded scholarly community, but if one wishes to extend it to an entire society—especially one so diverse and divided as Nigeria—"values" implies merely a collection of truisms, which often are difficult to apply because ambiguous and somewhat contradictory. One should not be oppressive. One should not deceive. One should not steal. One should be generous. One should show appropriate modesty and deference to one's superiors. Everyone can agree on such principles in the abstract, and even apply them in more detail: governors should not steal money. But there is more to it than that. Such principles do not combine into a workable code of conduct, nor do they provide the sort of accountability a scholarly community does its members. A moral economy is more than a system for applying moral condemnation, and discourses of "corruption" are more than a specific means of negotiating public life in Nigeria. The concept of moral economy and the Nigerian corruption-complex go together, but how? Applying the condemnatory label of "corruption" can discipline those who violate a shared set of norms, but the sociology of its applications is complex, and it always has been. For this reason, the Nigerian corruption-complex goes beyond a historically and culturally specific deformation of bureaucratic accountability. For one thing, it has limits. There is an emergent sense of crisis, a sense that something has gone very wrong in the Nigerian polity. That sense of crisis has been omnipresent ever since the First Republic, and it was even found during the fairly optimistic ethos that prevailed during the Murtala and Obasanjo military government preceding the Second Republic.

Since the presidential election of 2003, I have been struck by a nostalgia that has emerged for the Abacha regime of the 1990s, in large measure out of a conviction that the economy during the Fourth Republic has been worse than it was under the military and that corruption is more prevalent now than it was before. For example, I was chatting one evening in 2008 with a friend, a man in his forties who was highly educated but who had never secured a stable job. I first met him when Abacha was in power, and at that time he was not a fan, blaming the head of state for both the brutality and the rapacity of the regime. But on this evening (and it was a point he repeated many times subsequently) he said that really things had been better back then. There was not as much disorder on the streets, and people were not as desperately poor as they are now. I objected that, despite the considerable inflation that had taken place, incomes had also gone up. Why was it, I asked, that even salaried people who seemed objectively in better circumstances than they had been a decade previously thought things had become worse? Part of the difference, my friend suggested, was in how much more overt consumption was now among government actors. Even if a broader swath of the population is benefiting—at least to some extent—from Nigeria's potential riches, there is something maddening about having a tiny minority's disproportionate access to that wealth flaunted before all. And Abacha did not do that, at least not to the same extent. Nostalgia for Abacha is of a piece with a tendency that is well established in Nigerian political culture to invest earlier regimes with virtues almost in direct proportion to their temporal distance, and even more in proportion to their continuing political relevance. Thus during the Abacha period, everyone but apologists for the regime agreed that it was the worst military government ever. Its corruption dwarfed that of the Second Republic. The Babangida regime was similarly suspect, but the Buhari government was remembered with fondness, both for its relative lack of corruption and for its wars against indiscipline and against women, both considered increasingly problematic in the troubled social context of the 1990s, when chaos infected all aspects of public life and women had become increasingly wanton.[27] The Murtala regime was remembered with the greatest nostalgia as the epitome of governmental rectitude, though very few people have personally reminisced to me about the Gowon regime or the First Republic, except to the extent people have been nostalgic for the relative economic prosperity of the oil boom, which began under Gowon. Regarding the First Republic, the most common response to its leaders, at least from northern Muslims, has been a rather abstract admiration expressed for Ahmadu Bello and Abubakar Tafawa Balewa. Old NEPU and PRP activists felt differently, as did many Tijanis, who respectively tended to sympathize with Aminu Kano and Emir Sanusi. These complications to the side, the general sense is that matters get worse and worse.

The irony to this is that—as I argued with my friend—economic times have somewhat improved under the Fourth Republic. Public-sector employees received substantial increments under the civilian regime, and friends of mine from all walks of life are notably more comfortable than they were during the 1990s. Other than this slight anomaly, a general consensus that the Nigerian government grows worse and worse, under civilians and soldiers alike, might be considered somewhat compelling evidence for the proposition that practices of corruption are genuinely getting worse in absolute terms and that this is systematically eroding governmental legitimacy. Indeed, people's disinclination to credit the government for any improvement in living standards might be taken as evidence for an increasing outrage at politicians' violation of some absolute standard to the moral economy of corruption. In this regard, my friend's intuition that the problem is with the greater visibility of politicians' consumption suggests a part of what is at stake. The difficulty is that this is both impressionistic and inferential.

Is it possible to apply the notion of moral economy in some more precise way? Lonsdale's account of the moral economy of ethnicity is suggestive. Perhaps the conclusion is that one should look specifically at the historical emergence of particular public moral communities. Given that the Nigerian corruption-complex emerged through the intersection of a host of culturally specific modes of conceptualizing political community and patron-client ties, the extent to which the moral economy of corruption can be treated as one thing depends on how those discourses function as a disciplinary mechanism, a process not adequately comprehended by calling it either a "norm" or a "value." "Corruption" emerged as a political performative through its use as a justification for official condemnation of officeholders, as a strategy for achieving discrete political ends. Ordinary people do have deep-rooted ideas about how to evaluate official conduct, but these ideas are applied in complex, shifting ways. To the extent that condemnations of zalunci or deception or corruption reflect moral principles, they are always contextually dependent.

Malam Balarabe, for example, had a sophisticated political critique of the official structures that had made his life so very embattled. Like the NEPU activist he had been in his youth, he saw his travails in terms of a class divide between talakawa and masu sarauta, but unlike his more Marxist comrades, he saw that divide as instantiating a relationship of zalunci and for that reason a moral outrage. Balarabe was also a realist. Not only was he forced to make compromises in order to find patronage; he also recognized that left-wing politicians who attained office—the PRP during the Second Republic, the SDP during the abortive Third Republic—were inclined to steal money. Ultimately, he said, "it's necessary." A lot of people ask them for things, and they need respect. The challenge of the various intellectual systems comprising moral discourses within the corruption-complex is compounded by the problem of understanding the operation of a moral economy. An adequate account of this, then, would examine carefully the ways in which corruption discourse is applied to specific situations. What are its rules of formation; what manner of social work is being accomplished by discussing "corruption" (zalunci, deception) in the first place? It should be clear from part I of this book that discourses of corruption have accomplished a complex set of political ends across Nigeria's colonial history. Those discourses have changed with the institutional history of government, shifting paradigms of corruption itself (e.g., the move in Western technocratic thinking from Liberal reform and notions of crime prevalent in the early colonial period through the precipitation of Weberian paradigms in the 1960s and 1970s that resulted in the technocratic notions prevalent in global civil society today), the dramatic history of Nigeria's informal political structure, and changing trajectories in the rewards officials could reap from holding office. The discourse of corruption itself is a window onto this much more complex process through which corruption has been both constrained and enabled, and which today generates such a pervasive sense of crisis. To conclude this chapter, therefore, I shall consider one particular discussion of corruption as a means of thinking through the nature and the limits of the moral economy of corruption.

Taking Corruption Seriously

In order to trace how the moral economy of corruption can function, one must pay attention to the locations in which it is articulated, and some of the structural logic of the discourse itself. Nigeria has long possessed a dynamic civil society.

Even in periods of government repression (as during Sani Abacha's military administration, 1993–98, when journalists were regularly attacked and jailed), there has consistently been a freewheeling, very critical press, both domestic and expatriate. The press has a long history, from a small start along the coast in the early years of the twentieth century to the present day, when newspapers from a variety of perspectives are published in cities across the federation. In recent years, print publications have been supplemented by the Internet; electronic mailing lists, bulletin boards, and weblogs have extended debates yet further, and each has its own denizens, customs, and rules.[28] None is a transparent window onto a Nigerian moral economy, but for precisely the same reason, much of what is written provides insight into how such economies function. As an example of how this happens, consider one element common to much public discourse, speculation over the *real* motivations behind particular events and public decisions. What did particular officials intend, and what does this reveal about their characters? What might initially appear to be a kind of psychohistory is actually more profound and is indeed analogous to localized debates over the moral uprightness of village and district heads, and of LGA officials. At a national level, in the press and electronically, the analog to these debates often traces the conduct of officials in regional and ethnic context. The ultimate conclusions are not limited to an explication of the logic of patronage but instead are a way of claiming the official is moral or immoral and of positioning the writer in relation to the subject.

A similar trope is that of revealing the true story. Many events in Nigerian history are somewhat shadowy. It is not always possible to know what happened or when, and much political discourse is devoted to filling in the gaps. When Colonel Wase was killed in 1996 and petrol returned to Kano state's filling stations, there were many rumors about who precisely was involved with diverting the state's petrol allotment elsewhere and therefore was now maneuvering to cover up complicity. Nigeria's byzantine politics generate endless potential for rehearsing and retelling conspiracy theories, in no small part because a number of conspiracies undoubtedly take place. Elite groups from particular regions (like the group of northern officials who became known as the Kaduna mafia in the 1970s) *have* worked systematically to safeguard their individual, collective, and regional interests at particular moments in history, and stories therefore circulate about the role these groups have played in orchestrating particular incidents or thefts. These stories circulated endlessly, through a variety of media. They are a depiction of the moral economy of corruption, an account of how moral decisions were made, and a primary mechanism through which the moral economy functions.

To give one relatively simple example, General Abacha's death came as a surprise. He was taken ill and died suddenly on 8 June 1998. He was immediately succeeded by General Abdulsalami Abubakar, who was the chief of defense staff; the new head of state quickly began a transition to civilian rule. But why did Abacha die? Was his death natural, and if not, who was behind it? The story quickly circulated that Abacha had not been alone when taken ill; instead he had been consorting with women. The common elements of the stories I have heard most often involve prostitutes (two, three, and six are the frequent numbers), and they are usually supposed to have been Asian (typically Indian or Filipina) as a result of the general's fears that Nigerian women might attempt to cast spells or otherwise poison him. Sometimes the general is supposed to have taken an overdose of Viagra. Sometimes someone (one of the prostitutes, an army officer, a bodyguard) substituted a poisoned pill. Sometimes the "true" story is revealed not to involve prostitutes at all: General Abacha's enemies enlisted a former girlfriend to seduce him as part of an even more sinister plot. Trusting her and seduced by her beauty, the general did not notice when she introduced poison into his Gulder (a brand of beer) or gave him a poisoned Viagra.

The truth of the story and its variations is less interesting than the issue of what makes the story's various elements interesting, compelling, worth passing on.[29] By itself, the story does not involve corruption in the sense of General Abacha's misuse of office. But the structural logic of the story is nonetheless one of Nigerian political corruption. The question of *who* was responsible (army officers, government officials, other powerful men; the women are almost always faceless agents of others) provides a map for the moral evaluation of specific officials and classes of official: Was General Abubakar involved in the plot, or its innocent beneficiary? Does the complicity of officers whom Abacha had sponsored earlier in their careers indicate something bad about them, or something good? Telling or retelling the story is also a means of positioning the speaker in relation to the various actors involved. The "truth" about events in the past is compelling precisely to the extent that some retain present-day relevance. In addition to the implications for the living of their culpability in Abacha's death, the stories position the head of state himself as an actor, receiving or not—deserving or not—the loyalty of his subordinates. The "truth" of the story, and the endless variations of its details, are a way of creating and re-creating the moral terrain on which government actors function, and their organic relations with Nigerian society more broadly. Similarly, Abacha's having been poisoned, either literally or magically, does not just indicate the culpability of whoever did it. Someone as powerful as Abacha, and as powerfully destructive, is also easily understood as participating in magical practices himself. Tropes of magic and of sexual license position the story's tellers in relation to their evaluation of Abacha's conduct in office. Anyone who might occasion others' jealousy might fear magic, but those who commit widespread injustice are most likely to be described as fearing it.

In the end, stories about Abacha's death and narratives of corruption more generally are the means through which the moral economy functions. Both barometer of public sentiment and means of perpetuating or enforcing it, discussions of corruption are the way in which officials are subject to popular sanction. This web of culpability and innocence, the discursive positioning of current speakers in relation to past political figures, is thus more than a way of evaluating governmental corruption; it is the manifestation of political relationships themselves. In Nigeria, the oral economy of governance has become a moral economy of corruption.[30] While it is tempting to conclude such stories ultimately are a symptom of a more profound moral economy, that is not my point here. Such a conclusion would be powerful, suggesting that a sufficiently comprehensive and subtle reading of popular stories at any time would reveal whether officials had violated the moral economy—explaining perhaps that outrage over the cement armada and other instances of corruption in Yakubu Gowon's regime led to the coup that brought Murtala to power. Perhaps that could be done and moral economies described in a way that avoids circularity. Here I attempt a more modest claim, that an attentive reading to corruption discourse provides a window onto the moral economy of corruption, but only to the extent it reveals "corruption's" career as a political performative.

Let me demonstrate the point through a reading of the seven-part essay the poet Odia Ofeimun published in the newspaper *Vanguard* in 2003. To conclude this chapter, I shall consider this remarkable work. Setting aside its insight into what has happened in the past, what is currently wrong in Nigeria, and how it might be fixed, I shall instead consider how Ofeimun's essay reveals the logical structure of Nigerian corruption discourse *and* how that logical structure provides a useful window onto the interior logic of the Nigerian state. Entitled "Taking Nigeria Seriously," the essay is an analysis of the impasse the country has reached under the Fourth Republic. Reading it is not meant as an indication that the Nigerian corruption-complex is one and indivisible and can be uncovered through attention to Ofeimun alone. In some ways mine is a paradoxical choice given the start of my account in the northern emirates. However, Ofeimun's piece is one of the most insightful, most rhetorically dense pieces of writing on these topics that I have seen, and it has a quite unusual historical scope. While vernaculars of "corruption" necessarily inhere in specific communities, Ofeimun addresses a pan-Nigerian public, even if his mode of address is more localized. My exercise here is not one of cultural explication, nor is it an attempt to evaluate the truth or falsity of any of Ofeimun's empirical claims. Rather, it explores Ofeimun's text as a political performative, one that operates within a moral economy of corruption. Neither right nor wrong, Ofeimun's account simultaneously imagines a political future—attempting to describe and thus create a Nigeria that can be taken seriously—and intervenes to define and transform the moral politics of the Nigerian national community.

Ofeimun begins the article by lamenting the crisis of Nigerian universities before pivoting to a more general critique. The problems of Nigeria's cash-strapped, chaotic universities parallel a more general problem of political pedagogy: "Ours, at is happens, is a country being tutored to her death by foreign debt collectors, technical assistants and consultants, whose gain in management experience is our loss." He summarizes a report published in 2002 about human rights abuses in Nigeria, which lists "death penalties; judicial and ritual killings; assassinations; arbitrary arrests, assaults on the freedom of the Press and freedom of association; political unrests; strikes by the Police; non-payment of salaries and pensions; injudicious impositions on the educational sector and abuse of academic freedom; assaults on women and children's rights; brazen corruption and the disregard and abuse of the rule of law; and ethnic and communal conflict." He suggests the problem stems from a cynical move on the part of Nigeria's leadership, which attempts to inculcate a "pervasive feeling of hopelessness." Even a small portion of the money looted from Nigeria would be sufficient to ease its current woes. That Nigeria's troubles receive extensive coverage leads to a deadening effect on the body politic, in which all progressive change appears impossible. "The situation is worse than Thomas Hobbes' state of nature where life is nasty brutish and short; and where you have to eat someone or you are eaten. To be fair, the state of nature seems superior to the sheer barbarism of the current state of our society. Whereas those in the state of nature know what they are in for, nobody knows what rules are supposed to apply in our own civil jungle because those who make the rules do not obey them." The solution to this impasse, Ofeimun argues, is to "take Nigeria seriously," by which he means that Nigerians must consider the well-being of the entire polity as their point of departure rather than consider only the interests of some subsection.

Ofeimun's outline of the problem is provocative. Like many commentators, he suggests that the country's problems stem from lawlessness on the part of government officials. This is manifested both in monetary terms—the country's wealth has been systematically stolen, and what is not diverted by corrupt practices was paid as debt service[31]—and in the extralegal means through which politicians systematically stifle political dissent. Ultimately, however, these ills are a symptom rather than a cause. The failure to take Nigeria seriously boils down to a failure of the national imagination. The politicians of the Fourth Republic operate only within their own sectional interests, and even grassroots political pressure takes place in local contexts. With even dissidents failing to take Nigeria seriously, there is little hope for progressive change. Ofeimun's diagnosis is useful not so much because it is right, nor even because it eloquently expresses frustration and rage. Where others have condemned the effects of political sectionalism and the inadequacies of Nigeria's leaders, Ofeimun's formulation is novel in diagnosing the problem as a failure to imagine the nation. Politicians represent a narrow constituency or themselves only, rather than understand themselves as stewards of the country as a whole. The formulation is more interesting than a simple critique of the contemporary politics of culture. Read as a series of propositions, Ofeimun provides a familiar criticism of Nigerian political elites as both greedy and shortsightedly communalist. To the extent he offers a historical narrative, his account is undercut by an uncritical adulation of Obafemi Awolowo. However, the true brilliance of the essay lies in its rhetorical structure. His contribution to a Nigerian moral economy comes through very clearly when one examines the non-transparency of "Taking Nigeria Seriously," which demonstrates both the power and the limits of the moral economy of the corruption-complex.

In the body of the essay, Ofeimun examines what he terms Nigeria's "identifiable regions," which he lists as "Arewa [North], South West, South East, Middle Belt, and South South."[32] Ofeimun introduces the analysis by stating it will move through these zones systematically, identifying the "peculiar mode of selfishness and parochialism that have made it difficult for them to take Nigeria seriously." Provocatively, the actual text does something different. The Middle Belt is largely ignored (though it is mentioned in the sections on Arewa and South South). His story is one in which the northern aristocracy attempted to dominate the federation by systematically underdeveloping the south while only deepening its own regional misery. Meanwhile, the south was unable effectively to resist because the Igbo were determined to dominate the small ethnic groups near their own homeland while resisting Yoruba power. In outline, this is nothing new and would represent a pedestrian southwestern communalist view of Nigeria's ills.

In many ways the account of the South West is the most interesting. The analysis is structured around an opposition Ofeimun draws between President

Obasanjo and Chief Awolowo, by any reasonable measure the two most significant political figures the region has produced, and who are frequently contrasted with one another in popular discourse. For Ofeimun, they are almost precise opposites. Awolowo was the guiding figure of progressive southwestern politics for decades. Obasanjo was and remains a stalking horse for the elites of other regions, an "objective" Yoruba politician who "bargained for national offices by showing to people of other nationalities that they were not on Awolowo's side." Ofeimun's account proceeds from this opposition, as a tragic fall from grace. Awolowo is presented as an inspirational figure, one of the very few politicians ever to take Nigeria seriously. His political platform, Ofeimun avers, was based on a developmentalist vision in which federalism would allow Nigeria's ethnic groups to realize their own cultural potential while progressive social policies (universal primary education most notably) would bring them together in harmonious modernity. The first betrayal of this promise came even before independence, when he was prevented from becoming prime minister by British and northern machinations, and by Igbo cowardice. Under the First Republic Awolowo's southwestern base was then fractured by other Yoruba, who served outside interests and at the same time inaugurated a southwestern provincialism. After Awolowo, the dynamic has continued as other progressive southwestern forces attempt progressive reform but are forced to make the same accommodations. In contrast to Awolowo's failure, Obasanjo's success came as a result of his taking power as a military leader only after assuring northern leaders he would not disturb their regional privileges. He made precisely the same accommodation when he gained the PDP presidential nomination in 1999. This unfortunate route to power forced Obasanjo to reward his extraregional patrons with political appointments and the spoils of the state. Even if he had shared Awolowo's progressive goals, these political accommodations would have made them impossible.

This cannot be taken as an unproblematic representation of southwestern Nigerian history, though it is equally uninteresting to dismiss it as propaganda from an Awolowo partisan. I will return later to the portrayal of Awolowo and focus here on the many ironies to how President Obasanjo is portrayed. Here he is an almost antinomian figure, the fulfillment of a Yoruba politics of compromise pioneered by the Western Region's premier, S. L. Akintola, during the First Republic. Corruption and sectionalism go hand in hand: the rapacious demands of the political bosses Obasanjo was forced to accommodate in his bid for the presidency have led to continued looting of the state during the Fourth Republic. Government dysfunction can be attributed to its president's political base, and continued ethnic tension—even if not directly his fault—was nonetheless enhanced by his role in perpetuating the old politics. Obasanjo found the only successful route a Yoruba could take to power, but this was at the cost of undermining his own regional bona fides as well as his government's competence.

Ofeimun's discussion of the north lacks the complexity that structured his account of the west. Despite glancing references to "the horrid exploitation and repression that had hitherto been [the peasantry's] lot and against which Northern radicals fought many epic battles" and an acknowledgment that "Bala Usman and Balarabe Musa [were] among the best minds that Nigeria produced in the twentieth century," Ofeimun's story is a fairly straightforward depiction of northern reactionaries. The amalgamation of Nigeria conjoined southern Nigeria with a region dominated by aristocracies fearful that development or change would erode their power. By preventing progress the masu sarauta maintained their power, at the cost of deepening the north's disadvantage vis-à-vis the south. After 1970, class antagonisms in the north were ameliorated by oil revenue. For Nigeria as a whole this was a mixed blessing because this dependence on revenues of southern origin exacerbated the north's desire to keep control of the south because of the north's poverty and need for revenue. The zero-sum quality of Nigeria's ethnic politics is the direct result of this northern-aristocratic strategy of national domination-cum-class privilege. More damningly, even northern progressives fail to take seriously the claims of Nigeria's regions. Ethnic groups reified categories imposed by colonialism or, almost worse, national policy rewarded ethnic demands articulated through violence and riots at the expense of reasoned dialogue. This discussion of the north is structurally the antithesis of that of the west. Far from the Awolowo/Obasanjo polarity, northern political thought is represented as almost uniform. Even northern leftists tend to see the south in instrumental terms, as a resource for achieving their own ends. If the history of the west is a morality fable, a story of temptation and fall, the north appears as a hell that threatens to engulf the whole country. With even its progressive forces irremediably tainted by their failure to take Nigeria seriously, the north symbolizes a compromised political community no true patriot could ever accept.

Ofeimun's account of the southeast is if anything even more provocative. As with the west, the history turns around a historic figure, but in this case only one, Dr. Azikiwe, and he is neither as heroic as Awolowo nor as villainous as Obasanjo. In this account, the failure of southern progressivism during the First Republic was largely a result of Azikiwe's cowardice and his hope to dominate the entire south. The NCNC's decline from being a southern nationalist party to being largely an Igbo party was the consequence of a set of unfortunate strategems. Ofeimun's narrative posits Yoruba goodwill defeated by the inadequacy of Azikiwe and his Igbo supporters. The majors who perpetrated the coup in January 1966 are portrayed as heroic, largely because of their supposed ambition to place Obafemi Awolowo in charge, but Ofeimun explains they lost control to more provincial Igbo superiors. Ofeimun then makes a rhetorically powerful if logically tenuous transition, suggesting through juxtaposition that contemporary problems of electoral lawlessness emerge from precisely the same cowardice, a Machiavellianism undercut by timidity. Ofeimun ascribes the peculiar state-level coup through which the governor of Anambra state was kidnapped and forced to write a letter of resignation after falling out with his state's political boss. In the ensuing scandal and debate about the incident, a variety of charges of electoral irregularity affecting the governor's own election emerged.[33] This section has received much unfavorable comment from Igbo interlocutors, but what is really interesting here is how similar the analysis is to Ofeimun's description of the southwest. The lack of a figure as heroic as Awolowo is morally (if not historically) mitigated by the majors' purported ambition to make Awolowo head of state. Indeed, what separates the east from the west is a failure of leadership, something that might be overcome if only Igbos could be convinced to follow worthy leaders, even if of another ethnicity.

Most provocatively of all, Ofeimun devotes a considerable portion of his entire essay to the subject of the South South, which he terms the "deprived goose" of the federation. Under this rubric, however, his attention is not so much on the specific plight of the Niger delta peoples who occupy the empirical South South zone. Rather, he explores the multiple failures of ethnic reconciliation. While he does consider certain aspects of South South politics, particularly those involving the reluctance of Fourth Republic PDP governors to embarrass their president by making too-great claims on national resources, for the most part Ofeimun elides questions of the delta peoples, those of the old Mid-Western Region (also in the South South zone but who have had rather different experiences within the federation), and those of the Middle Belt as minority issues common to all. To some extent, the Mid-West escaped the travails of the delta peoples and the Middle Belters because of their earlier regional autonomy, which Ofeimun ascribes to the good graces of Obafemi Awolowo. Being a "deprived goose" would appear to place these areas outside the antinomian logics that otherwise suffuse Ofeimun's account. Reading his essay nearly a decade after it was written suggests that Ofeimun would now be forced to revise this aspect, especially with the presidency of the South South's Goodluck Jonathan.

The text's power is not in its provision of a transparent account of Nigeria's troubles, nor indeed because of the acuity of its political analysis. For while the notion of taking Nigeria seriously is compelling as a form of political critique, Ofeimun's analysis is neither systematic nor evenhanded enough to succeed in its own terms. However, the very non-transparency of Ofeimun's rhetoric offers something far more compelling. Ofeimun is too deliberate a stylist for his reliance on Obafemi Awolowo as a heroic figure to be read simply as a set of propositions about the historical politician. It is true Ofeimun served as Awolowo's private secretary; his admiration for his mentor is as clear as his practical gratitude for Awolowo's patronage. And it is undeniable that Awolowo is a compelling and admirable figure—though that may be partly the case because of the very limited periods he directly wielded power. But in treating Awolowo as progressivism's unblemished tribune, Ofeimun is not simply engaging in hagiography. The clue to Ofeimun's method lies exactly where he is least historically convincing. The plaster saint version of Awolowo is an unlikely compliment to the man from so deliberate a writer. Ofeimun's excesses suggest something else. Thus, he insists that Awolowo's role in the Egbe Omo Oduduwa and the foundation of the Action Group was not a careerist ploy appealing to Yoruba communalism—even creating an ethnic Yoruba party at the cost of a united nationalist front against colonial rule was a disinterested gesture because of Awolowo's taking Nigeria seriously. Ofeimun's "Awolowo" bears little resemblance to the politician, and the history of his career less to the strategies of a real-world political actor. Exactly at the moment when Awolowo was most clearly engaging in a politics of regionalism, Ofeimun claims he was at his most universal. Even politically motivated ethnogenesis becomes in this telling a strategy for pan-Nigerian political community. The audacity of this argument cannot mask the consequence, which is that Ofeimun's "Awolowo" becomes a figure of pure critique and renunciation. Ofeimun's "Awolowo" never had base motives, never acted except in Nigeria's national interests. He only failed when the machinations of others were too great. The account avoids any taint of Yoruba nationalism itself because it is always already critiqued by the example of "Awolowo."

This is not a realistic account of history or a prescription for political change. It is, however an almost uniquely powerful demonstration of how discourses of corruption can be applied in criticism of the body politic. Critique is not by itself either a politics or a policy, and in the end Ofeimun's essay is not just unconvincing because of his romanticism about Obafemi Awolowo. What is ultimately unconvincing about the essay is that he is able to exhort Nigerians to take Nigeria seriously, but in the end this is portrayed as an act of will, a simple case of deciding to do so. And in this it is no different from technocratic exhortations to prevent corruption. Take Nigeria seriously, take honesty seriously—what's the difference? At this juncture, it would perhaps be useful to try to bring together some of the strands Lonsdale so usefully spun out for Kikuyu identity.

Ofeimun's Awolowo is a utopian figure whose purpose is to suggest the contours of a Nigeria that *does* take itself seriously. And at the same time, it is the most explicit engagement I have ever found with the proposition that corruption has its own moral economy. Where most acknowledge the fact through denial ("corruption" is the quality of my enemies, but everyone knows compromise is a necessary part of the world, and that's what my friends and patrons do), Ofeimun does not use his condemnation of "corrupt" or cowardly politicians primarily as a means of signaling support for those within his patronage network—even if that is the ultimate effect of Awolowo's apotheosis. This Awolowo has as a point of departure that Nigeria is to be taken seriously, that the welfare of all depends on strong local ties, creating a political community cultural strand by cultural strand, where the welfare of one community is never ultimately subordinate to another's. In this formulation, what is wrong is not specific material acts per se but rather their being undertaken without regard for *Nigeria* as a whole. This is a vision of corruption in which means and ends need never be incompatible, but where neither can serve as excuse for the other. It is very much a form of critique—entirely a political performative—but its end is not to situate Ofeimun in a position of patronage and obligation or to privilege a network of his allies. Such aims are subordinate to the denial that such particularistic interests can ever be indulged before the Nigeria he has taken seriously. The clue to this subtle distinction lies in those moments Ofeimun must explain Awolowo's actions that might appear to be morally compromised: his seeming to engage in Yoruba sectionalism, his implication in coup plots, his various political compromises, the financial dealings that received unfavorable comment from the Coker Commission. Where others would deny or justify, Ofeimun lays bare the mechanism of the moral economy. Judging Awolowo's actions as legitimate or illegitimate, he argues, is possible through only one metric, that of his having taken Nigeria seriously. Corruption or lack of corruption does not reflect a system of norms or a system of values independent of this larger, more all-encompassing question.

Less relevant than the *details* of his exoneration of Awolowo is the fact of his insisting on them. For Ofeimun the possibility of taking Nigeria seriously depends on understanding how politicians have not done so, building their careers on and feeding the interests of only a portion of their entire constituency.

The problem is not one with politicians alone, for as long as Nigerians' political imagination is rooted in sectional interests, Nigerians will be incapable of achieving the kind of national rootedness that will allow them to demand accountability from their rulers. Only through a commitment to the national project will true democracy be achievable. And in that project, corruption will be eliminated. Ofeimun's romantic portrayal of Obafemi Awolowo, especially in his somewhat cavalier dismissal of the possibility that the findings of the Coker Commission were anything other than a plot against Awolowo by the NPC-dominated federal government, makes his account too easy to dismiss. Ofeimun's lionization of Awolowo as nothing but a progressive icon leaves his account open to the accusation that it is a defense of Yoruba sectional interests recast as an account of Nigerian universalism. This would miss the crucial lesson in his text.

Ofeimun's text is unusual in that it admits that Nigeria is plagued, in an almost biblical sense, by corruption but does not ascribe it to individual greed and the moral failure of cupidity. Many commentators recognize that corruption has a moral economy—some degree of malpractice is legitimate, but this has been far exceeded by the country's rulers. The brilliance of Ofeimun's contribution is that he has recognized the argument's analytic limits, its essential circularity, and located corruption in a broader political dilemma. He indicates why corruption is dysfunctional and suggests what might possibly ameliorate it. The corruption-complex (in my sense rather than Olivier de Sardan's) is not just individual "corrupt" acts; it is also the moral terrain on which they are condemned and is not by itself good or bad. The institutionalization of corruption discourse as a mode of conducting political battles, as Obafemi Awolowo learned so painfully in the early 1960s, demonstrates that the material and logistical problems arising from the diversion of state resources to private pockets and other consequences of material corruption are both driven by politicians' social circumstances and only very partially reflected in the discourses that excuse or condemn them.

Ofeimun is one of the very few people to understand that this cycle of obligation, action, and condemnation is not in itself the source of Nigeria's problems, nor of the intuition many now have that the country is in a state of crisis. Elite rapacity is a symptom rather than a cause. The failure to take Nigeria seriously not only encourages politicians to act for narrow sections of the country rather than in the interest of all; it also impedes ordinary people's ability to assess these actions. If one is always inclined to excuse the actions of one's confreres, it is impossible to hold leaders to account. By coupling this insight with his quasi-utopian veneration of Obafemi Awolowo, Ofeimun also suggests how Nigeria might move beyond its current problems. The secret does *not* necessarily lie in refraining from all material malpractices. It is in expanding one's focus of intimate identification to comprise all Nigeria. I am not certain that as a practical program this is more realistic than simply exhorting officials not to steal or attempting to create new systems of incentives to preclude corrupt actions. Nonetheless, the basic point that sectional competition and competition over national resources resulted in ratcheting up the absolute incidence of material corruption does suggest that anything to dampen the tendency would be helpful.

Ofeimun's careful lack of attention to litigating the details of particular corruption accusations points to his innovative stance on the moral economy of corruption. Ideally officials would not engage in malpractice, but the persistence of patron-clientage makes eradicating patterns of conspicuous consumption and redistribution a daunting project. But is it necessary? Ofeimun's political program inheres in his idealized figure of Awolowo, and it is noteworthy that portrait does not emphasize his status as some sort of ideal-typical bureaucratic officeholder. What if the ultimate problem with Nigerian political institutions was their dependence on a constitutive logic that presupposes disinterested, rule-bound, impersonal exercise of office? Might a different model of governance prove less dysfunctional? The only clue Ofeimun provides is in his suggestion that such officials should not be particularistic in outlook. Nonetheless, it is a powerful—and extremely innovative—vision. In the end, his essay does not just provide a portrait of how the moral economy of corruption exists and perpetuates Nigerians' suffering. It also provides a vision for what an alternative form of political community might entail. But the details of that alternative require looking in a different direction entirely.

FIVE. NIGERIAN CORRUPTION AND THE LIMITS OF THE STATE

On 14 May 2003, a group of eight men knocked at the gate of a house in Enugu, eastern Nigeria, belonging to Mrs. Amaka Martina Anajemba. Two of the men were uniformed police officers; the other six represented the Economic and Financial Crimes Commission. In a lawsuit Mrs. Anajemba filed against the EFCC, she alleged the official party brutalized a domestic servant and the guard at the gate, a plainclothes police officer who was inside the house providing extra security. The officers conducted a thorough search of the house, and the next morning they detained Mrs. Anajemba's children, who had been staying with a friend while their mother traveled.[1] The raid was the culmination of some months' investigation and resulted in the prosecution of Mrs. Anajemba and several colleagues for advance-fee fraud. This was an early and high-profile case for the EFCC, which had only come into existence toward the end of 2002. Mrs. Anajemba was convicted in July 2005 of having defrauded a Brazilian bank of U.S. $242 million. Coverage at the time called her the "queen" of the advance-fee fraud.[2] Mrs. Anajemba's legal woes and notoriety emboldened more humble 419 artists to circulate e-mails in her name: "We were accused of currupt [sic] enrichment, our money and assets confiscated in our base country and those abroad sorted after," and asking for help in laundering $55 million in still-hidden assets.[3]

The high-profile case was a telling illustration of Nigeria's confrontation with corruption during the first years of the twenty-first century. The EFCC had been created as the civilian president Olusegun Obasanjo was approaching the end of his first term and a campaign for reelection. The Independent Corrupt Practices Commission (ICPC) he had previously created to fight corruption had as yet made no convictions. The ICPC was mandated only to investigate official corruption, while the new EFCC was permitted to investigate "any person, corporate body or organization" suspected of economic or financial crimes and was authorized to trace the assets of anyone if "the person's lifestyle and extent of the properties are not justified by his source of income."[4] Dismissed as a "waste of the country's time and resources," the ICPC was handicapped by its considerably more limited mandate,[5] and the EFCC was able quickly to become the higher-profile body. This was politically advantageous for President Obasanjo and other officials facing reelection in 2003. Enthusiasm for the civilian administration had dissipated across the Fourth Republic's first three years, and the popular consensus was that corruption had only grown worse since the military had returned to the barracks. The EFCC's dynamic young chairman, Nuhu Ribadu, was an assistant commissioner of police.[6] He quickly garnered considerable public attention for EFCC raids such as that on Mrs. Anajemba, but tellingly the majority of cases were for crimes such as hers—committed by private individuals defrauding others. The EFCC's triumphs centered on private rather than state corruption, "corruption" in the broad Nigerian sense of the term but not the international technocratic one.

It is difficult to calculate the electoral dividends incumbent politicians reaped as a result of the EFCC's activities. The elections of 2003 were marred by such substantial malpractice that their actual outcome (as opposed to the official result) is somewhat ambiguous. Unlike national elections under previous regimes, the ruling PDP suffered high-profile losses and did not emerge having consolidated an overwhelming advantage against its political opponents. Even if anticorruption activities did not convince Nigerians of the president's or the PDP's rectitude, the EFCC itself received good publicity both at home and abroad. Hopes were high that its activities would finally improve Nigeria's international reputation: "It is undoubtedly successes like this that send strong messages to the international community of Nigeria's anti-corruption war. . . . I can already visualize Finance Minister Ngozi Okonjo-Iweala arguing with the Paris Club sharks next September that Nigeria is changing, business is no longer as usual and corruption is being frontally attacked."[7]

This goodwill lasted until after the election, when the EFCC and Chairman Ribadu began to receive unfavorable comment, which centered on observations of a tendency to prosecute private corruption more enthusiastically than state corruption, ordinary people rather than bigwigs, President Obasanjo's political enemies rather than his allies: "Viewed from all indices, the so-called image laundering motive of EFCC has been rendered ineffective, and hence counter-productive, simply because people are yet to see the big officials of government stealing public money and stashing them abroad apprehended. Only the small fries without godfathers are being paraded in front of cameras."[8] Praise still came from abroad: toward the end of 2004, Reuters cited the chairman as claiming, "Corruption became endemic in the 1990s under late dictator Sani Abacha, who personally banked $5 billion. But a culture of impunity spread throughout the political class when democracy returned . . . in 1999." Even so, as a result of EFCC activity, "Things have improved. About 70 percent [of oil revenues] used to go to waste and corruption, but the number is now maybe 40 percent."[9] Even if the EFCC's measures to control corruption attracted complimentary attention, the country's reputation did not significantly improve, at least by immediately obvious metrics. In 2004 Transparency International's Corruption Perceptions Index (CPI) listed Nigeria as the world's third-most-corrupt country, only a minimal improvement on 2003 when it had been deemed the second-most corrupt. The finance minister, Ngozi Okonjo-Iweala, was a widely respected technocrat who had been a senior official in the World Bank. When the rankings were announced, she held a press conference attacking the index's methodology as "unreliable, outdated, and misleading." The country's failure to improve stung.[10] A marginal improvement to number six in 2005 led the president's spokesman to respond, "Given the tremendous efforts that President Olusegun Obasanjo has made in fighting corruption, we don't accept the idea that we are the sixth most corrupt nation in the world."[11] Reservations about methodology were abandoned in 2006, however, when Nigeria did move up in that year's rankings. The triumph was palpable: "Nigerians, especially the authorities, who have been grappling with the monster of corruption since the last six years of the Obasanjo administration, can now heave a sigh of relief that all that great effort is at least yielding result."[12] This acute attention to the Transparency International Index was no fluke. Every year, TI's release of its new rankings occasions detailed coverage in the Nigerian press—and sorrow or rejoicing depending on Nigeria's location on it.

The improvement in 2006 of Nigeria's reputation (at least insofar as this can be read from its TI ranking) may have owed less to the country's war on corruption than to other developments only tangentially related to corruption as such. By 2006 word of the EFCC's prosecutions already had time to circulate internationally; the change in perception followed hard on the heels of success in a rather different arena. "Fiscal probity" in international terms was less a matter of reining in flamboyant official corruption than it was of running state finances in an internationally approved way. The EFCC's prosecutions and reformist legislation to the side, it would be hard to make a convincing case (or even to measure) changes in the incidence of corruption. The most important development in 2006 was not EFCC arrests but rather Dr. Okonjo-Iweala's management of the economy, particularly her success that April in paying off the country's long-standing Paris Club debt. If one is to ask the question of why Nigeria's ranking changed in 2006, EFCC activities are an unlikely answer because the commission's performance that year was of a piece with the several years previous. It is possible that word of them only influenced the "respected institutions" TI surveyed in the compilation of the index by 2006. The resolution of the debt and the international kudos Dr. Okonjo-Iweala received as a consequence are a more obvious watershed, suggesting the perception of corruption was more dependent on a certain neoliberal order than it was on concrete shifts in officials' material practices.

Press and popular perception of the index in Nigeria is more sophisticated than its reception in the West. Dr. Okonjo-Iweala was quite right to complain that the index did not seem to reflect substantive legal changes across several years, and critics post-2006 are not unreasonable in doubting whether high-profile prosecutions are discernably improving ordinary Nigerians' ability to benefit from state resources or staving off the looting of the national treasury. Despite this, Nigerians also recognize the CPI contributes to their country's reputation as corrupt and are accordingly pleased or displeased with the CPI as indicating how the country and its citizens are perceived. Meanwhile, foreigners and particularly Westerners often take the index as unproblematically indicating absolute levels of corruption around the world. Transparency International is candid that the corruption perception index is a measure of how corruption is *perceived*, and it is also transparent about its methodology. Thus in its discussion of the index for 2012, the organization warned, "The CPI scores and ranks countries/territories based on how corrupt a country's public sector is perceived to be. It is a composite index, a combination of surveys and assessments of corruption, collected by a variety of reputable institutions."[13] Western news reports generally collapse this description of perceptions into a metric of the relative prevalence of corrupt behavior. Both Nigerian and

Western stories often equate perceptions of corruption and corrupt practices, but the Nigerian press is more acutely aware of the index as a sign of their country's current and prospective *reputation*.

It is little surprise Nigeria's climb in the rankings lagged several years behind the EFCC's widely publicized actions. Taking the CPI to be what TI claims for it, a measure of how a knowledgeable international community views Nigeria, it must be understood to depend on news of substantive improvement, which would take time to spread or would initially engender some skepticism. However, the tight correlation of the improvement in the rankings with the triumph of Dr. Okonjo-Iweala's reforms suggests that the international community views "corruption" as the antithesis less of good governance than of a particular sort of economic regime, of which following bureaucratic norms may be a part but is perhaps a minor one. Such a conclusion is beyond the scope of this book. It is nonetheless intriguing that "corruption" may be as polyvalent beyond Nigeria as within it. The relationship between empirical acts of corruption and Nigeria's reputation for corruption is somewhat attenuated, and causality may go in both directions: although such a conclusion would necessarily be speculative, it would not be unreasonable to suppose that Nigeria's international reputation may also facilitate some large-scale acts of corruption. Even as reputation enabled the 419 scams of the 1990s and 2000s, a reputation for corruption might have been useful for officials looking for international collaborators or for ensuring they might be offered bribes as a matter of course. More than that, the ubiquity of talk about corruption and condemnation of it ensured the corruption-complex's centrality to Nigerian politics.

State Actors and the Politics of Reputation

The EFCC and its chairman created a splash in 2007 after President Obasanjo's retirement, when many governors retired as well due to term limits. In the process, all lost their immunity from prosecution. The EFCC proceeded to arrest a series of governors who had just stepped down, culminating in the former governor of Delta state, James Ibori, a powerful figure in the ruling People's Democratic Party.[14] The move was not calculated to endear the chairman to the new president, Umaru Yar'Adua, who was personally close to Governor Ibori. Chairman Ribadu was removed from office. He was then demoted in the police force and subsequently resigned from it, going into exile for a period. U.S. diplomatic cables released by WikiLeaks immediately speculated that the new EFCC chairman, Farida Waziri, had been mandated to end this most politically embarrassing investigation: "Critics allege Waziri's appointment was orchestrated by former Delta Governor James Ibori [and a number of other current and former governors under EFCC investigation] and Attorney General Michael Aondoakaa.... Rumors have also surfaced in the press that Waziri has been instructed to go after President Obasanjo and his family in an attempt to refocus attention away from the former governors."[15] Despite these rumors, the new chairman did not move against the former president, which presumably absolved her of the charges of naked intervention on behalf of her patron. However, her reputation as a political patsy and sluggish guardian of the public trust had already been established. The chair of the Ikeja branch of the Nigerian Bar Association commented that in the 1990s,

> Obasanjo farm was on the brink of bankruptcy, as at the time the man was languishing in the prison, but he eventually found his way to the palace. By the time the man was leaving office, Obasanjo farm was the most prosperous private farm in West Africa. Yet, he has no case to answer. About $16 billion was expended during his tenure on the power project. What was the result? The power sector collapsed, yet he has no case to answer. And you are arresting Aborishade and Fani Kayode for the stipend mismanaged at the aviation sector. We are having a mockery in Nigeria, a situation whereby a bus conductor is being arrested for the offence of the driver. If [Mrs. Waziri] is saying that Obasanjo has no case to answer in spite of petitions written by some human rights groups and in spite of the results of various probe panels set up by the National Assembly, then she has no business sitting as the Chairman of the anti graft agency.[16]

Whatever the justice of such conclusions, unfavorable comparison between the two EFCC heads was widespread. Waziri retained a reputation for sluggishness throughout her tenure. The unfavorable comparison to Ribadu was not entirely fair. Waziri's conduct in office was not substantively different from Ribadu's, even if their public personae were. As it had under her predecessor, Waziri's EFCC energetically pursued cases of advance-fee fraud, and it also vigorously prosecuted misconduct in banks. Its pursuit of malpractice among public officials was more delicate, as the attention to the former governors had demonstrated. Unlike Ribadu, however, Waziri did not receive much personal praise for many of the unequivocal successes on her watch. Some of the admiration of Ribadu was retrospective: complaints about his decisions in office were quieted by his travails afterward. His misadventures combined with dissatisfaction with Waziri to solidify his reputation as one of the great reformers of contemporary Nigerian politics. Indeed, Ribadu contested the presidential election of 2011 as the standard bearer of a party whose major strength was in southwestern Nigeria, which had been the stronghold of Obafemi Awolowo's progressive parties in the two previous republics. However, Ribadu ran a distant third in the popular vote.[17] By 2011 and indeed ever since, Ribadu had become something of a doyenne for progressive and reformist political opinion. Before the elections of 2015, both of Nigeria's major political parties hoped to attract him to stand as a candidate for the governorship of Adamawa state. He ultimately joined the PDP, losing to the APC candidate. Waziri, by contrast, has not been rehabilitated in the years after she left office. And yet, in a report on Nigerian corruption published in 2011, Human Rights Watch concluded that the EFCC's performance was very similar under both leaders, noting that the prosecution of political figures under both leaders was slow, selective, and often marked by incompetence.[18] Waziri's successor, Ibrahim Lamord, seems to have achieved a midpoint between these extremes—neither celebrated nor reviled.

Such debates took on new life in late 2013, when Olusegun Obasanjo gave an interview to *Zero Tolerance Magazine*, a publication of the EFCC. In that interview, the former president declared Waziri was the "wrong successor" to Ribadu: "I know that the woman they brought in to replace Ribadu was not the right person for that job because I understood that one of those who head-hunted her was Ibori. If Ibori, who is now in a UK . . . prison for fraud, head-hunts somebody who will fight corruption in Nigeria, then you can understand what happened."[19] Waziri's response was tart: "I would like to warn that those who live in a glass house don't throw stones and as such Obasanjo should not allow me to open up on him. Respectable elder statesmen act and speak with decorum."[20] The personal nature of this exchange cannot disguise the fundamental issues at stake. Waziri's being Ibori's client and Yar'Adua's lapdog and the "glass house" of Obasanjo's own history of corruption are not as significant as the normalization of EFCC activities as an integral part of the corruption-complex.

The different public profiles of Ribadu and Waziri point to an issue raised in the last chapter. There is a wide-ranging consensus that all forms of "corruption" in the Nigerian sense of improper acquisition of resources through pretense and misrepresentation are wrong and should be punished, and indeed a consensus that the thievery characterizing the Nigerian political class requires harsh punishment, but public opinion remains inflected by ties of patron-clientage and tends to shift across time. While there is general agreement that the diversion of large sums of money from government coffers is unacceptable, there is less agreement about who has committed such malpractices, and whether they might be excusable. Constituents evaluate public officials (or at least governors and legislators) on the basis of how well they bring development—for example, infrastructural improvements, schools, hospitals—to the areas they represent. Thus, the indigene of an area that has benefited from a politician's tenure is less likely to evaluate him or her as corrupt. Or rather, supporters may be more likely both to perceive a politician as having brought "development" *and* therefore to claim them as less "corrupt." But the diversion of public money to irregular uses is not the sticky point. The question is whether state resources have been used to make people's lives better. Thus, on a story about Governor Ibori's long-awaited extradition to London for trial in 2010, "Blackwell" commented,

> I find it very difficult to think that all what is said about Chief James Ibori are correct. As a young man who started life in Warri, we knew how Delta State was before he ascended into power in 1999. By the time he left office bridges and connecting roads have been built. Negative media hype and gang ups has compeltly [*sic*] ruined this once generous man. I remember the massive employment he did in primary and post primary schools in Delta State. I know someday he will work free again. By the grace of God. This is my prayers.[21]

There remains a tendency to idealize the conduct of figures who held office longer ago. As particular political actions recede into history, fewer people remember them as corrupt or problematic. Perhaps most noteworthy of all is the widespread consensus that General Buhari is the epitome of the honest public official, despite quiet reminders of how members of the general's inner circle enriched themselves while he was in power and complaints about his reliance on a Fulani coterie and determination to perpetuate Fulani dominance over the entire federation. It is noteworthy how little resonance "Army Arrangement" has with the general as a contemporary political figure. During the political transition leading to the start of the Fourth Republic, coverage of Olusegun Obasanjo had something of the same quality. News stories mentioned allegations of embezzlement, but the general's more recent history included a seat on Transparency International's advisory council, international advocacy against corruption, and his imprisonment under Abacha. Obasanjo's earlier criticisms of the Babangida administration received much greater attention than dark allegations about his official conduct in the 1970s. If corruption discourse is a set of stories one tells about people of current political relevance, and if its narratives are structured by ongoing relations of patronage, the EFCC (and corruption prosecutions more generally) serve simultaneously as a powerful mechanism for prosecuting political conflicts and for marketing domestic political gamesmanship internationally as a fight against corruption.

The role of the EFCC in contemporary Nigerian politics transcends stories of Ribadu versus Waziri or of how the moral economy of Nigerian public discourse evaluates officials, corruption, or efforts to discipline them. On one hand, the EFCC continues a long-standing feature of the Nigerian corruption-complex, in which attempts to contain corruption translate into accusations of corrupt behavior that are themselves a central strategy of political life. Scholars have tended to imagine that the solution to corruption lies in institutional reform and the inauguration of powerful and independent watchdog bodies— precisely what the EFCC was intended to be—or to maximize transparency. Part I of this book suggests a very different conclusion. Across Nigerian history, both the concrete practices that might be termed "corruption" *and* the intellectual and discursive traditions for describing them have been integral parts of politics and statecraft. In no sense is corruption epiphenomenal or incidental. Neither is it something that could be legislated away through an appropriate raft of policies. Indeed, policy approaches to corruption have tended to posit ideals of independence that real-world institutions are unlikely ever to attain. They discount the historical overdetermination of existing material practices labeled "corruption." A more modest appreciation of "corruption" and the corruption-complex would recognize the constraints of making real-world decisions. Rather than imagining corruption to be a determinate set of (mal)practices, conceiving of it as a set of labels brings into focus its status as a discourse that describes and in part enables a set of material activities. The lessons to be drawn from the EFCC, therefore, must be read from within this more delimited frame. And even if the EFCC's activities are not new, its presence in twenty-first-century Nigeria is significant. The Nigeria of 2015 is not the Nigeria of 2002, and this is due in part to the EFCC.

Corruption and the Problem of the State

The EFCC captures in microcosm a general tendency of the Nigerian state, perhaps of all states. The EFCC has become a disciplinary mechanism within Nigerian politics and appears to instantiate the PDP's commitment to control corruption. It is thus a political tool and a public-relations icon, but one need not assume its architects were cynics who saw no worth in anticorruption agencies except as camouflage. The war of words between Obasanjo and Waziri was a symptom of the EFCC's much greater importance: its activities *are* politics, though perhaps an unusual genre. The great sensitivity of Nigerian public discourse to Transparency International's rankings stems from the fact the country's unfavorable position on them is an international embarrassment: it confirms a stereotype of Nigeria held around the world. Acutely aware of the great difficulties corrupt practices pose to their own lives, people also hate the embarrassment of living in a kleptocracy. Ironically, to the extent that improvement in Nigeria's international perception is a result of the enactment of neoliberal prescriptions, doing better on the corruption-perception index is at best a mixed blessing. It is far from clear that the EFCC or anyone else has greatly decreased the incidence of grand corruption. Decisions taken by Dr. Okonjo-Iweala and by then–central bank governor Sanusi Lamido Sanusi (grandson of Emir Sanusi I of Kano and now himself Emir Sanusi II), such as 2011's abortive decision to lift the national subsidy on petrol, were massively unpopular, even though such measures demonstrate the "business-friendly climate" likely to make TI's experts improve their rating for the CPI. Even if these measures play a role in garnering Nigeria a greater reputation for fiscal probity, they do little to ameliorate practices Nigerians agree are problematic. Appearing to combat corruption while forming an integral part of the corruption-complex, the EFCC epitomizes the multiple paradoxes of Nigerian politics, thus bringing together the issue of corruption discourse as politics with the structural logic of political life.

The introduction proposed that the corruption-complex's power stemmed from its performative location in the gap between the illocutionary and the perlocutionary. The illocutionary power of the charge of corruption is the force it exerts simply by being uttered. Over and over again, corruption accusations have been key turning points in political careers. Royals like Aliyu of Zaria or Sanusi I of Kano, politicians like Nnamdi Azikiwe and Shehu Shagari, faced political watersheds at precisely the moment when accusations of corruption were taken seriously. The emirs lost their thrones; Azikiwe's position as premier of the Eastern Region became precarious; Shagari had been overthrown by the military. When whispers become public inquiries (or, as in the case of the 1970s military, Afrobeat songs), discourse itself is action. Corruption discourse besmirches what might otherwise be an unblemished reputation. Making an accusation positions the speaker vis-à-vis the complex ties of affiliation and patronage structuring all Nigerian politics.[22] Corruption discourse can structure political discourse through an inflection of how previous events and officials' conduct in office can be remembered. Illocutionary effects encompass both speaker and subject. Accusations have perlocutionary consequences as well. Even if not every official—indeed, perhaps not most officials—are tried for their corrupt activities, some are. The EFCC prosecutes—sometimes it even convicts—public officials. Criminal penalties are not the only perlocutionary consequences of corruption discourse. Technically, Emir Sanusi resigned instead of being removed from office, but his resignation was not voluntary. The First Republic's minister of finance, Festus Okotie-Eboh, was notorious for his corruption and was killed during the majors' coup in 1966. Many government officials were killed that January, especially from within the ruling coalition, but it is striking that Okotie-Eboh died while other prominent NCNC officials, such as President Azikiwe or Eastern premier Michael Okpara, survived. The perlocutionary force of corruption discourse may itself have been the difference between life and death.[23] Umaru Dikko's flamboyant attempted kidnapping from London was an effort to bring him to trial in Nigeria, but it was blatantly illegal, a ploy to circumvent the need for British extradition proceedings. Corruption accusations served to make the incident more a farce than a humanitarian outrage. Dikko's performance as a critic of the Buhari government and representative of a legitimate civilian regime was undercut by lurid stories of warehouses full of rice, bloated infrastructure projects, and an ignominious exit across international borders.

The critical political work of corruption discourse is somewhere between the immediate effect of corruption talk and the long-term consequences of its deployment. The EFCC's greatest power lies neither in its immediate activities—investigation, public relations, prosecution—nor in success at making activities labeled "corrupt" illegal in practice as well as in theory. Rather, the unstable terrain between these effects is where the EFCC—and the corruption-complex itself—is most powerful and most effective. Corruption discourse opens up new possibilities while foreclosing others. To the extent that Nigerian public life has become permeable to EFCC scrutiny, the possibility of being charged with corruption can dictate people's actions, and it can make others risky. Corruption discourse can tarnish people's public personae and dampen popular outrage about killing, detaining, or kidnapping them, even if such measures are not legal. In this regard, "corruption" has consequences analogous to those of "terrorism." The EFCC and contemporary Nigerian politics have pushed this logic further than previous regimes, but this is a difference of degree rather than kind. It also brings a powerful challenge to paradigms of liberal democracy and public choice. The current state of Nigerian political life is the outcome of a long history of regional and political competition, and it is shaped by an unfortunate constitutional legacy. This institutional conjuncture is in no way the result of any series of collective choices or democratic deliberations, though it has constituted corruption discourse as a weapon within Nigerian politics. "Corruption" is thus not a problem to be solved so much as a label for a series of practices and dilemmas that must be understood within the contexts that gave rise to them. Such conclusions about corruption demand more than a revision of paradigms that take it to be a malformation of universal bureaucratic rules. These conclusions pose the question of what a state is, and how one can be understood. One cannot understand the intellectual legacies of corruption discourse without paying attention to the ways it maps onto more comprehensive discussions about the nature of the state.

Corruption and the State

More than eighty years ago, the anthropologist A. R. Radcliffe-Brown dismissed the state as analytically vacuous, "a fiction of the philosophers" used to designate collections of people and established relationships engaged in political affairs. He argued instead for a more precise attention to actors, political roles, and the institutions within which they operated. That suggestion contrasted with traditions following Marx that posited the state as an instrumentality enforcing the interests of a dominant class, often as an expression or embodiment of the social relations and ideologies of class society. Equally it challenged followers of Weber, who viewed the state as the entity with a monopoly on the legitimate use of force in a defined area. Radcliffe-Brown's exhortation to greater precision was attractive in the aftermath of World War II for Western (and particularly American) social scientists eager to guard against the spread of state socialism. The apparent rigor of a "political system" suggested that even the most urgent political questions were susceptible to scientific understanding and technical solution.[24] The definitional agnosticism implied by invoking "political systems" rather than "states," however, made the approach vulnerable to the critique of modernization theory's historical accuracy.[25]

As the introduction argued, the scholarly literature on corruption that emerged in this period was deeply involved in this strand of modernization theory. The earliest work in this vein, such as Wraith and Simpkins's book, tended to view corrupt practices as having both positive and negative effects— distorting state decision making while potentially also strengthening social ties[26]—but they were increasingly understood as being a developmental problem or pathology, or even as epiphenomenal to appropriate state practice. Joseph Nye's formulation of corruption as "behavior which deviates from the formal duties of a public role because of private-regarding . . . pecuniary or status gains; or violates rules against the exercise of certain types of private-regarding influence"[27] was a significant turning point, making a truly influential importation of modernization theory's appropriation of Weberian sociology. Nye's choice of vocabulary demonstrates his reliance on Weber's account of the modern bureaucratic state. According to Weber, human societies go through a transition in government structure; one can discern a transformation in how government officials obtain and retain recognized authority—acquire legitimacy, to use Weber's term. The development of states demonstrates a tendency to move from a logic of what he termed patrimonialism to a logic of bureaucratic officeholding. In a patrimonial system, individuals hold and exercise power through personal ties. A chieftaincy or kingdom is the quintessential patrimonial state, because officeholders enjoy power through their relation to the monarch and because they retain his or her favor. The primary characteristic of offices in such a system is that the officeholder needs patronage. In a bureaucracy, by contrast, the organizing logic inheres in offices. A bureaucratic office consists of a set of rule-governed duties, which one fulfills more or less perfectly. Personal relations to one's superiors are incidental. Nye's formulation posits the position of corrupt officials as being within a bureaucratic state— they play a formal role, have a public duty. The implications of invoking Weberian bureaucracy are more wide-ranging than might be immediately obvious. Weber observes, "Bureaucratization offers above all the optimum possibility for carrying through the principle of specializing administrative functions according to purely objective considerations. Individual performances are allocated to functionaries who have specialized training and who by constant practice increase their expertise. 'Objective' discharge of business primarily means a discharge of business according to *calculable rules* and 'without regard for persons.'"[28] Deviations from the rules of office are not by themselves evidence of criminal malpractice. My job performance might deviate from my official duties for any number of reasons, because of incompetence, for example. But incompetence is not in itself corruption. For Nye, the deviations that can be considered "corrupt" are "private-regarding": I am corrupt because I make decisions in office on the basis of hopes for personal gain, because of my personal regard for a superior, or to benefit someone with whom I have a personal connection. This formulation invokes Weber's bureaucracy "without regard for persons" as a way of explaining the constitutional logic of political office within the modern state. There is more to it. "Pecuniary or status gains" and "certain types of private-regarding influence" are more than the confusion of "private" interests for "public" ones. They signal the persistence of patrimonial political logics within a formally bureaucratic state.[29] Corruption, however functional or useful it might be in particular circumstances, is quintessentially a problem of imperfect or incomplete transitions. Nye and, decades later, Transparency International use the term "corruption" in precisely this sense. According to bureaucratic norms, an official should execute his or her duties only with regard to the public interest. Any personal considerations should be excluded. The paradigm implies the development of modern bureaucracies depended on a double transition: a reorientation of the logic of offices so that they were rule-bound rather than personalistic *and* the development of a distinction between public and private.

This discussion of Weber represents the role his work played in modernization theory, and thus in the corruption literature. It is not entirely fair to the man himself. Weber's account is one of ideal types, heuristic devices that are to be used analytically. They "cannot be found empirically anywhere in reality."[30] He does not claim a teleological progression from patrimonialism to bureaucracy. Quite the contrary, Weber describes how institutions that could be described as patrimonial gave way to more or less bureaucratic ones, particularly with the expansion of democratic accountability in nineteenth-century Europe, but this is a way of characterizing a host of grounded political developments, not an inevitable transition from one system to another. Commentators on corruption influenced by Weber have tended instead to view corruption as a problem of bureaucratic states that retain within themselves earlier modes of political organization. Under bureaucratic norms, officeholders should be selected for their competence at fulfilling the requirements of their offices, which they should then perform in a disinterested manner. The persistence of patrimonialism inscribes a personalistic and self-interested logic into the workings of the bureaucratic system. This is not a particularly inspired reading. It substitutes a strong and deterministic historical trajectory—a teleology, really—for Weber's far subtler set of paradigms and case studies. For Weber, bureaucratization is a consistent feature of wealthy empires, even ones from the distant past. It occurs and recurs. His description of bureaucracy (even when he associates bureaucracy with modernity) is meant to elucidate extant states of affairs rather than to provide a model to which modern states conform, or from which they might deviate.[31] This modernization-inflected appropriation of Weber has persisted until the present, most recently under the label of "neo-patrimonialism," denoting a political system in which patrimonial logics persist within the structures of the bureaucratic state.[32]

This focus on a patrimonial or neo-patrimonial state took place in the context of a resurgence of attention to the state as such—"bringing the state back in," as a celebrated collection memorably put it.[33] The return to the state, as opposed to broader formulations of a political system, fit well with the interests of commentators on Nigeria and on corruption in the 1970s and 1980s. Where earlier studies had concentrated on Nigeria's problematic or incomplete process of modernization,[34] new generations of scholars, many using Marxist and materialist approaches, considered Nigerian state institutions and placed them in the context of the global political economy (Nigeria as an oil rentier state) or ethno-national politics.[35] Richard Joseph's study of Nigerian prebendalism was a particularly subtle contribution to this strand of the literature. He suggested that Nigerian politics had become characterized by a very particular form of patrimonialism, which went beyond a simple patron-client system. In Nigerian prebendalism, offices themselves were a resource, because they had become the primary way in which state resources—oil money, most specifically— became available to Nigerian citizens. Not only did Joseph's insight capture something central to Nigerian politics; it touched off a cottage industry,[36] to such an extent that Peter Lewis influentially proposed a progressive typology, arguing that patrimonialism gave way to prebendalism (usually around the start of the oil boom), and since Babangida's ascent to power gave way again to "predation" in which offices are not just used as a source of wealth but as a way systematically to loot state resources.[37]

Corruption and the "Weak State"

Lewis's account is compelling in its ability to capture the changes that have occurred in Nigeria since the end of the Second Republic. These included an increasing politicization of the military, especially during the Babangida and Abacha regimes, and an increased importance of retired military officers in second careers in business and politics.[38] As some military officers exploited their political roles in the 1980s and 1990s, enjoying precisely the prebendal benefits civilians had used under the Second Republic, the ideological utility of the "army arrangement" faded: no longer might the military appear to be a guarantor of governmental probity while in practice rehabilitating civilian politicians and enriching officers. Instead, the inauguration of the Fourth Republic enabled the circulation of people and of networks of patronage between the military and civilians to spawn an intensified brand of local patronage politics dubbed "godfatherism."[39] Where civilian politics have always been structured around great men and their constellations of followers, the recent and noteworthy development is the complex relationship between political dominance and political office. While Nigeria's current godfathers do sometimes hold office, often they do not and do not aspire to do so. This can have dramatic implications for the constitutional order.

A noteworthy illustration was in Anambra state. Anambra's politics had been controlled by a godfather, Chris Uba, who dominated the local branch of the ruling PDP. Uba's candidate for governor, Dr. Chris Ngige, had been declared the winner of a disputed election in 2003. Subsequently, the governor broke from his patron, whereupon he was kidnapped. During his captivity, the governor was forced to sign a letter of resignation, though this was abrogated after his release. The governor was deposed in 2006 when a court ruled his election invalid.[40] Afterward, the former governor reemerged under the banner of other parties and was elected to the national Senate in 2011. The godfather remains a potent and respectable force in state politics. Basic constitutional issues about gubernatorial tenures in office and how they should end have become increasingly detached from public affairs and the rule of law. By themselves, such extraconstitutional political pressures are nothing new: the Western Regional crisis of the First Republic demonstrated that point. Nonetheless, Chief Akintola's consolidation of his position as premier of the Western Region, however legally dicey, was negotiated with a broad spectrum of the region's political elite and members of the ruling coalition. Lewis's suggestion about the advent of predation goes alongside the politicization of the military and the era of godfatherism. But what does this have to do with corruption and the state? All three developments pose challenges to the modernization-theory-inflected appropriations of Weber that have informed much of the existing literature.

The protean quality of analysts' appropriation of Weber stems in part from their commitment to fine-grained empirical detail, but it also has the effect of creating a strange implicit sociology that naturalizes what is supposed to have occurred in European processes of state formation and universalizes it as *the* trajectory of modernization. While most of these commentators would not explicitly assert that Nigeria and other African countries deviate from such models or are intrinsically pathological, that is something of the effect of their initial theoretical assumptions. Aside from such abstract, teleological assumptions, why might that be the case? An important line of argument emerges from Robert Jackson and Carl Rosberg's discussion of the "weak" states of Africa, which suggested there is something distinctive (if not unique to Africa or the postcolony) in the role sovereignty plays in its own perpetuation. The "weak states" paradigm responded to the objective institutional incapacity of many African states. African governments have frequently failed to exercise a monopoly of violence in their territories, and the legitimacy of uses that did occur was often open to question. Many functions at the center of modern governance—censuses, policing mechanisms, agencies for ensuring social welfare—also were not able to function consistently or systematically. The most basic information about African populations and economies is unreliable.[41] Despite these obvious incapacities, African states nonetheless show considerable stability. At the time Jackson and Rosberg wrote, no African state that had attained full independence had lost its sovereignty or split into other states. One might have expected many more such incidents given the institutional weakness of many states and the relative prevalence of secessionist movements. Jackson and Rosberg suggest the relative stability of African borders and the persistence of African states can be explained by the international state system and its need for sovereign actors in Africa as anywhere else. The logic of interstate relations requires some instrumentality called "the state" to exercise sovereign authority. The order that has emerged is better served by predictability than by some more protean arrangement, and other African states are reluctant to support secessionists elsewhere lest success there fuel dissent at home. This international order creates a space African states can occupy and use to perpetuate their own institutional existence. The state is thus a function of its sovereignty rather than the reverse.[42] Since the time Jackson and Rosberg wrote, Eritrea has regained its independence from Ethiopia. More tellingly, South Sudan's recent independence from Sudan is an instance in which an entity unified across the colonial period split in two.

The model of the weak state can be applied to Nigeria only with great caution. A striking feature of the Nigerian polity is its extraordinary, if somewhat erratic, presence. Although state organs are frequently inefficient and vastly expensive given what they actually accomplish, they are also pervasive. The police and army are visible throughout the country. Police checkpoints stop traffic throughout Nigeria; the Federal Road Safety Corps maintains other surprise checkpoints, where they examine drivers' licenses and mandated aspects of automotive safety such as having the requisite flares and reflective safety panels in case of breakdowns. Police direct traffic and monitor vehicles passing through intersections. They jump in front of cars that flout traffic laws, sometimes playing a dangerous game of chicken with drivers disinclined to stop. The officer will enter a car that has stopped and will usually negotiate an on-the-spot "fine." Driving in Nigeria is a constant reminder of the ubiquity of officialdom, even and perhaps especially when these officials of the "everyday state" exercise their power in problematic or irregular ways. For while Nigeria has a highly developed system of traffic laws and rules for licensure and vehicle operation, in practice every aspect is highly negotiable. Obtaining a driver's license often requires bribery, a fact that also results in quasi-competent drivers succeeding in the examination. An unlicensed driver who is stopped will probably need to pay more than one with the appropriate credentials, but even the most law-abiding driver is likely to be stopped and fined on one pretext or other.

State hospitals and dispensaries are also everywhere, even if they are under-staffed, ill maintained, and ill equipped, and the government also maintains an impressive array of schools and universities, though these also suffer from a terrible shortage of resources. Cultural activity itself is overseen by state bodies that codify and regularize "tradition": herbalism, spirit possession, dance, music, other long-standing forms of artistic tradition—all are subject to governing boards and monitoring. Such supervision is often a source of pa-tronage for practitioners, but it is also a source of oversight. Nigeria has a cen-sus, taxing authority, and all the organs of the modern bureaucratic regulatory state. It also has a full panoply of agencies superintending development proj-ects and other public works. All these agencies employ world-class officials, who can represent Nigeria on a world stage and who understand their work in up-to-date technocratic terms.[43] State agencies are active, and Nigerians vig-orously discuss their undertakings and engage in public debate and political contestation about them. The Nigerian state is anything but nonexistent, but its shortcomings are grave.

Two great grievances are the diversion of public money to private ends—that is, the extraordinary gulf between Nigeria's rich (who have access to state resources) and everyone else—and a basic insecurity. With the former, there is a sense that something has changed, that corruption now is worse than it has ever been and that politicians' self-interested actions are more selfish and more parochial than ever before: whereas in the past, officials benefited their home communities, now they do not bother:

> What has Kano gained from producing presidents? The Aminu Kano International Airport is the worst you can find anywhere. The city is comatose at night. The talakawas are yet to find another Aminu Kano to give them hope. The streets are in pitch darkness most nights. All our leaders live in Abuja, yet this newly created city cannot boast of ordinary traffic lights. The proponents of zoning are yet to tell us that Minna has become as beautiful as Dubai for producing two heads of state. We are yet to see the physical progress that Yorubaland enjoyed in the eight years of their luckiest son in power. Not a single road was built or rehabilitated. What was the gain of Adamawa when her son became the most powerful vice president in Nigeria's chequered history? What

was the gain of Abeokuta and Ota with their most powerful man in the presidential villa? It would probably have been better if the people had no president in their midst.[44]

Such observations are telling in the failures of patronage they target. Kano has produced two heads of state—the still-popular Murtala Muhammed, and Sani Abacha. Minna's two were Babangida and Abdulsalami Abubakar, the military leader who briefly succeeded Abacha. The references to Yorubaland, Abeokuta, and Ota are a complaint that President Obasanjo did not help his home region or even the town where he famously owns a farm. Murtala aside, the complaints focus on heads of state who ruled since General Babangida's coup in 1985; that is, the period Lewis identifies as being characterized by "predation" rather than patrimonialism. Even as an ethos of benefiting one's immediate constituency degenerated, ordinary people's vulnerability increased. Crime is rampant, and daily life is patterned by the risk of terrible violence. And while the police are ubiquitous, they are believed to do little to combat this insecurity. As a result of these intertwined changes, interpenetration of state- and non-state institutions has been perceived to gather pace across the past two decades. Politicians have long surrounded themselves with unsavory characters, groups of young men who threaten opposing political parties with violence. During the 1990s, however, the institutional breakdown in the Nigerian police had reached such a point that groups of vigilantes emerged in many areas of Nigeria and took over policing functions. For a period they were perceived as being less corrupt, often somewhat more predictable, less liable to be in cahoots with criminals than the police. With the start of civilian politics in the Fourth Republic, these vigilante organizations have increasingly been co-opted by politicians. In the north, the vigilante *hisbah* organizations enforcing Islamic law were often granted quasi-official status—though that relationship frequently proved stormy. The vigilante leaders sometimes transitioned to more conventional political careers.[45]

The changes in Nigeria that have been unspooling ever since the start of the oil boom would initially appear to be a consequence of corruption's growing ever more powerful—the military politicized, politics dominated by godfathers, government assets looted. It is painfully obvious the country's impoverishment and the systematic underfunding of public institutions are intimately tied to the diversion of oil revenue to nonofficial ends, which has contributed to increasing dysfunctionality and chaos. However, it should also be clear that "corruption" is not such a transparent label. It is a discourse rather than a discrete thing and thus cannot be an explanatory device. The implications of viewing corruption in this way are illuminated through attention to the weak-states hypothesis: Nigeria (though not only Nigeria) demands a modification that focuses less on the persistence of Nigeria as a formally unified, independent state and more on the dysfunction of government institutions and on the blurry boundary between "state" and "non-state." Such an approach demonstrates the limits of the paradigms of patrimonialism or neo-patrimonialism, or indeed of how and whether "the state" enjoys a degree of autonomy from society. All of these paradigms treat a heuristic device as normative model. Contemporary Nigeria underlines the conceptual challenges thrown up by a place where it is unclear what counts as "the state." The formal framework of state sovereignty makes obvious the worth of recognition as an actor of the Nigerian state. It suggests less that the Nigerian state is weak than that the ideological nature of all state institutions has acquired a high value in Nigeria, where the state itself heavily depends on its location within broader international structures of sovereignty and recognition. Godfatherism, for example, need not be viewed as a pathology or an index of state dysfunctionality. Indeed, it might appear less disruptive if only godfathers' political maneuvers were more predictable or the constitutional order were better suited to the patronage structures undergirding their activities. The corruption-complex creates problems because the constitutional order presupposes a different mode of politics. To the extent that critiques of corruption—up to and including prosecution—are integral to that mode of politics, exhortations toward honesty and transparency will not help.

Others have made similar observations about the persistence of patronage. William Reno has described the situation of Liberia, whose pre-1980 government was quite corrupt in the sense that its rulers benefited personally from office and irregularly diverted state funds for their own purposes, but it was remarkably stable over a long period. Reno attributes this stability to its presidents' ability to control other members of the elite through tight ties of patronage. When Master Sergeant Samuel Doe overthrew that regime in a military coup, he was unable to achieve a similar degree of control through patronage, partly because he was a member of an indigenous ethnic group rather than the Americo-Liberian elite. Doe's successor, Charles Taylor, did manage to construct a greater degree of control over a patronage network, but he was limited by the extremity of warfare during his period in power. In post-conflict Liberia, figures from the Taylor regime have reemerged, using remnants of Taylor's network to aid their rise. Reno suggests that even though such structures are overtly incompatible with norms of good governance and with the eradication of corruption, they also represent a potential for control and stability which the state would be well advised to co-opt.[46]

The principle requires careful application. In her study of informal networks of shoe and garment manufacturers in Aba, Kate Meagher argues there can be no one-size-fits-all accommodation of patronage. Under some circumstances networks provided small- and mid-size manufacturers access to social resources, stable credit, input, and markets, all of which allow them to expand their operations. In others, such networks have the effect of making it difficult for successful firms to consolidate their success because they were subject to egalitarian pressures making innovation and expansion difficult to sustain. The transition in 1999 to civilian government strengthened this unfortunate tendency by enabling entrepreneurs to seek patronage, thereby exacerbating tensions between those who enjoyed it and those who did not, even while heightening the demands of the networks themselves.[47]

Nigeria is often held up as prototypical of a kind of pathological, African, or Third World state. While it is too well financed to be a clear instance of a "weak" state that persists mainly because of its place in the international order,[48] the power of its rulers does not emerge directly from their ability to monitor, control, or even significantly influence what goes on inside the country's borders. Neither is it a simple consequence of the demands of the international system of states that every country have a government. Nigerian oil is controlled by the Nigerian government. That obvious fact gives outsiders a considerable incentive to recognize those in charge of the government as legitimate. Nonetheless, the Nigerian state does suffer from the dysfunction of its most basic institutions. Its politicians often use violence and threats as political tools. Organized criminal activity is frequently protected by state officials, and officials often themselves commit criminal acts. The inability of the police to ensure public order has resulted in public support for vigilante groups, who in some areas have begun to enjoy quasi-official status, blurring institutional distinctions between the police, vigilantes, and politicians' followings.

The seeming paradox of a ruling class whose power rests on international recognition ties in to a much broader literature on what is specific to African states. The weak-state approach is not incompatible with this literature but requires a tweak, since the figure of the weak state implies something pathological about African states in that they deviate from "normality." This literature, largely francophone and centered on francophone Africa, neither euphemizes the suffering corruption can cause nor blames it on a specifically African failure to remove patrimonialism from state bureaucracies. Jean-François Bayart argues that understanding African politics has been hampered by ethnocentric, ahistorical attempts to shoehorn African polities into developmentalist Western categories, from which they fall short. Bayart's brand of historicism avoids recapitulating a teleological paradigm of progress from patrimonialism to bureaucracy by positing there has been an enduring logic to African political relationships, which colonialism did little to disrupt. Bayart terms this logic the "politics of the belly," in which political elites demonstrate their power through conspicuous consumption. Ties of patronage channel wealth to ordinary people, but political power cannot be separated from gaudy consumerism. More than mere patrimonialism, the politics of the belly are a mode of politicking intertwined with public culture—an ethics and esthetic as well as an organizing principle. From the start of political competition (according to Bayart this was the late-colonial period, though earlier in some areas), politicians competed for access to office and the resources necessary to ensure continued success. Political competition forced regional elites to come to terms with one another, created complex networks of alliances, with both vertical and horizontal linkages. Politicians and their constituencies maneuvered within this culturalized distributive and consumptive framework.[49] Bayart's is a subtle reworking of neo-Weberian paradigms. Instead of focusing on a model of political structures that real systems approximate at least to some extent, Bayart emphasizes a mode of political maneuver. He conjoins institutional analysis with ethnography. For Bayart, the African state is distinctive because its contours diverge from formal institutions and political practice. In a rather darker vein, Mbembe has extended these insights, pointing out that this politics of the belly has a complex aesthetic of the vulgarity of power and is based on a very deep authoritarian logic he terms "commandement."[50]

In a book that takes issue with Bayart but finishes in a somewhat similar position, Patrick Chabal and Jean-Pascal Deloz suggest that such *longue durée* pictures of a generic African political mentality are an inadequate solution to empty ahistoricism. Where Bayart suggests a utility to the politics of the belly, Chabal and Deloz emphasize the failure of the African state to become autonomous from society. The African state in their formulation is "essentially vacuous": it holds no Weberian monopoly on the legitimate use of force; it is not distinct from society; and formally bureaucratic structures instantiate rather than replace patrimonial ones. The result is a politics resting on politicized cultural distinctions, very often ethnic groups that channel political competition, and a reliance on political disorder—extralegal behavior, the use of violence by formally non-state actors like rioters or vigilantes. This situation, Chabal and Deloz conclude, helps to explain the political difficulties of contemporary African states but does little to suggest how these woes might be ameliorated.[51] A similarly glum conclusion emerges from Jean-François Bayart, Stephen Ellis, and Béatrice Hibou's *Criminalization of the State in Africa*, which notes that the increasing imbrication of African states in criminal activity has led to the disappearance of distinctions between state and non-state, sovereign and criminal.[52]

Despite their differences, these authors collectively furnish an important reminder about the travails of postcolonial politics, and they have gone far beyond paradigms that might attribute the difficulties to African primitivism. One might criticize a tendency to homogenize disparate historical and cultural experiences, though in part this is a consequence of the books' relative brevity and of the challenges of comparative work.[53] These writers have proposed a valuable extension of neo-Weberian paradigms, avoiding the teleological trajectories that often were the legacy of modernization theory. Nonetheless, an issue remains with the ideological figure of the state in their work. To the extent the secondary literature on corruption depends on an implicit model of the state, the question is how to reconcile oneself to the confusion emerging from nearly sixty years of conflating descriptive and normative appropriations of Weberian ideal types.[54]

Corruption is yet more complicated because it is moralizing: corruption discourse is about matters of right and wrong. In a country like Nigeria, "corruption" has typically been used to criticize practices dictated by forces formally epiphemomenal to the constitutive logic of the state. A politician's distribution of state resources to his clients is not part of his formal responsibilities, and yet it can be an act of political survival, necessary but forbidden. To the extent that both grand and petty corruption are built into everyday practice, they are an informal aspect of normal government processes, an often-pricey surcharge on state services. The diversion of resources is burdensome given ordinary Nigerians' poverty. While commentators have noted the potential utility of some corrupt practices, they also complain that widespread corruption makes government decision making unpredictable. It is one thing to budget for substantial cost overruns as the normal order of business, quite another for half the world's concrete supply to arrive in Lagos. Corruption discourse is useful to the extent it enables moral claims instead of naturalizing representations of an idealized state. Searching for something specific to African states, or neo-patrimonial regimes, gets beyond unproductive binaries of right-wrong, legal-illegal, or utilitarian-pathological, but it also implicitly claims European countries abide by them, and suggests the only hope for Africa is to begin to accord with political forms in the outside world. Trying to go beyond simple condemnation requires being more precise about what one means by invoking "the state."

During the 1980s a group of scholars followed Philip Abrams in developing Radcliffe-Brown's proposal beyond its original ethnographic application. Abrams underlined the elusiveness of the state/society distinction, and he proposed that resulting questions about the nature of the state might be addressed through Radcliffe-Brown's methodological proposal of viewing it as a collection of institutions and individuals. For Abrams, the state was an ideological project rather than an analytic artifact. Abrams placed equal weight on the "philosopher's fiction" that it was also an idea of a coherent, powerful whole. For him, the fiction was not trivial; the state's various components depend on the notion of its unity and coherence as a way to legitimate their own actions.[55] So a police officer who devotes all working hours to extorting bribes from motorists is more than a criminal in official garb because he or she exercises power as an agent of the state. The power is real even if its basis is illusory. Paradoxically "state" power is most purely manifested in interactions where agents invoke the power that the state apparently gives them. The state appears to legitimate individual action when in fact those actions are its only concrete manifestation.[56]

Timothy Mitchell pointed out that this "state-effect" went beyond legitimation or creating a sense of omnipresent, unified state power. The ideological project of making a heterogeneous network of people and instrumentalities appear to be unified also had the effect of making the state appear to be distinct from society and from the economy. These distinctions and the centrality of the state are the defining features of modern political society.[57] The state-effect is a matter of ideology and appearance, but the appearance of unity and autonomy has real-world consequences. It makes state actors more powerful as part of a much larger whole.[58] Moreover, the state-effect's symbolic density shapes our perceptions; metaphors become experiential realities. Thus, Akhil Gupta and James Ferguson have argued the very move that brings together dispersed instrumentalities, locations, and agencies also makes the state appear to possess particular spatial characteristics—it is "above" local agencies, or "encompasses" them.[59] Similarly, Deborah Poole and Veena Das have argued that the state's margins—both literal and the social domains excluded from the real official politics which therefore serve as the state's constitutive outside—are critical for understanding the nature and the limits of state power.[60]

This approach provides a different optic on the nature of the Nigerian state. Instead of being a set of real-world institutions that approximate Western models more or less well, the Nigerian state is an ideological project of labeling the activities of particular actors as being those of "state" officials. The ideological project of "the state" makes the institution appear to be more than the sum of its parts, to have spatializing characteristics, or to have the quality of not being political or nakedly extractive. This ideological work plays out in unexpected ways given the political-economic logic of Nigeria's government. An approach that retains many of the utilities of the weak-states paradigm is Cooper's influential description of the "gatekeeper state" characterized by elites who control the relatively constricted interface of the national and global economies. Cooper argues that the prevalence of gatekeeper states in Africa arises not from anything intrinsic to Africa's political institutions but as a consequence of the legacy of many centuries of economic dependence. Africa's relationship to the global economy has long been one of export: human beings, gold, ivory, and other minerals and agricultural goods. Colonial regimes intensified this dynamic while refusing to capitalize anything but the most minimal infrastructure necessary to enable exports. That political-economic relationship between African economies and the world economy created states whose authority neatly mirrored their capacities and incapacities. The colonial state and its postcolonial successors exist to maintain existing patterns of export, and they owe their continued authority through their tenure in that economically critical choke point. Beyond that, their success can be more limited. Bayart terms this quality Africa's "extraversion," and it helps to explain how African states persist despite institutional weakness.[61] This is a useful insight, given the caveat that the extraverted, gatekeeping state is neither peculiarly African nor uniform. Modes of engagement with the global economy arose because of contingent, local historical processes: both Nigeria and, for example, Rwanda can be considered extraverted and gatekeeping, but they bear little resemblance to one another.

Corruption discourse underlines one aspect of Nigeria's extraversion. James Scott has influentially argued that "modernist" systems of government have a tendency to reengineer social systems in order to make them more orderly and thus more transparent and susceptible to external monitoring and regulation.[62] Whatever happened elsewhere in the world, government projects in Nigeria have been characterized less by *seeing* like a state than by *looking* like one. Many incidents in the history of Nigerian administrative reorganization were aimed to make social and political relationships more regular and transparent, from the creation of districts and reorganization of the tax system in the north during the early colonial period to the reorganization and standardization of market stalls or initiatives toward governmental transparency more recently. Such initiatives cannot be taken at face value, or at least their overt purpose was not some ordered regularity, as with the revenue survey for the land tax described in chapter 1. Revenue maps bore an attenuated relationship to actual patterns of occupation or ownership because they were the product of negotiation between farmers, survey officials, and local administrators. In this instance and many others, "modernist" administrative techniques were a fantasy with serious consequences.[63] To the extent that corruption discourse condemns practices for deviating from the norms of bureaucratic governance, it is a political performative. However, when bureaucratic structures themselves are problematic, corruption discourse is no simple tool of technocratic critique. It underpins the ideological process through which the Nigerian state-effect functions at all. A condemnation of "corruption" implies a vision of a non-corrupt alternative, not degenerated, properly bureaucratic, fully modernized. It is a legitimating fiction, all the more powerful because it operates through its own denial.

If most African states are noteworthy for their extraversion, or for the way in which their political elites situate themselves at the juncture between the domestic and world economies, the state's ideological function is determined by the ways in which these gatekeeping elites attain and invoke their legitimacy as "state" authorities. And to the extent the state is extraverted, elites will assert their power through an appeal to the international community, recognizing themselves in and through outside recognition. Nigerians' careful attention to the country's international reputation becomes more immediately explicable, since that external audience is critical to the state's ability to claim its own existence. Corruption is not a set of distinct, definable malpractices but a stance individuals take toward and within the ideological project of the state. In a decision of whether to prosecute or not, the considerations are more delicate than whether any individual is guilty of a particular malpractice. Ultimately, the ideological overlay of his or her actions as "state" actions is in question, which is overdetermined by a set of political struggles within patronage networks involving elites and paralleling governmental institutions.

The problem of corruption is domestic, and it is thus most importantly and immediately mediated through the moral economies of corruption discussed in chapter 4. It is also an international embarrassment, a matter for Transparency International, a problem that precludes international investment, and a roadblock to development. Nigeria's dependence on international institutions—financial, governmental—places its political elites in a peculiar and vulnerable position. It is no coincidence that an elite which depends on its mediating role with the external economy should be marked domestically with its consumption of imported goods. Elites drive fancy (imported) cars, wear imported clothes. They eat imported food. They travel internationally. Nigeria is one of the world's greatest per capita consumers of champagne, though needless to say only a tiny percentage of the country actually consumes it.[64] Ordinary Nigerians are even more perilously situated. Their livelihoods are also dependent on Nigeria's position within the global economy, but they reap fewer benefits. This acute vulnerability to the external does bring a distinctive quality to Nigerian extraversion, though its manifestation as a particular kind of state is somewhat indirect. Instead of seeing Nigeria as an instance of some sort of distinctive African ideal type—as the weak-states paradigm would have it—one must see what is distinctive as a particular quality to the ideological process through which state actors are identified as such, in the meanings that being an official of the state takes on, and how those intersect with the legalities and moral evaluations of official conduct. This approach provides a very different angle on the nature of the state itself, and corruption discourse is almost unique in revealing this process.

"Corruption" designates something more than simply oppressive, self-interested, accumulative, illegal actions by state actors—that is, as practices *epiphenomenal* to the state. In this way of thinking, corruption marks the failure of the state, to the extent that the state is an ideological device, an entity that relabels individual activity as supra-local and disinterested. But it is a failure that presupposes a state dependent on this practice of euphemization. "Corruption" can be applied as a label precisely when officials' practices, even though supported by the machinery of the government, are perceived as interested, local, and oppressive. This possibility of labeling suggests the state succeeds through failure and fails through success, when state actors violate the canons of official behavior and when an official's status as such makes irregular action possible. Corruption is the mark of a category error. The history of local administration in northern Nigeria demonstrates this contention. The local-government reorganization increased the ability of officials of the Sokoto Caliphate's emirate hierarchy to extract revenue from commoners while removing some of the checks on their doing so. The colonial conceit was that retaining African officials would result in a retention of their legitimacy, and in this way the modernizing colonial regime would enjoy the ideological and political benefits of state authority and euphemization.

The implacable presence of popular condemnation of official actions—as being "corrupt" in one sense or another—in Nigerian narratives of government activity in the end demonstrates that the Nigerian state is active, but in a highly problematic way. Officials are able to operate as "state" actors, but their actions are also perceived as illegitimate. Ironically, the Nigerian government has proven fully able to exercise its coercive function in particular instances, but only at the cost of achieving a regime of systematic or regularized control. The euphemizing and legitimating state-effect has never functioned successfully. To no small extent, the colonial regime assumed all was well when revenue targets were met and when there were no overt political disturbances. Minimal markers of effectiveness denoted a functional state. But the regulative and legitimating functions of state, resulting in a delocalizing effect and dependent on a highly artificial distinction between public and private, never really worked.

The history of state formation in Northern Nigeria, then, is not (as Scott would have it) one of a government's coming to "see like a state" but rather of a transformation that enabled it to *look like* one. The euphemizing quality of the state-effect never got off the ground, though forms of state practice did emerge and did create an administration that could function, for outsiders, as a convincing stand-in. The logic of the state structure acts, at least in part, to cover over the state's inability to act as it "ought," and this does have consequences. The state-effect masks ordinary people's cynical and resigned appreciation that government officials are bent on personal enrichment and on the maintenance of personalistic chains of patron-client ties. The state-effect constitutes the Nigerian state as it appears to outside eyes, and so makes the country explicable within the context of the international state system. In doing so, it covers over a more complex process by which governmental actions are evaluated internally, a most complex moral economy in which some "corruption" can appear acceptable and other corruption not, in which the oppression of some can appear admirable to others, and in which the politics of identity emerge from the politics of position—ethnic, religious, regional.

Even if the euphemizing aspect of the state-effect has not resulted in much popular mystification, it has nonetheless been useful for *external* claims to legitimacy. State actors can identify themselves as state actors, if sometimes corrupt ones. Thus, officials can make claims on the coercive machinery of the government with exterior legitimacy. The ideological isolation of the Nigerian state calls into question the utility of the state as an analytic concept, or rather it underlines the necessity of clearly differentiating between empirical state actors and ideological projects or claims. The Nigerian state may do no more than look like a state. Is this so terribly unusual? The history of corruption in northern Nigeria underlines the necessity of agnosticism toward official accounts of what state agents are doing. Perhaps more interestingly, the distinction between the empirical and the ideological calls into question the utility of "legitimacy" as an explanatory force. To the extent that legitimacy is used to explain popular acquiescence to state actions, it can only be inferred from states of affairs it is supposed to explain. If people do not overtly protest, the state is "legitimate."

The circular quality to invocations of state legitimacy underlines the necessity of being clear on what states legitimate to whom, and what these maneuvers actually accomplish. The failure of the Nigerian state-effect has consequences. Even as state agents are able to mobilize the government's coercive machinery—and to appropriate its resources to their own ends—they remain cut off from the networks of grassroots authority that might temper their actions. The net result is that "the state" is, except in a grossly empirical sense, an illusion. The tragedy of this situation is that the distribution of various public goods—such as development money, revenue from oil exports, and basic commodities such as petrol—is dependent on a disinterested and rationalized bureaucratic system that does not actually exist. This, in the last analysis, is a most important and most unfortunate legacy of the past century.

But where does that leave us? If the material practices of corruption are as much a symptom of Nigeria's political troubles as a cause, and if the political system that generates so much of this concrete corruption depends on corruption discourse as an integral part, am I arguing ultimately for stopping the attempt to rein in corruption altogether? While I would argue that the various strategies proposed for reining it in—everything from legal strategies like the War against Indiscipline or the EFCC to initiatives in civil society—are ultimately insufficiently attentive to the historical causes of today's problems, that does not imply one must simply accept the status quo. Pieces of a more realistic and more enduring solution become evident from the arguments of the preceding chapters. One aspect is Odia Ofeimun's exhortation about taking Nigeria seriously discussed in the last chapter. As chapters 2 and 3 demonstrated, one of the reasons that corruption became institutionalized within the Nigerian government was the pattern of sectional competition that began with the inauguration of a federal parliament after World War II. Although Nigeria's vastly more complicated federal system has considerably defused the pattern of zero-sum regional competition, it still inflects political practice, and political malpractice. However, it is clearly insufficient simply to exhort Nigerians to take the country seriously. But what is the alternative? Although the current political system continues to institutionalize regional difference through doctrines of state residency, Nigerians continue to be extremely mobile. Not only the elite, but people from every walk of life travel regularly around the country, and a very considerable percentage of the population does not live in the states of which they are indigenes. In the long run, this pattern of national cosmopolitanism, along with aspects of national popular and consumer culture, will combine with patterns of interethnic and interreligious sociality to detach patron-client chains from geography. This is not a policy so much as an organic development, but I think it will have more profound legacies than any state-mandated program of national integration.

Another obvious factor is the Nigerian economy's dependence on oil export, and more broadly on the classic gatekeeping role of the Nigerian state and elite. To the extent that access to state office is the primary means by which one can get access to large-scale capital, corruption in the Nigerian government is a nearly inevitable by-product of economic structure. The key to getting around it is not so much to attempt to diminish the role the state plays in the economy (as Larry Diamond among others advocated many years ago)[65] as it is to expand and diversify Nigeria's economic contacts with the outside world. Access to state resources—and diverting them to private ends—will be less of an object if there are other ways to become rich and powerful. Again, this is not necessarily something that can be achieved through a concerted program. Nonetheless, a changing relationship to the international economy will, I think, in the long run have surprising effects on the incidence of material corruption.

CONCLUSION

In April 2013, Transparency International issued a press release disavowing connection with a group called Transparency in Nigeria (TIN). The latter organization had recently issued a "Budget Discipline Perception Index" that ranked the budgets and accomplishments of Nigeria's state governments. Transparency in Nigeria strongly implied its report issued ultimately from the international body. Transparency International protested it "has no links with 'Transparency in Nigeria,' nor does it currently have an affiliate in Nigeria."[1] The relationship was slightly closer than TI asserted: Transparency in Nigeria had been a TI affiliate until 2011, when it was disaffiliated from the international organization.[2] Transparency in Nigeria garnered additional attention in July 2013, when press coverage of Transparency International's Global Corruption Barometer inaccurately suggested Nigeria had just been ranked as the eighth-most-corrupt country in the world.[3] Nigeria ranked eighth in the barometer's question about whether a country's citizens considered corruption to be a major problem, but its performance in other metrics varied considerably. Nonetheless, the Nigerian government responded defensively, pointing out TI had published no such ranking.[4] The special assistant to the president (New Media) proceeded to recount Transparency in Nigeria's disavowal by the international secretariat, going on to note that many media outlets were controlled by opposition politicians. His press release did not assert that TIN was behind the news stories or that the organization was controlled by the opposition, but the implication was clear.

While there is no evidence to suggest TIN had choreographed the unflattering interpretation of the Global Corruption Barometer, the incident demonstrated once again the country's sensitivity to international coverage of Nigerian corruption and the deeply political nature of all discussions of the subject. Transparency in Nigeria itself is a prime exhibit of this domestic politics of reputation. The Budget Discipline Perception Index (BDPI) had been distributed by a journalist named Abba Anwar, and its contours demonstrated Nigerian domestic political concerns. The BDPI was complimentary to Governor Rabi'u Kwankwaso of Kano state, which came out at the top of the index,[5] something a movement of his supporters called the Kwankwasiyya was quick to trumpet.[6] Transparency International's disavowal of the index received a fast response on the Kwankwasiyya Facebook page, noting that the study was objectively accurate, whatever its author's institutional affiliations, and that the ties between TI and TIN were more enduring than the international body would admit: "Who sponsored . . . Abba Anwar to some training programmes in United Kingdom and United States of America (USA), among other nations of the world, sometimes in the past? So to even say Transparency in Nigeria has no link with Transparency International is nothing but a misnomer."[7] Although TIN might be tightly tied to Governor Kwankwaso, its members claimed international cachet because of training received through TI sponsorship. The extraversion of the Nigerian elite, the importance of a reputation for fighting corruption, and the central importance of ties of patronage and affiliation were all nakedly illustrated in the incident.

One could take this exchange as an "only in Nigeria" moment, when even Transparency International became an object of 419 posturing by a state government. There is doubtless something particularly extreme in Nigeria's "culture of corruption," as Daniel Jordan Smith has termed it. Material acts termed "corruption" are not restricted to state and public institutions. Private enterprise and nongovernmental organizations alike have been plagued by bribe taking and other forms of malpractice, which would easily be termed "corruption" were they in the public sector. Part I one of this book developed an account of how this state of affairs came about. This history requires some emendation of the implicit histories much of the literature on corruption has assumed in order to develop an account of corruption as a global phenomenon. Conceptualizations of corruption as a species of patrimonialism and allied notions of corruption as rent seeking rely on an implicit figure of a "normal" state to which the Nigerian (or other corrupt) state might be contrasted. The implicit history such an account develops of Western states—assumed gradually to have purged themselves of corruption—misses the role corruption discourse played in processes of political change in those states. Nigerian history demonstrates that corruption is not simply a persistence of older processes of politics, nor is it an ongoing pattern of economic behavior that could be discouraged given adequate incentives.

The history of corruption discourse in Nigeria demonstrates the country's deep particularity. Historicist accounts of corruption have tended to take one of two approaches. The first, emerging from intellectual history and political theory, historicizes the paradigms through which "corruption" has been understood, an intellectual trajectory moving from Aristotle through Machiavelli and culminating in the "modernist" moment of the present. In this view, "corruption" is a popular form of political philosophy in which notions of good and appropriate political behavior can be described and debated. Much of the social science literature remains caught in a second historicist notion emanating from modernization theory. Following early commentators like Joseph Nye or Wraith and Simpkins, they suppose that "corruption" is a problem all modernizing countries have been forced to deal with.[8] In that case, Nigerian history could be interpreted as an extreme instance of a common pattern in which political systems centering on patron-clientage were drawn into a modern constitutional order. Such an account would be compatible with an acknowledgment that the Nigerian state has been gravely handicapped by its peripheral location in the world economic order, its corruption exacerbated and entrenched by its gatekeeping role. Indeed, one can also acknowledge the role played by Nigeria's sectional and ethnic conflicts and by its status as an oil-rentier state.

Part I of this book demonstrated that such a view was insufficient. The story of Nigerian corruption is not simply one in which the country followed a trajectory traced by countless others—either all "modernizing" states or perhaps postcolonial ones. The contemporary Nigerian state emerged from institutions pioneered by the British colonial regime. In these institutions "corruption" was a label that might be used to explain getting rid of officials in political trouble. Persistent patronage and incomplete modernization are inadequate glosses for a more intricate set of political struggles. That legacy helped to constitute Nigeria's specific history of "corruption" as a political performative. More than a shifting set of malpractices, the Nigerian corruption-complex became central to state practice; deploying the charge of "corruption" served political ends. Corrupt practices were inseparable from the *charge* of corruption, which itself has been inseparable from patterns of political contestation. That history is deeply rooted in the legacies of Nigerian federalism and political competition. Then in the postcolonial period and particularly after 1970, Nigeria's notoriety for corruption created new opportunities for corrupt behavior. If nothing else, the 419 e-mails would not have been possible without that reputation. Corruption is inexorably tied to the history of the Nigerian polity, and in particular its complex regional and ethnic politics, and the logistical demands of administering and distributing oil revenue.

What aspects of this history can be generalized? The specifics cannot. Some might find it useful to construct typologies of countries and to trace the ways in which analogous histories create similar trajectories of national corruption-complexes. The historical account developed in part I of this book made a more modest contribution to comparative discussions of corruption. By demystifying the history of corruption in Nigeria, it demonstrated that corruption cannot be taken as a simple or straightforward set of political malpractices. It is a political performative whose importance can only be assessed in local historical context. So corruption cannot be viewed as one problem but as a family of problems and as a genre of political discourse demanding evaluation. Nigerian history shows corruption politics can illuminate political life more generally. Corruption cannot be fully appreciated without a relatively systematic attention to the history not just of corrupt practices but of the ways in which "corruption" has functioned as a means of engaging in politics and political critique. Part of that account must be a history of the ways in which external forces and paradigms of corruption have impinged on local ones. To this extent, it would be a mistake to attempt to describe a particularly "African" or "Third World" corruption. While obviously there are family resemblances between forms of corruption, and while there are historical parallels across Africa and beyond, the development of corruption-complexes is inextricably tied to the histories of individual polities. Generalization requires caution. In the past several decades, international discourse about corruption and political pressures on countries accused of permitting it have increased tremendously. *Corruption* may not be a label that has *analytic* purchase beyond local usage, but it nonetheless must frequently be addressed as a general problem: that is how actors around the world use the term, not infrequently while also relying on localized systems of meaning. By itself, the historical analysis of corruption can only cautiously be generalized.

Part II took up that challenge, using the previous discussion of Nigerian history to develop two broader points that might find application elsewhere. Chapter 4 developed a critical analysis of the moral economy of corruption-discourse. Have Nigeria's rulers transgressed a collective consensus about a permissible degree of diverting public resources to private ends, and if so when? This is an important question given the sense of crisis that has long pervaded Nigerian popular discourse: corruption is worse than ever before, the people's situation more desperate. As chapter 4 argued, the moral economy is something of a mirage, an explanation that is satisfying only at a distance. Corruption discourse appears to be the expression of outrage over the violation of norms, but in the end it perpetuates and entrenches precisely the modes of politics that outrage it. Only the most exceptional critiques, such as Odia Ofeimun's, promise something different from further entrenchment of the corruption-complex. Similarly, chapter 5 argued that the history of corruption in Nigeria requires a reevaluation of paradigms of the state. Paralleling recent work in the tradition of Philip Abrams, it argued that the state was ideological figure more than objective reality, and that the Nigerian state was striking in the starkness of its contradictions. That argument's important caveat is that this contradictory quality should not be presumed to be unique to Nigeria, or Africa, or postcolonial states. Instead, it suggests the need for agnosticism about the nature of states everywhere.

That points back to the question of whether Nigeria is so unusual that its experience cannot be generalized. Is corruption in Nigeria simply an extreme form of more general tendencies and historical experiences? My analysis points to radical particularism. Corruption in Nigeria cannot be disentangled from the institutional history of its politics, from the trajectory of its economy and its patterns of political and regional competition, or from the ways political actors engage with the corruption-complex. If corruption is a political performative, it cannot be extracted from the specific contexts in which corruption discourse is deployed. At the same time, corruption remains a global discourse, and particularly since the start of the oil boom the international reception of Nigerian corruption has been an integral part of even its domestic dynamics. So perhaps one could conclude that Nigerian corruption is a local phenomenon, but one that grew up in relation to a global counterpart.

While the argument in this book emphasizes the local and particular, its implications are of wider scope. Nigerian corruption can only be understood by juxtaposing local, national, and global scales of analysis and following them across time; that mode of analysis would apply elsewhere. Taking corruption not to be an objective fact or a determinate body of practices but rather a shifting array of practices labeled "corrupt" and an ever-changing terrain of moral discourse suggests that academic approaches to corruption must themselves acknowledge their own political ends. Instead of imagining that one offers disinterested policy advice—conceptualized as an objective array of strategies that could be adopted in order to achieve proper politico-economic development—one might view policy proposals in a broader, always-politicized frame. "Corruption" is not an analytic category; rather it is itself deployed to particular ends. While the political grounding of corruption discourse varies from one historical and cultural context to another, the lesson applies generally.

Corruption should therefore be viewed as a source for interpreting the cultural history of politics. This is not a surprising conclusion from an academic historian. Many scholars and policy makers have more practical concerns. What is one to do if one wishes to start a factory in Nigeria (or anywhere else) and is being extorted for bribes from different competing government agents? What is one to do if one wants to attract such international investment without deterring investors by subjecting them to such demands? How might a country like Nigeria achieve patterns of economic change that improve the lives of a greater percentage of its citizens? Calling the problem "corruption" and attempting to wipe it out—whether through exhortation or enforcement—will be unlikely to make much practical change given the broader context. It would also not work to attempt to emulate other experiences. There are countries—Malaysia, for example—that have emerged from extreme poverty. That country's ruling coalition has suffered from political scandals; accusations of cronyism are rampant and compelling. However, it has not fallen into the same pattern of political looting as Nigeria, and while there is a rich, politically connected elite, the lives of ordinary people have also changed profoundly.[9] The import of a historicist approach is that the distinction between Malaysia and Nigeria cannot be boiled down to a set of "lessons" that the latter could learn from the former. The riddle for all concerned is to find ways to bring the basic logic driving practices labeled "corruption" into accordance with the institutional demands that might be placed on them. The trick is not to assume Nigerian political society must change. Rather, it is to bring into being a better, more cooperative, and probably more egalitarian future.

International discourses on corruption have a long history. I am not the first writer to point that out. We know that corruption has changed over time. As one recent commentator put it, "Corruption is not what it used to be. While corruption used to imply a wide variety of morally dishonorable acts . . . [now it] refers to a set of actions of a distinctly material character which was not always shared by older conceptions."[10] However, it is not helpful to imagine that history is one of changing analytics for approaching a more-or-less constant object. Scholars have long known that ancient, medieval, and early modern notions of corruption are not equivalent to those of the present: paradigms of decay and degeneration gave way to other methods of understanding government malpractice. Nonetheless, a strong current of theorization of corruption depends on notions of transformation and deviance. Mark Philps, for example, has influentially argued that all definitions of political corruption depend on "some 'naturally sound condition' (variously described) from which corrupt acts deviate," suggesting that the key to understanding corruption is the notion of the ethical value of politics that one adopts.[11]

Similarly, scholars have detailed how conceptions of government misconduct have changed over time. The choice to call such genealogies of political critique "histories of corruption" is already to engage in an unfortunate nominalism. "Corruption" is not one thing. Discussions of corruption will thus vary depending on one's aims. Viewing corruption as crime or malpractice leads one to presuppose a set of moral principles, losing track of their contingency. My point is not that corruption is a social construct and thus imaginary, or that because corruption is historically and culturally contingent it is thus not open to condemnation on the basis of universal principles. The corruption-complex is a set of practices and ways for describing them that simultaneously critique and enable those practices to happen in the first place. There is nothing wrong with condemning corruption. Doing so is sensible, and often morally imperative. But condemning discrete instances of corruption necessarily involves the commentator in the phenomena she is attempting to describe. If one takes historical figures—Nuhu Ribadu, for example, or Farida Waziri—and describes their fights against corruption, one is forced to take a position on the legalities of the crimes they investigated and prosecuted. One *also* interprets Ribadu and Waziri as successful or not successful, genuine campaigners against corruption or servants of power. The problem is that doing so naturalizes a set of ideological presuppositions that are themselves part of the problem. Whether one thinks of corruption as being the persistence of patrimonialism or considers it to be a species of rent seeking insufficiently constrained by norms of good governance, the solution to the problem is distressingly elusive. The frustration perceptible in most public discussion of corruption one hears in Nigeria stems from the fact that they boil down to little more than condemnation and exhortation. Corruption is bad, and it can be avoided through sufficient willpower, greater awareness, and dedication to its eradication.

The prescriptions offered by economists and by organizations like Transparency International are similarly unconvincing. On one hand, these prescriptions include the inauguration of investigative, prosecutorial, or quasi-judicial forces, and initiatives like crowd-sourcing corruption reports. On the other, they involve initiatives for greater transparency in government in the hopes that corrupt practices will not be able to take place under public scrutiny. Such prescriptions are carefully thought through, and if fully implemented might work. For a historian, the problem with them is that real-world institutions do not emerge because of some disembodied process of public choice. Policy

makers do not simply pick from a menu of alternatives according to their preference orderings or those of others. Laws and institutions emerge through
contingent and often haphazard processes. Public-choice theorists do not pretend their models are manuals of political strategy, but they also often avoid
the problem of creating initiatives within a political culture that produced the
problems in the first place. And the empirical history of Nigerian corruption
demonstrates nothing if not that the charge of corruption is a central facet of
Nigerian politics. Even if political actors were genuinely committed to eradicating corruption—many are, at least in the abstract—it is difficult to escape
the multifaceted utilities of Nigerian corruption discourse. While it would be
difficult for any observer to laud both Nuhu Ribadu and Farida Waziri for
their anticorruption bona fides, considering either as historical figures requires more than hagiography or even balancing genuine judiciousness and
political calculation. The problem is that corruption discourse itself is part of
the system it is also attempting to critique and control. That is where moral
economy and of the ideological contradictions of the Nigerian state become
pressing and relevant.

Nigerians can almost universally agree that corruption is bad and that
the country's rampant corruption is largely responsible for its current woes.
There is less agreement on who precisely is corrupt. One is most likely to absolve
figures enmeshed in one's own chains of patronage and obligation. People are
likely to absolve figures in inverse proportion to their contemporary political
relevance. Thus, First Republic politicians are discussed more charitably than
Second Republic politicians. Government figures from the military regimes of
the 1980s and 1990s are discussed more leniently than Fourth Republic politicians. In my own experience, the most stunning development is the partial
rehabilitation of Sani Abacha's reputation. My first visit to Nigeria began immediately after the annulled election of 12 June 1993, but I truly came to know
the country after Sani Abacha took power later that year, during an eighteen-
month stay in 1996–97, when the Abacha regime had really shown its repressive character.

During that time, the only people I met who had kind words to say about
the government were its own officials and people with close government ties.
Driving past police barracks, people discussed the atrocities that had been
committed by the police and security forces, and they spoke quietly about people who had disappeared or been taken away. Such stories were intertwined
with those of rampant government theft and more quotidian violence from
state agents. Since then, there has been an effort to rehabilitate General Abacha's
reputation, and meanwhile many people remember his regime with greater

fondness than they exhibited at the time. I have discussed narratives of petrol shortages and black marketing, and people's relationships to the various actors involved helped to determine their investment in the stories of who was to blame. During the Abacha regime, Olusegun Obasanjo was remembered as having been fairly honest as a head of state, and indeed he was admired as an opponent of what was then understood to be a much more brutal military regime. His winning the presidency changed people's attitudes, and he is now often vilified as one of the most corrupt heads of state Nigeria has ever had. His continued involvement in Nigerian politics doubtless tends to compound that ongoing lack of admiration.

Akhil Gupta has suggested that *narratives* of corruption are part and parcel of corrupt practices, that indeed such narratives constitute much of ordinary people's affective relationship to state institutions.[12] This is an important point, but it does not fully acknowledge the degree of political work that discourses of corruption accomplish. Corruption reveals an entire moral economy of citizen-state relations, a normative scheme for evaluating official practices and how much might "legitimately" be diverted to unofficial ends. But the concept of moral economy encourages circular logic. Outrage requires a supplementary evaluation, because there is no consensus about an "appropriate" degree of corruption beyond which it becomes immoral. More to the point, there is an epistemic murkiness to actual corrupt practices. It would be difficult to argue that any particular figure has transgressed a boundary for "legitimate" amounts of corruption because it is nearly impossible to be certain how much has been stolen. Acknowledgment of a figure's corruption is a signal of disapprobation and a sign of positioning oneself in opposition to him or her. Under circumstances that make it very difficult to be certain of the truth or falsity of any given set of charges, one's conclusions are often ultimately a matter of faith. Thus, for example, one of the primary bits of evidence cited against President Obasanjo is the wealth and success of his farm, a mechanized, vastly profitable concern. How, ask his detractors, is this to be explained given its relative lack of success during the Abacha period? How could the president have managed to capitalize his farm so successfully during his time in office, when the farm really took off as a profit-making enterprise? The farm's success would only have been possible due to massive investment, and this would have been possible only by misappropriating public money.

As the investigations into officials accused of corruption have been regularly discovering for over a century, it is difficult to reach definitive conclusions about such accusations. Only the most naïve would conclude they had ever been disproven. Given the tenor of absolute conviction that undergirds most corruption allegations, it is clear that the corruption-complex does not operate as a mechanism for *limiting* or constraining the absolute scope of "corrupt" activities. That is not to say that a supporter's optimistic assessment of a politician's probity stems from a desire to euphemize or minimize his or her crimes, nor to assert that the politician's malpractices fell below the threshold of unacceptability. Rather, as Odia Ofeimun so brilliantly demonstrated, the moral economy of corruption suggests ultimately the nature of Nigerian political society. The issue is not what level of political malfeasance might be tolerated but rather the far deeper and more troubling question of how the political economy distributes resources, and particularly how the claims of different regions of Nigeria might be balanced against one another. That, similarly, stands behind the normative vision undergirding "Army Arrangement." At stake is a future in which rampant thievery is ubiquitous. The vision of a future in which young people "see and hear" is ultimately a vision of economic enfranchisement, and one in which public scrutiny is able to serve as an effective check on official malfeasance. The critique is of the "gatekeeper" system in which a political elite controls the international economy's access to Nigerian resources and is then able to use its position to extract enormous rents. "Seeing" and "hearing" are not simple synonyms for greater governmental transparency or an appropriate set of incentives for that political elite. They constitute a vision of substantive democracy and enfranchisement. By itself this vision is not a realistic political program, but it does suggest the corruption-complex is more than a pathology, more than a cultural stance that enables political malpractice even while condemning it.

This is where my suggestions about the state as an ideological device came in. Part I took "the state" in a substantive sense, to denote the institutions of the Nigerian government, glossing over their ineluctable heterogeneity. Chapter 5 underlined the conceptual incoherence of such a position and demonstrated that corruption emerges from and depends on the state's ideological aspects. "Corruption" is the sign of an action that is contained within the state's ideological process—it is the "improper" action of a person whose actions should be considered impersonal, the agency of "the state" rather than of a person's will. But by being improper, it is simultaneously enabled by and excluded from the scope of "the state." Narratives of corruption contain within themselves signs of this device's simultaneous success and failure, and they also point to the political work corruption talk accomplishes and some ways of addressing the problem that may in the long term prove more productive than exhortations to good behavior or the creation of reformist institutions. Corruption signals the failure of the state-effect because it requires viewing officials' practices as *not* being legitimate or appropriate state actions but rather as being private crimes. But it is also a success, because it presupposes there are norms and codes that are part of being a state actor, not just an individual maker of contingent decisions.

What does this tell us about corruption as a comparative phenomenon? The argument of this book is that corruption discourse has a long history as a global occurrence, and that history is well known. There is also a long history of articulations between that global discourse and its political use in particular locales. Understanding corruption requires understanding this history of intellectual and political interaction around the world, all taking place as if corruption were applied to a discrete and coherent object. The history of corruption around the world is a history of global politics, and it is a history bringing together myriad local histories. This relatively grand claim about historical processes can coexist with a number of more modest practical implications. For reformers, ameliorating corruption will require dealing with issues fundamental to the logic of local political culture, and these will vary tremendously from context to context. In Nigeria, the issues involve the intersection of patronage and political life and the distributive issues of revenue across a culturally diverse country. Instead of attempting to prevent officials from diverting public revenue to self-interested ends, Nigerians must face a constitutional challenge: how can public ends be served by accommodating patronage as a fundamental political principle? Exhortation is ineffective, as are investigations and judicial interventions. Instead, the constitutional order must be brought into alignment with political culture. Webs of patronage must be able to constrain official behavior and demand more from it, and the needs of regions must be brought into harmony. That is easier said than done.

NOTES

Introduction

1. "Switzerland to Give Back Abacha Millions," BBC News, 17 April 2002, http://news.bbc.co.uk/2/hi/africa/1935646.stm.
2. "Maryam Abacha Launches a Major Offensive to 'Save' the Abacha Loot," *Tempo* (Lagos), 23 September 1999.
3. For an excellent ethnography of these schemes in southeastern Nigeria, see Smith, *Culture of Corruption*.
4. Federal Republic of Nigeria, Criminal Code, section 419.
5. See Pierce, "Punishment and the Political Body."
6. Smith, *Culture of Corruption*, 5.
7. Transparency International, http://www.transparency.org/about_us, accessed 20 July 2011.
8. Olivier de Sardan, "Moral Economy of Corruption in Africa?" Olivier de Sardan uses "corruption-complex" to designate a variety of practices (not simply the diversion of money but nepotism, influence peddling, deviations from the norms of bureaucratic rules), all of which would fall under what I have termed material practices interpreted through a technocratic paradigm.
9. Anderson, *Imagined Communities*; Vail, *Invention of Tribalism in Southern Africa*; Ranger, "Invention of Tradition"; "Invention of Tradition Revisited"; Young, *Ethnicity and Politics in Africa*.
10. Philps, "Defining Political Corruption"; Barcham, Hindess, and Larmour, *Corruption*.
11. Johnston, "Search for Definitions"; Kreike and Jordan, *Corrupt Histories*.
12. van Klaveren, "Corruption as a Historical Phenomenon."
13. My thanks to Tomoko Masuzawa for her insight on the intellectual context of nineteenth-century Europe.
14. Gash, *Politics in the Age of Peel*; Key, *Politics, Parties and Pressure Groups*; Parrillo, *Against the Profit Motive*; Guyer, "Representation without Taxation."

15. Progressive-era authors wrote about the phenomenon with considerable insight. See, for example, Steffens, *Shame of the Cities*. A pioneering political scientist wrote about the corruption Steffens and other crusading journals condemned with considerable insight. Brooks, "Nature of Political Corruption"; "Attempted Apologies"; *Corruption*.

16. Dirks, *Scandal of Empire*; Nechtman, *Nabobs*.

17. Stoler, *Carnal Knowledge and Imperial Power*; Wilson, *Island Race*; Ballhatchet, *Race, Sex, and Class under the Raj*.

18. On this ambivalence, the classic work is Stoler, *Carnal Knowledge and Imperial Power*. On the dialectic of scandal and reform, see Rao and Pierce, "Discipline and the Other Body."

19. On the relationship between vernacular and specialized uses of political terms, see Pierce, "Pointing to Property."

20. See, for example, Lugard, *Dual Mandate*; Temple, *Native Races and Their Rulers*; Geary, *Nigeria under British Rule*.

21. For a discussion of how modern technocratic views of corruption have depended on a public-private distinction, see Bratsis, "Construction of Corruption." For a more extended discussion of the complexities of the political extension of "public" and "private" in colonial northern Nigeria, see Pierce, "Public, the Private, and the Sanitary."

22. Most influentially Rostow, *Stages of Economic Growth*. It is a slight exaggeration to say he posited a universal sequence, since part of his object was to posit a capitalist trajectory to development in the twentieth century as opposed to state socialism. For slightly earlier (and also very influential) discussions of political development, see Apter, *Ghana in Transition*; Lipset, "Some Social Requisites of Democracy." At this late date, it is unnecessary to rehearse the complex history of modernization theory and its critics. For the initial critique of the "dependency" theorists, see Frank, *Capitalism and Underdevelopment in Latin America*; Amin, *Neo-Colonialism in West Africa*; Rodney, *How Europe Underdeveloped Africa*. For a celebrated overview, see Cooper, "Africa and the World Economy."

23. Wraith and Simpkins, *Corruption in Developing Countries*.

24. van Klaveren, "Comment."

25. McMullen, "Theory of Corruption."

26. Leys, "Corruption"; McMullen, "Theory of Corruption."

27. Nye, "Corruption and Political Development," 419.

28. Much of the later literature retains these assumptions, though imported in a somewhat indirect way. See Williams, *Political Corruption in Africa*; Rose-Ackerman, "Democracy and 'Grand' Corruption"; *International Handbook on the Economics of Corruption*; *Corruption and Government*; *Corruption: A Study in Political Economy*. Rose-Ackerman in particular has been important in touching off a vast literature in economics, starting with a famous article, "Economics of Corruption." But though the formal innovation of the approach was viewing corruption as rent-seeking behavior usually (though not inevitably) within govern-

ment, the approach was nonetheless substantially similar to Nye's. See Williams, "New Concepts for Old?"

29. Here I borrow Fredric Jameson's famous term. Jameson, *Political Unconscious*.

30. Smith, "Political Corruption among the Hausa," 164; Ottenberg, "Local Government and the Law in Southern Nigeria."

31. For an excellent and far more comprehensive overview focusing on Africa and anthropology, see Blundo, "Corruption in Africa." See also Andvig and Fjeldstad, "Corruption"; Debiel and Gawrich, "(Dys-)Functionalities." A comprehensive collection of key works is available in Johnston, *Public Sector Corruption*.

32. Rose-Ackerman, "Economics of Corruption," 187. For Africa specifically, see Mbaku, *Bureaucratic and Political Corruption in Africa*; Gyimah-Brempong, "Corruption, Economic Growth and Income Inequality in Africa"; Blackburn, Bose, and Haque, "Endogenous Corruption in Economic Development"; Vicente, "Does Oil Corrupt?"

33. Rose-Ackerman, "Political Economy of Corruption."

34. Rose-Ackerman, "Corruption: Greed, Culture, and the State."

35. I am grateful to Obi Ojimiwe, whose work on how governments are determined to be "serious" about development has shaped my own thinking. Ojimiwe, "Malaria Control."

36. This included politically canny descriptions of political struggle during the nationalist period. See Sklar, *Nigerian Political Parties*; Coleman, *Nigeria*; Dudley, *Parties and Politics*; Whitaker, *Politics of Tradition*. An important early synthesis was Scott, "Analysis of Corruption."

37. Leys, *Underdevelopment in Kenya*; Schatz, "Pirate Capitalism." For a more recent application of the insight, see Cooper, *Africa since 1940*.

38. Ekeh, "Two Publics."

39. For an early formulation, see Zolberg, *Creating Political Order*. More recently, Christopher Clapham's formulation of neo-patrimonialism has been extremely influential. Clapham, *Third World Politics*. On corruption in particular, see Medard, "Public Corruption in Africa." For a criticism of such approaches, see Wai, "Neo-Patrimonialism."

40. Joseph, *Democracy and Prebendal Politics*. On ethnicized politics and corruption in Nigeria, see also Diamond, *Class, Ethnicity and Democracy in Nigeria*; Graf, *Nigerian State*. For a recent assessment of Joseph's book, which concludes it has stood up remarkably well, see Adebanwi and Obadare, *Democracy and Prebendalism in Nigeria*.

41. See also Laitin, *Hegemony and Culture*.

42. Reno, *Corruption and State Politics in Sierra Leone*; *Warlord Politics and African States*; "Crisis and (No) Reform in Nigeria's Politics." See also Hoffmann, "Fairy Godfathers."

43. Mamdani, *Citizen and Subject*; Herbst, *States and Power in Africa*; Bates, *Markets and States*.

44. Jackson and Rosberg, "Why Africa's Weak States Persist"; Herbst, *States and Power in Africa*.

45. Chalfin, "Border Zone Trade"; "Global Customs Regimes"; Hasty, "Pleasures of Corruption"; Chalfin, *Neoliberal Frontiers*. Chalfin's book *Neoliberal Frontiers* makes an important argument about the episodic and highly negotiable exercises of authority (both proper and improper) being the paradigmatic demonstration of state sovereignty. See chapter 5. For a somewhat similar discussion of the contours of state authority in Cameroon, see Roitman, *Fiscal Disobedience*. Beyond Africa, a useful and influential literature on India makes a similar point. Fuller and Benei, *Everyday State*; Gould, *Bureaucracy, Community and Influence in India*; Gould, Sherman, and Ansari, "Flux of the Matter"; Gupta, *Red Tape*.

46. Smith, *Culture of Corruption*.

47. Ellis and MacGaffey, "Research on Sub-Saharan Africa's Unrecorded International Trade"; MacGaffey, *Entrepreneurs and Parasites*; MacGaffey and Bazenguissa-Ganga, *Congo-Paris*; MacGaffey et al., *Real Economy of Zaire*.

48. Blundo and Olivier de Sardan, *Everyday Corruption and the State*.

49. Mauss, *Gift*; Malinowski, *Argonauts of the Western Pacific*; *Crime and Custom*; Sahlins, *Stone Age Economics*; Parry, "The Gift."

50. Fuller and Benei, *Everyday State*. See also Brownsberger, "Development and Governmental Corruption."

51. Gupta, *Red Tape*. This work builds on Gupta's important earlier work, some in collaboration with James Ferguson, on the ways in which such narratives also give the state the appearance of a particular spatial structure, one with "higher" levels, in which power is centralized, even as this accords imperfectly with the complex web of actors and actions which in fact constitute state activity. Ferguson and Gupta, "Spatializing States"; Gupta, "Blurred Boundaries." See also Ferguson, *Anti-Politics Machine*.

52. Rose-Ackerman, "Corruption: Greed, Culture, and the State," 131, 137.

53. Gould, Sherman, and Ansari, "Flux of the Matter"; Saha, "Male State"; "Mockery of Justice"; *Law, Disorder and the Colonial State*; Ochonu, "Corruption and Political Culture"; Bridenthal, "Hidden History"; Burgess, "Crisis"; Hibou, "Economic Crime"; Lindemann, "Dirty Politics"; Siniawer, "Befitting Bedfellows"; Waquet, *Corruption*.

54. Mamdani, *Citizen and Subject*; Bayart, *Politics of the Belly*; Bayart, Ellis, and Hibou, *Criminalization of the State*; Herbst, *States and Power in Africa*.

55. Austin, *How to Do Things with Words*. For a more recent use of the concept in relation to political speech, see Butler, *Excitable Speech*. Butler discusses political speech, the power of words to injure (as those concerned with regulating hate speech have argued) or conversely the ability of sovereign authority to act through saying. As chapter 5 will discuss at length, the ideological underpinnings of state authority are crucially tested, and for that reason usefully revealed, by discourses of corruption. Butler provides a singularly useful account of the productive space between intention and effect in which speech acts do their work, which is the location in which much routine governance takes place.

56. Austin, *How to Do Things with Words*, 98–102.

57. Daston, "Moral Economy of Science"; Lonsdale, "Moral Economy of Mau Mau"; Olivier de Sardan, "Moral Economy of Corruption in Africa?"; Scott, *Moral Economy of the Peasant*; Thompson, "Moral Economy of the English Crowd"; "Moral Economy Reviewed."

Chapter One: A Tale of Two Emirs

1. Usman, *Transformation of Katsina*, 152.
2. Barth, *Travels and Discoveries*, 1, 452. Barth consistently termed Emir Bello (and other emirs of the Sokoto caliphate's component emirates) "governor" to indicate their status as subjects of the sultan of Sokoto. I follow the modern convention of rendering them as "emir." Both emirs in the caliphate and the pre-jihadic Hausa kings are termed *sarki* in Hausa, which can be variously translated as "chief," "king," and "emir"—or indeed sultan, for the sultan of Sokoto is the Sarkin Musulmi.
3. Barth, *Travels and Discoveries*, 1, 453–54.
4. Barth, *Travels and Discoveries*, 1, 460.
5. Barth, *Travels and Discoveries*, 1, 462.
6. Barth, *Travels and Discoveries*, 1, 464.
7. Barth, *Travels and Discoveries*, 1, 466–69.
8. Barth, *Travels and Discoveries*, 1, 468–69.
9. Usman, *Transformation of Katsina*, 150–75.
10. Smith, *Culture of Corruption*, 56–61.
11. In Hausa there is a linguistic and conceptual distinction between masu sarauta and *talakawa* (sing. *talaka*), which would normally be translated as "commoners," while masu sarauta might be rendered as "aristocrats." Some offices might be reserved for the royal lineage or might be hereditary in another family, but for the most part the "aristocracy" was not a discrete group a talaka could never aspire to enter. M. G. Smith points out that although the masu sarauta/talakawa distinction is ideologically important, it does overlook large numbers of intermediate people— deposed masu sarauta, holders of minor offices rather than great offices of state, and so on. He argues for a much more nuanced appreciation of hierarchies of social status within Hausa society—a point that is well taken but that does not obviate the basic importance of this distinction. Smith, "Hausa System of Social Status."
12. Smith, *Affairs of Daura*; *Government in Kano*; *Government in Zazzau*; Usman, *Transformation of Katsina*; Mahadi, "State and Economy"; Nast, *Concubines and Power*.
13. Adeleye, *Power and Diplomacy*; Last, *Sokoto Caliphate*; Smith, *Writings of Professor Abdullahi Smith*; Sa'id, "Revolution and Reaction."
14. Lovejoy, *Transformations in Slavery*; Lovejoy and Hogendorn, *Slow Death for Slavery*; Hogendorn, "Slave Acquisition and Delivery in Precolonial Hausaland"; Mason, "Population Density"; Smith, *Baba of Karo*.
15. In the text I make a distinction between northern Nigeria, which is the northern part of what is now the Federal Republic of Nigeria, and Northern Nigeria, which

is a political unit. It was created with the proclamation of the Royal Niger Company protectorate, and it persisted (under different guises, including the Northern Provinces and the Northern Region) until 1967, when what was then a federation of four regions was broken up into a twelve-state federal system.

16. Miers and Roberts, *End of Slavery*; Cooper, Holt, and Scott, *Beyond Slavery*.

17. Kirk-Greene, "Thin White Line." See also Bull, "Indirect Rule in Northern Nigeria."

18. Burbank and Cooper, *Empires*.

19. Lugard, *Dual Mandate*; *1918 Political Memoranda*; *1906 Political Memoranda*.

20. Perham, *Lugard*; Orr, *Making of Northern Nigeria*; Temple, *Native Races and Their Rulers*.

21. "Lord Lugard."

22. About Lugard as propagandist, see also Nwabughuogo, "Role of Propaganda." Nwabughuogo contends Lugard's propaganda in favor of his system did not stem from an attempt to euphemize an extreme strategy emerging from colonial poverty but rather was an attempt to make distinctive a tenure that otherwise would have appeared a failure given the protectorate's lack of economic development. He suggests indirect rule was then picked up by Liberal critics of the colonial enterprise such as Mary Kingsley and E. D. Morel, a position that somewhat oversimplifies the context of early twentieth-century politics. The governor who followed Lugard (and who was aligned with reformist factions) adopted indirect rule as a rhetoric to explain policies that differed greatly from Lugard's. They were, he claimed, necessary for achieving true indirect rule, which was the overarching (and entirely Lugardian) imperative. See Pierce, *Farmers and the State*, chapter 3.

23. Miles, *Hausaland Divided*; Perham, *Lugard*; Robinson, Madden, and Perham, *Essays in Imperial Government*; Spear, "Neo-Traditionalism and the Limits of Invention."

24. The following summarizes arguments developed in Pierce, *Farmers and the State*, chapters 1 and 3.

25. National Archives, Kaduna (NAK) Kanoprof FC vol. I, C.111/1908.

26. For good descriptions of the process in Kano, see Ubah, *Administration of Kano*; Fika, *Kano Civil War*; Watts, *Silent Violence*.

27. Umar, *Islam and Colonialism*, 119–43.

28. Smith, *Government in Zazzau*, 201–2.

29. Smith, *Government in Zazzau*, 188–96.

30. Backwell, *Occupation of Hausaland*, 70–71; Umar, *Islam and Colonialism*, 116–17.

31. Northern Nigeria, *Annual Report*, 1902, para. 18.

32. Northern Nigeria, *Annual Report*, 1902, para. 19.

33. Arnett, *Gazetteer of Zaria Province*.

34. Northern Nigeria, *Annual Report*, 1902, para. 20.

35. Miller, *Autobiography*, 37–45.

36. Northern Nigeria, *Annual Report*, 1905–6, para. 226.

37. Northern Nigeria, *Annual Report*, 1907–8, 36, Zaria Province. It was really only through the emir's intervention that the school received any Muslim students

who paid attention to the curriculum at all. Graham, *Government and Mission Education*, 50–51.

38. By contrast, Brian Larkin's interpretation of early-colonial attitudes toward Western technology reads *Wakar Diga* as evidence of the "colonial sublime," a local northern Nigerian appreciation of the ultimately indescribable power of colonial technologies. *Signal and Noise*, 38–39.

39. This paragraph is based on Smith, *Government in Zazzau*, 178–93.

40. Smith, *Government in Zazzau*, 207–9.

41. Unless otherwise noted, this paragraph is based on Smith, *Government in Zazzau*, 212–21.

42. Pierce, "Punishment and the Political Body."

43. Arnett, *Gazetteer*, 26.

44. NAK SNP 8/4 58/1917. Palmer quoted in Lieutenant Governor to Governor, 26 May 1917.

45. NAK SNP 8/8 6/1921, Acting Lieutenant Governor to Resident Zaria, 15 January 1921.

46. National Archives (UK), Public Record Office (TNA PRO) CO 583/99 Conf. 7 February 1921, Aliyu, Emir of Zaria: Deposition of, Clifford to CO, 7 February 1921.

47. Arewa House (AH) file no. 15,346, Slaves (Females), Attorney General to Chief Secretary, 26 May 1921.

48. AH file no. 15,346, Acting Lieutenant Governor, 16 July 1921.

49. Miller to Lugard, 29 July 1903, cited in Ayandele, *Missionary Impact*, 145, emphasis in original.

50. Miller, *Reflections*, 124.

51. Miller, *Reflections*, 127–28.

52. Miller, *Reflections*, 128.

53. Miller, *Reflections*, 133–38.

54. Cf. Baba of Karo's account of raids sponsored by the emirs of Maradi and Kontagora. Smith, *Baba of Karo*, 66–73. The latter was in the caliphate rather than outside of it, but there was some justification because of the questionable legal status of Emir Kwassau's regime. Similarly, even if Wombai Aliyu had sponsored raids against Muslims, it is likely these also could have had some pretext.

55. Miller, *Reflections*, 139.

56. TNA CO 583/94 Tel, 3 December 1920, Charges against Emir of Zaria.

57. TNA CO 583/99, Conf. 7 February 1921.

58. NAK SNP 8/8 6/1921, Byng-Hall to Lieutenant Governor, 17 December 1920.

59. NAK SNP 8/8 6/1921, Lieutenant Governor, Northern Provinces, to Resident, Zaria Province, 15 January 1921.

60. NAK SNP 8/8 6/1921, W. F. Gowers, 16 February 1921. When the decision was questioned in the House of Lords some years later, the Parliamentary undersecretary of state claimed that the reason for the deposition was Aliyu's interference in a court case. *Hansard*, 11 March 1925, Lords Sitting.

61. TNA PRO CO 583/99 Conf. 7 February 1921, Aliyu, Emir of Zaria: Deposition of.

62. TNA PRO CO 583/99 Conf. 7 February 1921.

63. TNA PRO CO 583/99, Conf. 7 February 1921.

64. TNA PRO CO 583/99, Conf. A, 11 March 1921, Emir of Zaria.

65. Pierce, "Punishment and the Political Body."

66. During the colonial period, taxes were payable after the harvest came in at the end of the rainy season, which generally ended in September. From the second decade of colonial rule, taxes were levied in sterling rather than in kind or in cowries. Thus, the tax season ran into the new year, and there were occasions in which farming families increasingly needed to convert a portion of their crops into cash in order to meet their tax burdens. As Michael Watts notes, even without the increase in the absolute incidence of tax that accompanied colonial rule, this schedule substantially increased the burden taxation placed on families' food supply. In the precolonial period, tax was levied toward the end of the dry season. Thus, in the colonial period poor families were forced to sell agricultural produce to cover their tax liabilities at harvest time, just when produce prices were at their lowest. Watts, *Silent Violence*.

67. NAK SNP 17/8 K.761, vol. II, Complaint by Mohama Sani, 18 June 1924. NB The complainant's name is rendered as "Mohama Sani" in the documentation, which is a highly unusual form. I take this as a typo for the more common Muhammad Sani, even though it is used twice, in the heading of the file and in the heading of his complaint itself.

68. NAK SNP 17/8 K. 761, vol. II, Resident Kano to Secretary Northern Provinces, 24 September 1924, pp. 1–3.

69. NAK SNP 17/8 K. 761, vol. II, Resident Kano to Secretary Northern Provinces, 24 September 1924, pp. 3–4.

70. NAK SNP 17/8 K. 761, vol. II, Resident Kano to Secretary Northern Provinces, 24 September 1924, pp. 5–6.

71. Pierce, *Farmers and the State*.

72. Smith, *Government in Kano*, 452; Fika, *Kano Civil War*, 176.

73. Dokaji, *Kano Ta Dabo Cigari*, 95. Translation mine.

74. Smith, *Government in Kano*, 452.

75. NAK SNP 17/8 K. 761, vol. II, Resident Kano to Secretary Northern Provinces, 24 September 1924, p. 2.

76. HCB SNP 9 603/1924, Sumaila District, Kano Emirate, Re-Assessment Report.

77. As it turned out, the regime's hopes for cotton production were dashed, and what cotton was grown was absorbed by the local textile industry, which paid higher prices than merchant exporters would offer. Instead, both small producers and large landholders concentrated on producing groundnuts for export. Okediji, "Economic History"; Hogendorn, *Nigerian Groundnut Exports*; Salau, "Slave Labor in Groundnut Production."

78. Pierce, *Farmers and the State*, chapter 3.

79. I am using "farm" as the most graceful equivalent for the Hausa term *gona*, which might also be rendered as "farm plot." Individual farmers often cultivate several *gonaki*, which are frequently not contiguous and indeed may be at some remove from one another. Forms of tenure are also complex. Some farmers have access to their land because they have a clear and unambiguous right to cultivate it. Some are loaned

it by others, some cultivate it on behalf of someone else (this is particularly true of gonaki owned by women), and some engage in a form of cash cropping. See Pierce, *Farmers and the State*, chapters 2, 3, 6; Starns, "Land Tenure among the Rural Hausa."

80. Pierce, "Looking like a State."
81. NAK SNP 10 844P/1913, Kano. Report on Taki Assessment.
82. Pierce, *Farmers and the State*, chapter 6; Garba, "Taxation in Some Hausa Emirates"; Watts, *Silent Violence*, 274–305.
83. Kano State History and Culture Bureau (HCB) SNP 9 603/1924, Sumaila District, Kano Emirate, Re-Assessment Report.
84. NAK SNP 17/8 K.5093, Kano Emirate Assessment, 30 April 1927.
85. See Pierce, "Looking like a State."
86. NAK Kanoprof 5/1 2953, Emir's Instructions to District Headmen (1922–48). The most pointed warning, dated 6 February 1922, reads "Any hakimi or dagaci, or ward head, or subordinate of theirs who takes land or cattle tax, except for that written in the land or cattle tax register, has committed a crime." Translation mine.
87. Northern Nigeria Annual Report, 1910–11, 738. See also Smith, *Government in Kano*, 429; Ubah, *Administration of Kano*, 178–83.
88. Ubah, *Administration of Kano*; Fika, *Kano Civil War*; Smith, *Government in Kano*. Peter Tibenderana is perhaps too extreme in his characterization of the sultan of Sokoto as having lost control of the structures of his own emirate government, but his basic point is well taken, that extreme characterizations of indirect rule as having allowed emirs absolute latitude are quite inaccurate. Instead, British authorities intervened consistently and systematically into emirate affairs, and the modes of government that emerged were different from those in the precolonial period. Nonetheless, Nigerian authorities retained considerable freedom to maneuver in these new circumstances. See Tibenderana, "Irony of Indirect Rule in Sokoto Emirate."
89. Sean Stilwell develops an insightful and subtle account of this process of bureaucratization in the Kano Native Authority, with particular attention to the manner in which the new apparatus substituted for the old system of royal slavery. Stilwell, "Constructing Colonial Power." Moses Ochonu's study of indirect rule in the "minority" middle belt of the North provides an important account of how the process played out in a culturally distinct area. Ochonu, *Colonialism by Proxy*.
90. Watts, *Silent Violence*, 282.
91. See Ochonu, *Colonial Meltdown*.

Chapter Two: The Political Time

1. Reprinted in Yahaya, *Native Authority System*, 223–29.
2. The outlines of these developments have been admirably traced by a number of scholars. See Sklar, *Nigerian Political Parties*; Whitaker, *Politics of Tradition*; Dudley, *Parties and Politics*; Yakubu, *Aristocracy*; Paden, *Ahmadu Bello*; *Religion and Political Culture in Kano*; Reynolds, *Zamanin Siyasa*.
3. Paden, *Religion and Political Culture in Kano*.

4. This was only a temporary defeat for the emirs and their supporters. The system of indirect election was conducted through a series of electoral colleges that began among adult men at the village level and culminated at the provincial level, which selected representatives to send to the House of Assembly. The native authorities were allowed to "inject" up to 10 percent of the members of the final electoral college by appointment, and these appointees became a disproportionate number of the final members of the assembly. See Sklar, *Nigerian Political Parties*, 30; Bello, *My Life*, 70–72.

5. Cooper, "Writing the History of Development." The 1950s saw a considerable transformation in the implications of the term "development." For key works, see Lewis, *Theory of Economic Growth*; Apter, *Gold Coast in Transition*; Rostow, *Stages of Economic Growth*.

6. Lugard, *Dual Mandate*; 1918 *Political Memoranda*.

7. For an extended discussion, see Pierce, *Farmers and the State*. Sara Berry has argued for viewing colonial representations of tradition as continually in flux, an ongoing topic of debate that constrained government practice rather than a positive system in its own terms. *No Condition Is Permanent*; *Chiefs Know Their Boundaries*. See also Ranger, "Invention of Tradition Revisited"; Spear, "Neo-Traditionalism and the Limits of Invention."

8. Paden, *Ahmadu Bello*, 115–19.

9. Bello, *My Life*, 49, 58.

10. Adebayo, "Jangali."

11. Paden, *Ahmadu Bello*, 119.

12. There certainly were African employees of the British colonial administration—clerks, soldiers, teachers, medical doctors, and many other categories—but there were limits to how far such employees could advance, and they were always under the administrative supervision of British officials.

13. In a somewhat sensational memoir published only online, Harold Smith, who had worked in the Labour Department in Lagos during the 1950s, recalled considerable bribe taking among British officials and claimed a colleague told him, "You can't stop these people taking money. If you make a fuss, which you do, they just keep your share! You can have as many black girls as you want . . . [or] boys if you fancy some black bum." Smith, *Blue-Collar Lawman*, chapter 8. The colonial government was extremely delicate in disciplining British officials who did not properly observe the strictures of administrative behavior. The case of J. F. J. Fitzpatrick, who served as a political officer in a number of provinces, is instructive in this regard. Fitzpatrick became an embarrassment to the regime because he had a penchant for flogging, and in several instances his activities touched off international scandals. He was finally separated from the colonial service because of a government-owned typewriter, which he sold for private profit. In this case, the typewriter was clearly a pretext for dispensing with an official who was problematic for other reasons. Nonetheless, even in this instance the government was careful *not* to label his activities as "corrupt," merely as "improper." Pierce, "Punishment and the Political Body."

14. Low and Lonsdale, "Introduction"; Cooper, "Reconstructing Empire in Post-War French and British Africa"; "Writing the History of Development."

15. Ochonu, *Colonial Meltdown*, 100–120. Ochonu demonstrates that a set of popular responses to the Great Depression created a set of institutions and a political tradition of dissent that was not itself nationalist but that then was taken up for nationalist purposes after World War II. I am deeply indebted to his brilliant, innovative account.

16. East, "Recent Activities"; Imam, "Nigerian Constitutional Proposals"; Hayatu, *50 Years*.

17. Anderson, *Imagined Communities*. More generally, see Warner, "Publics and Counterpublics"; Habermas, *Structural Transformation of the Public Sphere*.

18. Dudley, *Parties and Politics*, 165–71.

19. CO 554/237, Political Situation in the Kano Emirate of Nigeria, R. J. Purdy, "Appreciation of the Situation in Kano on the Death of the Emir" (1953).

20. CO 554/237, Political Situation, Governor's Deputy to Secretary of State, 16 November 1953. In fact, on the Nigerian government's advice, the Colonial Office supported Sanusi in response to a parliamentary question from a Labour MP who noted Sanusi was more a Machiavellian prince than a Hitler but that policing in Kano was conducted "in a way which we have come to accept as normal in a Fascist and police State, but which ought not to be permitted under the British flag." *Hansard* HC Deb., 17 November 1953, Vol. 520, c. 1678, Mr. George Wigg (Dudley).

21. Pierce, "Farmers and 'Prostitutes.'"

22. CO 554/237, Political Situation.

23. Reynolds, *Zamanin Siyasa*. NAK KADMIN JUSTICE S/MOJ/45, N.R. Native Courts—Interference in by Political Bodies and Others.

24. For example, in a discussion of district heads who improperly included young boys on lists of taxpayers, the senior district officer for Kano wrote to the madaki saying, "This is exactly the sort of injustice which they like to find. They know that it is both illegal and contrary to accepted principle and they know well how to profit from it." HCB COSL R.583, District Taxation—Principles Governing Exemption from Assessment: Instruction Policy, SDOK, to Madakin Kano, 5 April 1957.

25. TNA CO 554/596, The Activities of the Northern Elements Progressive Union (1951).

26. Umar, "Fatwa and Counter-Fatwa"; Hutson, "Women's Authority."

27. Ibrahim, "Traditional Ruling Families in the Politics of Kano State, Nigeria"; Paden, *Ahmadu Bello*; *Religion and Political Culture in Kano*.

28. Yakubu, *Aristocracy in Political Crisis*. See also Dudley, *Parties and Politics*, 215–17.

29. Paden, *Religion and Political Culture in Kano*.

30. Dudley, *Parties and Politics*, 213–14. The assistant treasurer of the Kano Native Authority at the time would later allege the shortfall had come about because the NA was developing an industrial area under instructions from the regional government. The regional government withdrew its guarantee for the NA's letter

of credit, which was what created the notorious overdraft. Alhaji Usman Nagado, "Letter to the Editor re: Muhammadu Sanusi, 1899–1991," *New Nigerian*, 24 June 1991.

31. HCB MLG NAF/361, Warning to Kano NA Officials by North Regional Government on Muffett Inquiry.

32. TNA DO 186/13, Relations between the Emir of Kano and the Northern Regional Government, H. A. Twist to J. O. Moreton, 20 September 1962.

33. TNA DO 186/13, Relations between the Emir of Kano and the Northern Regional Government, H. A. Twist to J. O. Moreton, 20 September 1962.

34. TNA DO 186/13, Relations between the Emir of Kano and the Northern Regional Government, Twist to Moreton, 7 November 1962.

35. TNA DO 186/13, Telegram Kaduna to Lagos, 5 December 1962.

36. Yakubu, *Aristocracy*, 196–205.

37. Yakubu, *Aristocracy*, 197–98.

38. TNA DO 186/13, Twist to Moreton, 7 November 1962.

39. TNA DO 186/13, Secret Letter to Sir Henry Lintott, 6 February 1963.

40. Umar, "Fatwa and Counter-Fatwa."

41. Muffett, "Legitimacy and Deference."

42. Yakubu makes precisely this point. Yakubu, *Aristocracy*, 193. His assertion that Muffett was "erroneous" in calling Tukur "the usurper" goes too far. That succession did lead to the Kano civil war, and the events of the time demonstrate Tukur suffered from a certain lack of legitimacy. The issue was more complex than popular dissatisfaction with the lineage position of rival claimants to Kano's throne, which does demonstrate Muffett's position was disingenuous at best. See Fika, *Kano Civil War*. Regardless, the succession of Usman I after the death of his father Ibrahim Dabo in 1846 also would undermine the thesis.

43. Oyediran and Gboyega insightfully discuss the process of democratization in southern local councils during this period but suggest that the retention of a chiefs-in-council model of local governance retarded the process in the north. I would agree that the transfer of direct administrative authority to elected local councils took place in a later period in the Northern Region, to such an extent that emirs and their subordinates remained the embodiment of local government. Nonetheless, the shift between native authorities and the secular state during this period had powerful consequences. Oyediran and Gboyega, "Local Government." See also Olufemi Vaughan's excellent study of chiefship in southwestern Nigeria, *Nigerian Chiefs*, for an account of how politics in that region actually worked to strengthen chiefly institutions.

44. Cf. Tignor's important argument that "corruption" had long been a charge leveled at indigenous African systems of government that took on new coloration as Nigeria moved to self-government. Where I have emphasized the ubiquity of official practices susceptible to being called "corrupt," Tignor suggests a degree of skepticism. Most of the direct evidence for corruption, he argues, comes from commissions of inquiry, and these turned up many rumors but relatively little legally actionable malpractice. As is clear from my argument up to this point, I agree with him that the actual extent of malpractice is epistemically murky but

disagree on whether legal admissibility is the correct standard for assessing its prevalence. Tignor, "Political Corruption in Nigeria."

45. Richard Joseph famously termed this political logic "prebendal politics." See *Democracy and Prebendal Politics*. His argument will be addressed more systematically in chapters 3 and 5, below.

46. Vaughan, *Nigerian Chiefs*; Achebe, *Farmers, Traders*; *Female King*; Afigbo, *Warrant Chiefs*; Ochonu, *Colonialism by Proxy*; Nadel, *Black Byzantium*; Apter, *Black Critics and Kings*.

47. Ochonu, *Colonialism by Proxy*.

48. Lloyd, "Development of Political Parties in Western Nigeria"; Sklar, *Nigerian Political Parties*; Nolte, *Obafemi Awolowo*.

49. See Sklar, *Nigerian Political Parties*, 35–38. Abba has stressed that Nigerian politics must not be seen solely through an ethnic lens, emphasizing the class and ideological dimensions of party contests both in this period and during the Second Republic in the 1970s and 1980s. His point is well taken, particularly since the dominance of the big three parties in their home regions partially masks other tendencies—NEPU's class-based challenge to the NPC in the north, for example. This is an important reminder, though Abba's account tends to ignore appeals to ethnic sentiments retailed by politicians as a part of their electoral strategy and to view ethnicity as a constant identity that exists or not. The difficulty with such an argument is that ethnic identities themselves shift, becoming more and less salient over time, consolidating and fragmenting. Nigerian politicians have not just capitalized on identities that objectively existed but acted to consolidate and make them politically relevant. Abba, "Misrepresentation of Nigeria by Nigerians and Others." See Cohen, *Custom and Politics in Urban Africa*; Laitin, *Hegemony and Culture*; Young, *Ethnicity and Politics in Africa*.

50. Cooper, *Decolonization and African Society*; "Modernizing Bureaucrats."

51. Ochonu, *Colonial Meltdown*; "African Colonial Economies."

52. Colonial Office, *Report on Nigeria for the Year 1949*, p. 40. On cash cropping, see Berry, *Cocoa, Custom, and Socio-Economic Change*; Korieh, *Land Has Changed*; Lynn, "Profitability of the Early Nineteenth Century Palm Oil Trade"; Meredith, "Government and the Decline of the Nigerian Oil-Palm Export Industry, 1919–1939"; Olukoju, "United Kingdom and the Political Economy of the Global Oils and Fats Business during the 1930s"; Hogendorn, *Nigerian Groundnut Exports*; Okediji, "Economic History."

53. Helleiner, "Fiscal Role."

54. Cooper, *Africa since 1940*. Cf. formulations of the comprador state, for example, Nore and Turner, *Oil and Class Struggle*; Graf, *Nigerian State*.

55. Diamond, *Class, Ethnicity and Democracy in Nigeria*; Graf, *Nigerian State*.

56. There is an immense literature on ethnicity and the role politicians and retail politics have played in the mobilization of ethnic tension. See, for example, Anthony, *Poison and Medicine*; Diamond, *Class, Ethnicity and Democracy in Nigeria*; Young, *Ethnicity and Politics in Africa*; Cohen, *Custom and Politics in Urban Africa*; Laitin, *Hegemony and Culture*; Melson and Wolpe, *Politics of Communalism*.

57. Sklar, *Nigerian Political Parties*.

58. *Report of Coker Commission of Inquiry into the Affairs of Certain Statutory Corporations in Western Nigeria* (Lagos: Federal Ministry of Information, 1962).

59. Nigeria, *Report of the Tribunal Appointed to Inquire into Allegations Reflecting on the Official Conduct of the Premier of, and Certain Persons Holding Ministerial and Other Public Offices in, the Eastern Region of Nigeria*, [Cmnd. 51, 1957], 42.

60. Comments of the Federal Government on the *Report of Coker Commission of Inquiry into the Affairs of Certain Statutory Corporations in Western Nigeria* (Lagos: Federal Ministry of Information, 1962), 17.

61. *Report of Coker Commission of Inquiry into the Affairs of Certain Statutory Corporations in Western Nigeria*, vol. III (Lagos: Federal Ministry of Information, 1962), 24–26.

62. *Coker Report*, 31–33.

63. *Coker Report*, 33.

64. Coker Comments, 16.

65. *Coker Report*, 33.

66. Coker Comments, 4.

67. Coker Comments, 16.

68. Soyinka, *You Must Set Forth at Dawn*, xiii.

Chapter Three: Oil and the "Army Arrangement"

1. Ahmad Khan, *Political Economy of Oil*; Ikein and Briggs-Anigboh, *Oil and Fiscal Federalism*; Nore and Turner, *Oil and Class Struggle*; Watts, *State, Oil, and Agriculture in Nigeria*. Michael Watts's more recent scholarship has been the most important and insightful examination of the implications of oil for Nigeria's political economy. See, for example, "Shock of Modernity"; "Resource Curse?"; "Oil as Money."

2. Joseph, *Democracy and Prebendal Politics*. For an important recent reassessment of Joseph's paradigm, see the essays in Adebanwi and Obadare, *Democracy and Prebendalism in Nigeria*.

3. Apter, *Pan-African Nation*. Apter discusses of the transformative effects of oil revenue and in particular the ways in which the petro-naira reworked systems of value; the Nigerian state increasingly operated through what Apter terms a politics of spectacle, channeling goods bought with oil rents and thus affecting the Nigerian public in their capacity as consumers. For an influential account of a similar process in Venezuela, see Coronil, *Magical State*.

4. Amnesty International, "Fela Kuti, PoC, Nigeria," http://static.amnesty.org/ai50/fela_kuti_en.pdf, accessed 20 August 2013. On the background of the composition, see Moore, *Fela*; Olaniyan, *Arrest the Music!*

5. Nigeria has had three elected civilian regimes, the First Republic (1960–66), Second Republic (1979–83), and Fourth Republic (1999–present). The presidential election that would have completed the transition to the Third Republic was annulled in 1993, and the short-lived "transitional" government that year was also

headed by a civilian, Ernest Shonekan. In addition to these republics, Nigeria has had six distinct military governments: those headed by General Ironsi (January–July 1966), General Gowon (1966–75), Generals Muhammed and Obasanjo (1975–79; Muhammed was assassinated during a coup attempt in 1976), General Buhari (1984–85), General Babangida (1985–93), and Generals Abacha and Abubakar (1993–99; Abacha died in 1998).

6. Ogbondah and Onyedike, "Nigerian Press Laws," 61.

7. Obi Nwakanma, "Probe Obasanjo Too," *Vanguard*, 23 May 2010.

8. "The *Sun* Exclusive: Buhari Bares It All," *Sun*, 24 December 2012. Solarin and Awojobi were both prominent critics of the Nigerian government and played key roles in publicizing the missing money. Awojobi died soon after the coup in 1984, of hypertension, at the age of forty-seven. Solarin was imprisoned.

9. The other brother to be detained, Dr. Beko Ransome-Kuti, was repeatedly jailed under the Babangida and Abacha governments as well. Ironically, he would testify before the Oputa Human Rights Violations Investigations Committee and compel the testimony of then-President Obasanjo on the subject of the 1977 raid. The irony stems from Ransome-Kuti's simultaneous complaint about his imprisonment in 1995 under General Abacha, which came about because of Dr. Ransome-Kuti's activism about Obasanjo's imprisonment, for allegedly plotting a military coup.

10. Notably, on 27 August 2012 Seun gave an interview to Lagos's Channels Television objecting to Funmilayo's portrait on the new ₦5,000 note, calling it an inappropriate gesture toward a woman the government had murdered. See http://www .channelstv.com/home/2012/08/27/hangout-with-seun-kuti-on-google-plus/, interview available at http://www.youtube.com/watch?v=Rn-3hPQZLGk, accessed 22 August 2013.

11. Elaigwu, *Gowon*, 135–39; Clarke, *Gowon*, 135–43.

12. Adamolekun and Ayo, "Evolution of the Nigerian Federal Administration System"; Siollun, *Oil, Politics and Violence*.

13. There were members of "majority" ethnicities living in these states, but they did not make up a majority of the population.

14. "Corruption Disrupts Relief in Nigeria," *Irish Times*, 17 November 1970.

15. Stanley Meisler, "Corruption in Nigeria Has Double Edge," *Los Angeles Times*, 14 February 1971.

16. Stolper, *Inside Independent Nigeria*, 252.

17. Anthony Sampson, "Mac, Zik, Awo and Co," *Observer*, 17 January 1960.

18. Lloyd Garrison, "Corruption the Main Enemy as New Army Rulers Chart Nigeria's Future," *New York Times*, 4 February 1966.

19. Salubi, *T. E. A. Salubi*, 37.

20. Chief Bobson Gbinjie, "Festus Okotie-Eboh and History," *National Mirror*, 18 January 2013.

21. Smith, *Blue-Collar Lawman*.

22. Smith, *Blue-Collar Lawman*. Smith's memoir caused a great stir in the Nigerian and Nigerian diasporic public sphere when it went online in 1998. Smith's major

contention was that the British colonial government had systematically falsified the census and conspired to rig the elections of 1956 in order to marginalize the Action Group and its leader Obafemi Awolowo.

23. Ahmad Khan, *Political Economy of Oil*, 50.

24. Iwayemi, "Military and the Economy," 67.

25. Usman, "Revenue Sharing," 73–80. See also Ikein and Briggs-Anigboh, *Oil and Fiscal Federalism*; Ashwe, *Fiscal Federalism in Nigeria*.

26. See Kirk-Greene and Rimmer, *Nigeria since 1970*; Rimmer, *Economies of West Africa*; Nore and Turner, *Oil and Class Struggle*; Watts, "Shock of Modernity"; *State, Oil, and Agriculture in Nigeria*; Beckman, "Neo-Colonialism"; "Whose State?"

27. The formulae did not reflect the areas from which revenue was derived for a considerable period, which led to grievances among the Niger Delta peoples, whose land was degraded from oil production. It was not until the violence began there during the 1990s that the federal government began again to move toward compensating states for the wealth produced within them.

28. Usman, "Middlemen, Consultants, Contractors and the Solutions to the Current Economic Crisis."

29. Okolo, "Nigerian Census."

30. Ahonsi, "Deliberate Falsification and Census Data in Nigeria."

31. Awolowo, *Voice of Courage*, 2, 69–74.

32. Siollun, *Oil, Politics and Violence*, 170.

33. Azikiwe, *Democracy with Military Vigilance*.

34. Quoted in Siollun, *Oil, Politics and Violence*, 173.

35. Siollun, *Oil, Politics and Violence*, 191–94.

36. "Nigeria: Anti-Corruption Crusade; Bold but Not Decisive," *Post-Express* (Lagos), 9 July 2000.

37. *Report of the Tribunal of Inquiry into the Importation of Cement* (Lagos: Federal Ministry of Information, 1976), 8. Subsequent citations to the report will be made parenthetically in the text.

38. Osoba, "Corruption in Nigeria," 378–79.

39. This allegation was first made in 1969, but Stonehouse denied it at the time. It was only confirmed by a Czech defector in 1980. The Conservative government in power at the time did not publicize the tidbit, which was not released until 2010, after Stonehouse's death. Alan Travis, "Margaret Thatcher in Cover-Up after Czech Spy Exposed John Stonehouse," *Guardian*, 30 December 2010.

40. The accounts invoke Princess Jeanne but do little other than use the glamour of royalty to make the story more exotic. The princess was a colorful figure by any measure. Born in Tennessee and named Thelma Jeanne Williams, Princess Jeanne married Prince Carol of Romania, whose legitimacy was questionable. Carol's father, crown prince at the time of Carol's conception, either was not married to Carol's mother or was married morganatically. Carol was not acknowledged as a member of the royal family by his father or his half brother, King Michael. The couple traded on their royal connections for the bulk of their marriage, leasing a mansion near Poole from the local council and running up debts with the surety

of their royal connections and the fortune they claimed to possess back home. Hounsome, *Very Nearly Man*, 223–26. Prince Carol and Princess Jeanne had separated by the time of the cement scandal. They would ultimately divorce. Just before his death, Prince Carol would have his legitimacy affirmed by a Romanian court. "Obituary: HRH Prince Carol of Romania," *Daily Telegraph*, 9 February 2006. Later that decade, Princess Jeanne was arrested for car theft in New Jersey. "Self-Proclaimed Princess Jailed for Car Theft," *Lakeland Ledger*, 10 December 1979. She died in Vermont in 1988.

41. "The Great Cement Mixer," *Guardian*, 11 February 1975; "Okereke's Death Accidental—Inquest," *Irish Times*, 18 February 1975.

42. See, for example, Richard Keatinge, "Hitch with Cement's Nigerian Contract," *Irish Times*, 14 October 1975.

43. "Nigeria Probes Possible Fraud in Cement Deal," *Boston Globe*, 14 October 1975.

44. "All Ports in Nigeria Clogged by 250 Ships that Carry Cement," *Wall Street Journal*, 16 October 1975.

45. Peter Niesewand, "Concrete Jungle," *Guardian*, 17 October 1975. The "black cultural Olympics" was a reference to the plans for FESTAC, the spectacular festival held in Lagos in 1977.

46. "Nigeria: The Cement Block," *Time*, 27 October 1975. This story, though primarily about Nigeria, notes at the end that it is not the only oil producer suffering from a certain inefficiency in processing its imports, quoting a U.S. Defense Department official who noted Iran's ports made him think of "a chaotic flea circus."

47. Peter Kilborn, "Nigeria's Glut of Cement Epitomizes Growing Pains of an Underdeveloped Nation," *New York Times*, 4 December 1975.

48. Kilborn, "Nigeria's Glut."

49. Patrick Keatley, "Nigeria Sacks London Envoy in Cement Scandal," *Guardian* May 15, 1976.

50. Karen DeYoung, "Firms Feeling Weight of Nigeria's Cement Scandal," *Washington Post*, 6 June 1976.

51. Apter argues that this process was driven by wide-ranging transformations of value brought on by the oil economy, which created the *appearance* of development and an industrialized economy by enabling the purchase of consumer goods and building a facade of modernity while in practice channeling the bulk of oil rents through ethnicized chains of patronage. Apter, *Pan-African Nation*, 40–45.

52. First, *Barrel of a Gun*.

53. Nigeria Lagos to Secretary of State, 1 August 1975, Wikileaks.

54. Oyovbaire, *Federalism in Nigeria*; Suberu, *Federalism and Ethnic Conflict in Nigeria*.

55. The provision touched off a lawsuit, since President Shagari's victory only arguably met that requirement. Two-thirds of 19 is 12-2/3, and the NPN candidate only met his quota in twelve states. The Supreme Court, however, ruled that since he had won two-thirds times one-fourth of the vote in a thirteenth state, his victory precluded a runoff. Nigeria, "Awolowo V. Shagari and Others."

56. Except where otherwise noted, the following is based in the superb account of Second Republic party politics in Joseph, *Democracy and Prebendal Politics*.

57. The zoning question is particularly troubled at the time of this writing. The president in office at the time of Nigeria's 2015 elections, Goodluck Jonathan, was from the south-south zone, and he first came to the presidency to complete President Yar'Adua's 2007–2011 term. Yar'Adua came from the northwest zone, and his death in office foreshortened the north's claim to the presidency after eight years in which it was occupied by an incumbent from the southwest zone. President Jonathan's maneuvers preparing to contest the presidential election of 2015 precipitated a split in his People's Democratic Party (PDP) and the departure of a significant percentage of its leadership to an emergent national rival, the All-Progressives Congress. This crisis was central to the PDP's devastating defeat in 2015.

58. In the NPN's scheme, the zones were north, east, west, and minorities, though Joseph notes that in practice the "minorities" zone, which did not have an easy or straightforward geographical expression, became conflated with the southeastern groups in the Niger Delta.

59. Funk, *Life*, 272–73. Before his career as a political consultant, Funk had served in the Jimmy Carter administration as a specialist in the National Security Council for Africa. If anything, he comes across as inclined to give NPN politicians the benefit of the doubt, opining at some length about the excellence of the elections of 1983 and the legitimacy of the ruling party's victory in them. That position required a certain credulity, but it does demonstrate Funk was not inclined to exaggerate the personal failings of Second Republic officials.

60. Othman, "Classes, Crises and Coup."

61. Joseph, *Democracy and Prebendel Politics*, 178 ff.

62. Umaru Dikko, "Buhari, Danjuma and I," *Tell*, 13 September 1999.

63. Cameron Duodu, "Nigeria's 'Most Wanted Man' Declares War," *Observer*, 22 January 1984.

64. Dikko, "Buhari, Danjuma and I."

65. Human Rights Violations Investigation Commission [Oputa] Report, vol. 5, 47–48.

66. "Umaru Dikko: Return of Another Old Political Warhorse," *Guardian* (Nigeria), 10 August 2013.

67. "Agonies of Choice," *West Africa*, 28 July 1986, 1576.

68. "Curtains on the Civilian Past," *West Africa*, 18 August 1986.

69. Obotetukudo, *Inaugural Addresses*.

70. "Student Riots against SAP," *West Africa*, 5–11 June 1989.

71. "Clampdown on Riots," *West Africa*, 12–18 June 1989.

72. "A Season of Discontent," *West Africa*, 17–23 July 1989.

73. "Forces of Instability," *West Africa*, 7–13 August 1989.

74. Odimegwu Onwumere, "Amaechi, David-West and I," www.modernghana.com /news/324162/1/amaechi-david-west-and-i-html, accessed 27 May, 2015.

75. "OPEC Allows Nigeria to Raise Oil Output by 150,000 Barrels a Day over Its Quota," *Wall Street Journal*, 12 July 1984.

76. "Former Petroleum Minister Released after Detention," Associated Press, 17 October 1989.

77. "The Trial of Tam David-West," *New Nigerian*, 14 December 14 1990. The *New Nigerian* was owned by the Nigerian government, and its coverage of the David-West affair was generally supportive of the prosecution and government policy. This article, however, was the first installment of its summary of the complete prosecution and defense cases, along with the eventual verdict.

78. "The Trial of David-West," *New Nigerian*, 15 December 1990.

79. "The Trial of David-West," *New Nigerian*, 25 December 1990.

80. Editorial, *Guardian* (Nigeria), 17 December 17 1990; Editorial, *New Nigerian*, 27 December 1990.

81. Joshua Jaja, "David-West Freed," *New Nigerian*, 9 August 1991.

82. "The Trial of David-West," *New Nigerian*, 18 December 1990.

Chapter Four: Moral Economies of Corruption

1. At the time, the ₦50 note was the largest denomination available, equal to about U.S. $0.60 at exchange rates then prevailing.

2. There were two military governors between Colonel Wase's death and the advent of civilian rule, but they are not much discussed either.

3. During his second term (2011–2015), Governor Kwankwaso left the then-ruling PDP and went over to the new opposition alliance, the APC. Former governor Shekarau, who held office under the aegis of the ANPP, recently joined the PDP.

4. The reason for going to court in the absence of a dispute is to have the judge assign the proper proportion of the state to each inheritor, which then (at least in theory) allows the family to divide up the "hidden" portion appropriately. This does not always work: some families are forced to go to court several times when they are unable to agree on how to divide parts of the estate not already allocated. Pierce, *Farmers and the State*, chapter 4.

5. Interview 23e, ser. 2:30. Anonymized interview, conducted Ungogo Town, Kano State, 1997.

6. Yakubu, *Aristocracy*; Stilwell, "Constructing Colonial Power."

7. Balarabe is based on a real individual, though in the interest of protecting his anonymity I have substituted a composite of others' experiences for certain details of his story.

8. The question of land litigation is explored in more detail in Pierce, *Farmers and the State*.

9. "Oppression" by itself is not necessarily an official act. It is something anyone with more power may do to anyone with less.

10. M. G. Smith made a very similar point in a classic article on corruption in the Zaria emirate (Smith, "Political Corruption among the Hausa"), though our emphases are somewhat different.

11. Cited in Whitaker, *Politics of Tradition*, 98.

12. Adamu, "Understanding the Balogun Effect," *Daily Trust*, 15 July 2005.

13. To give just one instance of how difficult such an estimate would be, consider how influential Transparency International's annual ranking of most- and least-

corrupt countries is. For Nigeria, a major point of transition was 2004. In years previous to that, it had always been listed among the most corrupt countries. Following that, it has tended to be twenty or thirty countries down the list. The reason for the change was not some sort of absolute decrease in the incidence of corruption (or at least, TI has not claimed that to be the case) but rather the passage of a raft of legislation aimed at curbing corruption, including the institution of the Economic and Financial Crimes Commission (EFCC). While the EFCC and especially its first chairman, Nuhu Ribadu (who ran for president in 2011 as candidate of a major party), did engage in a number of high-profile prosecutions, including that of Tafa Balogun, the real effects have been largely cosmetic. For a challenging and wonderfully detailed contrary argument that Ribadu's EFCC *was* extremely effective, see Adebanwi, *Authority Stealing*.

14. Thompson, "Moral Economy of the Crowd," 79.
15. Polanyi, *Transformation*, 46.
16. Polanyi, *Dahomey*; Polanyi, Arensberg, and Pearson, *Trade and Market*.
17. The case of Dahomey has received particular attention, for Polanyi made a very strong case the Dahomeyan crown reserved for itself the right to determine the price of slave exports and to determine the price of key commodities. Africanist scholars who have done extensive work in the area, however, have demonstrated his contentions were based on a set of misunderstandings and that market mechanisms were critically important even during periods that Polanyi claimed must be archaic. Johnson, "Polanyi"; Hogendorn and Johnson, *The Shell Money of the Slave Trade*; Law, "Posthumous Questions"; *Ouidah*; "Royal Monopoly." For a similar criticism of Polanyi's discussion of the ancient Middle East, see Silver, "Karl Polanyi." These criticisms should not be taken as implying that all human societies depend on a fundamentally similar set of market mechanisms. Quite the contrary, modes of establishing and reworking equivalence and valuation are historically contingent and culturally complex. The difficulty of Polanyi's work is that it ultimately boils down to one historical transformation that is replicated through human societies and that ultimately results in modern market mechanisms. For a state-of-the-art discussion, see Guyer, *Marginal Gains*.
18. Thompson, "Moral Economy Reviewed."
19. Fassin, "Économies morales revistées," 1247.
20. Roitman, "Économie morale, subjectivité et politique."
21. Roitman, *Fiscal Disobedience*, 7.
22. Daston, "Moral Economy of Science," 4.
23. Lonsdale, "Moral Economy of Mau Mau."
24. Olivier de Sardan, "Moral Economy of Corruption in Africa?," 26. Emphasis in original.
25. "Moral Economy of Corruption in Africa?," 26–27.
26. It would be possible to argue that various uprisings—from the Maitatsine riots in 1980 through the Niger Delta conflicts to the Yusufiyya violence current at the time of this writing—represent precisely the violent response to corruption one would expect when moral-economic consensus had been abrogated.

27. I emphasize: the claim that female sexual morality had degenerated was not my own conclusion but rather a point made by any number of friends and acquaintances. See Pierce, "Farmers and 'Prostitutes'"; "Identity, Performance, and Secrecy"; "Public, the Private, and the Sanitary"; "Prostitution, Politics, and Paradigms."
28. See Reynolds, *Zamanin Siyasa*; Ochonu, "Critical Convergence."
29. White, *Speaking with Vampires*.
30. In this, I agree with Gupta on the centrality of narrative of corruption to experiences of the everyday state. Gupta, *Red Tape*.
31. The Paris Club debt was retired in 2006, three years after the essay's publication.
32. This usage presents something of a contrast to the six-zone system that had been worked out for the constitution written under Abacha, which was never fully implemented but which has informed the ruling PDP's allocation of major offices. That scheme terms the Middle Belt "North Central," and Ofeimun's Arewa is divided into "North West" and "North East."
33. Hoffmann, "Fairy Godfathers."

Chapter Five: Nigerian Corruption and the Limits of the State

1. Godwin Ijijeh and Andrew Ahiante, "Crimes Commission: Charges of Human Rights Breaches Soar," *This Day*, 23 May 2003.
2. Ujudud Shariff, "The Amaka Martina Anajemba Story," *Daily Trust*, 26 July 2005.
3. https://groups.google.com/forum/?fromgroups#!topic/news.admin.net-abuse .sightings/d1N-Klx9GDQ%5B1-25%5D, accessed 17 August 2012.
4. Economic and Financial Crimes Commission (Establishment) Act, 2004, which revised the original legislation of 2002.
5. Kabeer M. Adamu, "Obasanjo's Anti-Corruption Campaign: Reality or Myth?" *Daily Trust*, 10 October 2003.
6. For a detailed and well-informed account of EFCC investigations under Ribadu, see Adebanwi, *Authority Stealing*. It is based on extensive interviews with Ribadu and many officials and anticorruption activists, though it suffers from a tendency toward hagiography. See also Obuah, "Combatting Corruption"; Lawson, "Politics of Anti-Corruption Reform."
7. Shariff, "Anajemba Story."
8. Soji Omotunde, "Still Chasing Shadows," *This Day*, 25 November 2004.
9. "Corruption Costs Nigeria 40 percent of Oil Wealth, Official Says," *Boston Globe*, 17 December 2004. Both ideas are attributed to Ribadu, but only the second is reported as a direct quotation.
10. Pini Jason, "Transparency Int'l, Nigeria, and Corruption Index," *Vanguard*, 26 October 2004.
11. George Oji, "Nigeria, 6th Most Corrupt Country," *This Day*, 18 October 2005.
12. "Our New TI Corruption Ranking," *Daily Champion*, 14 November 2006.
13. http://cpi.transparency.org/cpi2012/in_detail/#sthash.DC9KzLqh.dpuf, accessed 6 November 2013.

14. Governor Ibori garnered international notoriety several years later, when he pleaded guilty in a British court to charges of money laundering. In his plea, the governor admitted to laundering $50 million, but many commentators claimed the actual amounts abstracted from the Delta state government were far higher. One aspect to the story that received enormous attention was that the governor had perjured himself in his affidavit before running for governor in 1999 by claiming he had no previous convictions, a requirement for political candidates. In fact, the governor had a considerable record of petty theft from a previous stay in the United Kingdom. He avoided the records of those convictions by falsifying his passport. Thus in retrospect, it turned out the governor was ineligible for the office that he subsequently misused.

15. American Embassy Abuja to Secretary of State, 16 May 2008, Wikileaks, www.wikileaks.org/plus/cables/08ABUJA898_a.html, accessed 5 July 2013. The cables were reported in the Nigerian press in March 2011, just before Waziri was forced from office.

16. Dave Ajetomogi, "EFCC Can't Fight Corruption Where It Matters—Ajetomobi," *Daily Independent*, 12 November 2008.

17. Political parties in the Fourth Republic have been somewhat fluid, apart from the ruling PDP. Nonetheless, the southwest has been a center of strength for a party called the Action Congress, later the Action Congress of Nigeria, which bears continuities to Obafemi Awolowo's old Action Group and Unity Party of Nigeria.

18. Albin-Lackey, "Corruption on Trial?" Researchers who sampled a multiethnic sample of people living in the southwestern Nigerian town of Abeokuta in 2009 found that people believed the EFCC had succeeded in reducing public corruption and advance-fee fraud, though the body was subject to interference from senior government figures. Sowunmi, Adesola, and Salako, "Performance."

19. "Ibori Recommended Waziri for EFCC job—Obasanjo," *Punch*, 11 September 2013.

20. "Angry Farida Waziri Fires Back at Obasanjo," *Premium Times*, 11 September 2013.

21. "James Ibori Extradition Ruling for Next Sunday, October 17, in Dubai," *Sahara Reporters*, 10 October 2010.

22. On this topic Leena Hoffmann provides a particularly insightful recent analyst. See Hoffmann, "Fairy Godfathers"; "Big Men and the Pot at the Centre." See also Ikpe, "Godfatherism and the Nigerian Polity."

23. Chief Okotie-Eboh's death is equally explicable as a matter of ethnicity and of NCNC factional politics, so one would not wish to press the point of corruption discourse too strongly.

24. See, for example, Almond, "Comparative Political Systems."

25. For an intellectual history of this development, see Mitchell, "Limits of the State"; "State Effect." See also Hansen and Stepputat, *States of Imagination*; Sharma and Gupta, "Rethinking Theories of the State."

26. For a much earlier discussion in a similar vein, see Brooks, "Attempted Apologies."

27. Nye, "Corruption and Political Development," 419.

28. Weber, *Economy and Society*, 3: 975.

29. McMullen, "Theory of Corruption."

30. Weber, *Methodology*, 90.

31. Peter Ekeh's famous essay on the two publics predominant in postcolonial Africa is an interesting variation on this theme, suggesting the coexistence of patrimonial and bureaucratic notions of public life and public office. Ekeh, "Two Publics."

32. Eisenstadt, *Traditional Patrimonialism and Modern Neopatrimonialism*; Clapham, *Private Patronage and Public Power*; Medard, "L'état néo-patrimonial"; Bratton and van de Walle, "Neopatrimonial Regimes and Political Transitions in Africa"; Bach, "Patrimonialism and Neopatrimonialism."

33. Evans, Rueschemeyer, and Skocpol, *Bringing the State Back In*.

34. Very fine works on Nigerian politics written in the 1950s and 1960s are distorted by this clumsy framework. See, for example, Coleman, *Nigeria*; Sklar, *Nigerian Political Parties*. Even Whitaker's admirably subtle study of the imbrication of the northern native authorities in First Republic politics, which in no way assumed "traditional" emirate structures, were in the process of giving way to "modernity," nonetheless depended on somewhat teleological assumptions. Whitaker, *Politics of Tradition*.

35. For example, Beckman, "Neo-Colonialism"; "Whose State?"; Oyediran, *Nigerian Government*; Oyovbaire, *Federalism in Nigeria*; Schatz, *Nigerian Capitalism*; Shenton, *Development of Capitalism*; Ikpe, "Patrimonialism and Military Regimes in Nigeria"; "Godfatherism and the Nigerian Polity"; Watts, *State, Oil, and Agriculture in Nigeria*; " Shock of Modernity"; Diamond, *Class, Ethnicity and Democracy in Nigeria*; Graf, *Nigerian State*; Laitin, *Hegemony and Culture*; Elaigwu, *Shadow of Religion on Nigerian Federalism: 1960–93*; Kalu, *State Power, Autarchy, and Political Conquest in Nigerian Federalism*; Suberu, *Federalism and Ethnic Conflict in Nigeria*; Ojo, "Patrimonialism, Sultanism, and Nation-Building in Nigeria"; Onwudiwe, Suberu, and University of Ibadan, Programme on Ethnic and Federal Studies, *Nigerian Federalism in Crisis*; Osaghae, "Structural Adjustment and Ethnicity in Nigeria"; *Crippled Giant*.

36. For an excellent assessment, see Adebanwi and Obadare, *Democracy and Prebendalism in Nigeria*.

37. Lewis, "Prebendalism to Predation."

38. Adekanye, *Retired Military*.

39. Ikpe, "Godfatherism and the Nigerian Polity"; Hoffmann, "Big Men and the Pot at the Centre"; Albert, "Explaining Godfatherism"; Omotola, "Garrison 'Democracy.'" Onwuzuruigbo usefully points out that political patrons and patronage as such are nothing new in Nigerian politics but less convincingly argues that contemporary political problems come about because of distortions engendered by the colonial period. Onwuzuruigbo, "Concept of Godfatherism."

40. Hoffmann, "Fairy Godfathers"; "Big Men and the Pot at the Centre." Ultimately, a court overturned Governor Ngige's 2003 election, and he left office after three years in power.

41. Hill, *Development Economics on Trial*; Jerven, *Poor Numbers*.

42. Jackson, *Quasi-States*; Jackson and Rosberg, "Why Africa's Weak States Persist."

43. For a stimulating discussion of the complexities of this situation, see Ojimiwe, "Malaria Control."

44. Dele Momodu, "Nigeria: Our Time Will Come," *This Day*, 10 April 2009.

45. Nolte, "Ethnic Vigilantes"; Pratten and Sen, *Global Vigilantes*; Gore and Pratten, "Order and Disorder in Southern Nigeria"; Harnischfeger, "Bakassi Boys."

46. Reno, "Anti-Corruption Efforts in Liberia."

47. Meagher, "Social Capital." Meagher has also developed a very useful assessment of the utility of Tillyan approaches to the state as a variety of protection racket, one which potentially becomes institutionalized across long periods. "Strength of Weak States?"

48. Jackson and Rosberg, "Why Africa's Weak States Persist."

49. Bayart, *Politics of the Belly*, 235.

50. Mbembe, *On the Postcolony*. For a brilliant analysis of how the Togolese dictator Gnassingbe Eyadema enacted and epitomized this mode of power, see Piot, *Nostalgia for the Future*. For a discussion of magic and religious powers undergirding some Nigerian political networks, see Ellis, "Okija Shrine" Marshall, *Political Spiritualities*. Despite many points of similarity, Bayart has condemned Mbembe (and the entire field of postcolonial studies), for a lack of subtlety or appreciation for variation. Mbembe's reply points out that few of Bayart's objections to postcolonial studies accurately describe the field, and he implicitly suggests their substantive positions (on anything other than perhaps considering France to be the center of the world of theory) are quite similar. Mbembe, "Provincializing France?" See also Young, "Bayart's Broken Kettle." For a more successful criticism of postcolonial studies (though with only indirect bearing on the positions outlined above), see Cooper, *Colonialism in Question*.

51. Chabal and Deloz, *Africa Works*, 1.

52. Bayart, Ellis, and Hibou, *Criminalization of the State*. Olivier de Sardan's suggestion that African corruption has a distinct moral economy also fits neatly into this approach. My use of the term "moral economy" is indebted to Olivier de Sardan's formulation but differs from it profoundly. See chapter 4. Olivier de Sardan, "Moral Economy of Corruption in Africa?"

53. For a similar critique, see Ochonu, "Corruption and Political Culture," 32–33.

54. For an allied critique of such approaches, see Pitcher, Moran, and Johnston, "Rethinking Patrimonialism." They suggest the problem is commentators' tendency to take patrimonialism as being a particular type of state rather than being a mode through which states are legitimated.

55. Radcliffe-Brown, "Preface"; Abrams, "Notes on the Difficulty of Studying the State."

56. This argument was influentially laid out in Althusser, "Ideological State Apparatuses." See also Butler, *Psychic Life of Power*.

57. Mitchell's first formulation was in Mitchell, "Limits of the State." A revised version that underlined the congruence of his work with Abrams's was published as "State Effect."

58. Fernando Coronil has perhaps pushed this line of reasoning to its ultimate conclusion in *The Magical State*. See also Sharma and Gupta, "Rethinking Theories of the State"; Hansen and Stepputat, *States of Imagination*; Brown, *States of Injury*.

59. Ferguson and Gupta, "Spatializing States." See also Harris, "State as Socio-Natural Effect"; Roitman, "Africa, Otherwise."

60. Das and Poole, *Anthropology in the Margins of the State*. For important studies of how these dynamics play out at the edges of Cameroon and Ghana, see Roitman, *Fiscal Disobedience*; Chalfin, *Neoliberal Frontiers*.

61. Cooper, "Africa and the World Economy"; *Africa since 1940*; Bayart, "Extraversion."

62. Scott, *Seeing like a State*.

63. Pierce, "Looking like a State."

64. Arukaino Umukoro, "Nigerians Fuel Champagne Lifestyle with Billions of Naira," *Punch*, 19 May 2013.

65. Diamond, "Class Formation in the Swollen African State."

Conclusion

1. "Transparency International Asks Nigerian Organisation to Stop Using Its Name and Logo," press release, 12 April 2013, http://www.transparency.org/news/pressrelease/20130412_ti_asks_nigerian_organisation_to_stop_using_logo, accessed 16 July 2013.

2. "Transparency International Disowns Nigerian Clone," *Premium Times*, 13 April 2013.

3. The Corruption Barometer is a measure distinct from the Corruption Perceptions Index. The latter is based on a variety of measures taken from experts in the field—businesspeople, nongovernmental organizations (NGOs), and the like. The former is the result of public opinion surveys conducted in countries around the world.

4. Reno Omokri, "Re: 8th Most Corrupt Nation—Transparency International," 12 July 2013, http://presreleasenigeria.com/general/, accessed 28 August 2013. Omokri is special assistant to the president (New Media).

5. Abubakar Saliki, "Kano Emerges Best in Fiscal Responsibility," *Leadership*, 2 April 2013.

6. "Kano Most Budget Disciplined State," *Kwankwasiyya Online*, http://www.kwankwasiyyaonline.org/index.php/9-uncategorised/188-kano-most-budget-disciplined-state, accessed 28 August 2013.

7. Uba Danzainab, "Re: Transparency International Dissociating Self from Transparency in Nigeria's Budget Discipline Assessment Where Kano State Emerges as the Most Budget Disciplined State in Nigeria," 14 April 2013, https://www.facebook.com/KwankwasiyyaOnline/posts/560581330643150, accessed 28 August 2013. The author of this post is a special assistant to Kano's governor. A more measured op-ed making similar points appeared more than a month later, Umar Farouq Tafida, "Nigeria: That TIN Report Kano's Budget Discipline," *Daily Trust*, 24 May 2013.

8. Nye, "Corruption and Political Development"; Wraith and Simpkins, *Corruption in Developing Countries*. James Scott's early work included an admirably subtle synthesis of the political science literature from this period. Scott, "Analysis of Corruption."

9. Case, "Malaysia in 2007."

10. Mikkelsen, "In Murky Waters."

11. Philps, "Defining Political Corruption," 446.

12. Gupta, "Narrating the State of Corruption"; *Red Tape*.

BIBLIOGRAPHY

Primary Sources

ARCHIVAL COLLECTIONS

Arewa House, Kaduna (AH)
Kano State History and Culture Bureau (HCB)
Nigerian National Archives, Kaduna (NAK)
Rhodes House, Oxford (RH)
United Kingdom National Archives, Public Record Office (TNA PRO)

PUBLISHED REPORTS

Federal Republic of Nigeria. Comments of the Federal Government on the *Report of Coker Commission of Inquiry into the Affairs of Certain Statutory Corporations in Western Nigeria.* Lagos: Federal Ministry of Information, 1962.

Federal Republic of Nigeria. *Report of Coker Commission of Inquiry into the Affairs of Certain Statutory Corporations in Western Nigeria.* Lagos: Federal Ministry of Information, 1962.

Federal Republic of Nigeria. *Report of the Tribunal of Inquiry into the Importation of Cement.* Lagos: Federal Ministry of Information, 1976.

Nigerian Democratic Movement. *Report of the Human Rights Violations Investigation Commission.* Washington, DC: NDM, 2002.

Nigeria. *Annual Report on Nigeria for the Year 1949.* London: HMSO, 1950.

Nigeria. *Report of the Tribunal Appointed to Inquire into Allegations Reflecting on the Official Conduct of the Premier of, and Certain Persons Holding Ministerial and Other Public Offices in, the Eastern Region of Nigeria.* London: HMSO, 1957.

Northern Nigeria. *Report for 1902.* London: HMSO, 1903.

Northern Nigeria. *Report for 1905–6.* London: HMSO, 1907.

Northern Nigeria. *Report for 1907–8.* London: HMSO, 1909.

Northern Nigeria. *Report for 1910–11.* London, HMSO, 1911.

United Kingdom. *Hansard Parliamentary Debates.* 1953. http://hansard.milbanksystems
.com.

NEWSPAPERS

(Newspapers are Nigerian unless otherwise noted.)
Boston Globe (USA)
Daily Champion
Daily Independent
Daily Telegraph (UK)
Daily Trust
Guardian
Guardian (UK)
Irish Times (Ireland)
Lakeland Ledger (Florida, USA)
National Mirror
New Nigerian
New York Times (USA)
Observer (UK)
Post-Express
Premium Times
Punch
Sahara Reporters
Sun
Tell
This Day
Time (USA)
Vanguard
Wall Street Journal (USA)
Washington Post (USA)
West Africa (UK)

Secondary Sources

Abba, Alkasum. "The Misrepresentation of Nigeria by Nigerians and Others." In *Nige-
ria UN Reform Committee.* Ahmadu Bello University, Zaria, 2005.
Abrams, Philip. "Notes on the Difficulty of Studying the State (1977)." *Journal of His-
torical Sociology* 1, no. 1 (1988): 58–89.
Achebe, Nwando. *Farmers, Traders, Warriors, and Kings: Female Power and Authority
in Northern Igboland, 1900–1960.* Portsmouth, NH: Heinemann, 2005.
———. *The Female King of Colonial Nigeria: Ahebi Ugbabe.* Bloomington: Indiana
University Press, 2010.
Adamolekun, Ladipo, and S. Bamidele Ayo. "The Evolution of the Nigerian Federal
Administration System." *Publius* 19, no. 1 (1989): 157–76.
Adamu, Adamu. "Understanding the Balogun Effect." *Daily Trust,* 15 July 2005.

Adebanwi, Wale. *Authority Stealing: Anti-Corruption War and Democratic Politics in Post-Military Nigeria.* Durham, NC: Carolina Academic Press, 2012.

Adebanwi, Wale, and Ebenezer Obadare, eds. *Democracy and Prebendalism in Nigeria: Critical Interpretations.* New York: Palgrave, 2013.

Adebayo, A. G. "Jangali: Fulani Pastoralists and Colonial Taxation in Northern Nigeria." *International Journal of African Historical Studies* 28, no. 1 (1995): 113–50.

Adekanye, Bayo. *The Retired Military as Emergent Power Factor in Nigeria.* Ibadan, Nigeria: Heinemann Educational Books, 1999.

Adeleye, R. A. *Power and Diplomacy in Northern Nigeria, 1804–1906.* London: Longman, 1971.

Afigbo, A. F. *The Warrant Chiefs: Indirect Rule in Southeastern Nigeria, 1891–1929.* London: Longman, 1972.

Ahmad Khan, Sarah. *Nigeria: The Political Economy of Oil.* Oxford: Oxford University Press, 1994.

Ahonsi, Babatunde A. "Deliberate Falsification and Census Data in Nigeria." *African Affairs* 87, no. 349 (1988): 553–62.

Albert, Isaac Olawale. "Explaining Godfatherism in Nigerian Politics." *African Sociological Review* 9, no. 2 (2005): 79–105.

Albin-Lackey, Chris. "Corruption on Trial? The Record of Nigeria's Economic and Financial Crimes Commission." New York: Human Rights Watch, 2011.

Almond, Gabriel A. "Comparative Political Systems." *Journal of Politics* 18, no. 3 (1956): 391–409.

Althusser, Louis. "Ideology and Ideological State Apparatuses (Notes toward an Investigation)." Translated by Ben Brewster. In *Lenin and Philosophy, and Other Essays,* 127–88. New York: Monthly Review Press, 1972.

Amin, Samir. *Neo-Colonialism in West Africa.* Translated by Francis McDonagh. Baltimore, MD: Penguin Books, 1973.

Anderson, Benedict. *Imagined Communities: Reflections on the Origin and Spread of Nationalism.* Rev. and extended ed. London: Verso, 1991.

Andvig, Jens, and Odd-Helge Fjeldstad. "Corruption: A Review of Contemporary Research." *Development Studies and Human Rights* Report Series. Bergen: Chr. Michelsen Institute, 2001.

Anthony, Douglas. *Poison and Medicine: Ethnicity, Power, and Violence in a Nigerian City, 1966 to 1986.* Portsmouth, NH: Heinemann, 2002.

Apter, Andrew. *Black Critics and Kings: The Hermeneutics of Power in Yoruba Society.* Chicago: University of Chicago Press, 1992.

———. *The Pan-African Nation: Oil and the Spectacle of Culture in Nigeria.* Chicago: University of Chicago Press, 2005.

Apter, David. *Ghana in Transition.* Rev. ed. New York: Atheneum, 1963.

———. *The Gold Coast in Transition.* Princeton, NJ: Princeton University Press, 1955.

Arnett, Edward J. *Gazetteer of Zaria Province.* London: Waterlow and Sons, 1920.

Ashwe, Chiichii. *Fiscal Federalism in Nigeria.* Canberra: Centre for Research on Federal Financial Relations, 1986.

Austin, J. L. *How to Do Things with Words*. Cambridge, MA: Harvard University Press, 1962.

Awolowo, Obafemi. *Voice of Courage: Selected Speeches of Chief Obafemi Awolowo*. Vol. 2. Akure: Fagbamigbe Publishers, 1981.

Ayandele, E. A. *The Missionary Impact on Modern Nigeria, 1842–1914: A Political and Social Analysis*. London: Longman, 1966.

Azikiwe, Nnamdi. *Democracy with Military Vigilance*. Lagos: African Book Company, 1974 [1972].

Bach, Daniel C. "Patrimonialism and Neopatrimonialism: Comparative Trajectories and Readings." *Commonwealth and Comparative Politics* 49, no. 3 (2011): 275–94.

Backwell, H. F. *The Occupation of Hausaland, 1900–1904, Being a Translation of Arabic Letters Found in the House of the Wazir of Sokoto, Bohari, in 1903*. London: Frank Cass, 1969.

Ballhatchet, Kenneth. *Race, Sex, and Class under the Raj: Imperial Attitudes and Policies and Their Critics, 1793–1905*. New York: St. Martin's Press, 1980.

Barcham, Manuhuia, Barry Hindess, and Peter Larmour, eds. *Corruption: Expanding the Focus*. Canberra: ANU E Press, 2012.

Barth, Heinrich. *Travels and Discoveries in North and Central Africa: Being a Journal of an Expedition under the Auspices of H.B.M.'S Government in the Years 1849–1855*. Vol. 1. New York: Harper and Brothers Publishers, 1857.

Bates, Robert H. *Markets and States in Tropical Africa: The Political Basis of Agricultural Policies*. Berkeley: University of California Press, 1981.

Bayart, Jean-François. "Africa in the World: A History of Extraversion." *African Affairs* 99, no. 395 (2000): 217–67.

———. *The State in Africa: The Politics of the Belly*. London: Longman, 1993.

Bayart, Jean-François, Stephen Ellis, and Beatrice Hibou. *The Criminalization of the State in Africa*. Translated by Stephen Ellis. Bloomington: Indiana University Press, 1999.

Beckman, Bjorn. "Neo-Colonialism, Capitalism, and the State in Nigeria." In *Contradictions of Accumulation in Africa: Studies in Economy and State*, edited by Henry Bernstein and Campbell Bonnie K. Beverly Hills, CA: Sage, 1985.

———. "Whose State? State and Capitalist Development in Nigeria." *Review of African Political Economy* 9, no. 23 (1982): 37–51.

Bello, Ahmadu. *My Life*. Cambridge: Cambridge University Press, 1962.

Berry, Sara. *Chiefs Know Their Boundaries: Essays on Property, Power, and the Past in Asante, 1896–1996*. Portsmouth: Heinemann, 2001.

———. *Cocoa, Custom, and Socio-Economic Change in Rural Western Nigeria*. Oxford: Clarendon Press, 1975.

———. *No Condition Is Permanent: The Social Dynamics of Agrarian Change in Sub-Saharan Africa*. Madison: University of Wisconsin Press, 1993.

Blackburn, Keith, Niloy Bose, and M. Emranul Haque. "Endogenous Corruption in Economic Development." *Journal of Economic Studies* 37, no. 1 (2010): 4–25.

Blundo, Giorgio. "Corruption in Africa and the Social Sciences: A Review of the Literature." In *Everyday Corruption and the State: Citizens and Public Officials in Africa*, edited by Giorgio Blundo, 15–68. London: Zed Press, 2006.

Blundo, Giorgio, and J.-P. Olivier de Sardan. *Everyday Corruption and the State: Citizens and Public Officials in Africa*. Translated by Susan Cox. London: Zed Books, 2006.

Bratsis, Peter. "The Construction of Corruption, or Rules of Separation and Illusions of Purity in Bourgeois Societies." *Social Text* 21, no. 4 (2003): 9–33.

Bratton, Michael, and Nicolas van de Walle. "Neopatrimonial Regimes and Political Transitions in Africa." *World Politics* 46, no. 4 (1994): 453–89.

Bridenthal, Renate. "The Hidden History of Crime, Corruption, and States: An Introduction." *Journal of Social History* 45, no. 3 (2012): 575–81.

Brooks, Robert C. "Attempted Apologies for Corruption." *International journal of Ethics* 19, no. 3 (1909): 297–320.

———. *Corruption in American Politics and Life*. New York: Dodd, Mead, 1910.

———. "The Nature of Political Corruption." *Political Science Quarterly* 24, no. 1 (1909): 1–22.

Brown, Wendy. *States of Injury: Power and Freedom in Late Modernity*. Princeton, NJ: Princeton University Press, 1995.

Brownsberger, William N. "Development and Governmental Corruption—Materialism and Political Fragmentation in Nigeria." *Journal of Modern African Studies* 21, no. 2 (1983): 215–33.

Bull, Mary. "Indirect Rule in Northern Nigeria, 1906–1911." In *Essays in Imperial Government*, edited by Kenneth Robinson and Frederick Madden. Oxford: Oxford University Press, 1963.

Burbank, Jane, and Frederick Cooper. *Empires in World History: Power and the Politics of Difference*. Princeton, NJ: Princeton University Press, 2010.

Burgess, Douglas R. "A Crisis of Charter and Right: Piracy and Colonial Resistance in Seventeenth-Century Rhode Island." *Journal of Social History* 45, no. 3 (2012): 605–22.

Butler, Judith. *Excitable Speech: A Politics of the Performative*. New York: Routledge, 1997.

———. *The Psychic Life of Power: Theories in Subjection*. Stanford, CA: Stanford University Press, 1997.

Case, William. "Malaysia in 2007: High Corruption and Low Opposition." *Asian Survey* 48, no. 1 (2008): 47–54.

Chabal, Patrick, and Jean-Pascal Deloz. *Africa Works: Disorder as Political Instrument*. Bloomington: Indiana University Press, 1999.

Chalfin, Brenda. "Border Zone Trade and the Economic Boundaries of the State in North-East Ghana." *Africa* 71, no. 2 (2001): 202–24.

———. "Enlarging the Anthropology of the State: Global Customs Regimes and the Traffic in Sovereignty." *Current Anthropology* 47, no. 2 (2007): 243–76.

———. *Neoliberal Frontiers: An Ethnography of Sovereignty in West Africa*. Chicago: University of Chicago Press, 2010.

Clapham, Christopher, ed. *Private Patronage and Public Power: Political Clientelism in the Modern State*. New York: St. Martin's Press, 1982.

———. *Third World Politics: An Introduction*. London: Crook Helm, 1985.

Clarke, John D. *Yakubu Gowon: Faith in a United Nigeria*. London: Frank Cass, 1987.

Cohen, Abner. *Custom and Politics in Urban Africa: A Study of Hausa Migrants in Yoruba Towns*. Berkeley: University of California Press, 1969.

Coleman, James S. *Nigeria: Background to Nationalism*. Berkeley: University of California Press, 1958.

Cooper, Frederick. "Africa and the World Economy." *African Studies Review* 24, no. 2/3 (1980): 1–86.

———. *Africa since 1940: The Past of the Present*. Cambridge: Cambridge University Press, 2002.

———. *Colonialism in Question: Theory, Knowledge, History*. Berkeley: University of California Press, 2005.

———. *Decolonization and African Society: The Labor Question in French and British Africa*. Cambridge: Cambridge University Press, 1996.

———. "Modernizing Bureaucrats, Backwards Africans, and the Development Concept." In *International Development and the Social Sciences: Essays on the History and Politics of Knowledge*, edited by Frederick Cooper and Randall Packard. Berkeley: University of California Press, 1997.

———. "Reconstructing Empire in Post-War French and British Africa." *Past and Present* 210, no. Supplement 6 (2011): 196–210.

———. "Writing the History of Development." *Journal of Modern European History* 8, no. 1 (2010): 5–23.

Cooper, Frederick, Thomas C. Holt, and Rebecca J. Scott. *Beyond Slavery: Explorations of Race, Labor, and Citizenship in Postemancipation Societies*. Chapel Hill: University of North Carolina Press, 2000.

Coronil, Fernando. *The Magical State: Nature, Money, and Modernity in Venezuela*. Chicago: University of Chicago Press, 1997.

Das, Veena, and Deborah Poole, eds. *Anthropology in the Margins of the State*. Santa Fe: School of American Research Press, 2004.

Daston, Lorraine. "The Moral Economy of Science." *Osiris* 10 (1995): 3–24.

Debiel, Tobias, and Andrea Gawrich. "(Dys-)Functionalities of Corruption: Comparative Perspectives and Methodological Pluralism." *Zeitschrift für Vergleichende Politikwissenschaft* 7, supplement 1 (2014): 1–11.

Diamond, Larry. *Class, Ethnicity and Democracy in Nigeria: The Failure of the First Republic*. Syracuse, NY: Syracuse University Press, 1988.

———. "Class Formation in the Swollen African State." *Journal of Modern African Studies* 25, no. 4 (1987): 567–96.

Dirks, Nicholas B. *The Scandal of Empire: India and the Creation of Imperial Britain*. Cambridge: Belknap, 2006.

Dokaji, Alhaji Abubakar. *Kano Ta Dabo Cigari*. Zaria: Gaskiya, 1959.

Dudley, B. J. *Parties and Politics in Northern Nigeria*. London: Frank Cass, 1968.

East, R. M. "Recent Activities of the Literature Bureau, Zaria, Northern Nigeria." *Africa* 14, no. 2 (1943): 71–77.

Eisenstadt, S. N., ed. *Traditional Patrimonialism and Modern Neopatrimonialism*. Beverly Hills, CA: Sage, 1973.

Ekeh, Peter. "Colonialism and the Two Publics in Africa: A Theoretical Statement." *Comparative Studies in Society and History* 17, no. 1 (1975): 91–112.

Elaigwu, J. Isawa. *Gowon: The Biography of a Solder-Statesman.* Ibadan: West Books, 1985.

———. *The Shadow of Religion on Nigerian Federalism: 1960–93.* National Council on Intergovernmental Relations Monograph Series. Garki, Abuja, Nigeria: NCIR, 1993.

Ellis, Stephen. "The Okija Shrine: Death and Life in Nigerian Politics." *Journal of African History* 49, no. 3 (2008): 445–66.

Ellis, Stephen, and Janet MacGaffey. "Research on Sub-Saharan Africa's Unrecorded International Trade: Some Methodological and Conceptual Problems." *African Studies Review* 39, no. 2 (1996): 19–41.

Evans, Peter, Dietrich Rueschemeyer, and Theda Skocpol, eds. *Bringing the State Back In.* Cambridge: Cambridge University Press, 1985.

Fassin, Didier. "Les économies morales revistées." *Annales* 64, no. 6 (2009): 1237–66.

Ferguson, James. *The Anti-Politics Machine: "Development," Depoliticization, and Bureaucratic Power in Lesotho.* Cambridge: Cambridge University Press, 1990.

Ferguson, James, and Akhil Gupta. "Spatializing States: Toward an Ethnography of Neoliberal Governmentality." *American Ethnologist* 29, no. 4 (2002): 981–1002.

Fika, Adamu Mohammed. *The Kano Civil War and British over-Rule 1882–1940.* Oxford: Oxford University Press, 1978.

First, Ruth. *The Barrel of a Gun: Political Power in Africa and the Coup D'Etat.* London: Allen Lane, 1970.

Frank, Andre Gunder. *Capitalism and Underdevelopment in Latin America: Historical Studies of Chile and Brazil.* New York: Monthly Review Press, 1969.

Fuller, C. J., and Veronique Benei, eds. *The Everyday State and Society in Modern India.* London: Hurst, 2001.

Funk, Jerry. *Life Is an Excellent Adventure: An Irreverent Personal Odyssey.* Victoria: Trafford, 2003.

Garba, Tijjani. "Taxation in Some Hausa Emirates." Ph.D. thesis, University of Birmingham, 1986.

Gash, Norman. *Politics in the Age of Peel: A Study in the Technique of Parliamentary Representation 1830–1850.* London: Longman, 1953.

Geary, William. *Nigeria under British Rule.* London: Methuen, 1927.

Gore, Charles, and David Pratten. "The Politics of Plunder: The Rhetorics of Order and Disorder in Southern Nigeria." *African Affairs* 102, no. 407 (2003): 211–40.

Gould, William. *Bureaucracy, Community and Influence in India: Society and the State, 1930s–1960s.* London: Routledge, 2010.

Gould, William, Taylor C. Sherman, and Sarah Ansari. "The Flux of the Matter: Loyalty, Corruption and the 'Everyday State' in the Post-Partition Goverment Services of India and Pakistan." *Past and Present* 219, no. 1 (2013): 237–79.

Graf, William. *The Nigerian State: Political Economy, State, Class and Political System in the Post-Colonial Era.* London: James Currey, 1987.

Graham, Sonia F. *Government and Mission Education in Northern Nigeria, 1900–1919, with Special Reference to the Work of Hanns Vischer.* Ibadan: Ibadan University Press, 1966.

Gupta, Akhil. "Blurred Boundaries: The Discourse of Corruption, the Culture of Politics, and the Imagined State." *American Ethnologist* 22, no. 2 (1995): 375–402.

———. "Narrating the State of Corruption." In *Corruption: Anthropological Perspectives*, edited by Dieter Haller and Cris Shore, 173–93. London: Pluto Press, 2005.

———. *Red Tape: Bureaucracy, Structural Violence, and Poverty in India*. Durham, NC: Duke University Press, 2012.

Guyer, Jane. *Marginal Gains: Monetary Transactions in Atlantic Africa*. Chicago: University of Chicago Press, 2004.

———. "Representation without Taxation: An Essay on Democracy in Rural Nigeria, 1952–1990." *African Studies Review* 35, no. 1 (1992): 41–80.

Gyimah-Brempong, K. "Corruption, Economic Growth and Income Inequality in Africa." *Economics of Governance* 3 (2002): 183–209.

Habermas, Jurgen. *The Structural Transformation of the Public Sphere*. Translated by Thomas Burger. Cambridge, MA: MIT Press, 1991.

Hansen, Thomas Blom, and Finn Stepputat, eds. *States of Imagination: Ethnographic Explorations of the Postcolonial State*. Durham, NC: Duke University Press, 2001.

Harnischfeger, Johannes. "The Bakassi Boys: Fighting Crime in Nigeria." *Journal of Modern African Studies* 41, no. 1 (2003): 23–49.

Harris, Leila M. "State as Socio-Natural Effect: Variable and Emergent Geographies of the State in Southeastern Turkey." *Comparative Studies in South Asia, Africa and the Middle East* 32, no. 1 (2012): 25–39.

Hasty, Jennifer. "The Pleasures of Corruption: Desire and Discipline in Ghanaian Political Culture." *Cultural Anthropology* 20, no. 2 (2005): 271–301.

Hayatu, Husseini, ed. *50 Years of Truth: The Story of Gaskiya Corporation, 1939–1991*. Zaria: Gaskiya Corporation, 1991.

Helleiner, Gerald K. "The Fiscal Role of the Marketing Boards in Nigerian Economic Development, 1947–1961." *Economic Journal* 74, no. 295 (1964): 582–610.

Herbst, Jeffrey. *States and Power in Africa: Comparative Lessons in Authority and Control*. Princeton, NJ: Princeton University Press, 2000.

Hibou, Beatrice. "Economic Crime and Neoliberal Modes of Government: The Example of the Mediterranean." *Journal of Social History* 45, no. 3 (2012): 643–60.

Hill, Polly. *Development Economics on Trial: The Anthropological Case for a Prosecution*. Cambridge: Cambridge University Press, 1986.

Hoffmann, Leena. "Big Men and the Pot at the Centre: Patronage Politics and Democracy in Nigeria." Ph.D. thesis, University of Birmingham, 2011.

———. "Fairy Godfathers and Magical Elections: Understanding the 2003 Electoral Crisis in Anambra State, Nigeria." *Journal of Modern African Studies* 48, no. 2 (2010): 285–310.

Hogendorn, Jan S. *Nigerian Groundnut Exports: Origins and Early Development*. Zaria: Ahmadu Bello University Press, 1978.

———. "Slave Acquisition and Delivery in Precolonial Hausaland." In *West Africa Culture Dynamics*, edited by Ben Swartz and Raymond Dumett, 477–93. The Hague: Mouton, 1980.

Hogendorn, Jan S., and Marion Johnson. *The Shell Money of the Slave Trade.* Cambridge: Cambridge University Press, 1986.

Hounsome, Robert. *The Very Nearly Man: An Autobiography.* Leicester, UK: Matador, 2007.

Hutson, Alaine S. "The Development of Women's Authority in the Kano Tijaniyya, 1894–1963." *Africa Today* 46, no. 3–4 (1999): 43–64.

Ibrahim, Omar. "The Fabric of Rule: A Study of the Postion of Traditional Ruling Families in the Politics of Kano State, Nigeria, 1960–1983." Ph.D. thesis, Rutgers University, 1988.

Ikein, Augustine A., and Comfort Briggs-Anigboh. *Oil and Fiscal Federalism in Nigeria: The Political Economy of Resource Allocation in a Developing Country.* Aldershot: Ashgate, 1998.

Ikpe, Ukana B. "Godfatherism and the Nigerian Polity." In *Nigeria's Democratic Experience in the Fourth Republic since 1999: Policies and Politics,* edited by A. Sat Obiyan and Kunle Amuwo, 111–26. Lanham: University Press of America, 2013.

———. "Patrimonialism and Military Regimes in Nigeria." *African Journal of Political Science* 5, no. 1 (2000): 146–62.

Imam, Abubakar. "Nigerian Constitutional Proposals." *African Affairs* 45, no. 178 (1946): 22–27.

Iwayemi, Akin. "The Military and the Economy." In *Nigerian Government and Politics under Military Rule, 1966–1979,* edited by Oyeleye Oyediran, 47–73. London: Macmillan, 1979.

Jackson, Robert H. *Quasi-States: Sovereignty, International Relations, and the Third World.* Cambridge: Cambridge University Press, 1990.

Jackson, Robert H., and Carl G. Rosberg. "Why Africa's Weak States Persist." *World Politics* 35, no. 1 (1982): 1–24.

Jameson, Fredric. *The Political Unconscious: Narrative as a Socially Symbolic Act.* Ithaca, NY: Cornell University Press, 1981.

Jerven, Morten. *Poor Numbers: How We Are Misled by African Development Statistics and What to Do about It.* Ithaca, NY: Cornell University Press, 2013.

Johnson, Marion. "Polanyi, Peukert, and the Political Economy of Dahomey." *Journal of African History* 21, no. 3 (1980): 395–98.

Johnston, Michael, ed. *Public Sector Corruption.* 4 vols. Beverly Hills, CA: Sage, 2011.

———. "The Search for Definitions: The Vitality of Politics and the Issue of Corruption." *International Social Science Journal* 48, no. 149 (1996): 321–35.

Joseph, Richard A. *Democracy and Prebendal Politics in Nigeria: The Rise and Fall of the Second Republic.* Cambridge: Cambridge University Press, 1987.

Kalu, Kalu Ndukwe. *State Power, Autarchy, and Political Conquest in Nigerian Federalism.* Lanham, MD: Lexington Books, 2008.

Key, V. O. *Politics, Parties and Pressure Groups.* New York: Thomas Y. Crowell, 1942.

Kirk-Greene, A. H. M. "The Thin White Line: The Size of the British Colonial Service in Africa." *African Affairs,* no. 314 (1980): 25–44.

Kirk-Greene, A. H. M., and Douglas Rimmer. *Nigeria since 1970: A Political and Economic Outline.* London: Hodder and Stoughton, 1981.

Korieh, Chima. *The Land Has Changed: History, Society and Gender in Colonial Eastern Nigeria*. Calgary: University of Calgary Press, 2010.

Kreike, Emmanuel, and William Chester Jordan, eds. *Corrupt Histories: Studies in Comparative History*. Rochester, NY: University of Rochester Press, 2006.

Laitin, David D. *Hegemony and Culture: Politics and Religious Change among the Yoruba*. Chicago: University of Chicago Press, 1986.

Larkin, Brian. *Signal and Noise: Media, Infrastructure, and Urban Culture in Nigeria*. Durham, NC: Duke University Press, 2008.

Last, Murray. *The Sokoto Caliphate*. London: Longman, 1967.

Law, Robin. *Ouidah: The Social History of a West African Slaving Port, 1727–1892*. Athens: Ohio University Press, 2005.

———. "Posthumous Questions for Karl Polanyi: Price Inflation in Pre-Colonial Dahomey." *Journal of African History* 33, no. 3 (1992): 387–420.

———. "Royal Monopoly and Private Enterprise in the Atlantic Trade: The Case of Dahomey." *Journal of African History* 18, no. 4 (1977): 555–77.

Lawson, Letitia. "The Politics of Anti-Corruption Reform in Africa." *Journal of Modern African Studies* 47, no. 1 (2009): 73–100.

Lewis, Peter. "From Prebendalism to Predation: The Political Economy of Decline in Nigeria." *Journal of Modern African Studies* 34, no. 1 (1996): 79–103.

Lewis, W. Arthur. *The Theory of Economic Growth*. Abingdon: Routledge, 2003 [1955].

Leys, Colin. *Underdevelopment in Kenya: The Political Economy of Neo-Colonialism*. Berkeley: University of California Press, 1974.

———. "What Is the Problem about Corruption?" *Journal of Modern African Studies* 3, no. 2 (1965): 215–30.

Lindemann, Mary. "Dirty Politics or 'Harmonie'? Defining Corruption in Early Modern Amsterdam and Hamburg." *Journal of Social History* 45, no. 3 (2012): 582–604.

Lipset, Seymour Martin. "Some Social Requisites of Democracy." *American Political Science Review* 53, no. 1 (1959): 69–105.

Lloyd, Peter C. "The Development of Political Parties in Western Nigeria." *American Political Science Review* 49, no. 3 (1955): 693–707.

Lonsdale, John. "The Moral Economy of Mau Mau: Wealth, Poverty and Civic Virtue in Kikuyu Political Thought." In *The Unhappy Valley: Conflict in Kenya and Africa*, edited by Bruce Berman and John Lonsdale, 315–504. Athens: Ohio University Press, 1992.

"Lord Lugard, G.C.M.G." *Nature* 142 (November 1938): 865.

Lovejoy, Paul E. *Transformations in Slavery: A History of Slavery in Africa*. 2nd ed. Cambridge: Cambridge University Press, 2000.

Lovejoy, Paul E., and Jan S. Hogendorn. *Slow Death for Slavery: The Course of Abolition in Northern Nigeria, 1897–1936*. Cambridge: Cambridge University Press, 1993.

Low, D. A., and John Lonsdale. "Towards the New Order, 1945–1963." In *History of East Africa*, edited by D. A. Low and Alison Smith, 1–64. Oxford: Clarendon Press, 1976.

Lugard, Frederick. *The Dual Mandate in British Tropical Africa*. Edinburgh: W. Blackwood and Sons, 1922.

———. *Instructions to Political and Other Officers on Subjects Chiefly Political and Administrative*. London: Waterlow and Sons, 1906.

———. *Political Memoranda: Revision of Instructions to Political Officers on Subjects Chiefly Political and Administrative 1913–1918*. 3rd ed. London: Frank Cass, 1970.

Lynn, Martin. "The Profitability of the Early Nineteenth Century Palm Oil Trade." *African Economic History* 20 (1992): 77–97.

MacGaffey, Janet. *Entrepreneurs and Parasites: The Struggle for Indigenous Capitalism in Zaire*. Cambridge: Cambridge University Press, 1987.

MacGaffey, Janet, and Remy Bazenguissa-Ganga. *Congo-Paris: Transnational Traders on the Margins of the Law*. Bloomington: Indiana University Press, 2000.

MacGaffey, Janet, Vwakyanakazi Mukohya, Rukarangira wa Nkera, Brooke Gundfest Schoepf, Makwala ma Mavambu ye Beda, and Walu Engundu. *The Real Economy of Zaire: The Contribution of Smuggling and Other Unofficial Activities to the National Wealth*. London: James Currey, 1991.

Mahadi, Abdullahi. "The State and the Economy: The Sarauta System and Its Roles in Shaping the Society and Economy of Kano with Particular Reference to the 18th and 19th Centuries." Ph.D. thesis, Ahmadu Bello University, 1982.

Malinowski, Bronislaw. *Argonauts of the Western Pacific: An Account of Native Enterprise and Adventure in the Archipelagoes of Melanesian New Guinea*. London: G. Routledge, 1922.

———. *Crime and Custom in Savage Society*. London: K. Paul Trench Trubner / New York: Harcourt Brace, 1926.

Mamdani, Mahmood. *Citizen and Subject: Contemporary Africa and the Legacy of Late Colonialism*. Princeton, NJ: Princeton University Press, 1996.

Marshall, Ruth. *Political Spiritualities: The Pentecostal Revolution in Nigeria*. Chicago: University of Chicago Press, 2009.

Mason, Michael. "Population Density and 'Slave Raiding'—the Case of the Middle Belt of Nigeria." *Journal of African History* 10, no. 4 (1969): 551–64.

Mauss, Marcel. *The Gift*. New York: Norton, 1967.

Mbaku, John Mukum. *Bureaucratic and Political Corruption in Africa*. Malabar, FL: Krieger Publishing, 2000.

Mbembe, Achille. *On the Postcolony*. Berkeley: University of California Press, 2001.

———. "Provincializing France?" *Public Culture* 23, no. 1 (2011): 85–119.

McMullen, M. "A Theory of Corruption." *Sociological Review* 9, no. 2 (1963): 181–201.

Meagher, Kate. "Social Capital, Social Liabilities, and Political Capital: Social Networks and Informal Manufacturing in Nigeria." *African Affairs* 105, no. 421 (2006): 553–82.

———. "The Strength of Weak States? Non-State Security Forces and Hybrid Governance in Africa." *Development and Change* 43, no. 5 (2012): 1073–101.

Medard, Jean-François. "L'état néo-patrimonial en Afrique noire." In *Etats D'afrique Noire: Formation, Mecanismes et Crises*, edited by Jean-Francois Medard, 323–53. Paris: Karthala, 1991.

———. "Public Corruption in Africa: A Comparative Perspective." *Corruption and Reform* 1, no. 2 (1986): 115–31.

Melson, Robert, and Howard Wolpe, eds. *Nigeria: Modernization and the Politics of Communalism*. East Lansing: Michigan State University Press, 1971.

Meredith, David. "Government and the Decline of the Nigerian Oil-Palm Export Industry, 1919–1939." *Journal of African History* 25, no. 3 (1984): 311–29.

Miers, Suzanne, and Richard L. Roberts. *The End of Slavery in Africa*. Madison: University of Wisconsin Press, 1988.

Mikkelsen, Kim Sass. "In Murky Waters: A Disentangling of Corruption and Related Concepts." *Crime, Law and Social Change* 60, no. 4 (2013): 357–74.

Miles, William F. S. *Hausaland Divided: Colonialism and Independence in Nigeria and Niger*. Ithaca, NY: Cornell University Press, 1994.

Miller, Walter. *Reflections of a Pioneer*. London: Church Missionary Society, 1936.

———. *Walter Miller, 1872–1953: An Autobiography*. Zaria: Gaskiya, 1953.

Mitchell, Timothy. "The Limits of the State: Beyond Statist Approaches and Their Critics." *American Political Science Review* 85, no. 1 (1991): 77–96.

———. "Society, Economy, and the State Effect." In *State/Culture: State Formation after the Cultural Turn*, edited by George Steinmetz, 76–97. Ithaca, NY: Cornell University Press, 1999.

Moore, Carlos. *Fela: This Bitch of a Life*. Chicago: Chicago Review Press, 2009.

Muffett, D. J. M. "Legitimacy and Deference in a Tradition Oriented Society: Observations Arising from an Examination of Some Aspects of a Case Study Associated with the Abdication of the Emir of Kano in 1963." *African Studies Review* 18, no. 2 (1975): 101–15.

Nadel, S. F. *A Black Byzantium: The Kingdom of Nupe in Nigeria*. London: Oxford University Press, 1946.

Nast, Heidi J. *Concubines and Power: Five Hundred Years in a Northern Nigerian Palace*. Minneapolis: University of Minnesota Press, 2005.

Nechtman, Tillman W. *Nabobs: Empire and Identity in Eighteenth-Century Britain*. New York: Cambridge University Press, 2010.

Nigeria, Supreme Court of. "Awolowo v. Shagari and Others." *Journal of African Law* 23, no. 2 (1979): 175–82.

Nolte, Insa. "Ethnic Vigilantes and the State: The Oodua People's Congress in Southwestern Nigeria." *International Relations* 21, no. 2 (2007): 217–35.

———. *Obafemi Awolowo and the Making of Remo: The Local Politics of a Nigerian Nationalist*. Edinburgh: Edinburgh University Press, 2009.

Nore, Petter, and Terisa Turner, eds. *Oil and Class Struggle*. London: Zed Press, 1980.

Nwabughuogo, Anthony I. "The Role of Propaganda in the Development of Indirect Rule in Nigeria, 1890–1929." *International Journal of African Historical Studies* 14, no. 1 (1981): 65–92.

Nye, Joseph S. "Corruption and Political Development: A Cost-Benefit Analysis." *American Political Science Review* 61, no. 2 (1967): 417–27.

Obotetukudo, Solomon Williams, ed. *The Inaugural Addresses and Ascension Speeches of Nigerian Elected and Non-Elected Presidents and Prime Minister, 1960–2010*. Lanham: University Press of America, 2011.

Obuah, Emmanuel. "Combatting Corruption in Nigeria: The Nigerian Economic and Financial Crimes (Efcc)." *African Studies Quarterly* 12, no. 1 (2010): 17–44.

Ochonu, Moses. "African Colonial Economies: Land, Labor, and Livelihoods." *History Compass* 11, no. 2 (2013): 91–103.

———. *Colonialism by Proxy: Hausa Imperial Agents and Middle Belt Consciousness in Nigeria*. Bloomington: Indiana University Press, 2014.

———. *Colonial Meltdown: Northern Nigeria in the Great Depression*. Athens: Ohio University Press, 2009.

———. "Corruption and Political Culture in Africa: History, Meaning, and the Problem of Naming." *Law and Development Review* 4, no. 3 (2011): 26–58.

———. "Critical Convergence: The Great Depression and the Meshing of Nigerian and British Anti-Colonial Polemic." *Canadian Journal of African Studies* 43, no. 2 (2009): 245–281.

Ogbondah, Chris, and Emmanuel U. Onyedike. "Origins and Interpetation of Nigerian Press Laws." *African Media Review* 5, no. 2 (1991): 59–70.

Ojimiwe, Obi. "Malaria Control and Its Discontents: A Critical Examination of the Emerging Discourse of Seriousness in Development Assistance." Ph.D. thesis, University of Manchester, 2013.

Ojo, O. J. B. "Patrimonialism, Sultanism, and Nation-Building in Nigeria." *Scandinavian Journal of Development Alternatives* 6, no. 2–3 (1987): 191–210.

Okediji, Florence A. "An Economic History of Hausa-Fulani Emirates of Northern Nigeria, 1900–1939." Ph.D. thesis, Indiana University, 1972.

Okolo, Abraham. "The Nigerian Census: Problems and Prospects." *American Statistician* 53, no. 4 (1999): 321–25.

Olaniyan, Tejumola. *Arrest the Music! Fela and His Rebel Art and Politics*. Bloomington: Indiana University Press, 2004.

Olivier de Sardan, J.-P. "A Moral Economy of Corruption in Africa?" *Journal of Modern African Studies* 37, no. 1 (1999): 2–52.

Olukoju, Ayodeji. "The United Kingdom and the Political Economy of the Global Oils and Fats Business During the 1930s." *Journal of Global History* 4, no. 1 (2009): 105–25.

Omotola, J. Shola. "'Garrison' Democracy in Nigeria: The 2007 General Elections and the Prospects of Democratic Consolidation." *Commonwealth and Comparative Politics* 47, no. 2 (2009): 194–220.

Onwudiwe, Ebere, Rotimi T. Suberu, and University of Ibadan. Programme on Ethnic and Federal Studies. *Nigerian Federalism in Crisis: Critical Perspectives and Political Options*. Ibadan: Programme on Ethnic and Federal Studies, Department of Political Science, University of Ibadan, 2005.

Onwuzuruigbo, Ifeanyi. "Recontextualisation of the Concept of Godfatherism: Reflections on Nigeria." *Africa Development* 38, no. 1–2 (2013): 25–50.

Orr, Charles William James. *The Making of Northern Nigeria*. 2nd ed. London: Frank Cass, 1965.

Osaghae, Eghosa E. *Crippled Giant: Nigeria since Independence*. London: Hurst, 1998.

———. "Structural Adjustment and Ethnicity in Nigeria." In *Research Report*. Uppsala: Scandinavian Institute of African Studies, 1995.

Osoba, Segun. "Corruption in Nigeria: Historical Perspectives." *Review of African Political Economy* 23, no. 69 (1996): 371–86.

Othman, Shehu. "Classes, Crises and Coup: The Demise of Shagari's Regime." *African Affairs* 83, no. 333 (1984): 441–61.

Ottenberg, Simon. "Local Government and the Law in Southern Nigeria." *Journal of Asian and African Studies* 2, no. 1/2 (1967): 26–43.

Oyediran, Oyeleye, ed. *Nigerian Government and Politics under Military Rule, 1966–1979*. London: Macmillan, 1979.

Oyediran, Oyeleye, and E. Alex Gboyega. "Local Government and Administration." In *Nigerian Government under Military Rule, 1966–1979*, edited by Oyeleye Oyediran, 169–91. London: Macmillan, 1979.

Oyovbaire, S. Egite. *Federalism in Nigeria: A Study in the Development of the Nigerian State*. New York: St. Martin's Press, 1985.

Paden, John N. *Ahmadu Bello, Sardauna of Sokoto: Values and Leadership in Nigeria*. London: Hodder and Stoughton, 1986.

———. *Religion and Political Culture in Kano*. Berkeley: University of California Press, 1973.

Parrillo, Nicholas. *Against the Profit Motive: The Transformation of American Government, 1780–1940*. New Haven, CT: Yale University Press, 2013.

Parry, Jonathan. "The Gift, the Indian Gift and the 'Indian Gift.'" *Man* 21, no. 3 (1986): 453–73.

Perham, Margery. *Lugard*. London: Collins, 1956.

Philps, Mark. "Defining Political Corruption." *Political Studies* 45, no. 3 (1997): 436–62.

Pierce, Steven. "'Farmers and 'Prostitutes': Twentieth-Century Problems of Female Inheritance in Kano Emirate, Nigeria." *Journal of African History* 44, no. 3 (2003): 463–86.

———. *Farmers and the State in Colonial Kano: Land Tenure and the Legal Imagination*. Bloomington: Indiana University Press, 2005.

———. "Identity, Performance, and Secrecy: Gendered Life and the 'Modern' in Northern Nigeria." *Feminist Studies* 33, no. 3 (2008) 539–65.

———. "Looking like a State: Colonialism and the 'Modernity' of Corruption in Northern Nigeria." *Comparative Studies in Society and History* 48, no. 4 (2006): 887–914.

———. "Pointing to Property: Colonialism and Knowledge About Land Tenure in Northern Nigeria." *Africa* 83, no. 1 (2013): 142–63.

———. "Prostitution, Politics, and Paradigms." *Journal of Colonialism and Colonial History* 5, no. 3 (2004).

———. "The Public, the Private, and the Sanitary: Domesticity and Development in Northern Nigeria." *Journal of Colonialism and Colonial History* 13, no. 3 (2013).

———. "Punishment and the Political Body: Flogging and Colonialism in Northern Nigeria." In *Discipline and the Other Body: Correction, Corporeality, Colonialism*, edited by Steven Pierce and Anupama Rao, 186–214. Durham, NC: Duke University Press, 2006.

Piot, Charles. *Nostalgia for the Future: West Africa after the Cold War*. Chicago: University of Chicago Press, 2010.

Pitcher, Anne, Mary H. Moran, and Michael Johnston. "Rethinking Patrimonialism and Neopatrimonialism in Africa." *African Studies Review* 52, no. 1 (2009): 125–56.

Polanyi, Karl. *Dahomey and the Slave Trade: An Analysis of an Archaic Economy*. Seattle: University of Washington Press, 1966.

———. *The Great Transformation*. Boston: Beacon, 1957 [1944].

Polanyi, Karl, Conrad M. Arensberg, and Harry W. Pearson, eds. *Trade and Market in the Early Empires: Economies in History and Theory*. Glencoe: Free Press, 1957.

Pratten, David, and Atreyee Sen, eds. *Global Vigilantes:*. London: Hurst, 2007.

Radcliffe-Brown, A. R. "Preface." In *African Political Systems*, edited by E. E. Evans-Pritchard and Meyer Fortes, xi–xxiii, 1969 [1940].

Ranger, T. O. "The Invention of Tradition in Colonial Africa." In *The Invention of Tradition*, edited by E. J. Hobsbawn and T. O. Ranger. Cambridge: Cambridge University Press, 1983.

———. "The Invention of Tradition Revisited." In *Legitimacy and the State in Twentieth-Century Africa: Essays in Honor of A.H.M. Kirk-Greene*, edited by T. O. Ranger and Olufemi Vaughan. Houndmills: Macmillan, 1993.

Rao, Anupama, and Steven Pierce. "Discipline and the Other Body: Humanitarianism, Violence, and the Colonial Exception." In *Discipline and the Other Body: Correction, Corporeality, Colonialism*, edited by Steven Pierce and Anupama Rao, 1–35. Durham, NC: Duke University Press, 2006.

Reno, William. "Anti-Corruption Efforts in Liberia: Are They Aimed at the Right Targets?" In *Corruption and Post-Conflict Peacebuilding: Selling the Peace?*, edited by Christine S. Cheng and Dominik Zaum, 126–43. London: Routledge, 2012.

———. *Corruption and State Politics in Sierra Leone*. Cambridge: Cambridge University Press, 1995.

———. "Crisis and (No) Reform in Nigeria's Politics." *African Studies Review* 42, no. 1 (1999): 105–24.

———. *Warlord Politics and African States*. Boulder, CO: Lynner Rienner Publishers, 1998.

Reynolds, Jonathan T. *The Time of Politics (Zamanin Siyasa): Islam and the Politics of Legitimacy in Northern Nigeria, 1950–1966*, 2nd ed. Lanham: University Press of America, 1999.

Rimmer, Douglas. *The Economies of West Africa*. London: Weidenfeld and Nicolson, 1984.

Robinson, Kenneth, A. F. Madden, and Margery Perham, eds. *Essays in Imperial Government*. Oxford: B. Blackwell, 1963.

Rodney, Walter. *How Europe Underdeveloped Africa*. Washington, DC: Howard University Press, 1974.

Roitman, Janet. "Africa, Otherwise." In *African Futures*, edited by Charles Piot, J. Obarrio, and B. Goldstone. Durham, NC: Duke University Press, forthcoming.

———. "Économie morale, subjectivité et politique." *Critique internationale* 6, no. 6 (2000): 48–56.

———. *Fiscal Disobedience: An Anthropology of Economic Regulation in Central Africa*. Princeton, NJ: Princeton University Press, 2005.

Rose-Ackerman, Susan. *Corruption and Government: Causes, Consequences, and Reform*. Cambridge: Cambridge University Press, 1999.

———. *Corruption: A Study in Political Economy*. New York: Academic Press, 1978.

———. "Corruption: Greed, Culture, and the State." *Yale Law Journal Online* 125 (2010): 125–140. Published electronically 9 November 2010. http://yalelawjournal .org/2010/11/10/rose-ackerman.html.

———. "Democracy and 'Grand' Corruption." *International Social Science Journal* 48, no. 3 (1996): 365–80.

———. "The Economics of Corruption." *Journal of Public Economics* 4, no. 2 (1975): 187–203.

———. *International Handbook on the Economics of Corruption*. Cheltenham: Edward Elgar, 2006.

———. "The Political Economy of Corruption." In *Corruption and the Global Economy*, edited by Kimberly Ann Elliott, 31–60. Washington, DC: Institute for International Economics, 1997.

Rostow, W. W. *The Stages of Economic Growth: A Non-Communist Manifesto*. Cambridge: Cambridge University Press, 1960.

Saha, Jonathan. *Law, Disorder and the Colonial State: Corruption in Burma c. 1900*. London: Palgrave, 2013.

———. "The Male State: Colonialism, Corruption and Rape Investigations in the Irrawaddy Delta c. 1900." *Indian Economic and Social History Review* 47, no. 3 (2010): 343–76.

———. "A Mockery of Justice? Colonial Law, the Everyday State and Village Politics in the Burma Delta, c. 1890–1910." *Past and Present* 217, no. 1 (2012): 187–212.

Sahlins, Marshall. *Stone Age Economics*. Hawthorne: Aldine, 1972.

Sa'id, Halil Ibrahim. "Revolution and Reaction: The Fulani Jihad in Kano and Its Aftermath, 1807–1919." Ph.D. thesis, University of Michigan, 1978.

Salau, Mohammed Bashir. "The Role of Slave Labor in Groundnut Production in Early Colonial Kano." *Journal of African History* 51, no. 2 (2010): 147–64.

Salubi, T. E. A. *T. E. A. Salubi: Witness to British Colonial Rule in Urhoboland and Nigeria*. Buffalo: Urhobo Historical Society, 2008.

Schatz, Sayre P. *Nigerian Capitalism*. Berkeley: University of California Press, 1977.

———. "Pirate Capitalism and the Inert Economy of Nigeria." *Journal of Modern African Studies* 22, no. 1 (1984): 45–57.

Scott, James C. "The Analysis of Corruption in Developing Nations." *Comparative Studies in Society and History* 11, no. 3 (1969): 315–41.

———. *The Moral Economy of the Peasant: Rebellion and Subsistence in Southeast Asia*. New Haven, CT: Yale University Press, 1976.

———. *Seeing Like a State: How Certain Schemes to Improve the Human Condition Have Failed*. New Haven, CT: Yale University Press, 1998.

Sharma, Aradhana, and Akhil Gupta. "Rethinking Theories of the State in an Age of Globalization." In *The Anthropology of the State: A Reader*, edited by Aradhana Sharma and Akhil Gupta. Malden: Blackwell, 2007.

Shenton, Robert W. *The Development of Capitalism in Northern Nigeria*. London: James Currey, 1986.

Silver, Morris. "Karl Polanyi and Markets in the Ancient near East: The Challenge of the Evidence." *Journal of Economic History* 43, no. 4 (1983): 795–829.

Siniawer, Eiko Maruko. "Befitting Bedfellows: Yakuza and the State in Modern Japan." *Journal of Social History* 45, no. 3 (2012): 623–41.

Siollun, Max. *Oil, Politics and Violence: Nigeria's Military Coup Culture (1966–1976)*. New York: Algora Publishing, 2009.

Sklar, Richard L. *Nigerian Political Parties: Power in an Emergent African Nation*. Princeton, NJ: Princeton University Press, 1963.

Smith, Abdullahi. *A Little New Light: Selected Historical Writings of Professor Abdullahi Smith*. Zaria: Abdullahi Smith Center for Historical Research, Gaskiya Corporation, 1987.

Smith, Daniel Jordan. *A Culture of Corruption: Everyday Deception and Popular Discontent in Nigeria*. Princeton, NJ: Princeton University Press, 2007.

Smith, Harold. *Blue-Collar Lawman*. c. 1998. http://www.biafraland.com/harold _smith/harold_smith_frm.htm, last revised 27 March 2001.

Smith, M. G. *The Affairs of Daura: History and Change in a Hausa State, 1800–1958*. Berkeley: University of California Press, 1978.

———. *Government in Kano, 1350–1950*. Boulder, CO: Westview Press, 1997.

———. *Government in Zazzau, 1800–1950*. London: Oxford University Press, 1960.

———. "The Hausa System of Social Status." *Africa* 29, no. 3 (1959): 239–52.

———. "Historical and Cultural Conditions of Political Corruption among the Hausa." *Comparative Studies in Society and History* 6, no. 2 (1964): 164–94.

Smith, Mary F. *Baba of Karo: A Woman of the Muslim Hausa*. New Haven, CT: Yale University Press, 1981.

Sowunmi, Fatai Abiola, Muniru Adesola Adesola, and Mudashiru Abiodun Salako. "An Appraisal of the Performance of the Economic and Financial Crimes Commission in Nigeria." *International Journal of Offender Therapy and Comparative Criminology* 54, no. 6 (2010): 47–69.

Soyinka, Wole. *You Must Set Forth at Dawn*. New York: Random House, 2007.

Spear, Thomas. "Neo-Traditionalism and the Limits of Invention in British Colonial Africa." *Journal of African History* 44, no. 1 (2003): 3–27.

Starns, William. "Land Tenure among the Rural Hausa." In *Occasional Papers, No. 6*. Madison: African Studies Program, University of Wisconsin, 1974.

Steffens, Lincoln. *The Shame of the Cities*. New York: McClure, Phillips, 1904.

Stilwell, Sean. "Constructing Colonial Power: Tradition, Legitimacy and Government in Kano, 1903–1963." *Journal of Imperial and Commonwealth History* 39, no. 2 (2011): 195–225.

Stoler, Ann Laura. *Carnal Knowledge and Imperial Power: Race and the Intimate in Colonial Rule*. Berkeley: University of California Press, 2002.

Stolper, Wolfgang. *Inside Independent Nigeria: Diaries of Wolfgang Stolper, 1960–1962*. Aldershot: Ashgate.

Suberu, Rotimi T. *Federalism and Ethnic Conflict in Nigeria*. Washington, DC: United States Institute of Peace Press, 2001.

Temple, Charles. *Native Races and Their Rulers: Sketches and Studies of Official Life and Administrative Problems in Nigeria*. Cape Town: Argus, 1918.

Thompson, E. P. "The Moral Economy of the English Crowd in the Eighteenth Century." *Past and Present* 50 (1971): 76–136.

———. "The Moral Economy Reviewed." In *Customs in Common*, 259–351. New York: New Press, 1991.

Tibenderana, Peter K. "The Irony of Indirect Rule in Sokoto Emirate, Nigeria, 1903–1944." *African Studies Review* 31, no. 1 (1988): 67–92.

Tignor, Robert. "Political Corruption in Nigeria before Independence." *Journal of Modern African Studies* 31, no. 2 (1993): 175–202.

Ubah, C. N. *Government and Administration of Kano Emirate, 1900–1930*. Nsukka: University of Nigeria Press, 1985.

Umar, M. Sani. "Fatwa and Counter-Fatwa in Colonial Northern Nigeria: The Islamic Legality of Broadcasting Qur'an Recitation on Radio." *Journal for Islamic Studies* 21 (2001): 1–35.

———. *Islam and Colonialism: Intellectual Responses of Muslims of Northern Nigeria to British Colonial Rule*. Leiden: Brill, 2006.

Usman, Philip. "Resource or Revenue Sharing in Nigeria." In *Fiscal Federalism in Nigeria: Facing the Challenges of the Future*, edited by J. Isawa Elaigwu. London: Adonis and Abbey, 2008.

Usman, Y. B. "Middlemen, Consultants, Contractors and the Solutions to the Current Economic Crisis." *Studies in Politics and Society* 2 (1984): 8–34.

———. *The Transformation of Katsina*. Zaria: Ahmadu Bello University Press, 1978.

Vail, Leroy, ed. *The Invention of Tribalism in Southern Africa*. Berkeley: University of California Press, 1989.

van Klaveren, Jacob. "Corruption as a Historical Phenomenon." In *Political Corruption: Readings in Comparative Analysis*, edited by Arnold J. Heidenheimer. New Brunswick: Transaction Books, 1978.

———. "Historical and Cultural Conditions of Political Corruption among the Hausa: Comment." *Comparative Studies in Society and History* 6, no. 2 (1964): 195–98.

Vaughan, Olufemi. *Nigerian Chiefs: Traditional Power in Modern Politics, 1890s–1990s*. Rochester: University of Rochester Press, 2000.

Vicente, Pedro C. "Does Oil Corrupt? Evidence from a Natural Experiment in West Africa." *Journal of Development Economic* 92, no. 1 (2010): 28–38.

Wai, Zubairu. "Neo-Patrimonialism and the Discourse of State Failure in Africa." *Review of African Political Economy* 39, no. 131 (2012): 27–43.

Waquet, Jean-Claude. *Corruption: Ethics and Power in Florence, 1600–1770*. Cambridge: Polity Press, 1992.

Warner, Michael. "Publics and Counterpublics." *Public Culture* 14, no. 1 (2002): 49–90.

Watts, Michael. "Oil as Money: The Devil's Excrement and the Spectacle of Black Gold." In *Reading Economic Geography*, edited by Trevor J. Barnes, Jamie Peck, Eric Shappard, and Adam Tickell, 205–19. Oxford: Blackwell, 2004.

———. "Resource Curse? Governmentality, Oil and Power in the Niger Delta, Nigeria." *Geopolitics* 9, no. 1 (2004): 50–80.

———. "The Shock of Modernity: Petroleum, Protest, and Fast Capitalism in an Industrializing Society." In *Reworking Modernity: Capitalisms and Symbolic Discontent*, edited by Allan Pred and Michael Watts. New Brunswick, NJ: Rutgers University Press, 1992.

———. *Silent Violence: Food, Famine and Peasantry in Northern Nigeria*. Berkeley: University of California Press, 1983.

———, ed. *State, Oil, and Agriculture in Nigeria*. Berkeley: Institute of International Studies, University of California, 1987.

Weber, Max. *Economy and Society: An Outline of Interpretive Sociology*. Translated by Ephraim Fischoff, Hans Gerth, A. M. Henderson, Ferdinand Kolegar, C. Wright Mills, Talcott Parsons, Max Rheinstein, et al. Vol. 3. New York: Bedminster Press, 1968.

———. *The Methodology of the Social Sciences*. Translated by Edward Shils and Henry Finch. New York: Free Press, 1949.

Whitaker, C. S. *The Politics of Tradition: Continuity and Change in Northern Nigeria, 1946–1966*. Princeton, NJ: Princeton University Press, 1970.

White, Luise. *Speaking with Vampires: Rumor and History in East and Central Africa*. Berkeley: University of California Press, 2000.

Williams, Robert. "New Concepts for Old?" *Third World Quarterly* 20, no. 3 (1999): 503–13.

———. *Political Corruption in Africa*. Aldershot: Gower, 1987.

Wilson, Kathleen. *The Island Race: Englishness, Empire and Gender in the Eighteenth Century*. New York: Routledge, 2003.

Wraith, Ronald, and Edgar Simpkins. *Corruption in Developing Countries*. New York: W. W. Norton, 1963.

Yahaya, A. D. *The Native Authority System in Northern Nigeria, 1950–1970: A Study in Political Relations with Particular Reference to the Zaria Native Authority*. Zaria: Ahmadu Bello University Press, 1980.

Yakubu, Alhaji Mahmood. *An Aristocracy in Political Crisis*. Aldershot: Avebury, 1996.

Young, Crawford. *Ethnicity and Politics in Africa*. Boston: Boston University African Studies Center, 2002.

Young, Robert. "Bayart's Broken Kettle." *Public Culture* 23, no. 1 (2011): 167–75.

Zolberg, Aristide. *Creating Political Order: The Party-States of West Africa*. Chicago: Rand McNally, 1966.

INDEX

Moba, 96–97

modernization theory, 12–15, 199–201, 210, 221, 232n22

moral economy, 22–23, 169–180, 185–87, 196, 216, 222–23, 227–28

Moran, Mary H., 254n54

Mossad, 140–41

Muffet Commission. *See* Muffet, David

Muffet, David, 78–82

Muhammed, Murtala, 110, 206; military regime of, 124–27, 129–32, 174, 178

National Bank of Nigeria, 96, 98

National Council of Nigeria and the Cameroons, 66, 85–92, 99–103, 111, 118, 134, 136, 182–83, 252n23

National Council of Nigerian Citizens. *See* National Council of Nigeria and the Cameroons

National Investment and Properties Company, 96, 98

National Party of Nigeria, 110, 135–41, 247n55, 248n58–59

NCNC. *See* National Council of Nigeria and the Cameroons

neo-patrimonialism. *See* patrimonialism

NEPU. *See* Northern Elements Progressive Union

newspapers, 1, 64, 75–76, 98, 111, 116–18, 122, 131–32, 147, 176, 178–78, 188, 190–96, 219–20, 249n77

Niger delta, 2, 101–2, 111, 153, 183, 246n27, 248n58, 250n26

Nigerian National Democratic Party, 100

Nigerian National Petroleum Corporation, 108–11, 146

Nigerian People's Party, 134–36

Nigerian Protectorate Ram, 75

NNDP. *See* Nigerian National Democratic Party

NNPC. *See* Nigerian National Petroleum Corporation

Northern Elements Progressive Union, 65–67, 76–79, 85–86, 88, 91–92, 100, 102, 154–57, 159, 164, 174, 175, 243n49

Northern People's Congress, 64–68, 74–78, 80–86, 90–92, 100–103, 134–36, 157, 160, 164–65, 186, 243n49

Northern Region, 66, 76–83, 85, 88, 90–92, 97, 100, 105, 114, 134, 161, 164, 166, 212, 235–36n15, 242n43

northern states, 108, 114–15, 120, 123, 125, 134–36, 157, 162–63, 174, 176, 180, 182, 206, 248n57, 251n32

NPC. *See* Northern People's Congress

NPN. *See* National Party of Nigeria

NPP. *See* Nigerian People's Party

Nwabughuogo, Anthony, 236n22

Nye, Joseph, 14, 199–200

Obadare, Ebenezer, 233n40, 251n6

Obasanjo, Olusegun, 139, 181–82, 206, 227, 245n9; characterization of in "Army Arrangement," 110; military government of, 125, 127–28, 136, 143, 145, 173; presidency of, 107, 111, 189–96

Ochonu, Moses, 239n89, 241n15

Ojukwu, Chukwuemeka Odumegwu, 101–2, 113–14

Okereke, Sylvester, 129

Okonjo-Iweala, Ngozi, 189–92, 197

Okotie-Eboh, Festus, 117–19, 149, 198

Okpara, Michael, 101, 198

Olivier de Sardan, Jean-Paul, 8, 168, 171–72, 186, 231n8, 254n52

oppression: Hausa concept of, *see* zalunci; official malpractice conceptualized as, 5–6

Orkar, Gideon, 143

Ottenberg, Simon, 15

palm oil. *See* marketing boards

patrimonialism, 17–18, 23, 166, 200–202, 206–10, 220, 225, 233n39, 254n54

patronage: emirate patterns of and party politics, 84; and ethnicity, 17–18, 87–88, 106–7, 114–15; and moral evaluation, 158–63, 175–76, 184–85, 195–97, 213, 226–29; and political position in Zaria, 42; and politicians' need for resources, 90, 200–209, 220–21; in precolonial Sokoto Caliphate, 32; in western countries, 10–11; and zoning, 135–37, 141–42

PDP. *See* People's Democratic Party

People's Democratic Party, 107–8, 181–83, 189, 194, 196, 203, 248, 249, 251, 252